THE GAMES PLAYERS

FICTION

The Big Wheel
A Pride of Lions
The Man Who Broke Things

NONFICTION

The Seven Fat Years
The Fate of the Edsel
The Great Leap
Business Adventures
Once in Golconda
The Go-Go Years
Telephone

JOHN BROOKS

THE GAMES
PLAYERS

*Tales of
Men and Money*

```
$$$$$$$$$$$$$
$$$$$$$$$$$$$
$$$$$$$$$$$$$
$$$$$$$$$$$$$
$$$$$$$$$$$$$
$$$$$$$$$$$$$
$$$$$$$$$$$$$
$$$$$$$$$$$$$
```

•

A Truman Talley Book

𝕿imes BOOKS

New York

•

All the material in the book with the exception of Chapter IV has previously appeared in THE NEW YORKER *in somewhat different form.*

The author is indebted for translation and research help on Chapter V to Patti Hagan, Kenneth Krabbenhoft, and Elizabeth Macklin.

Published by *Truman Talley Books · Times Books,* a division of Quadrangle/The New York Times Book Co., Inc. Three Park Avenue, New York, N.Y. 10016

Published simultaneously in Canada by Fitzhenry & Whiteside, Ltd., Toronto

Library of Congress Cataloging in Publication Data

Brooks, John, 1920-
  The games players.

  Includes index.
  1. Capitalists and financiers. 2. Finance.
I. Title.
HG172.A2B73   1973   332'.092'2   79-51452
ISBN 0-8129-0864-3

Manufactured in the United States of America

To Barbara Mahoney

Contents

PART I: U. S.—THE FIFTIES

1 The Great Proxy Fight   *3*
ROBERT R. YOUNG AND THE NEW YORK CENTRAL

2 The Adventure of Morgan Stanley & Co.   *30*
GM MEETS MESSRS. HALL AND BALDWIN

PART II: EUROPE

3 The City of London   *63*
THAW ON THREADNEEDLE STREET

4 The Amsterdam Cradle   77
THE TOWN WHERE STOCK TRADING WAS BORN

5 Spanish Privateer   *93*
THE CURIOUS CAREER OF SEÑOR JUAN MARCH

PART III: U. S.—THE SIXTIES

6 The Gentlemanly Junket   *219*
BROWN BROTHERS THROWS THE ULTIMATE PARTY

7 Confrontation   *249*
STEINBERG/LEASCO VERSUS RENCHARD/CHEMICAL BANK

PART IV: U. S.—THE SEVENTIES

8 Starting Over   *285*
THE NEW INTERNATIONAL MONETARY GAME

9 It Will Grow on You   *301*
THE ESSO—EXXON NAME CHANGE

10 Retaking Pittsburgh   *310*
BARON GUY DE ROTHSCHILD COMES TO COPPERWELD

11 The Law School and the Noodle Factory   *324*
HOW N.Y.U. GOT RICH

12 Funds Gray and Black   *337*
GREASING THE WHEELS AT GULF OIL

Index   *365*

PART ONE

U. S.—The Fifties

The Great Proxy Fight

ON THE AFTERNOON of Sunday, January 17, 1954, William White, the president and chief executive officer of the New York Central Railroad, received a telephone call from Palm Beach at his home, in Scarsdale. The caller, as White suspected the moment he learned that Palm Beach was on the wire, was Harold S. Vanderbilt, who had been a member of the New York Central's fifteen-man board of directors for forty years and whose great-grandfather, Commodore Cornelius Vanderbilt, almost a century ago first brought fame both to the Central (as it then was; much later it became part of the Penn Central) and to his family name. How was the weather in Palm Beach, White wanted to know. Splendid, said Vanderbilt, and how was it in Scarsdale? Terrible, White said, and he wished he were in Palm Beach. Then Vanderbilt got down to business. "Bill," White later recalled him as saying, "Bob Young is here in Palm Beach, and he told me this afternoon that he and Allan Kirby have been buying a lot of Central stock. They're getting out of Chesapeake & Ohio, because Young wants to be chairman of the board and chief executive officer of the Central, and bring Kirby along."

White, a tall, heavyset man then in his late fifties with graying temples and a stolid oval face, recalled later that it took him a few seconds to recover from his shock at what he considered the effrontery of the demand; after all, the company's setup at that time did not even provide for a chairman of the board. Vanderbilt seemed taken aback, too. "Do you owe him some sort of an answer?" White asked, finally.

Vanderbilt said yes, he guessed he did. Both he and Young divided a good deal of their time between Palm Beach and Newport, and the two men had been on socially friendly terms for some years.

"I suggest you tell him that his request and Mr. Kirby's will be taken up at our next regular monthly directors' meeting, on February 10th," said White. "Would you agree to that?"

Vanderbilt said that he would, and added that he would call again after he had spoken to Young. An hour or so later, he did call again. "Well," he said, "it looks as if we're going to have a proxy fight on our hands at the next annual meeting."

Two days later, Young announced publicly that he, his partner Kirby, and the Alleghany Corporation, a railroad holding company they dominated, had got rid of the stock they had held in the Chesapeake & Ohio Railway, in order to leave themselves legally free to seek control of the New York Central.

THE nineteenth-century attitude of management toward the public was succinctly and resoundingly summed up on October 8, 1882, by William H. Vanderbilt, son of the Commodore and president of the New York Central & Hudson River Railroad, as the New York Central was then called. On that date, he was riding in his private car between Michigan City, Indiana, and Chicago when a reporter challenged him to say whether or not he ran trains for the benefit of the public. In reply, as almost every schoolboy knows and as four subsequent generations of Vanderbilts were not allowed to forget, William H. said, "The public be damned!" In a way, the proxy fight that began with Harold S. Vanderbilt's calls from Palm Beach may be looked upon as the lifting of that seventy-two-year-old curse. For while certain segments of the public believe they have reason to feel that they are still being damned by the men who run the railroads, in the case of the New York Central ruckus, management seemed to be admitting once and for all that the public—or at any rate the not inconsiderable portion of the public that holds stock in railroads—had become so influential as to make damning it inconsistent with keeping one's job. Devices that in the past had been applied chiefly to political elections, revival meetings, and tent shows were used to beguile the Central's forty-one thousand stockholders, many of whom knew nothing of railroading but every one of whom was entitled to cast one vote for each share of stock he owned at the annual election of members of the board of directors. Old William H. would have found it hard to understand that each side in the battle thought it judicious to spend over half a million dollars on presenting itself and its slate of candidates to the public in the best possible light.

In a broad sense, the information conveyed in Vanderbilt's two calls from Palm Beach that Sunday hardly came as a surprise to White. It had been well known for some time that, more than anything else in the world, Robert R. Young, a small, dapper, fifty-seven-year-old Texan with white hair, blue eyes, and a face that suggested a worldly-wise cherub, wanted control of the New York Central, a railroad system second in size only to its future partner, the Pennsylvania. To White, what was news in Vanderbilt's calls was that Young had decided to strike at once for the chairmanship of the board, instead of trying to work his way up to it gradually, and that he had picked the 1954 annual stockholders' meeting, to

be held on May 26th in Albany, where the Central has its headquarters, as the time for a showdown. Primarily a financial pro-
moter and speculator, Young had been involved in railroad
management since 1937, when he acquired control of the Chesapeake & Ohio, and he had come to think of himself as an expert on
"sick railroads"; he felt that control of a big line like the Central
would enable him to give a really practical demonstration of some
of his pet railroading ideas, such as mechanically refrigerated cars,
roller-bearing freight cars, and a low, lightweight, high-speed train
of two-wheeled cars, built along aircraft lines, which he called
Train X. Young also regarded the Central as the key link in a
transcontinental railroad system—something he had long agitated
for. (His name was first brought to the attention of the public, in
1946, by his newspaper advertisements stresssing the theme, "A
Hog Can Cross the Country without Changing Trains—But You
Can't.") Young had been invited to sit on the Central's board of
directors in 1947, when the line was under the presidency of
Gustav Metzman, but he was unable to do so, the Interstate Commerce Commission having ruled that since he was then chairman
of the Chesapeake & Ohio, it would be a violation of the antitrust
laws. Knowing all this, White, from the time he became president
of the Central, in 1952, had had a pretty strong hunch that sooner
or later Young was going to be heard from, and in order to prepare
himself for the struggle he had been keeping a file on Young's
actions and transactions. In the weeks following the calls from
Vanderbilt, White consulted this file frequently and thought a
great deal about his prospective antagonist's weapons. He was well
aware that, regardless of Young's qualifications as a railroad man,
the special talents the insurgent had revealed both for inspiring
confidence in investors, small and large, and for enlisting public
support would be useful in a proxy fight. White, a self-made professional railroad man of Dutch ancestry, who had started in the
business at the age of sixteen as a freight auditor on the Erie, had
little experience in high finance and a conservative businessman's
distaste for publicity of any kind. His qualifications were experience in railroad management and a stubbornness inherited from
his forebears. He decided to stand on these.

On February 2nd, Young, having flown up to New York, invited White to lunch at the Cloud Club, the private dining room in the Chrysler Building for executives who, like Young, had offices there. At first, the talk dealt with the railroad business in general. Then White said that there were apparently some things about the Central that Young did not know. For example, what about the claim some of Young's aides had been making during the past few weeks that he could eliminate the railroad's passenger-service deficit? That deficit, White said, was a great problem, and one that he had been doing his best to solve. Maybe the deficit could be reduced some, but, what with the prevailing government-fixed fare rates, it simply could not be eliminated. Young replied placatingly that he hadn't been claiming he would wipe out the passenger-service deficit. He was a much misunderstood man, he protested, and his aides had got it all wrong. Then he proposed a compromise. If White would step down as the Central's chief executive officer, giving place to Young, he could stay on with the title of chief operating officer; in addition, White would be given stock options—an opportunity to buy Central stock at a fixed price and without any obligation to pay for it unless it went up. White refused the proposal in its entirety. Weeks later, he was asked whether the parting after the Cloud Club lunch had been cordial. "Well, I didn't kiss the guy," he said.

Not long after this lunch, White showed how strongly he felt by announcing that he would abrogate his contract with the Central if Young should win out. The contract, which was the reward of a lifelong career as a railroad man, stipulated that White was to be paid a hundred and twenty thousand dollars a year as president until he reached the age of sixty-five, that for the next five years he was to receive an annual seventy-five thousand dollars as a consultant, and that from then on he would have a lifetime pension of forty thousand dollars a year. Although the contract was binding on the Central no matter what changes might be made in the board of directors, White felt that he could not work with Young under any circumstances and preserve his self-respect.

At the directors' meeting on February 10th, which was held at the University Club, it was unanimously decided that it would be "inimical to the best interest of the company" to bow to Young. The decision brought the controversy out into the open. Young, back in Palm Beach, declared that he would wage an all-out proxy fight to gain control at the stockholders' meeting in May. He also released the first of numerous broadsides against what he called "banker control" of the incumbent board, whose members included George Whitney, chairman of J. P. Morgan & Co.; Lawrence N. Murray, president of the Mellon National Bank & Trust Co.; Alexander C. Nagle, president of the First National Bank of the City of New York; and Percy J. Ebbott, president of the Chase National Bank.

White was ready—or hoped he was—to launch a counterattack. At the close of the directors' meeting, he had gone straight to his office, on the thirty-second floor of the Central Building, at 230 Park Avenue, and made two telephone calls. One was to Willard F. Place, his vice-president for finance, whom he instructed to engage the services of Georgeson & Co., the largest of several firms of professional proxy solicitors in the Wall Street area. The other was to Joseph Copps, the president of the public-relations firm of Robinson–Hannagan Associates, with whom he arranged to engage that company's services for a year, at a fee of fifty thousand dollars plus expenses. Then White got in touch with the Central's advertising department, which was operating on a million-and-a-quarter budget for the year, and ordered it to suspend all its scheduled advertising; there were going to be a lot of expensive ads coming up, he said, and every one of them would be a part of the proxy fight. When he quit work that day, he felt that he had set up a good, strong defense all along the line. Five days later, he assembled a group of trusted associates in his office for the first in a series of strategy meetings, which he thereafter held regularly, on Mondays and Thursdays, right up to the end. According to a man who was present, White opened the meeting by saying, "Since we have a contest on our hands, we'll conduct it in a bare-fisted manner—with decency, honor, and in such a way as to retain our self-respect and that of our friends, yes, but there will be no holding back on any other grounds. This could be the begin-

ning of a technique in which we find an astute trader with a
certain popular appeal moving in on the professional management
of big firms. American business right now has the most widespread
ownership that it's ever had in history, and that's a fine, democratic thing. It would be, to say the least, unfortunate if this widespread ownership were allowed to be used as a tool by demagogues.
We're not only fighting to keep control of the Central, we're fulfilling an overall responsibility to American business."

IT was early in December, 1953, during a conversation with Kirby,
that Young decided the time had come to make his bid for
control of the Central. (Kirby, an heir to the Woolworth fortune
who had long been a Young backer, suffered from a heart ailment
and was, moreover, retiring by nature, so he took little active part
in the fight itself.) Young stated later that he couldn't recall where
the conversation took place or whether it was held face to face or
by telephone. In any case, Young told Kirby that he thought their
Alleghany Corporation should sell its Chesapeake & Ohio stock,
"to get our house in order," and that then, if they could do it
without running the market up too much, they should begin buying Central stock, preparatory to making the big push in May.
Kirby agreed, and the two men then discussed at some length a
block of eight hundred thousand shares of Central stock that the
Chesapeake & Ohio had bought as an investment during Young's
chairmanship of that line. So that there might be no violation of
the antitrust laws, the C. & O. had placed these shares, which,
representing twelve and four-tenths per cent of the 6,447,410
shares of Central stock outstanding, were by far the largest single
block, with the Chase National Bank under a voting trusteeship.
This arrangement provided that the C. & O. could collect dividends on the stock and could sell it at any time, but ceded the
stock's voting rights to Chase. Kirby asked Young whether he
thought Chase would vote the stock in their favor. Young said he
wasn't sure, but he believed that Chase would take a neutral position. On January 18th, the day after he told Vanderbilt that he
wanted to take over the Central, Young came to New York from

Palm Beach and went to see Ebbott, the president of Chase, to ask
him how the stock was going to be voted. Ebbott, according to
Young, replied pointedly that he certainly did like sitting on the
Central's board, and hoped he would be sitting there for a long
time; he added, however, that the last thing the bank wanted was a
fight, and that it would undoubtedly try to remain as nearly neutral as possible. Taking this to mean that the bank would not vote
the shares against him, Young flew happily back to Palm Beach.
Three weeks later, he recounted afterward, he was "shocked" to
learn what had happened at the Central directors' meeting. What
shocked him was not the fact that he and Kirby had been turned
down—he had expected that—but the fact that the vote had been
unanimous. This meant that Ebbott had voted against him, and
therefore the future voting strength of the eight hundred thousand
shares could be presumed lost.

The eight hundred thousand shares made a big difference.
Young calculated that with them, plus the two hundred thousand
or so that he and Kirby owned personally, he would need about
forty per cent of all the other outstanding votes in order to win. If
they were voted against him, he would need about fifty-five per
cent. Grieved by Ebbott's action but resilient, he set to work to
contrive a means of prying the eight hundred thousand shares out
of Chase hostile hands by finding a friendly buyer and persuading
the C. & O. to sell its Central stock to him. On Thursday, February 11th, David Baird, a friend of Young's who was a member of
the New York Stock Exchange and who happened to be in Palm
Beach, offered to try to organize a syndicate to buy the stock.
Young was delighted. But then, after two critical days, during
which Baird had nothing conclusive to report, he began to get
nervous. Central stock was churning around on the Stock Exchange in anticipation of the proxy fight; it had jumped from
twenty to twenty-five. If Young couldn't arrange to have the C. &
O.'s block bought quickly, its price might be so high that no one
would want to buy it.

On the third day, Young, still in Palm Beach, received a caller
—an old friend of his named Don H. Carter, who was a business

representative of Clint W. Murchison, the freewheeling Texas oil-man and investor. In the past, acting through Carter, Murchison had found Young's promotions profitable to the extent of several million dollars. As Young later recalled it, Carter came to see him about another business matter, and while they were in the middle of discussing it, the following cryptic bit of dialogue took place:

YOUNG: Don, I think the New York Central represents the greatest speculative opportunity in American business—under new management.

CARTER: Bob, what's going to happen to all that Central stock that Chase is holding for C. & O.?

That started the ball rolling. Young, trying not to seem eager, asked Carter if he thought Murchison might be interested in buying the stock. Carter said perhaps, and, after telephoning Murchison, reported to Young that Murchison did indeed seem interested. Young then put in a call to Walter J. Tuohy, president of the C. & O. and Young's former subordinate there, and asked him whether the C. & O. might care to sell its Central stock at a price rather higher than the twenty dollars or so a share that the company had paid for it. Maybe, said Tuohy, if the price was twenty-six.

Young was now in the ticklish position common to brokers in big deals. The market price of Central stock was fluttering around twenty-four just then, and because of the uncertainties of the proxy fight, it might soar or sink at any moment. If it soared, Murchison would not buy, and if it sank, the C. & O. would not sell; either way, the deal would be off. On Monday the fifteenth, Young arrived in New York—to stay, he said, "for the duration." By then, Central stock had touched twenty-six. After shaking his fist symbolically for the benefit of photographers at the airport, Young went to his office in the Chrysler Building and began negotiating with Murchison by telephone. He had reason to suspect that Tuohy would come down to twenty-five dollars a share, and he pointed out what a bargain the stock would be at that price— perhaps a whole point lower than the figure quoted on the Exchange. Murchison said the price was all right; he also said that he

would need a partner in the deal, and had one ready in the person
of Sid W. Richardson, another Texan with a penchant for shorten-
ing his given name and enlarging his bank roll. Young approved;
he had never done business with Richardson, but he had visited
him at his ranch in Texas. So far, so good. But neither of the
Texans liked the idea of putting up all that cash. Young thereupon
undertook to raise the cash for them. Within a few days, he had
arranged for a seven-and-a-half-million-dollar loan from the Alleghany Corporation, secured by four-and-a-half-per-cent short-
term notes signed by Murchison and Richardson, and a loan of
five million from Kirby. That made twelve and a half million in
hand, and Young and the two Texans then set about borrowing
from various banks the additional seven and a half million that
was needed to buy the eight hundred thousand shares at twenty-
five. Tuohy, confronted by the prospect of twenty million dollars
in cash, finally agreed to sell at that figure. On February 25th,
twelve days after Young's meeting with Carter, the C. & O. directors, at a special meeting in Cleveland, announced that they had
approved the sale.

Not only were Murchison and Richardson, each of them reput-
edly worth over three hundred million dollars, able to buy the
stock without putting up any of their own money but, as an added
inducement, Young saw to it that they were given an option to sell
half of the eight hundred thousand shares to Alleghany at any
time between July 15th and September 15th for twenty-five dollars a share, or the same price they had paid. Moreover, Richardson had a separate option to sell half the remaining four hundred
thousand shares at cost to Kirby. There was actually a risk, then,
on only two hundred thousand shares.

It was quite a deal. C. & O. got a substantial profit on the sale,
Murchison and Richardson got a practically foolproof speculation
without putting up any cash, and Young, who presently placed the
Texans on his slate of prospective directors, got his eight hundred
thousand votes in the Central proxy fight. The only possible loser
appeared to be Alleghany, which was now shouldering half the
risk involved in the Texans' speculation; Young, who dominated

Alleghany with personal holdings of no more than seven-tenths of one per cent of the common stock, seems to have shown a tendency to treat the company, with its almost twenty thousand stockholders, as his personal property. One might think that those stockholders would have been incensed enough to start a proxy fight of their own, but to think that would be to reckon without their devotion to their leader, and their unbounded confidence that he would eventually bring them, as well as himself, home safe and solvent. To demonstrate their devotion and confidence, they met in Baltimore on May 5th and adopted a resolution expressing their gratitude to Young for everything he had done for them.

WHITE learned of the big Texas deal on February 24th, when Ebbott called him from the Chase Bank to say that the eight hundred thousand shares of Central stock had been released from trusteeship. That was bad news, because White knew that there was only one likely reason for such a maneuver. It was worse news when Ebbott went on to say that the stock had been bought by Murchison and Richardson, because White, who had, of course, heard of them, knew that Murchison, at least, had been associated with Young. White called in a battery of lawyers—headed by Harold H. McLean, his general counsel, and Chauncey H. Hand, of the law firm of Dorr, Hand & Dawson—and asked them if there wasn't something illegal about it all. The battery retired to think it over, and returned not with an answer but with a question: Since the sale seemed to indicate that the C. & O. still did what Young wanted it to, even though he no longer owned any of its stock or sat on its board, would not his control of the Central mean that he was running two railroads at once, and thereby violating the antitrust laws and circumventing the Interstate Commerce Commission? On March 3rd, the Central filed a petition asking the I.C.C. to investigate this situation.

On the ninth, a Tuesday, White received a telephone call from John J. McCloy, a chairman of the board of the Chase Bank. "Where can we talk?" McCloy asked. White replied that he was going downtown to attend a board meeting of the First National

Bank at noon that day, and wouldn't McCloy meet him there? McCloy said he would, and they arranged to get there at half past eleven and have their talk then. When White arrived at the First National, McCloy told him that Murchison wanted to meet him. White replied that he'd be glad to meet Murchison anywhere, at any time, but that he'd prefer to have Richardson on hand, too. O.K., said McCloy. McCloy put in a call to Murchison, in Texas, and White talked to him briefly. Murchison then put in a call to Richardson, in California. By the time the First National board meeting was over, an hour and a half later, White had received word that Murchison and Richardson were flying to New York the next day and would come to his office at nine-thirty Thursday morning.

The meeting was held, and lasted two hours. The Texans, White said later, were affable, gentlemanly, and businesslike. At the outset, White asked whether Young knew they were there. Yes, said Murchison; the pair had got in touch with him on the phone the night before, upon their arrival in New York. Murchison said that at that time Young had told him he had no objection to the meeting, but that he called back early that morning and urged him not to see White, because "it will damage our cause." Murchison reported that he had replied, "I've made an appointment, I've come from Texas to keep it, and I'll keep it." The next topic of conversation at the meeting, according to White, was the possibility of a compromise between him and Young. The Texans said that they were saddened by the spectacle of a quarrel within a company of which they now owned twelve and four-tenths per cent. White replied that there would be no basis for a compromise except an agreement on the part of Young to back down unequivocally as a candidate for any position at all on the Central board. When it became evident that there was nothing further to discuss along that line, the three men sat talking amiably for a while about general affairs, and then Murchison and Richardson shook hands with White and departed—one for Texas, the other for California. From that time on, White left the matter of the eight hundred thousand shares up to his lawyers and the I.C.C., and turned his whole attention to the matter of rounding up proxies for the 5,647,410 other shares in the Central.

THE word "proxy," which is of fifteenth-century origin, is a contraction of "procuracy," as "proctor" is of "procurator." Section 19 of the New York State General Corporation Law provides that holders of stock that carries with it the right to vote on company affairs must be permitted to vote by proxy, and most other states have similar laws. Proxy fights for control of large American corporations were in 1954 a comparatively recent development—a result of widespread stock ownership and strict government control of speculation. Back in the days when ownership of the railroads was in the hands of a relatively few individuals, the leaders of the industry gained their ends by other means than the rounding up of proxies. Small stockholders were considered a nuisance, if they were considered at all, and the common welfare meant nothing. Commodore Vanderbilt, for instance, won control of the New York Central not in a proxy fight but by getting hold of the New York & Hudson, a line that connected New York with Albany. In those days, the Central ran only between Albany and Buffalo. Vanderbilt, in the dead of winter, ordered his Hudson trains to use East Albany as their terminal, instead of the Albany depot, and this left the Central's passengers to cover the two miles to and from the Central's Albany terminal as best they could. By this maneuver, Vanderbilt battered the Central's stock down to a level at which he could buy control outright for a mere eighteen million dollars.

Young and White prepared for their battle in a manner that the old Commodore would have thought hopelessly weak-kneed—by pleading with stockholders to vote for them. In the course of the fight, Young's side spent some $305,000 on newspaper advertisements, most of them appearing in the New York papers and the others in Washington and Chicago; White's side spent some $340,000. Typical of the Young ads were the headings "A Dismal Dividend Record," "Why New Top Direction of the New York Central Is So Urgently Needed," and "Beware This Ruse! Last

Minute Tricks to Whitewash Central's White." White's ads, mostly
in the same newspapers and slightly more restrained, bore such
headings as "Destination—Dividends," "Which Way Up for New
York Central Stock?," and "Too Good for Stockholders? How
Does Mr. Young Make This Inside Deal Jibe with Morals and
Methods?" In one rather disarming Central ad, Harold S. Vanderbilt wrote, "You do not learn railroading relaxing at Palm Beach.
. . . I know, because in recent years, I have spent a good deal of
time engaged in more or less similar pursuits. But then, I do not
aspire to be chief executive officer." The actual soliciting of proxies
was carried out in several ways. For White's side, Georgeson &
Co., which employed for the purpose around a hundred solicitors,
spread out from coast to coast, set about reaching stockholders by
telephone and in person. Georgeson's solicitors, most of them retired financial men, were augmented by several hundred employees
of the railroad, who volunteered their services, and went to work
calling up stockholders—presumably on their own time, rather
than the company's. Young engaged the services of the Kissel
Organization, of 25 Broad Street, another professional proxy-
soliciting firm, which had served him on several previous occasions. Kissel supplied about fifty solicitors. In addition, Young had
six hundred and twelve volunteers among the Central stockholders
soliciting for him. And he had other sources of manpower, too—
one, in particular, that his rival could not match.

On Saturday, May 1st, all the Eastern branch managers and
star salesmen of Diebold, Inc., a firm that manufactured office
equipment, convened at the Waldorf-Astoria as Young's guests.
They had not been officially notified of the purpose of their visit,
but they suspected that they knew what it was. Diebold was one of
a hundred or more far-flung companies in which Murchison was a
major stockholder, and the unsettling fact appeared to be that
Murchison had offered the services of Diebold's sales force to
Young as proxy solicitors in the Central fight. The salesmen understood that they were to be reimbursed for the time they spent
soliciting, but many of them were unhappy at the prospect, because
selling office equipment was their line and soliciting proxies
wasn't.

At the close of a glum sales conference at the Waldorf Saturday morning, the branch managers and star salesmen marched, forty strong, down Lexington Avenue to the Chrysler Building. There they rode up to the Cloud Club and had a sumptuous filet-mignon lunch, for which Young footed the bill. After the dessert, Young addressed them for a few minutes, in an easygoing, conciliatory manner. "There are two sides to every question," he said. "I'm only going to tell you what are the good things about my side." He then went on to tell them some good things about Alleghany and the C. & O. Over cigars and brandy, the guests mellowed somewhat.

Finally, the branch managers and star salesmen rode down again and trooped back up Lexington to the Waldorf. Upon entering the suite where they had held their sales meeting, they were confronted by a table on which were stacked thousands of sheets of paper. These were lists of New York Central stockholders, classified in two ways—by states and by the number of shares represented. There was an Alleghany man on hand to explain the rudiments of proxy soliciting. Start with Group A, the holders of a thousand or more shares, he said; when you have worked through that group, take up Group B, representing 99 to 999 shares; and so down. "Always try to get there in the evening, when both husband and wife are there," the Alleghany man concluded brightly. "That way, you can get a quicker decision."

Carter, Murchison's man, was also present, and he delivered a warning. "Don't carry this thing too far," he said. "That is, if you're dealing with a Diebold customer and he's dead set against Young or in favor of White, let it go—don't press the point. Never insult a customer, even in a proxy fight."

Despite Young's filet-mignon lunch, his cigars and brandy, and his amiable manner, some of the branch managers and star salesmen still felt put out. "I get it," one of them said to another. "Murchison's Central investment needs a transfusion, and Diebold's the blood bank."

Daniel Maggin, chairman of the board of Diebold, attempted to soothe them. "Look at it this way," he said. "We're in the big time now. This is really *big* business." There was another angle, too, Maggin said. Diebold had been trying to sell equipment to the

Central for years, without much luck. If Young should win, there would be a new board of directors, and one friendly to Diebold. That might mean new business. The branch managers and star salesmen perked up considerably.

WHITE, who was also busy with the routine of running a railroad, masterminded his side of the proxy fight mostly on the basis of information he received at his twice-a-week strategy meetings. These were held in White's office, a northwest corner room affording a view of the Hudson and furnished with a large mahogany desk, several leather-covered chairs and sofas, an Oriental rug, and an antique grandfather's clock. A man who was present at these meetings later outlined the group's customary procedure. White, always looking calm and cheerful and stolid, would lean back in his chair and call on his department heads, one by one, for reports of progress, if any. Raymond F. Blosser, the Central's public-relations chief, or William E. Robinson, chairman of Robinson–Hannagan Associates, would report on Young's latest appeals to the public and recommend ways of countering them—usually by staging a television appearance to balance one by Young. Then Place, the Central's vice-president for finance, would give the meeting the increasingly bad news on how much the campaign was costing the railroad. Richard S. Nye, senior partner of Georgeson & Co., would report on the success, or lack of it, that his staff of solicitors had been having in getting firm promises of proxy votes. McLean and Hand, the lawyers for the Central, would report on the status of various litigations bearing on the fight. Harry W. Frier, an account executive for Foote, Cone & Belding, which was the Central's advertising representative, would discuss newspaper advertisements, and these were considered so important that practically everybody would get into the act before the subject was dropped. The topic of the next ads would be decided on—an answer, perhaps, to Young's frequent charge that the Central's board was banker-controlled, or some statistics calculated to ridicule Young's claim that under his management Central stock would pay dividends of from seven to ten dollars annually instead of the prevailing one dollar. Then the precise wording of the advertising copy would be thrashed out, with White himself doing most of the actual writing.

At one meeting, late in April, there was an argument about how to take advantage of an unexpected bonanza, in the form of two thoroughly pro-White pieces—one an article, one an editorial —in the May issue of *Fortune*. "We couldn't have done better if we'd written those ourselves," Blosser told the others, with a chuckle.

"Well, how are we going to make the most of them?" White wanted to know.

The lawyers began talking about copyright infringements. Only a limited number of words in the two articles could be quoted, they said, without incurring the risk of a lawsuit.

"Damn it all!" White said impatiently. "Don't tell me what I *can't* do! That's the way all lawyers are—always in the negative. Tell me something I *can* do!"

Malcolm Johnson, a member of the Robinson–Hannagan crew and a former Pulitzer-Prize-winning journalist, spoke up. "The way I look at it is this," he said. "If we're going to infringe on copyrights, let's do it up brown. Let's reproduce the two articles verbatim, and send them to every stockholder."

"*There's* a man who talks my language," White said, and the decision was made. After the article and editorial had been reproduced and distributed, Time, Inc., the publishers of *Fortune*, sued the Central for copyright infringement. The case was settled for seven thousand dollars, and the Central management considered the money well spent.

At the time this particular meeting broke up, one of the conferees lingered to speak to White. "How are you standing it, Bill?" he asked. "Getting any recreation?"

White grinned. "Know what my recreation's been since this thing started?" he said. "One evening of bridge in Scarsdale and one night at the theatre. And at that the theatre night was a busman's holiday. My wife came into town last Saturday, and I asked the ticket-reservation desk at the Barclay to choose a couple of tickets for us. Well, what do you think they came up with? *The Solid Gold Cadillac*. And I thought *I* had stockholder trouble!''

YOUNG's campaign headquarters were the offices of the Alleghany Corporation, on the forty-fifth floor of the Chrysler Building. His chief of staff was Thomas J. Deegan, Jr., a suave public-relations man, whom Young thought so highly of that he had made him a vice-president of the C. & O. in 1948, and who, in the days when he had been a newspaperman with part-time connections as a press agent, had extolled the charm and talents of Sonja Henie and had once sent out invitations to a party at Roosevelt Raceway in the name of a horse. So adroit were Young and Deegan at making headlines favorable to their side that tributes to their skill were occasionally heard at the opposition's strategy meetings. One notable stroke came early in the contest, when Young announced that he planned to include a woman on his slate of directors; he was publicly commended for this by Mrs. Wilma Soss, president of the Federation of Women Shareholders in American Business. A month later, he announced his choice—Mrs. Lila Bell Acheson Wallace, co-editor, with her husband, of the *Reader's Digest*. White meanwhile bogged down on this salient; he told Mrs. Soss there were no vacancies on his slate of directors. Young pressed his advantage. The day after the Wallace announcement, he gave a luncheon at the Bankers Club, at 120 Broadway, for about a hundred proxy clerks, including a dozen or so female ones, from various New York brokerage houses; the ladies—just in case they had not been sufficiently impressed with Young's good intentions toward their sex by his selection of Mrs. Wallace—were all given nosegays. Wall Street critics of this beau geste later suggested that many of these clerks, whose employers were holding forty-two per cent of all outstanding Central shares in the interests of customers, had some leeway as to exactly when they sent out the material supplied them by the two sides, and could, if they wanted to, give their host last bats. Later in the contest, Young declared that he had chosen another candidate on his slate of directors—William P. Feeley,

president of the Great Lakes Dredge & Dock Co., of Chicago—
not only because of his qualifications as an executive and financier
but because he was a Catholic. "Gad, the gall of it!" a man in the
Central camp exclaimed, not without a certain stunned admiration, upon hearing of this.

Young's campaign to woo the public reached its apogee on
Monday, May 17th, when, at not only the busiest but the most
critical moment in his career, he welcomed a crew from C.B.S.
Television Newsfilm to his canary-colored private office and spent
the whole day before the camera while carrying on approximately
as usual. The crew and its equipment consisted of a cameraman, a
producer, two lights men, a sound man, a motion-picture camera
mounted on a dolly, three sets of floodlights, a hand camera, and a
sound-recording machine. Young, dressed in a dark-blue suit and
the loafers he customarily wore to work, sat at his eighteenth-
century desk, which, set diagonally across one corner of the office,
commanded a view of both the East River and the spires of Wall
Street. On the desk was a Texas flag, presented to him several
years back by a governor of that state. Although it was a warm
day, the windows of the office were kept closed, to shut out street
noises, and there were beads of sweat on Young's forehead as he
faced the floodlights. The telephone on his desk rang, he answered
it, and a long conversation ensued involving the Pittston Company,
a subsidiary of Alleghany, during which Young made frequent
references to "a million six." Next, he put through a call to Kirby,
in Morristown, New Jersey. "Hello, Allan," he said. "Let's go
forward with that matter I discussed with you. . . . Well, forget
that now. . . . That's correct. . . . And will advise you. Righto.
Thanks a lot. Goodbye."

Joseph Routh, the president of the Pittston Company, entered
the office. He started at the sight of all the television equipment,
but quickly grasped the situation and beamed. He and Young had
a rather lengthy talk about the relationship between railroading
and trucking. At the end of it, Young asked Routh, "Joe, are you
coming to the big meeting in Albany on the twenty-sixth?"

"If my arthritis doesn't kick up," Routh said.

"Gentlemen, could we have that once more?" a television man interrupted.

"Joe, are you coming to the big meeting in Albany on the twenty-sixth?" said Young.

"If my arthritis doesn't kick up," said Routh.

This odd little drama, with the characters playing themselves, went on all day while the temperature in the office—or on the stage—mounted to a scarcely bearable level. The camera followed Young to lunch at the Cloud Club and back to his office for the afternoon. At five o'clock, the television men began packing up their equipment. One of them asked Young, who was by now drenched in perspiration, how he was enjoying the proxy fight. "It's meat and drink to me," he said. "I work hard at it all day, and at night I go home and read about the Greeks—Durant's *The Life of Greece*. You know, I don't *have* to do all this. I enjoy it, or I wouldn't do it. I'm like the fellow playing golf. It's a hot day and he's in a sand trap and he's muffed about three shots, and suddenly he says to himself, 'Damn it, I don't *have* to play this game!' But he goes on playing it anyhow."

IN the last few weeks of the campaign, several currents began to run against White. The Central's petition for an I.C.C. investigation was turned down; so was a subsequent civil suit asking the New York Supreme Court to forbid the issuance of proxies on the eight hundred thousand shares to Murchison and Richardson. Around this time, too, the first reports from Wall Street were coming in, and they were not favorable to White. As the big brokerage houses received signed proxies from their customers, they tabulated the results, and some of them passed their tallies along to the principals in the dispute. More often than not, Young was leading by better than two to one.

The Central men were growing grim and discouraged—all except White, who showed no signs of despondency. "The news all seemed to be bad," a man who attended two or three of White's final strategy meetings later said. "The lawyers reported that they were losing their cases. It was too late to do much more with newspaper advertising. Young was getting most of the space in the newspaper write-ups. At those last meetings, of course, Dick Nye, of Georgeson, was the key man. Everybody was wondering what reaction the solicitors were getting and how the proxies were coming in. We all kind of held our breath until the moment came for Bill White to say, 'All right, what about proxies, Dick?' Nye was a rather dour, gloomy-looking fellow to begin with, and when he said, 'Fahnestock is going against us,' or 'Our Pittsburgh man isn't making out so well,' you could see faces falling all around the room. But not White's. That was the extraordinary thing. He'd be sitting up there behind that big desk, and when Dick had told us the bad news, he'd just nod and smile, and get on with the business. He gave you the feeling he was determined not to let anyone get the impression for one moment that he thought there was a chance we might lose. Maybe he was even determined not to let himself get that impression."

On the evening of May 24th, with the annual meeting only thirty-six hours away, White was host to thirty or forty members of the New York press, most of whom had been covering the contest from day to day, at a dinner at the Biltmore, which is a New York Central property. In inviting them, he had made it emphatic that as far as he was concerned the battle was over except for the counting of the ballots, and he was no longer trying to sell anything. Looking worn, almost sick, but resolutely serene, he circulated among his guests while drinks were being served before the meal. "It's the first day I've felt really tired," he said. "I guess it's the letdown at the end. I don't know. I think maybe I'm running a fever. Maybe this is what I need." He took a whiskey-and-soda from a tray.

A stranger from the *Wall Street Journal* introduced himself to White and explained that he was substituting for the regular man, who was sick. "Sure he's not having dinner with Allan Kirby?" White asked. Several Central representatives who were standing around—vice-presidents, lawyers, public-relations men—laughed wanly. They had all been involved in the fight against Young, and all their jobs would possibly be in jeopardy if he won.

White seemed to brighten after his little joke. "You know, our famous editorial in *Fortune* was called 'The Sound and Fury of Robert R. Young,' " he said. "I'm not a literary fellow and I wouldn't have known that quotation. It took my publicity people to tell me what it is. It's from *Macbeth*—'a tale told by an idiot, full of sound and fury, signifying nothing.' Pretty good, eh?"

After dinner, White made a brief speech. "I get messed up when I talk about this thing," he said. "But anyway, everything's off the record tonight, or, hell, on the record—either way you want it. No one's ever engaged in a slugging match with Mr. Young before. He's always succeeded in ruling by fear. He was surprised when he couldn't do that this time. If we should get licked in this fight—I mean in the unlikely event that we should get licked—I want to see Mr. Young up there on the thirty-second floor meeting our day-to-day problems. I'd just like to see him sit down, by God, and stick it out five years." Then White looked at his watch, said good night, and walked across Vanderbilt Avenue to catch his train to Scarsdale.

THE day of wrath and glory for the small stockholder—so long pushed aside as a nuisance, so often belittled by epithets like "Aunt Jane"—began with a commotion near the gateway to Track 27, on the upper level of Grand Central Station, at a few minutes before eight o'clock on the morning of the twenty-sixth. A train was about to leave from that track—the first of two sections of the Shareowners' Special that the Central ran once a year to Albany. (On the theory that it has less of a speculative ring to it, the word "shareowners" is preferred to the word "stockholder" by many financial people, including speculators.) At the center of the commotion was Young, standing beside a gateman, smiling fixedly, and giving the Churchill V sign for a swarm of photographers. The gateman had the disturbed look of a man who isn't sure whether or not he is being compromised. Young's aides were industriously distributing campaign buttons bearing the legend "YOUNG AT HEART" to a crowd of well-wishers, ill-wishers, and idly curious bystanders.

Just as Young walked down the ramp to the train, followed by an eager horde, White showed up at the gate, smiling faintly as he clenched a pipe in his teeth. The photographers bore down on him, and, upon request, he, too, gave the V sign, but in a deprecatory, mechanical way, contrasting sharply with the zest Young had put into the gesture. White seemed anxious to get on the train. As he stood at the entrance to the first car, somebody shouted, "We want White!"

"I hope you're a stockholder," White said.

Some three hundred and fifty stockholders, or shareowners, boarded the first section of the train, along with White and Young. White and his entourage occupied the first car; Young and his chose a car near the middle. It was a tumultuous, almost hysterical journey. After the stop at Harmon, to change engines, White and Young began walking back through the cars and shaking hands with stockholders. Each was followed by a constantly growing throng of admirers. The two men had met only once since their February lunch at the Cloud Club, and that meeting—on a television program—had been brief and formal. Now, since both were making their way toward the last car of the train, it seemed inevitable that they would meet again. Young, having the shorter distance to go, got there first, and when word came that White was approaching, there was a frenzy of excitement. "They've got to meet!" someone shouted. "My God, it's going to be like Stanley and Livingstone!" White, pushing slowly rearward, seemed to debate at one point whether to kiss a baby a stockholding matron had brought along, and to decide against it. He was now only two cars away from the end of the train. At this point, the train stopped at Poughkeepsie, and White quietly got off and waited for the second section to take him on to Albany.

The meeting, which was held in the drill shed of the Washington Avenue Armory, was attended by about fifteen hundred stockholders. White, flanked on the speakers' platform by McLean and Place, called it to order at noon. Clustered in the three front rows of chairs facing the platform and to the right of a center aisle sat the management's candidates for membership on the board, including Harold S. Vanderbilt, William H. Vanderbilt (a great-grandson of the man who damned the public), James A. Farley, and several of the bankers Young had made an issue of in his campaign. In the corresponding rows to the left sat Young and most of the members of his slate; among the absent candidates were two that some of the stockholders might have been rather curious to get a look at—Murchison and Richardson. In the front corner on the Young side were the ballot boxes, presided over by inspectors and monitors from each faction. Young's proxies had been taken to Albany in two armored cars on the twenty-fourth, White's in a guarded Central freight car on the same day; early in the morning of the twenty-sixth, both sides had brought their proxies to the Armory and deposited them with the inspectors. At the meeting itself, stockholders who had not mailed in their proxies, or who wished to change the votes they had cast by proxy, could vote in person. The counting of the ballots would not begin until the next day.

When the list of Young's candidates was read, the names of Murchison and Richardson were greeted with rebel yells. That set the tone. Stockholders began walking around the floor, making speeches without being recognized by the chair, introducing themselves to whatever notables they came upon, and in general asserting their independence. "Mother!" a stockholder called to his wife. "I just shook hands with all the Vanderbilts!" Mrs. Soss raised a scolding voice to say that White was not running the meeting properly. A Texan stockholder got up and complained that he had heard some White supporters call Murchison and Richardson uncouth. "Clint and Sid will have to look that word up in their dictionaries," he said. Box lunches were served, but they stilled the clamor only temporarily. Farley stood at his place in the front row, shaking hands and remembering names. Elderly ladies marched up to ballot boxes, cast their votes, and marched back to their seats. White tried to read his annual report on the railroad's progress, but the loudspeaker betrayed him and kept letting out bloodcurdling shrieks. Mrs. Soss climbed onto the platform and waggled a forefinger under White's nose, and then was escorted down by a policeman, whose presence did not deter her from smiling brilliantly for cameramen as she went.

At four-seventeen, Young, having gone to the ballot boxes to vote his personal holdings, stood up and announced that the total number of shares voted for his side represented a clear majority of the outstanding stock. "Shareholders," he said, "I am happy to tell you you have won."

From the platform, White asked, "Has Mr. Young the authority to make such an announcement?" Since the votes and proxies had not yet been verified, it appeared that Young did not have it.

At four-forty-seven, after most of the stockholders, sensing that the best of the show was over, had straggled out, White let the gavel fall for adjournment.

THE counting and verifying of the ballots, by three law professors, got under way the next morning behind the locked doors of the Siena Room, on the twelfth floor of Albany's Ten Eyck Hotel. It was a long and tedious job, complicated by the circumstance that during the campaign each side had, by a coincidence, distributed no fewer than seven proxy forms to every stockholder and that any stockholder who changed his mind had had the privilege of reversing his previous vote by sending in a new proxy; the proxy with the latest date on it was the one that counted. It developed that some stockholders had impartially filled out all fourteen proxy forms—seven for White, seven for Young—and a few had topped off this performance by personally casting a fifteenth ballot at Albany.

On Monday morning, June 14th, the meeting was reconvened in Albany, with only a handful of stockholders present, and the results were officially announced. (The press had got wind of the outcome a couple of days earlier.) White had a wide margin in the number of stockholders voting for his side—23,033 to 12,522. But in the number of shares cast—which is, of course, what pays off—Young won, with a plurality of 1,067,273. Since that was enough to insure his victory even without the disputed eight hundred thousand shares—the legality of voting them was still being questioned, but, of course, they had been voted anyhow—White conceded defeat, saying that he did not intend to contest the results in the courts, and adding that he was going home to sit in a rocking chair for a while.

Later that Monday, Young and his board, except for the still absent Murchison and Richardson, held an organization meeting in the Central's board room, on Park Avenue, under the baleful eye of Commodore Vanderbilt, whose portrait hung on a wall there. It had been announced that the new board would assemble that morning at the Alleghany office in the Chrysler Building, march in a body uptown to the Central Building, and triumphantly advance upon the board room, but this project was called off at the last minute. Perhaps one of Young's supporters was right when he said afterward, "Bob's got a prudent streak in him, and I guess he realized that the flourish and the grand gesture—indispensable though they are—can be overdone."

THE story of Young's dashing conquest has a somber ending. White, who wanted to see Young "up there on the thirty-second floor . . . five years," saw him stick it out three years and seven months. Keeping the chairmanship himself, Young immediately delegated Central's presidency to a capable and experienced railroadman named Alfred Perlman. (As for White, that autumn he accepted the presidency of the Delaware and Hudson Railroad at a salary of $90,000.) Under the new leadership, Central at first flourished. Its stock sold well up in the forties. Dividend payments increased, although they never reached anything approaching the levels Young had promised, and some of his other promises went unfulfilled, too. Even so, with the stock up and most of the displaced leaders of the White faction settled in other jobs, it appeared that almost everybody had won the proxy fight.

Then during 1957, things went badly for all of the nation's railroads, Central included. Its stock took a nose-dive. In October, Young was reported to have sold fifty thousand shares of his personal Central holdings—about half the total—in order to satisfy creditors. Later that fall, word came out that he had sold practically all the rest. On January 21, 1958, the Central board met and decided to pay no dividend for the current quarter. It was the first time such a thing had happened under Young's chairmanship. On the morning of January 25th, Young went to the billiard room of his mansion in Palm Beach and killed himself with a twenty-gauge shotgun.

He left no notes; his friends said he had been despondent about the state of the economy in general and the fortunes of Central in particular. In the days following, there were rumors that he had died ruined, like Ivar Kreuger and many a less celebrated plunger, but when his will was probated it turned out that in spite of his reverses he was still over eight million dollars in the black. His complaint to White at the Cloud Club took on a new force: He had indeed been, and now remained, a much misunderstood man. If in life he had been something of an enigma, his death made him something of a figure of tragedy.

$$\$\$\$\$\$\$\$\$\$\$\$\$\$\$\$\$\$\$$$

2

The Adventure of
Morgan Stanley & Co.

ON JANUARY 3, 1955—or just about the time a good deal of the country suddenly rediscovered Wall Street, and something like a national speculative fever was abroad for almost the first time since 1929—Harlow H. Curtice, president of the General Motors Corporation, and Alfred P. Sloan, Jr., chairman of its board, announced in a statement to the press that at a meeting held earlier that day in the corporation's executive offices, at Broadway and Fifty-seventh Street, New York City, the board of directors had decided to raise about three hundred and twenty-five million dollars of additional capital funds through the sale of common stock. Curtice and Sloan—they did not actually manifest themselves, but permitted their words to be delivered through the medium of public-relations oracles—explained that the money was required "to enable production facilities to keep pace with the continued demand for the corporation's products, including replacement and modernization of machinery and equipment, provision for advances in design and styling and to meet customer preference for automatic transmissions, power steering, power brakes and V–8 engines." Although the oracles' syntax appeared to be nearly as cloudy as the Delphic oracle's ever was, their meaning was fairly clear. The money, the announcement went on, was to be raised by offering all holders of General Motors stock the privilege, for a certain period, of buying one new share of the company's common stock, at a yet-to-be-determined price, for each twenty shares of the stock that they already held. (The directors evidently assumed that anyone astute enough to hold General Motors stock was also astute enough to know that the price of the new shares, though yet to be determined, would be alluringly below the current market price.) Furthermore, the oracles revealed, the sale of the stock was to be underwritten by a nationwide syndicate of investment-banking firms headed by Morgan Stanley & Co., as manager. The issue, it was duly noted by financial writers during the next few days, would be the largest industrial financing, by means of either bonds or stock, ever undertaken up to that time. The significant and unusual feature of the issue, the writers also noted, was that the money was to be raised by offering new stock (asking stockholders to increase their investment in the corporation), rather than by issuing bonds (borrowing money to be paid back later, with interest). This was taken to be evidence of a bold and farsighted financial policy on the part of General Motors.

Although in those days my mind tended to boggle at sums running into the millions, let alone the hundreds of millions, I nevertheless decided to go down to Wall Street and see what I could find out about how the movers and shakers of the financial world go about helping a giant corporation raise a record-breaking sum in order to cater to the public's whim in such matters as advanced design and styling, automatic transmissions, power steering, power brakes, and V–8 engines. Other things kept coming up, however, so it was not until a couple of weeks after the flurry over the January 3rd announcement had subsided that I got around to making the plunge. By that time, I had established, with the help of the telephone book and a not very stimulating volume called *Directory of Directors*, that Morgan Stanley & Co. had its offices at 2 Wall Street and was buttressed by no fewer than nineteen partners. An exploratory telephone call to the firm proved to be not the glacial experience I had rather imagined it might be but instead resulted in a cordial invitation to stop around. Accordingly, early in the afternoon of the last day of January, nine days before the scheduled opening of the period in which stockholders could avail themselves of General Motors' offer, I made my way down to 2 Wall, where I discovered by studying the directory in the lobby that Morgan Stanley was installed in the three top floors of the building—the nineteenth, twentieth, and twenty-first. Getting off the elevator at the twentieth floor, as I had been instructed, I found myself in a handsome reception room furnished with black leather chairs and sofas, polished brass standing lamps, and framed prints of old New York. A young lady at the reception desk was telling a friend over the telephone how to do a home permanent. She smiled at me and interrupted her call to ask me what I wanted, and when I told her, she ushered me into a large, rectangular, carpeted room. Near the entrance was a flat-top mahogany desk, which seemed to be headquarters for several messenger girls, and ranged along the sides of the room were ten enormous mahogany roll-top desks, about half of them occupied by men busily writing or telephoning. Each of the roll-tops, I learned later, was the preserve of a Morgan Stanley partner, except for the two on the right side nearest the entrance; these were assigned to Hudson Lemkau and Robert Baldwin, who were two of the partners' assistants. (They were both later admitted to partnership, and Baldwin became managing partner.) The room itself, as I was also to find out, was called the Platform—a harking back to the days when the officers of a bank and their staff all worked together in one big office and the officers were set off from the rest in a section that was raised a few inches above the floor.

Baldwin, with whom I had made an appointment, was talking on the telephone when the receptionist led me to his desk, and he motioned to me to take a chair beside him. "We just can't tell you for sure, Ed," he was saying to the person at the other end of the wire. "Oh, we've got you in mind—in fact, we want to give you all we possibly can. But it all depends on what happens down in Wilmington. Keep your fingers crossed. We'll let you know, Ed. . . . Bye."

Hanging up, Baldwin turned to me. An athletic-looking young man, he was wearing a conservative brown suit, neatly pressed. "That was a securities dealer in Houston, wanting to buy General Motors stock," he said. "Everything is up in the air right now. Depends on which way Du Pont decides to go."

I said it might be best if he began at the very beginning. "Perry Hall, our managing partner, is the man to do that," Baldwin said. "But he's in a conference at the moment in the partners' private dining room upstairs, and while we're waiting for him to be free, I'll tell you some of the rules of the game, and the names and numbers of some of the players. O.K. General Motors has about 88,000,000 shares of common stock outstanding—88,513,817, to be exact. Its current price on the Stock Exchange is not quite a hundred dollars a share. The corporation wants to raise $325,000,000 or so for additional plant needs. They've decided to do it by issuing 4,380,683 new shares and giving their stockholders rights to buy one new share for every twenty shares held, at a price below the going market price. The offer will be good for one month. The subscription price hasn't been decided on yet—and won't be, because of the chanciness of market conditions, until the very last moment, which is February 7th—but let's say for the sake of argument that it will be around seventy-five or eighty. Since that's below the current price, the rights, which will be mailed out to the stockholders, will have cash value. If the stockholders don't want, or are unable, to exercise their rights and subscribe for their additional stock, they can sell the rights to somebody else, who will then either exercise them or try to resell them at a profit himself. Either way, General Motors eventually sells its new stock and gets the money it needs.

"Fair enough. Now, where does Morgan Stanley come in? Well, the point is that raising corporate funds involves risk. Suppose—knock on wood—that during the subscription period the stock market goes blooey for some reason or other, and the price of General Motors stock goes down below our hypothetical offering price. Then the rights become worthless, the new stock won't be subscribed for, and the issue turns out to be a failure. So General Motors pays Morgan Stanley to take that risk. For a fee, Morgan Stanley underwrites the entire issue; that is, it agrees to buy up any stock that isn't subscribed for. By the way, when I've been saying 'Morgan Stanley' what I've actually meant is a syndicate of three hundred and thirty investment-banking firms—coast to coast—headed by us. No one firm can assume the whole risk. The syndicate, you see, would be out about four and a third million dollars for every dollar the market price of the stock dropped below the offering price, and you can imagine what effect that would have on any single underwriter. The members of the syndicate are known legally as the joint adventurers."

I told Baldwin I was still with him, whereupon he looked at me challengingly and said that taking a share of the risk and managing the syndicate was only half of Morgan Stanley's job; the other half was actively selling the new stock. Among General Motors' four hundred and sixty thousand stockholders were some with huge holdings, worth millions of dollars. Though rich as Midas and loyal as Achates, these stockholders would not all be expected to scare up the vast amounts of cash they would need to exercise all their rights. Consequently, some of them—as well as some of the small stockholders—could be expected to sell at least part of their rights, and this might have an unsettling effect on the market. To forestall such a possibility, Baldwin told me, Morgan Stanley would undertake to buy up these rights as rapidly as they became available, exercise them, and then dispose of the stock thus acquired to syndicate members and other securities dealers, all over the country. For each share of stock thus disposed of, or "laid off," Morgan Stanley and their associates would get an additional fee. The syndicate would hope to break about even on these transactions. If it made a profit on them, so much the better; if a loss, so much the worse.

I was pondering the term "laid off," which I had previously associated with a hedging operation of race-track bookmakers, when Baldwin's phone rang. It was another dealer, this one in California, and Baldwin told him that a lot depended on which way Du Pont was going to go. After he had hung up, I asked where Du Pont came into it, anyhow. "Well," he replied, "E.I. du Pont de Nemours & Co., as everybody in the financial swim knows, owns twenty million shares of General Motors—nearly twenty-three per cent of the total, in fact, which makes it by far the largest single stockholder. Exercising its rights for a million shares would cost it—still assuming the hypothetical price—seventy-five or eighty million dollars. And that," Baldwin added, gazing at me soberly, "is a great deal of money in any man's language." As of that moment, he went on, Morgan Stanley hadn't the faintest idea whether the Du Pont rights would be exercised or sold, in whole or in part. The general expectation around the office was that they would be sold.

Morgan Stanley, Baldwin said, had to proceed with its underwriting and selling plans without knowing what the Du Pont decision would be. "You see, if the Du Pont rights were to be put up for sale without someone being ready to buy them, it's quite possible that such a large block of rights would depress the market," he told me. "To avoid this, the underwriting group is busy building up a 'book' of dealer-customers who will stand ready to take up the stock. Then if the Du Pont people sell, Morgan Stanley will negotiate with them to buy the rights, exercise them, and sell the stock without causing any repercussions on the market." Baldwin paused. "And that's about it, as far as *I'm* concerned," he said. "Wait a minute while I see if that conference upstairs has broken up."

BALDWIN went and stuck his head in at an open doorway near the entrance to the Platform. After a moment, he beckoned to me to follow him, and led me into an office that was furnished, like the reception room, with leather chairs and sofas; on the walls, in addition to prints of old New York, were framed copies of several of those institutional advertisements that investment bankers habitually run on the financial pages of certain publications to describe a new issue of stock or bonds and to announce the firms sponsoring it. These advertisements are known in the business, because of their inert, graven quality, as tombstones. In the middle of the room, in a swivel chair behind a massive flat-top desk, sat a heavyset, strenuous-looking man, who had a freckled, wind-burned face and was wearing a midnight-blue suit. Baldwin introduced him to me as the managing partner, Perry Hall.

When Baldwin had returned to the Platform, Hall waved me to a chair and said, "I understand you want to hear the story of the General Motors issue." (His pronunciation of "General" sounded to me very much like "Genal," and as time went on and I paid more visits to Morgan Stanley, I noticed that the partners tend to elide the middle syllable of the corporation's first name, in more or less the same way, I suppose, that the British, as a sign of long familiarity and healthy respect, elide syllables in some of their country's most venerable names.) I told Hall that I did indeed, at which he pulled over a nearby leather-covered straight chair, put his feet up on it, and stared across his office toward the Platform.

"Here's the guts of the thing," Hall began. "The directors of General Motors have decided to do common stock. A fine decision, and not too usual a one in recent years. Last year only ten per cent of American corporate financing was done by stock. Stock is good for the economy, but it's often risky, and it's a lot more hard physical work than bonds, for both the investment bankers and the issuing company. All right, here's how the thing got started. We've done work for General Motors before. That three-hundred-million-dollar bond issue in '53 was the biggest—the biggest any industrial company ever did up to this one, as a matter of fact. Well, one day toward the end of last October, I was talking on the phone with Frederic Donner, their financial vice-president, and we made a lunch date for a Wednesday in November. On that

Wednesday morning, Albert Bradley, chairman of their Financial Policy Committee, called and asked me if I could come back to his office with Donner after the lunch, to discuss, as he put it, 'certain matters.' I said sure. When we got there, Bradley said, 'Well, we want some more money.' " Bradley, Hall went on, remarked that the Financial Policy Committee—which included Curtice and Sloan and other General Motors directors, in addition to Bradley and Donner—had met the previous Monday, as it always met on the first Monday of each month, to take a look at the corporation's financial situation; the fact that the Hall–Donner lunch date came right after the monthly meeting was pure coincidence. During 1954, Bradley said, it had become increasingly apparent that General Motors was going to need more capital in the course of the next few years; at the November meeting, the Financial Policy Committee had decided that the time had come to move, and did so by making a formal request to the corporation's management that it explore the various means of raising money.

Hall put his feet back on the floor and looked at me earnestly. "Well, after that meeting up at Fifty-seventh Street the work began," he said, his eyes lighting up. "There are a lot of ways for a corporation to raise money—mortgage bonds, debentures, serial bonds, preferred stock, convertible bonds, convertible preferred, straight preferred with a sinking fund. Permutations and combinations. I came back down here and got together with my partners, and we worked up a memorandum on the subject. It ran to some thirty pages, packed with facts and figures. Practically everybody around here worked on it day and night for about a month. We finally got it up to Fifty-seventh Street on December 10th. In it, we discussed every method of raising the money. Of course, the General Motors people knew all the methods, but they wanted our ideas on which would be best under prevailing conditions. First of all, we asked, hypothetically, could they do it with straight debt? Sure they could—even after that big '53 issue, General Motors has an enviably low debt ratio. But why lose an asset like that when you don't have to? O.K., how about bonds convertible into stock? Could they do that? Yes, they could—but with convertible bonds you've got to hope that the stock's going up, because if it doesn't, the holders won't convert, and you're left with bonds, not ownership money. Could they do a serial-bond issue, like U.S. Steel? Yes, they could—but that just doesn't fit General Motors' book. So what we finally said in the memo was 'Why not go the common-stock way?' " Hall had been speaking faster and faster as he came more and more under the spell of his subject, and now, his eyes brighter than ever, he was going at breakneck speed.

"What are the advantages of the common-stock way to the corporation?" Hall asked rhetorically, for my benefit. "First, it's ownership money, and doesn't ever have to be paid back to anybody. Second, not all the stockholders exercise their rights. Some of them sell, instead, and that means new stockholders, which, in turn, means new customers—a fellow wants to buy his own company's product. That was certainly a factor, General Motors being a sales-minded company. Third, that low debt ratio keeps the borrowing power in reserve for future needs, acting as a sort of anchor to windward."

At last, Hall paused, and drew a deep breath. "Well," he said then, again putting his feet up on the leather chair, from which he presently transferred them to the top of his desk, "you can be very sure that they know what they're doing up there at Fifty-seventh Street. They didn't just accept our advice. They *walked around* the problem first. As John Young, one of the partners here who has had the most to do with this issue, says, 'When General Motors takes up a question, they don't just discuss it, they pulverize it.' We didn't know what they were going to do for a long time. In fact, we never got the final word until January 3rd—same day as the public announcement. Right after the directors' meeting that afternoon, Donner called up and said, 'Well, Perry, the directors have decided that we're going the common-stock way.' " (Donner told me later that in the course of pulverizing the question, Bradley and the other members of the Financial Policy Committee had carefully considered each of the permutations and combinations mentioned in the Morgan Stanley memorandum and had abandoned all of them, one by one, except common stock. "Basically, we decided on stock because the corporation wanted additional permanent capital," he told me. "Of course, keeping the debt ratio low was a plus. Probable increase in number of stockholders was another plus.")

While Hall was talking to me, a calm-looking man had strolled into the office. "Meet my partner—Chester Lasell," Hall said. "He's in charge of the buying end of this issue, which, believe me, is important. Can you sit down and talk awhile, Chet?"

Lasell said he could. He then explained to me that Morgan Stanley's operations were divided into what are known as the selling department and the buying department. The terms are to some extent misnomers. The selling department, with its operations centered on the Platform, is concerned with lining up new business, forming syndicates, and negotiating, or bidding on, issues. The job of the buying department, which is on the floor below and receives the full-time attention of eight of the partners, is to assist client companies with the paperwork involved in setting up issues; in each case, this includes drafting a prospectus—the buying department's chef-d'oeuvre in connection with any issue—in such a way that it will satisfy the issuing company, the underwriters, and the Securities and Exchange Commission, in Washington.

Between December 10th, when Morgan Stanley submitted its memorandum to General Motors, and January 3rd, when Donner called up Hall and told him that the corporation had decided on common stock, Lasell and his men went up to Fifty-seventh Street several times and huddled there with the corporation's officers and staff over preliminary drafts of a prospectus. Then, back at 2 Wall, they huddled over the drafts with each other, day and night, while the General Motors men huddled, day and night, uptown. During this period, one of the foremost considerations at Morgan Stanley was secrecy. If word of negotiations between General Motors and Morgan Stanley on a huge new issue had leaked out, it might have caused all sorts of idle rumors that would have embarrassed General Motors, and it might also have led to erratic speculation in the stock. Every reasonable precaution was taken against the word getting around, but it was obvious to elevator boys and

messengers—and, in fact, to anyone who walked down the Street
late at night and saw the lights burning brightly on the nineteenth
and twentieth floors of 2 Wall—that something special was going
on at Morgan Stanley. People would say to Hall, "I hear you're
working on something, Perry." "Sure, we're always working on
something," he would reply, and change the subject. Hall kept his
notes on the General Motors issue in a folder marked simply
"Folder X," just in case an inquisitive dealer should drop in unexpectedly and see it lying on his desk. One of the tensest moments
of the whole transaction occurred late in the afternoon of the day
before Christmas, when a friendly dealer stopped by, in all innocence, to wish Lasell a merry Christmas. Lasell's desk, his chairs,
and even part of the floor of his office were strewn with papers,
many of which bore the incriminating heading "General Motors."
Lasell, with a somewhat sickly expression, returned the caller's
greeting. The two men shook hands, and as their eyes met, the
dealer winked broadly. But either the dealer did not grasp the full
significance of the untidy display or he was too imbued with the
spirit of Christmastide to take advantage of it. Whatever the case,
to Lasell's profound relief, there were no reverberations in the
days that followed.

After January 3rd, representatives of Morgan Stanley and General Motors set about thrashing out the exact wording of the
prospectus and of the registration statement—a more detailed document, which includes the prospectus and which must be submitted
to, and approved by, the S.E.C. They did this in a series of sessions
that were held in Room 2410 of the General Motors Building, a
conference room adjoining Donner's office. Sessions were held
almost every day—with many evening bouts, and several on
weekends, too—for approximately a fortnight. "It was a time-
consuming job," Lasell told me. "You see, under the Securities
Act, the issuing company, its officers and directors, and the members of the investment-banking syndicate can all be sued for any
loss sustained by stockholders if there is a material misrepresenta-
tion in the prospectus. The first draft of the prospectus ran to
about fifty closely typed pages. When you have ten or fifteen

people poring over a document of that size, the great problem is to keep everybody's mind on the same thing. What would happen was we'd be moving along, say, to the Corporation's Capitalization Statement, on page five, and suddenly one guy would pipe up, 'Now, wait a minute. I think there's something wrong with the Purpose of Issue Statement here on page four.' That would stop us all dead in our tracks, and we'd groan and turn our minds back to page four. We had thought we were *through* with the Purpose of Issue Statement. In the process of trying to reach an agreement on precisely the right word, differences of opinion are bound to arise. A fellow on either side can get stubborn about some minor point, and aside from that there's a lot of plain old-fashioned haggling involved. Sometimes these prospectus meetings develop into real hassles, but there were hardly any in this case. After all, those General Motors fellows really know their business. If tempers got short, somebody would crack a joke and we'd all be ready for another hour."

The job was finally finished in the middle of January, and the registration statement was filed with the S.E.C. on the twentieth. While General Motors and Morgan Stanley were waiting to hear whether the S.E.C. considered the document satisfactory, they busied themselves making arrangements for printing the prospectus. The print order was for five hundred and fifty thousand copies —four hundred and sixty thousand for General Motors stockholders and the rest for banks, brokers, and other interested parties. "General Motors just got the deficiency letter back from the S.E.C. today," Lasell told me. "Or perhaps I should say the 'letter of comment.' 'Letter of comment' is what the S.E.C. calls it, and 'deficiency letter' is what *we* call it. We haven't had a chance to study our copy of it yet, but it looks very light—only four pages. After we've all studied it, the company people will get together with us again to fix up the deficiencies before we go to press."

I had had about all the facts and figures I could absorb in one afternoon, but before leaving, I asked Hall whether he regarded the General Motors issue as, relatively speaking, a risky one. He lowered his feet to the floor and assumed a rather somber look.

"Sure it's risky," he said. "Consider it this way. Reduced to the simplest terms, if the market price of the stock stays above the subscription price during the offering period, the issue is successful. If the market price drops below, the issue is a failure, and we all get burned. Now, this will probably shock you, but last July, General Motors stock was selling in the low seventies, and in January, 1954—only a year ago—it was selling in the high *fifties*. Well, if the offering price turns out to be seventy-five, say, or eighty, you can see how much risk is involved. I wouldn't say it's quite as risky a commitment as that National City Bank issue last year, though." He paused and seemed to muse, and then went on, "Ran seventy-four days, as against a month for General Motors, and the rights offering was much heavier—one for three, as compared to one for twenty. Of course, you can't really compare a bank stock with an industrial, but, anyhow, that one was a beautiful job of handling by First Boston Corporation. Perfectly beautiful!"

Hall sat silent for a moment, as if in tribute to First Boston's handling of the National City Bank issue. Then he returned to reality. "Sure it's risky," he said. "I wish I knew what Du Pont's going to do!"

WHAT was Du Pont going to do? Would it subscribe for the million shares to which it was entitled, or would it sell them? If it sold, would Perry Hall and his men be able to lay off the million? And what about the shares of the other large stockholders? Back uptown, I found myself mulling over such unaccustomed questions —the cliffhangers in the strangest sort of soap opera. The Du Pont people had said they would try to reach a decision on Friday, February 4th. Monday, February 7th, was to be a busy day for all concerned. At ten that morning, the General Motors Financial Policy Committee was to meet to recommend a subscription price and underwriting terms to the board of directors. At two-thirty, the directors were to meet and act on the recommendation. At three-thirty, representatives of the syndicate firms were to converge on 2 Wall to sign their contracts with Morgan Stanley, and, almost simultaneously, Morgan Stanley was to sign *its* contract with General Motors, up at Fifty-seventh Street. The rights were to go on sale on the Stock Exchange at twelve noon on Tuesday, February 8th, even though they were not to be mailed out to General Motors stockholders until the next day. (Since transactions on the Stock Exchange are customarily not consummated until four days after they are orally agreed upon, rights and securities can be traded on a "when-issued" basis before the seller actually has them in hand.) The rights were to expire at 6 P.M. Monday, March 7th.

While I was waiting for time to bring the answers to my questions, I did some background reading on the investment-banking business. The syndicate system of underwriting stock and bond issues, I discovered, was evolved shortly before the start of this century. Prior to the First World War, a common-stock issue of ten million dollars was considered large; by the middle twenties, issues of twenty or twenty-five million were becoming fairly common but were still considered absolutely whopping. In those days, many commercial-banking firms were also in the investment-banking business; in the former capacity, they accepted deposits and backed commercial enterprises, and in the latter, they were primarily concerned with underwriting and used the capital of their depositors to back their speculative ventures. The 1929 crash and subsequent depression dealt a serious blow to many investment-banking firms, ruining both their finances and their reputations, and their depositors suffered accordingly. In an effort to prevent a repetition of this sort of thing, Congress passed the Banking Act of 1933 (also known as the Glass–Steagall Act), which decreed that institutions that had previously engaged in both commercial banking and investment banking must in the future operate exclusively in one field or the other; it was up to each of them to say which. Among the institutions affected were J. P. Morgan & Co. and Drexel & Co., its Philadelphia affiliate. J. P. Morgan & Co. chose commercial banking. So did Drexel & Co., but later it exercised a bank's prerogative to change its mind and switched over to investment banking. In September, 1935, three Morgan partners

(Harold Stanley, William Ewing, and Henry S. Morgan, a son of the younger J. P.), two Morgan staff men (John M. Young and A. N. Jones), and two Drexel partners (Perry Hall and E. H. York) resigned to form the new investment firm of Morgan Stanley & Co.

The most spectacular development in the field since that time had been a civil suit instituted by the federal government in November, 1950, against seventeen leading investment firms, of which Morgan Stanley was one, charging the defendants with being parties to a conspiracy to eliminate competition among themselves and to monopolize "the cream of the business." The essence of the government's case was that the defendant firms did not try—or did not try hard enough to satisfy the law—to get business away from each other, and were therefore in violation of the antitrust laws. Judge Harold R. Medina, after listening for nearly three years to evidence that filled 108,646 pages of transcripts, briefs, and exhibits, dismissed the case on September 22, 1953.

As for Morgan Stanley specifically, I learned that during the previous three years it had been one of the three top-ranking managers of investment-banking syndicates in the dollar volume of business handled, and this despite the fact that it was far smaller, both in its total capital and in the number of its employees, than either of its two leading rivals, the First Boston Corporation and Halsey Stuart & Co.; prestige, it seems, had a good deal to do with its landing the biggest issues. In a brochure that the firm had recently put out primarily to give an account of itself to past, present, and potential clients, I read that of the nineteen partners, five went to Princeton, three to Yale, two to Williams, and one each to Harvard, Columbia, Virginia Military Institute, Trinity, Chicago, Dartmouth, Pennsylvania, Massachusetts Institute of Technology, and Cornell. The brochure did not give the partners' ages, but it did give the years in which they graduated from college; by this criterion, the oldest was William Ewing (Yale '03), and the youngest Frank A. Petito (Princeton, '36). The average year of graduation, I calculated, was 1922. Further research also disclosed that the roll-top desks on the Platform were copies of those the original Morgan Stanley partners who came from J. P. Morgan & Co. used before they struck out on their own; the desks were worth nearly a thousand dollars apiece, and Morgan Stanley had never had an issue so disastrous that it had had to pawn them.

I RETURNED to Wall Street toward noon on Friday, February 4th, taking the West Side I.R.T. and getting off at the corner of Wall and William. Perhaps because of my recent researches, as soon as I reached the street level, I became more strongly aware than I had ever been before of the financial district's peculiar atmosphere, and for an instant the narrow, crooked streets with the tall buildings rising steeply on either side made me think, irrationally, of the paths in an informal garden. The smell of coffee reached me from the importing and roasting establishments along nearby Front Street, and I was suddenly impressed by the preponderance of men in the crowds pushing along the sidewalk—a consequence of the fact, of course, that the large number of women who worked down there were mostly tied to their typewriters, while swarms of male messengers plodded from building to building, carrying documentary evidence of deals previously made by telephone. I headed west, toward 2 Wall, which, with the other towering structures lining the street, helps frame the soot-blackened spire of Trinity Church for a person walking in the direction I was going. At the corner of Wall and Broad, I stopped to examine something that an uptown friend had told me about a few days before: pockmarks in the masonry of the J. P. Morgan & Co. building, at 23 Wall, souvenirs of the bomb that exploded there in the summer of 1920—the work of an anarchist, many people suspected at the time. The Morgan people have never smoothed them over, preferring, possibly, to wear them as a sort of Purple Heart.

Diagonally across the intersection, on the sidewalk next to the Bankers Trust Company and directly above the B.M.T. tracks, I saw a knot of twenty or thirty people gathered around a florid-faced man who was wearing a Homburg and holding an American flag. Crossing over, I found that a religious controversy was in progress. The topic was the textual accuracy of John 3:5; some members of the group were maintaining that the verse had been mistranslated in the King James Version, and others were cheerfully retorting that it had not. I was unable to make out where the man with the flag stood on the issue. Among the disputants were a second man in a Homburg, who was wearing a slightly seedy chesterfield and looked strikingly like John Foster Dulles; a sandwich man advertising a check-cashing emporium on Nassau Street; and several very young men, all of them holding packets of papers. These last I took to be messengers. There was a good deal of milling around; several men had small notebooks in their hands —or perhaps they were pocket Bibles—in which they made brief jottings from time to time with pencil stubs. The whole scene struck me as an unintentional parody of the scene at a post on the Stock Exchange floor where a particularly active stock is being traded, with a cluster of brokers milling around the specialist, calling out their bids and noting down transactions.

Leaving the theologians, I proceeded to 2 Wall, and was immediately admitted to the Platform by the friendly receptionist. "You've come at a big moment," she said. On entering the room, I saw that all of its occupants were standing up—most of them at their own desks, but a few forming a small cluster around a large, ruddy-faced man who had the next-to-last desk on the left.

"Well, what do you know!" this man was saying, in a voice that had traces of an Oklahoma drawl. "Why, our people go down there to Wilmington any number of times a year, and we have any number of old friends down there, and still none of us had the faintest idea they were going to do this. What do you know!"

Baldwin, who was standing at his desk beside a wavy-haired man with a pipe clenched in his teeth, beckoned me over. He introduced his companion to me as Tim Collins, who, he said, was spending a year in the United States and Canada as a representative of Morgan Grenfell & Co., the London associate of J. P. Morgan & Co.

After shaking hands, I asked Baldwin what was going on.

"Good news from Wilmington," he replied. "The Du Pont people have just announced that they're subscribing for their entire block of shares—provided, of course, that they're satisfied with the price and market conditions when the offering is made next week. It's the best thing that could have happened, from everyone's point of view." He went on to explain that the Du Pont finance committee had met in Wilmington that morning to hammer out a final decision on the General Motors stock. Morgan Stanley had been told about this meeting, and had been told that when a decision was reached, word would instantly be sent to Donner, since General Motors was the party most directly interested. Morgan Stanley had then arranged to have Donner relay the word to John Young—the Morgan Stanley partner at the next-to-last desk on the left—who had been handling the Du Pont angle of the issue. Just a minute or two before I had arrived, Baldwin said, Young's telephone had rung, and everybody, realizing that this was the crucial moment, had stood up at his desk and waited tensely. Then Young had announced the news, and everyone had begun to talk at once.

"It's the same in London," Collins remarked, puffing on his pipe. "Whenever there's a dramatic moment in banking, everyone stands up. Of course, one speaks of the Parlor at Morgan Grenfell, rather than of the Platform."

"What do you know?" Young said again. "We had a release all ready to make public stating that we would negotiate to buy the Du Pont rights. That's how much we thought they were going to sell. They were really close to the chest."

One of the other partners, a rugged-looking man with a mane of gray hair, called to a colleague across the room, "What's the latest on General Motors?"

"A hundred and one," the second partner replied. "Jumped three and an eighth on the first trade after the announcement—on a forty-two-thousand-share block. Pretty lively, eh?"

"Pretty lively," the gray-haired partner agreed. "You know, I never thought they were going to do it."

"Neither did I," the second partner said. "Matter of fact, I gave five to one that they wouldn't—in lunches. I'll be feeding the guy for a week."

Everybody on the Platform grinned happily.

on the afternoon of the following Monday—February 7th—I went downtown hoping to witness the formal organizing of the syndicate, at which members of the other participating firms, or their representatives, were to sign up with Morgan Stanley for their part in the issue. I had heard that this was scheduled to take place in a couple of rooms the firm rents on the twelfth floor at 2 Wall, but I first went up to the Platform to see if it would be all right for me to be present. As I got out of the elevator at the twentieth floor, I met Hall, waiting for a down car. He said he was on his way up to Fifty-seventh Street to sign the underwriting contract with General Motors on behalf of the syndicate. "By the way, don't get the idea that the Du Pont subscription means we're out of the woods," he added. "The fact that an issue gets off to a flying start—in this case, before it's even on the market—doesn't mean everything, by a long shot. When an issue goes wrong, it goes wrong *fast*. Suddenly nobody wants your securities. You just sit up here waiting for the phones to ring, and brooding."

An elevator arrived, and Hall waved to me and got into it. In the reception room, I met Baldwin, who said he was going down to the twelfth floor to have a look at the signing, and invited me to go along with him. On the way down, he glanced at his watch and said, "Exactly three-thirty now—Stock Exchange closing time, and the formal time for announcing the offering price. Here it is." He pulled out of his pocket a slip of paper on which the number "75" was written. "That's a little lower than was generally expected," Baldwin said. "It makes the offer very attractive to existing stockholders. At present prices, the rights will be worth more than a dollar for each share held."

On the twelfth floor, a couple of dozen underwriters, or their representatives, had already turned up and more were pouring in by the elevatorful. Morgan Stanley's accommodations down there, I found, contrasted sharply with those of the Platform—just two adjacent rooms, each about twenty by thirty feet and bare except for some filing cabinets against the walls, and in each room two long and battered tables, like those used for picnics, with long benches flanking them. The two rooms were reserved for just such syndicate signings as this, Baldwin said. On a table at the entrance to one of the rooms was a placard marked "A to K," and on a table at the entrance to the other was a placard marked "L to Z." As each underwriter arrived, he picked up his contract form at one table or the other, depending on the initial of his firm, and went in and sat down at one of the tables to glance over his contract and sign up. Most of the underwriters kept their hats on the whole time, and there was a good deal of kidding among them—a sort of rowdy conviviality that reminded me of a group of men in the Army taking a physical examination or signing the payroll. "Boy, kindly direct me to a seat," one underwriter said to another, obviously his peer, as he got off the elevator. A puckish-looking elderly man with a bowler pressed down on his ears came up to me and said, "Brother, this is *some* issue!"

A bespectacled young man with a jutting jaw was moving around confidently among the underwriters, passing out small slips of paper. Baldwin told me that he was Charles Francis Morgan, grandson of J. P. the younger and son of Henry S., the "Morgan" in Morgan Stanley. Young Morgan graduated from Harvard in 1950 and joined the firm a year and a half later. He was subsequently made a partner in 1956. "The underwriters don't know the price when they come in," Baldwin said. "But they *do* have a good enough idea of it so that it's highly doubtful any of them will balk at signing. The price and the terms are printed on Charlie's slips. There hasn't been time to put them in the contracts the underwriters will sign, but the underwriters trust Morgan Stanley to fill them in later." The slips, Baldwin went on to say, had been hastily printed up since noon, immediately after the General Motors Financial Policy Committee had recommended the price and the terms to the General Motors directors. Word that the directors had approved the recommendation had just come through.

By now, some of the underwriters were leaving, waved on their way by Morgan. "By God, I don't think they'll have to lay off any at all at that price," one departing underwriter said.

"Sure they will," said another. "The big fellows won't take up."

"Well, I'll see you when we sign on Kansas Gas & Electric, if I live that long," said the first.

Baldwin and I went back up to the twentieth floor, where he excused himself and made for his desk. In the reception room, I met Lasell, who proudly held up a large pamphlet. "Well, here it is," he said. "A dummy of the prospectus in its final form. The presses are already running on the inside pages, where there's no mention of the price. The first copies of the prospectus will go out to stockholders, along with the rights, on Wednesday." At the top of the first page of the pamphlet I read: "PROSPECTUS—4,380,683 Shares, General Motors Corporation, COMMON STOCK."

I asked Lasell how General Motors and Morgan Stanley had made out with the S.E.C. on the deficiency letter. He replied that there had been only two sticky points, one of which—a matter having to do with General Motors' relative position in the automotive industry—had been easily cleared up. The other sticky point had been on page fourteen, which carried a general statement about the General Motors bonus plan for executive and supervisory personnel. The S.E.C. had requested that several sentences be added there explaining how General Motors goes about acquiring the stock that it distributes as bonuses. The request was complied with, reluctantly. "General Motors had no objection to that information being put in," said Lasell. "But they wanted it further along in the text. What they, and we, objected to was putting it right there, where it doesn't belong. It doesn't follow the sentence before it. What the S.E.C. did, as I see it," he concluded, in an aggrieved tone, "was force us into a non sequitur."

Lasell went back to his office on the floor below, and I went on to the Platform. I found Baldwin and Lemkau busy on their telephones, answering queries from dealers about when Morgan Stanley expected to have some General Motors stock to lay off. Baldwin and Lemkau were replying that they didn't know, but that it would be no earlier than Wednesday—two days from then. Charles Morgan, still carrying a fistful of the little slips, was wandering around the room.

"What was the effect in San Francisco and Los Angeles?" one of the partners called down to a man in a room near the messenger girls' desk, where there was a Stock Exchange ticker.

"The latest in L.A. is ninety-nine—off more than a point," the man called back.

"That shows you never know," said the partner.

Baldwin pointed out to me that since, because of the difference in time, the exchanges on the West Coast had not yet closed for the day, the drop of more than a point in the price of General Motors stock out there reflected the immediate reaction of at least some investors to the announcement of the subscription price.

"What time do you expect to be through at the printer's tonight, Charlie?" a partner asked Morgan.

"God only knows," Morgan said. "This is such a big job, and such a rush one, that Pandick, our regular printer, has farmed out part of the run to Donnelley, in Chicago. They're going to be rushing nine thousand prospectuses an hour to New York, by airline."

"Rushing them in by airline reminds me of the summer of 1952," Baldwin remarked. "Some of us were at Tulsa, working out a prospectus for a pipeline issue. The issuing company was in a hurry to get to market, and when we'd finished the prospectus there weren't any airliners immediately available to get the Morgan Stanley party home, so the company lined up a converted bomber for us. We got home, all right, and the issue went to market on time, but we had to dodge a tornado on the way." He gave me a glance. "See what we mean when we speak of joint adventurers?" he said.

AT eleven o'clock the following morning—Tuesday, February 8th —the S.E.C. sent word to the Stock Exchange that everything was now formally O.K.'d, and at noon public trading in the rights began, on a when-issued basis. The rights opened with a block of five hundred thousand at a price of 1 3⁄32, or $1.09375. (When it comes to sums of less than a dollar, the Stock Exchange figures in terms not of cents but of fractions in which the denominators are powers of 2. Nobody knows why.) On Wednesday morning, General Motors began mailing out its rights and prospectuses, and Morgan Stanley, which had obtained permission from the Stock Exchange to deal directly with each stockholder who owned fifty thousand shares or more of General Motors, began getting in touch with the members of that fortunate group and making bids for their rights. Meanwhile, J. P. Morgan & Co., which was acting as the New York subscription agent for General Motors, took temporary space—a large ground-floor room—at 120 Wall, down at the other end of the Street from Morgan Stanley. Here it began welcoming in stockholders' rights and money, most of which were sent by mail, although a surprising number of investors turned up in person to see the thing through.

That same morning, Du Pont proved that its word was as good as its bond when a representative of the firm walked into J. P. Morgan & Co., at 23 Wall, and plunked down rights for one million shares, along with a check for seventy-five million dollars. A Morgan official thanked the representative, accepted the check —holding it fairly gingerly, even for a Morgan man—and carried it down to 120 Wall. Up the Street, on the Stock Exchange, General Motors stock that day went ex-rights and ex-dividend— meaning that from then on people who bought the stock would not be entitled to either the stock rights or the regular quarterly dividend of a dollar a share, which was payable in March. To a financial man, this action could logically be expected to knock the price of the stock down a little more than two points, which is just what it did—General Motors dipped from 99 1⁄8 to 96 3⁄4. Late that afternoon, Morgan Stanley found that it had bought up enough rights from the fifty-thousand-shares-or-more group for its first layoff, and thereupon laid off 101,883 shares without batting an eye.

A FEW days later, I heard that Hall had sneaked off to a place of his at Woods Hole for a short vacation, and Young to Hobe Sound, in Florida, for a longer one. From these portents, I assumed that everything must be going well with the issue. Right from the start of the four-week offering period, I had been watching the papers to see how General Motors stock was doing, keeping a weather eye out for repercussions. On February 10th, the stock was up to 99⅜. On the eleventh, it slipped to ninety-seven, and on the fourteenth—a weekend having intervened—to 95¼. On the sixteenth, it was down to 93½. The rights, meanwhile, had dropped from 1¹⁴⁄₆₄ to ⁵⁸⁄₆₄ or 90.625 cents. (The Stock Exchange always reduces its fractions to their lowest terms when the denominator is 4 or 8. However, when it is 16, 32, 64, or 128, the Exchange sometimes reduces them and sometimes doesn't.) At about this time, noting that while the decline in General Motors was in progress, the market averages had for the most part been holding steady, I decided to call Morgan Stanley and find out how the partners felt about the situation, and upon doing so I was connected with Lasell. "Don't worry too much," he said. "We think it's just the volume of rights that people are selling; they're hitting the bid and punishing the stock a bit. We think it will all blow over pretty soon."

It did. On February 25th, the stock was down to 92¼ and the rights to ⁵⁵⁄₆₄, but then a slow rise set in. On March 1st, with only a week of the offering period left, the stock climbed to 94⅜ and the rights to ⁶¹⁄₆₄, and I called Morgan Stanley again. "It looks a lot better," Lasell said. "To date, the public has subscribed for fifty-five percent of the issue, and we've successfully laid off another ten per cent. The chance of the stock falling to seventy-five looks pretty remote now. We expect things will be fairly quiet from here on until the very end. Human nature being what it is, a lot of stockholders and brokers will wait until the last day and then crowd into 120 Wall to exercise their rights."

Taking my cue from that, I waited until the last day myself, and then, shortly before noon on the morning of March 7th, headed for 120 Wall to see the stockholders—victims of human nature, one and all—throng in under the wire. On my way, I stopped in at the New York Stock Exchange visitors' gallery, which I found crowded with tourists staring down at the trading floor with glazed expressions. General Motors stock was selling at $97\frac{3}{4}$ and the rights at $1\frac{9}{64}$, I learned from a young woman who was acting as a guide in the gallery and who could interpret far better than I the symbols that were dancing across the illuminated ticker screens along the sides of the room high above the floor. Beside Trading Post 4, where both General Motors stock and the fast-expiring rights were being traded, stood two groups of men—one the stock group and the other the rights group, the guide said. The rights group was the larger and more active; its members were seething around and scribbling on their pads like mad. "It's the last minute for them," the guide explained. "At twelve o'clock sharp, the rights go off the board. That leaves time for the buyers to exercise their rights before expiration time, at six o'clock this evening."

Sure enough, on the stroke of twelve, the ticker reported, now in plain English, "DEALINGS SUSPENDED IN GENERAL MOTORS RIGHTS—FINAL SALES IF ANY FOLLOW." A minute or two later, it reverted to gibberish to announce, "GM RTS 2000S 1.8.64," which, with some help from the guide, I made out to mean that the last transaction had been two thousand rights at $1\frac{8}{64}$, or $1\frac{1}{8}$, or $1.12\frac{1}{2}$. After a round of backslapping, the members of the rights group dispersed, wandering off and soon melting into other groups around the trading floor.

Leaving the Exchange, I went on to 120 Wall, where the door to the ground-floor room bore the inscription, in gold letters, "J. P. Morgan & Co., Subscription Agent for General Motors Corporation." I went in and found myself in a scene of bustle and confusion. The whole place had been festooned with pictures of Chevrolets, Buicks, Oldsmobiles, Pontiacs, and Cadillacs. There were a dozen or so desks—less grand than the ones on the Platform—ranged along the walls, a row of straight chairs just inside the door, and a long counter at the rear. A line of men, each carrying a packet, was strung out before the counter; a man or woman sat expectantly beside each of the desks, while the Morgan man occupying it studied the papers he or she had brought; and several people were waiting in the straight-backed chairs. A tall, fatherly

Morgan man was welcoming the stockholders as they arrived, ushering them to chairs and assuring them that their wait would be short. "This way, lad," he said to the man ahead of me, patting him on the back. "You'll have your new stock in no time."

After I had persuaded the greeter that I was not a stockholder, he introduced me to a tall, white-haired man named Sydney J. Geismar, a Morgan assistant secretary and the man who was pretty much in charge of things at 120 Wall. Geismar explained that the people beside the desks were stockholders exercising their rights, and that the men in line at the counter were messengers from brokerage houses that were exercising *their* rights. "Morgan assigned fifty or sixty of its regular people to the rights job, and hired a hundred and forty more to help out," Geismar said. "We've been closing to the public at five o'clock, but then the clerical and statistical work—handling mail, counting the money, mailing the new stock, and so on—has gone on until two or three in the morning. Around midnight, they've been bringing down sandwiches from the bank's employee cafeteria, which is up on the fourteenth floor."

Looking around at the stockholders present, I noticed that while the majority of them were old ladies, both sexes and all adult ages were represented. I asked Geismar if he had any idea why they came in person, instead of exercising their rights by mail. "Well, let's ask Ware Cady, here," Geismar said, buttonholeing a young man from one of the desks who was taking time out to get a drink of water. Cady said in answer to my question that from what he had been able to learn by talking to the stockholders, they came because they didn't trust the mails, or because they had something to get off their chests, such as how they'd shrewdly bought General Motors back in 1949 for less than a third of what it costs now, or simply because they wanted to see what a man from J P. Morgan & Co. looked like. "Most of them are from Greater New York, but we've had stockholders in here from as far away as Nyack," Cady said. "I remember one man who said he was exercising his rights because he'd been buying securities all his life and General Motors was the only one that had ever gone up.

Some of them, of course, ask us what the market is going to do. And what do you do with a question like that? Parry it, parry it."

"We've had some curious requests," Geismar said. "There was a woman stockholder who was very anxious to send her new stock to her two daughters—divided evenly between them—as Valentine's Day presents. She came in a few days before February 14th, bringing the valentine cards that she wanted sent with the stock. Well, we checked up to see whether the cards would fit into the stock envelope all right. Fortunately, they did, so they were stapled to the customary letter from the bank that accompanies the stock, and mailed out. J. P. Morgan & Co., as I'm sure you know, has a tradition of service."

"Did you hear about the lady from Brooklyn?" Cady asked Geismar. "She evidently didn't understand about the stock issue, but she gathered that General Motors needed money. So she came in and said that the company had always treated her well, and since she happened not to have cashed her last two dividend checks, she wanted to give them back, to help out."

Geismar and Cady went on regaling each other with tales about General Motors stockholders. One woman, in exercising her rights for two shares, had sent in a check for fifteen thousand dollars, instead of for a hundred and fifty. J. P. Morgan & Co. had sent her a refund of $14,850, along with a courteous letter. Eighteen stockholders had sent in signed checks made out to the order of General Motors but with the amount left blank. The stockholder who had been most carried away by the spirit of the occasion, Geismar and Cady agreed, was a man who had mailed in not only his check but his whole checkbook with it.

As I was leaving 120 Wall, a garrulous broker who had been exercising his rights overtook me. "This is one deal the whole Morgan staff has been in on," he volunteered. "Right up to the board chairman—George Whitney. Did you hear about the other afternoon, when Whitney took over one of the desks? While he was on duty, a lady stockholder came in to exercise her rights for two shares and handed him a stack of bills that supposedly totalled a hundred and fifty dollars. Whitney, it seems, was too polite to count them in her presence, so he just took them, smiled, shook her hand, and gave her a receipt. Well, after she had left, he counted the money and was flabbergasted to find that it came to a hundred and *seventy* dollars. Everybody was in a terrible tizzy until it was discovered that the papers hadn't yet disappeared into the files, so they knew who the stockholder was and could send the overpayment back to her, along with her stock."

LATE that afternoon, just before the rights expired, I paid a final visit to Morgan Stanley. There was an ebullient atmosphere about the Platform, I noticed, as I made my way through it to Hall's office. I found Hall seated at his desk and radiating good cheer, and I asked him why he was in such high spirits. "Why not?" he said. "Look. The stock closed at around ninety-seven today, just about where it was when the issue started. This means we can easily resell any unsubscribed stock, and remit the twenty-two-dollar-a-share profit to General Motors, as our contract provides. A successful issue. Outstandingly successful!"

I inquired what Hall thought the chances were that all the stockholders had exercised their rights. At this, he started to put his feet up on the leather chair and then changed his mind, and said, "Well, of course, logically there shouldn't be any unsubscribed stock at all. But the problem is how are you going to *make* somebody take money that's his? Some unexercised rights are lying in unopened piles of mail right this minute, some are buried under bills, a few are in the mail of people who are abroad and haven't left their affairs in anyone's charge, some were thrown into wastebaskets by people who mistook them for nuisance mail. There's bound to be some unsubscribed stock—there always is. Matter of fact, just yesterday, upstairs in the partners' dining room, we got up a dollar-a-man pool on what percentage of the whole issue would be unsubscribed. I chose three per cent, because I thought it would be smart to shoot for the high field, but we did it by secret ballot and Cortelyou Simonson outfoxed me. He took about *six* percent."

Three men, their faces beaming, entered Hall's office, and he introduced them to me as Francis T. Ward, Walter W. Wilson, and Herbert Hall, his brother—all Morgan Stanley partners. The four partners jovially discussed the General Motors issue for a few minutes, enumerating some of the forces that might have, but had not, caused a disastrous market break—suppose, say, the break in the London stock market had caught on in New York, or Bill Martin, down at the Federal Reserve Board, had picked this particular time to raise the federal rediscount rate, or, worst of all, shooting had started in the Pacific.

"Did you hear about the stockholder who sent in his whole checkbook with his check?" one of the partners asked. "Sort of like throwing the baby out with the bath water."

The four men chuckled beatifically for a moment. Then Perry Hall said to me, "We wouldn't admit it at the time, but when the stock began to slide at about the middle of the offering period, we got kind of nervous. And there were several days when that China situation looked particularly bad." He stopped, and glanced briefly at the ceiling. Then he resumed, "But when the stock got down to ninety-two and a fraction, one of the partners came in here and said, 'Well, Perry, I think it's hit bottom.' He was dead right, but if he hadn't been, we might have got badly burned." A gleam came into his eye, and he went on, "You know, when I first started out in banking, it was making straight loans with the Guaranty Trust, and I thought, 'Gee, this is dull work.' Then one day I got over into the investment end, and I knew right away it was for me. Australia bonds one minute, American Telephone the next. It's got romance. But it's also damn hard work. It's a strain. You go to a price meeting on a big issue and you try to figure out what price is right for the market. Who's to say what price is right? Finally, you decide. You know what you *think* is right—101¼ on a bond, seventy-five on a stock, or whatever it is. It *seems* right; you feel it in your bones. Then, after you've decided, you say to yourself, 'I wonder if I *was* right. Shouldn't Australia be a quarter of a point higher? Or American Telephone a quarter of a point lower?' "

Perry Hall put his feet on top of his desk and grinned broadly.

A COUPLE of days later, the final box score of the issue was announced. Ninety-eight and a half per cent of the new stock had been subscribed for, either by the stockholders it was originally offered to or by persons who had bought rights and exercised them. Subscribing stockholders could be presumed to be happy, since they had paid seventy-five for shares that were currently selling for around ninety-five. General Motors' proceeds from the issue were $328,551,225, less the cost of underwriting, which came to a net of $2,790,814. That left the corporation the sum of $325,760,411, with which *it* could be presumed to be happy. (To be sure, from this sum had to be deducted various expenses, including a fine of five dollars levied against General Motors by Magistrate Louis Kaplan, in Lower Manhattan Court, after the corporation pleaded guilty to allowing seventy-eight employees in its stock-transfer department to work on Sunday, March 6th, in violation of the Penal Code, which forbade "all labor except works of necessity and charity" on the Sabbath; a summons was served on the corporation by a policeman whose attention was called to the situation by a passerby. Magistrate Kaplan considered transferring General Motors stock to be neither necessary nor charitable.) The underwriting syndicate's total fee for assuming the risk was $2,803,637.12. Morgan Stanley, as an underwriter, collected $82,439.04 for its share of the risk, and it also received $55,973.30 for managing layoffs, which had totalled 560,200 shares. These fees, together with its fee for its management services, presumably made Morgan Stanley happy, too. One and a half per cent, or 66,427 shares, of the stock had been unsubscribed, and this was bought by Morgan Stanley, for the underwriters, at seventy-five and resold at 94½, for a profit of $1,292,470, after commissions —a neat bundle that, by the terms of the contract, went to General Motors, presumably making the corporation even happier than it had expected to be. The Morgan Stanley partners' pool was won by Alfred Shriver, who had guessed that one and six-tenths per cent of the stock would go unsubscribed, and who smiled happily as he was congratulated by his colleagues for having come so close. At a dollar a partner, Shriver presumably cleared $18. All in all, just about everyone concerned could be presumed to be as happy as a clam, except the owners of the unsubscribed, and now worthless, rights lying in unopened piles of mail, or buried under bills, or, as ashes, at the bottom of incinerators. By carelessness or oversight, these stockholders had given the corporation $1,292,470, or nearly a third of its costs in getting out the whole issue. As for the public, it could be pretty sure that there would be no lack of advanced designs and styles, automatic transmissions, power steering, power brakes, and V–8 engines for some time to come.

PART TWO

Europe

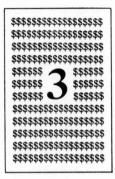

The City of London

THE NINETEENTH-CENTURY British economist Walter Bagehot called the City—that is, the old City of London, the British equivalent of Wall Street—"by far the greatest combination of economical power and economical delicacy that the world has ever seen." What Bagehot meant by "delicacy" undoubtedly embraced, among other things, a reserve sometimes bordering on iciness—particularly in dealings with strangers—that is still said to characterize London's financiers in the twentieth century not much less than it did in the nineteenth. Even the loyally British publication the *Economist*, of which I have been a reader for many years (and of which Bagehot was a famous editor), speaks a bit guardedly of the City's "veil of privacy." Such a reputation for cool imperviousness naturally tends to affect an inquisitive transatlantic visitor very much as Mount Everest affected Mallory. So when I found myself on the loose in London for a few days in the autumn of 1960, I resolved to have a go at cracking the City's reticence; before I was through, I ran into plenty of delicacy, no iciness to speak of, and intimations, at least, of power.

It might be thought that an American hoping to slip behind the City's veil would need some language training, the local dialect being what it is. I considered myself fortunate in this respect, for my years of puzzling over the *Economist* had amounted to a Berlitz course. As things turned out, though, I was given no opportunity to show that I knew how to translate into British such American terms as mutual funds (unit trusts), installment debt (hire-purchase debt), and investment and commercial banking (merchant banking). Nevertheless, my training served a purpose, for it enabled me to tackle the City with the knowledge that the same, or similar, institutions flourish on both sides of the Atlantic, however different the local folkways may be. A buck is a buck and a quid is a quid; introduce a factor of about 2.81, as the exchange rate stood in 1960, and bucks turn into quids or quids into bucks. Another confidence-builder was the fact that at the time I was in London, the stock market there was straining toward an all-time high. In Wall Street, there is nothing like a good market to thaw out economical delicacy, just as there is nothing like a bad market to freeze it up.

INDEED, when I emerged from the Underground station outside the Bank of England one drizzly morning, I got the impression that the City was in a friendly and expansive mood. Probably this feeling came in considerable part from the presence everywhere of flowers, which are so bleakly absent from Wall Street. Wandering around the central streets of the City, I discovered that almost every one of the buildings, however massive and soot-blackened,

had flowerboxes on its window ledges or out on the sidewalk—
mainly at that time containing late-blooming varieties, like chrys-
anthemums. As for the people on the streets, they looked cheerful
enough, in a self-possessed way. This was most notably true of
certain gentlemen wearing black suits and top hats; these men
were bill brokers—members of a small and ineffably respectable
fraternity whose function is to keep capital flowing around the
City by borrowing from firms that temporarily have too much
money on hand and lending to firms that haven't enough. Wall
Street has no bill brokers, and it could use some, if only to give the
place a little tone. Out of curiosity, I followed a bill broker at a
decent distance as he proceeded with a purposeful but unhurried
stride along Poultry, past Old Jewry, and on to the corner of
Queen Street, where he met another of his kind. The two of them
nodded, their hats giving the gesture a certain exaggerated quality,
and after conversing for a moment on the sidewalk they both
entered a building labeled Ghana Commercial Bank. Capital, it
was safe to assume, would soon be flowing.

   Circling back, I began to notice right and left the City's similarities to Wall Street—or, rather, to avoid provincial ethnocentrism,
Wall Street's similarities to the City. There were the same long
black cars disgorging men of substance in front of their offices.
There were the same little alleys largely monopolized by pedes-
trians, the same new glass-walled buildings interspersed here and
there among the predominant heavy old stone ones, the same non-
descript side streets lined with loft buildings whose ground floors
were occupied by shops selling luggage, office equipment, and
stamp collectors' items. (A natural law of money: The presence of
great quantities of it tends to impose a certain pattern on the
surroundings, the way a magnet imposes a pattern on iron filings.)
Furthermore, the old (and now no longer functioning) Royal
Exchange, a Corinthian temple standing at the key intersection of
the City, where Threadneedle Street and Cornhill meet, suggested
our Subtreasury Building—the Corinthian temple at the intersection of Wall and Nassau. Entering the Royal Exchange, I found it
largely given over to an exhibition of City antiquities, including
some coins from the time of Julius Caesar, and even earlier. (An-

other natural law: Money, once established in a certain place, tends to stay there.) Some of the old coins had been unearthed recently, and a sign urged anyone who found such coins, in the course of scrabbling in City soil, to turn them in. With British thoroughness, the sign invoked both authority and reason by pointing out that, in the first place, the law required that old coins be turned in, and that, in the second, it was to the finders' own advantage to turn them in, since they were worth more as museum pieces than as precious metal.

Glancing back after leaving the Royal Exchange, I observed on its architrave the quotation, "The Earth is the Lord's and the fulness thereof." It was hard—impossible, rather—to resist the cynical thought that insofar as gold bullion may be said to represent the earth's fullness, quite a bit of it just then was the Bank of England's (the Bank is the fiscal agent for the British government), and was at that very moment reposing in the depths of that institution, right across Threadneedle Street from where I was standing. There were some benches on the sidewalk opposite the Bank, and I sat there for a while looking at the building. It reminded me of a mammoth mausoleum, its high ground floor unrelieved by a single window, its doors like those usually found on vaults. Its custodians, however, had not felt impelled to adorn it with flowers. I was thinking that, to judge by the front it presented, the Bank carried reticence well beyond the point of economical delicacy when I saw with a sense of relief—almost of shock—a couple of blithe young secretaries sashay in through that seemingly impenetrable entrance. But they had certain advantages I lacked, and I recalled the experience of an Englishman I had read about who approached the Bank for reasons similar to mine and, on being ushered into the presence of one of its officers, asked what his duties were. "To protect Bank officials from the likes of you, if you don't mind my saying so," the officer replied. I decided to pass up the Bank—at least for that day.

INSTEAD, I started with the London Stock Exchange, knowing that, like all stock exchanges in this age of distributed wealth, it was democratically inclined, and had gone so far as to emulate the New York Stock Exchange by installing a visitors' gallery. One reaches the gallery by climbing one flight from an entrance at 8 Throgmorton Street, right around the corner from the Bank, and then walking through a couple of reception rooms decorated with modern furniture, pamphlets, and pretty girl guides. It was all just as it is in New York, except for one thing: In London you can scarcely look at any of the rooms' furnishings—a curtain, say, or a section of wallpaper—without finding a reproduction of the London Stock Exchange coat of arms and motto, *"Dictum Meum Pactum,"* or "My word is my bond." The gallery is very much like the New York gallery. As for the floor itself, though it is less capacious than New York's, the brokers and traders on it are just as fond of littering it with small pieces of paper and almost as fond of engaging in fake fist fights and other forms of horseplay. The London floor, however, is enviably brightened by the presence around the perimeter of numerous men wearing red-and-navy-blue uniforms and top hats with gold piping, who at intervals utter weird, singsong cries, audible even through the pane of glass and reminiscent of the cries of actors in Japanese *no* drama. Moreover, the London floor has a good many benches. In London, a Stock Exchange membership is called a membership, and it entitles the holder to take a seat; in New York, a Stock Exchange member-ship is called a seat, and it doesn't.

While I watched it all, along with a couple of dozen other visitors, one of the girls offered explanations. She told us that the garishly dressed men were attendants, that their unearthly cries summoned brokers to the telephone, and that they are called "waiters" out of deference to the coffeehouse origins of the Lon-don Stock Exchange. She also explained that the passage of time toward the end of each trading day is marked by a series of three rattles. The first, at two-fifteen, serves warning that no deals made thereafter will be settled until the following morning; the second informs the members that it is three-fifteen, and time for smokers to light up, if they wish; and the third, fifteen minutes later, an-nounces the closing. Lastly, our guide called our attention to twelve pillars on the floor, around which most of the trading was being done, and said they were known as pitches. Having finished her spiel, she wanted to know if there were any questions.

I had one ready. "Why are the pillars called pitches?" I asked.

"Why do you call them pillars?" she shot back, giving me a melting smile.

Since I couldn't think of anything to say to that, I assumed that the Old World had stolen a march on the New, until I found out later that she wasn't quite accurate. The pillars themselves aren't called pitches; the trading places at their bases are, because it is there that a dealer—or, to translate the word into British, a "jobber"—makes his pitch.

After the questions and answers, our girl guide led us into a small theatre, where we saw a twenty-three-minute film entitled *My Word Is My Bond*. In brilliant color, it outlined the history of the London Stock Exchange and went on to present a little sketch of an apple-cheeked British couple visiting a broker to make their first investment; supposedly showing how the Exchange works today, it was liberally laced with ringing affirmations driven home by kettledrums—affirmations like "The City and the Stock Exchange are synonymous with honesty, fair dealing, and integrity." (Bong! Bong!) The New York Stock Exchange had a film, too; it was twenty-seven minutes long, and before getting down, briefly, to the brass tacks of buying stock it presented a hazy pageant of American science and industry, accompanied by ringing affirmations like "Investors have helped create jobs for millions." (No kettledrums.) In cinematic art, it was a standoff between the two great institutions.

At the end of the film, I asked the guide what the chances were for me to round out my visit by spending five minutes or so with an official of the Exchange. She picked up a phone, and reported a moment later that Mr. Simon Preston, of the public-relations department, would see me right away in his office, on the first floor at 23 Throgmorton Street. I concealed my surprise at learning that the Exchange *had* a public-relations department, and simply thanked the girl and made my way to 23 Throgmorton, where I rose breathtakingly to the first floor (it's one flight up in England, of course) in a contraption that seemed the perfect embodiment of the Exchange's odd mixture of old and new—a nineteenth-century open-grillwork elevator that had been converted to self-service. Mr. Preston, a smiling, fair-haired, youngish man, debonair of manner and public-school of speech, told me apologetically that he might be interrupted while we were talking; one of the companies listed on the Exchange was suspected of some fishy dealings, the Exchange had just turned over certain information to the police, and, as a result of these developments, he was in a bash. He didn't look it, though; he looked as calm as Nelson at Trafalgar. "Been to the gallery, have you?" he said. "You saw *My Word Is My Bond,* I suppose, and the *'Dictum Meum Pactum'* wallpaper? They adopted that motto when the Exchange was organized, in 1773. Possibly it annoys you slightly? We emphasize it because that is considered one of the nicest aspects of this business —nothing written down, all deals made orally and later adhered to. Same thing on your Exchange, to be sure, but since we have the motto, we like to use it. Admittedly, we rather cherish our traditions. For example, dark suits to be worn on the floor at all times, and black hats, if any. Members occasionally show up wearing funny hats. They are immediately seized upon and torn to pieces by other members. I mean the hats. One old boy wears a straw boater once a year, on his birthday, for a lark. It gets destroyed regularly."

A moment later, a pleasant-looking man entered the room. Mr. Preston introduced him to me as Lord Ritchie of Dundee, chairman of the Stock Exchange Council, and the two men then engaged in a short conversation about the bash. I promised I wouldn't reproduce it, and I won't. *Dictum meum pactum.* When Lord Ritchie had left, Mr. Preston fell into a statistical mood and gave me some figures to account for the greatness of the London Stock Exchange. At the time it listed about 9,500 securities, while 1,500 were listed by the New York Stock Exchange. It had about 3,500 members to New York's 1,400. Its members included more than a dozen peers; New York gets whitewashed there. Becoming a member—and I'll drop the comparisons at this point—entails, among other things, buying a nomination from a retired member or the estate of a deceased one; the price of a nomination is regulated by supply and demand, and fluctuates wildly, depending on how appetizing a membership looks at any given time and on how many members have recently retired or died. A nomination cost sixteen hundred pounds in the autumn of 1960, but a few years earlier one went for three pounds. As I gulped at this vision of a lost opportunity, Mr. Preston was interrupted by the telephone, and while he was talking he tossed me a copy of the *Stock Exchange Journal,* from which I learned that an Exchange member named W. G. Barron was chairman of the Committee on Damaged Bonds and Irregular American Certificates. I thought of asking Mr. Preston what that committee was up to, but by the time he hung up, I had decided that the question might smack of economical indelicacy. Instead, I asked him how long the London Stock Exchange had been deigning to bother about public relations. "The visitors' gallery was opened in 1953, the guides were installed in it in 1958, and the film was first shown in 1959," he replied. "Our department didn't come into being as such until the beginning of this year, although the Exchange had been making some sort of stab at public relations ever since the end of the war. Not much was accomplished in that direction, I'm afraid, during the six years of Labour Party rule. The lean years, you know." Mr. Preston smiled a confiding smile, called a secretary, and asked her to bring two cups of tea. "Now, however," he went on, "we like to think we're setting the pace for our neighbors in the City, some of whom tend to be a bit backward in this respect."

DURING the next couple of days, I went on a whirlwind tour of the City, visiting N. M. Rothschild & Sons, the celebrated merchant-banking firm; Lloyd's, the—well, Lloyd's; Hoare & Company, which has the distinction of being the last surviving private-banking firm in London; and, finally, the Bank of England itself. Again and again, evidence was presented to me that economical delicacy is not necessarily incompatible with hospitality—at least, as long as the guest does not insist on talking specifically about matters economical. Perhaps one explanation of the City's easy self-assurance lies in the fact that it *is* a city, and no mean one; in contrast to Wall Street, London's financial district gets its nickname from something bigger than it is, rather than from something smaller. The City of London is an autonomous county within Greater London, consisting of 677 acres along the north bank of the Thames, and bounded by Temple Bar on the west, Aldgate on the east, and London Wall on the north. For centuries, it was the whole of London, and now, even though it is only a tiny section of the metropolis, it stubbornly retains its medieval form of government—a Lord Mayor (or, rather, the ceremonial official still known as *the* Lord Mayor of London), twenty-five aldermen, two hundred and six common councilmen, and a body of liverymen, who, as representatives of the City's trade guilds, are principally charged with the duty of nominating candidates for Lord Mayor. (The guilds haven't concerned themselves with trade for centuries, but they still earn impressive incomes from property and investments, and many of them have splendid headquarters and well-filled treasuries; as Paul Ferris, an Englishman who wrote a book on the City, put it, "Most of their money is spent on schools, charities, and good food and drink.") Again in contrast to Wall Street, the vote in the City is extended to owners and renters of property as well as to its few residents, and this means that its government is in the hands of the financiers who work there, even though nearly all of them live somewhere else. Just as a good part of London, run by the London County Council, is firmly Labour, so the City is firmly Tory, as what banker or broker wouldn't be who hopes for a chance to serve a year's term as Lord Mayor of London?

At Rothschild's, which occupies a stately old mansion off St. Swithins' Lane, I was led through countless paneled and portrait-hung rooms by the firm's secretary, a kindly gentleman who asked me to cloak him in anonymity. In one of the rooms, the secretary presented a young man, who had the look of knowing what he was about, as Mr. Evelyn. I shook hands with Mr. Evelyn. Not until somewhat later, when I became more accustomed to the secretary's idiom, did I realize that the man I'd met was Mr. Evelyn de *Rothschild*. After remarking that the firm, which was founded in 1804, had recently elected its first non-Rothschild partner ever, the secretary showed me the gold-fixing room, where, every morning, seated around an oval table and under the eyes of long-vanished European royalty looking down from the portraits on the walls, the City's four or five leading gold brokers meet to fix the day's gold price in London. Each broker has a miniature Union Jack mounted on a stand in front of him, and when, in the course of the dickering, he becomes satisfied with the price, he knocks his flag down. Nobody at Rothschild's is quite sure how the flag tradition started. All the flags are usually down within five minutes, the secretary said, but during the fevers of gold speculation that occur periodically, it sometimes takes as long as twenty or twenty-five minutes. And why is the price of gold fixed at Rothschild's? Perfectly simple, said the secretary; in the nineteenth century, between financing Wellington at Waterloo, helping to finance Britain's purchase of the Suez Canal, and putting up the cash for a few other little ventures, Rothschild's became bullion brokers for the Bank of England, and that was that.

Lloyd's is not an insurance company in the American sense but a society of individual insurers prepared to cover their losses by putting up their combined private fortunes. When I went to its headquarters on Lime Street, a fatherly sort of man named E. G. Chapman, who described himself as a clerk to the committee, led the way through a room—considerably larger and lighter than that of the London Stock Exchange—in which some men were walking around and talking to other men who were seated. Mr. Chapman explained that the rampant ones were brokers placing insurance risks and the couchant ones were underwriters assuming them. The room, he said, was called The Room. Until about five years earlier, when Lloyd's had moved to its present quarters from its old home on the other side of Lime Street, the brokers walked and the underwriters sat in what was really two rooms but was called The Room anyhow. On a cabinet near the center of the present Room lay a big volume full of reports on ships sunk or damaged, and Mr. Chapman advised me that entries are always made with a quill—not for the sake of tradition, but because a quill writes better on the parchment-like paper deemed appropriate for such records. He also pointed out a board suspended from one of the walls, where the names of prospective members are posted for a while prior to their admission—"like chaps being put up for a club," he remarked, leaning toward me confidentially as he spoke.

Mr. Chapman then escorted me to a large office a couple of stories above The Room, where I met Patrick Ward Milligan, deputy chairman of Lloyd's. "One decides which risks to assume on various bases," said Mr. Milligan genially. "First of all, experience. One has done an apprenticeship of perhaps ten years before becoming a member of Lloyd's. Then, too, perhaps the broker may be a pal of yours." The deputy chairman indicated, with a fractional grin, that he was being facetious, and went on, "Beyond that, there is your liver, the state of the weather, and so forth. Setting the premium in cases where there's no precedent is sometimes simply a matter of looking at a bare wall. The odd underwritings—insurance against holes-in-one at golf, against the capture of the Loch Ness monster, against the birth of twins, against damage to actresses' legs—are *not* an important part of our business, though I must say they are spoken of a great deal. We are rather placid here. We do not get ulcers from contemplating our liabilities. After a big storm that has cost a pretty penny in marine underwritings, you don't find everyone in The Room looking at the Loss Book. You find the crowd at the newsboard reading the test-match results."

"The deputy chairman is excessively modest," Mr. Chapman informed me as he escorted me to the front door. "It takes knowhow and flair to write insurance, that's what it takes."

I HAD a particular reason for wanting to go to Hoare & Company. I'd heard that among the items in a small museum of banking memorabilia that the firm has on the premises was one of the first checks, or cheques, ever written, and I was eager to see it. Accordingly, one of my telephone calls had been to the curator of this collection, making an appointment. The company's offices are in a fine old town house on Fleet Street—not as large as Rothschild's but impressive enough. An attendant led me through the ground-floor banking section, which had a sort of gaslit look, and up a long flight of stairs; on the way, he told me that one partner of the firm always lives in the building, so that clients suddenly in need of a bank in the middle of the night can get attention at once. The collection occupied a front room ornamented with a crystal chandelier, a marble mantel, and two eighteenth-century oil paintings, and there I was turned over to the curator—a peppy white-haired man, wearing a monocle and the air of a mischievous scholar, named R. McD. Winder.

"Ah, yes, the check," Mr. Winder said, going straight to the mantel, where a yellow scrap of paper was preserved under glass.

I followed, and read:

July 11, 1676

Mr. Hoare,

Pray pay to the bearer hereof Mr. Witt Morgan fifty-four pounds ten shillings and ten pence and take his receipt for the same.

Your loving friend,
Will Hale

54/10/10
for Mr. Richard Hoare
at the Golden bottle in Cheapside

"We can't say that it was the first British check—only one of the first," Mr. Winder said. "Incidentally, the Golden Bottle wasn't a pub, as you might expect. It was the Hoares' place of business. They were goldsmiths, with a sideline in banking."

I asked who Will Hale was.

"Why, a Hoare client," said Mr. Winder, plainly implying that any further identification would be superfluous.

He led me to a couple of large glass cases near the windows, and pointed out various documents enshrined there. "Over here," he said, "is a record of a fund to support the suffering clergy in America during your Revolution. Hoare & Company banked the fund. And, here, a judgment of one pound against Samuel Pepys, which I do not believe you will find mentioned in his diary." Mr. Winder chuckled, and his monocle fell out. Deftly replacing it, he continued, "Here we have a copy of a letter sent by our firm to the governor of the Bank of England on the occasion of their two-hundred-and-fiftieth anniversary, in July, 1944. We're considerably older than the Bank, of course. They opened in 1694, whereas Hoare & Company was founded sometime before 1673—it has never been ascertained just when—and has been on the present site since 1689." I read the 1944 letter to the bank, and could not detect in it the slightest note of patronage toward a junior institution. A forbearing house, old Hoare & Company.

On the way out, Mr. Winder guided me into the partners' dining room for a glimpse of the inevitable collection of family portraits, calling special attention to an old fellow who, he said, had been known as Good Henry Hoare. Good Henry looked rather self-satisfied, and no wonder. I inquired whether there had ever been a Bad Henry. "No, but there was a Naughty Richard," said Mr. Winder. "Happily, he had nothing at all to do with the bank."

MR. WINDER had reminded me of the Bank of England. Screwing up my courage, I now marched on it. Well, the Old Lady of Threadneedle Street could hardly have been more gracious. An employee at the main entrance inclined his top hat solicitously while he listened to my account of myself; another accompanied me across a vast expanse of marble floor to an armored lift; a third took me up an indeterminate number of stories and showed me into a little room, where I was left alone to contemplate leather furniture and old prints for a not excessive interval; and a fourth, a young lady, escorted me into the presence of a Bank officer, who did not tell me what his duties were. (I took pains not to ask.) The officer—I'll call him Harris, for he, too, asked me to suppress his identity—and I had half an hour of amiable talk, none of it about the bank rate and most of it about the Bank of England's

Guard. Mr. Harris said that the Guard, consisting of an officer, a sergeant, two corporals, twelve guardsmen, and a drummer or piper, arrived at the Bank every day at the end of business hours and remained until morning, as it had been doing regularly ever since the Bank was threatened by the Gordon Riots of 1780. A while back, the War Office, noting that the rioting seemed to have subsided, suggested discontinuing the Guard, on the ground that it was costly and caused traffic jams while en route to its post. The Bank expressed dismay at the mere thought of such a thing, and the War Office discreetly backed down.

"They generally arrive a bit after six o'clock," Mr. Harris said. "They're apt to come by truck if it's wet, but today's drizzle seems to be over, and they should be marching. It's not quite six. If you go right down, you should catch them all right."

That seemed to me an excellent idea, and after bidding Mr. Harris goodbye I went in reverse through the Bank's minuet of entrance. There was one hitch, though; neither I nor anyone else could remember at what stage somebody had taken my raincoat. This occasioned a good deal of whispering and scurrying around among Bank people, as the specter loomed of the Bank's being found guilty of having improperly appropriated an American raincoat. It finally turned up, and, to everyone's relief, the Old Lady and I parted all even.

I sat down on one of the benches across Threadneedle Street, and at five minutes past six the Guard arrived, marching smartly up in three admirably regular columns, all red-coated and busby-topped. True to Harris' count, there were seventeen men in all, but if one was a drummer or piper, he wasn't drumming or piping. The Guard came to a stamping halt in front of the Bank, and at the officer's command the guardsmen filed in through the entrance. I noticed that nearly all the civilian Britons who happened to be passing on their way home from work stopped to watch. Most of them were grinning the same sort of half-moved, half-sheepish grin that I was.

```
$$$$$$$$$$$$$$$$$$$$
$$$$$$$$$$$$$$$$$$$$
$$$$$$$$$$$$$$$$$$$$$
$$$$$$$$$$$$$$$$$$$$$
$$$$$$$          $$$$$$
$$$$$$$   4    $$$$$$
$$$$$$$        $$$$$$
$$$$$$$$$$$$$$$$$$$$$
$$$$$$$$$$$$$$$$$$$$$
$$$$$$$$$$$$$$$$$$$$$
$$$$$$$$$$$$$$$$$$$$$
$$$$$$$$$$$$$$$$$$$$
```

The Amsterdam Cradle

STOCK TRADING, the buying and selling of bits and pieces of other people's affairs in the hope of gain, was carried on for the first time anywhere in the world in Amsterdam in 1602. The reason it hadn't begun before that is simple enough; there had been no stock to trade—in Amsterdam or anywhere else. On March 20th of that year, the States General of the Netherlands chartered the Dutch East India Company; granted it a monopoly on trade and navigation east of the Cape of Good Hope and West of the Straits

77

of Magellan; empowered it to build forts, make alliances with
sovereigns, and appoint governors; and authorized an initial capital of 6.6 million guilders, to be raised by public subscription at
home. It was a time of general affluence in Holland—the beginning, indeed, of the century that would come to be called that
nation's golden age, in both commerce and art—and the shares
were bought up by thousands of citizens, many of whom instantly
took to trading them back and forth among themselves and with
newcomers to the market. At first, the chief arena for this activity
was the New Bridge, which spanned the Damrak in front of where
the Central Station of Amsterdam now stands. The custom of
trading on bridges derived from Italy, and the Venetian Rialto
evidently influenced the Dutch in choosing New Bridge as a commercial center. Meteorologically speaking, though, Amsterdam
was not a Venice, and on inclement days the traders took to
moving into St. Olof's Chapel, which was nearby, suitably roofed,
and seldom used on weekdays. They were soon evicted, not on
grounds of being moneychangers in the temple but because they
used bad language there. So in 1611, the municipality of Amsterdam built them and their fellow-traders in commodities their own
exchange—a splendid rectangular columed arcade resting on five
arches spanning the mouth of the Amstel, with, however, an open-
air central courtyard as the main trading area, using this time the
design of the old Royal Exchange in London as a model. The
traders were to use it, vigorously and in all weathers, for more
than two centuries.

The strangest aspect of the beginning of stock trading is that it
sprang into being practically fully developed. It went through no
primitive phase; on the contrary, almost all the mystifying complexities and Byzantine misfeasances that were to characterize it
in the twentieth century were there almost from the outset. By
1607, wild speculation, much of it on borrowed money—now
called margin—had driven Dutch East India Company stock to
twice its original price. By that time, too, short selling—the practice of selling shares one has borrowed but doesn't own, in Amsterdam picturesquely called the *windhandel,* or wind trade—was

a well-established practice on New Bridge and in St. Olof's. In 1609, the Amsterdam stock market suffered its first great bear raid, or organized attempt by a group of speculators to depress prices through short selling. Over the next few decades, Dutch East India shares gyrated as wildly, and for many of the same disreputable reasons, as Radio or Anaconda in Wall Street during the nineteen-twenties. In 1621, trading got a tremendous boost when the shares of a second institution, the Dutch *West* India Company, were introduced. These instantly became subject to fluctuations even wilder than those of the older firm, perhaps because the new one's profits, when they came at all, came chiefly not from trade or colonization but from the even riskier business of piracy. (There is no record that news of the bargain purchase of Manhattan Island by the West India Company in 1626 had the slightest effect on the price of its shares in Amsterdam.) Well before the end of the seventeenth century, put-and-call options, time bargains, dealings in fractional shares—practically the whole bag of tricks of latter-day stock traders—were well established. "Oh, what double-dealers!" exclaimed Joseph de la Vega, possibly the world's first stock-market writer, of the Amsterdam speculators in a book published in 1688. But at the same time he fulsomely described the stock-trading business as "a quintessence of academic learning," "a touchstone for the intelligent and a tombstone for the audacious," "a treasury of usefulness and a source of disaster," and, finally, "in this magnificent world theatre, the greatest comedy."

There seem to be two reasons why the seventeenth-century Amsterdam tyros operated at such a high level of sophistication. For one thing, many of their feints and subtleties were adapted from commodity trading, which had gone on in Amsterdam in grain, herring, spices, and whale oil well before 1600; and for another, the shares of the Dutch charter companies were by their nature about as speculative as could be, since the traders usually had nothing more than rumors as to where the fleets were or how they were faring. Even so, the almost Venus-like birth of a more or less modern stock exchange in 1602 does seem to suggest that stock

trading was and is no mere detail of industrial life but a previously
buried form of human behavior that must have been there all
along, waiting its time.

Its time has certainly come now; for tens of millions of fortunate
citizens of rich countries, it is, if seldom a living, a source of vast
satisfaction and one of the few entertainments that enjoy the sanc-
tion of social acceptability on grounds of utility. (The horse
player's protestation that he is generating taxes or improving the
breed rings hollow beside the stock player's that he is helping
finance industrial expansion.) It was with such notions in my head
that, on a visit to Amsterdam in 1969, I went around to the Stock
Exchange to see how the cradle of stock trading is getting along in
the second half of the twentieth century.

THE Amsterdam Stock Exchange's modern quarters consist of a
stately stone-and-brick building, topped with not only a roof but
also no fewer than five cupolas, that dates from 1914 and is situated in the Beursplein, or Bourse Square, just a few steps from the
site of the original exchange. Having entered it and taken an elevator to the fourth floor, where the executive offices are, I was
ushered by a man in a tailcoat down corridors and through ante-
rooms decked out in the international high-finance style (dark
paneling, old prints, stern-visaged portraits), and, eventually, into
the office of U. J. N. de Graaff, the Exchange's managing director,
with whom I had an appointment. Mr. de Graaff, a middle-aged
man with an air of calm precision, spent the next hour telling me
something about the Amsterdam Stock Exchange's place in the
world and its mode of operation. It was, he said, probably the
second most important stock exchange in the Common Market
countries, after the Paris Bourse—West Germany, a far more industrially powerful country than the Netherlands, lost its chance
for this distinction by spreading its stock trading over eight separate exchanges—and it was unquestionably the leading continental market for American shares, with the issues of more than two
hundred United States-based companies listed and regularly
traded. Its most active stocks, naturally enough, were those of

the giants of Dutch industry—Royal Dutch Petroleum, Unilever, Philips Gloeilamp, K.L.M., Heineken's—but not far behind came I.B.M., General Motors, General Electric, and other American blue chips. It had about five hundred members, somewhat more than a third of the number on the New York Stock Exchange's roster. In the period between the two World Wars it had had a woman member, who regularly appeared on the floor and engaged in trading—something that quite possibly had not happened up to then on any other major stock exchange anywhere. But her distinction turned out to be a temporary one; the lady fell in love with a fellow-member, married him, and gave up working. In 1969—through accident rather than design—the Amsterdam Stock Exchange had no women members at all. One of its more engaging characteristics, from an American point of view, was the shortness of its daily trading period. Until 1967, the opening bell rang at 1 P.M. and the closing bell at 2:15; that year, the hours were changed, so that trading took place from 11:30 to 1:15—an hour and three-quarters instead of an hour and a quarter. Even that working day seemed to represent sheer indolence by comparison with the New York Exchange's customary five-and-a-half-hour session. However, as Mr. de Graaff pointed out, Amsterdam had considerably less business to transact than New York—its daily turnover, or total value of stocks bought and sold, normally amounting to some three million dollars, while it was a slow day in 1969 at 11 Wall Street when the turnover didn't add up to a hundred times that much. Even so, though, the stock market in the Netherlands was a big enough affair to be of wide public interest; a survey made in 1963 showed that of all Dutch citizens between the ages of twenty-one and sixty-five, fifteen per cent owned stocks.

The most characteristic institution of the Amsterdam Exchange, I learned, is the *hoek*. A *hoek* is the equivalent of a trading post, and in 1969 there were eighty-two of them on the floor, at each one of which a given stock is traded—or, more often, several stocks are traded. Each *hoek* is presided over by several *hoekmen*, the Dutch equivalent of the New York Stock Exchange's specialists, or brokers' brokers, charged with keeping the books and making the market. What chiefly distinguishes an Amsterdam Stock Exchange *hoek* from a New York Stock Exchange post is its invisibility. The posts at 11 Wall Street consist of U-shaped desks ranged around the floor. At these desks orders are filed and records are kept, and from them completed transactions are reported to the ticker. In the Beursplein, however, the paperwork is handled at a single large central desk, right in the middle of the floor, while the various *hoeken* are simply arbitrarily chosen places, here and there around the marble floor, unmarked in any way. Every *hoekman* knows precisely where his *hoek* is, and so do the members who may want to trade in his stock. No one has ever been heard to suggest that palpable posts be erected—things work all right without them, and nobody gives the matter a thought. Another such tradition lies behind the rather unusual behavior of members and employees each September 10th. On that date, back in 1660, there was a Guy Fawkes-style bomb plot against the Stock Exchange, which was frustrated in the nick of time by a young man who gave warning by beating a drum. Now, on September 10th, members and employees are permitted to bring drums to the Exchange and beat them there—and many of them do.

Mr. de Graaff was a young employee of the Stock Exchange during the Second World War, and he recalled for me some of the Exchange's trials and accomplishments then. It stayed open right through the war period. The Gestapo entered the building only once—in the summer of 1940, right at the start of the Occupation. A detachment marched in, took the elevator to the fourth floor, and invaded the boardroom, where the executive board was in session. The Gestapo men asked various questions about the Exchange's operations, and these were answered by a Dutch Nazi who by German order had been put on the board. After an hour or so, the Gestapo men left, apparently satisfied. On February 25, 1941, trading on the Exchange was suspended for half an hour, during which time the members stood on the floor in silence, in formal protest against the first official anti-Semitic measure of the Germans in the Netherlands—an edict restricting the movements of Dutch Jews. (Among the Exchange's members and employees at the time were between forty and fifty Jews, of whom only a handful were to survive the war.) After this show of defiance, there came a long series of minor harassing measures against the Stock Exchange; in spite of them, however, it remained relatively free to operate as it always had, largely through the firm and deft diplomacy of its chairman, Carel Overhoff—who, far from being a Dutch Nazi, was functioning secretly at the same time as a leading underground organizer. Overhoff's story has a sour ending that I find suggestive about the nature of man's behavior in war and in business: In 1948, de Graaff told me, Overhoff's firm went into bankruptcy, and he was sent to prison for improper dealings in stocks.

ONE of the most striking things that I learned from my talk with Mr. de Graaff and from some subsequent reading was that in the matter of government regulation the evolution over the years of the stock exchanges of the Netherlands and the United States has been in opposite directions. The Amsterdam Exchange, which began life as in many ways the most rigidly regulated that ever existed, has become one of the freest from regulation, while the New York Exchange, which for its first hundred and forty-one years was an almost classic arena of free-for-all competition, has evolved into the most firmly regulated in the modern world. The New York Exchange got along—far from well, from a public point of view—with almost no federal, state, or city policing (apart from that applicable to all citizens) from the time of its founding, in 1792, until the passage of the Securities Act of 1933. The Amsterdam Exchange, at its inception, functioned entirely by leave of the city of Amsterdam—the city owned its building, and a municipal official had absolute power to levy fines on traders and otherwise discipline them. In the early years, for example, trading was restricted to the hour between 11 A.M. and noon; anyone who failed to leave promptly at noon was subject to a fine, and anyone caught still loitering on the premises at twelve-thirty was punished by being confined there until three o'clock, as if he were a naughty schoolboy. As early as February, 1610, in reaction to speculative excesses, the city authorities issued an edict flatly forbidding short selling—the *windhandel*. This, as things have turned out, was as drastic a governmental restraint on stock trading as has ever been imposed anywhere, at least up to the present. Subsequent attempts to ban short selling—or to restrict it so severely as effectively to ban it—for more than brief periods of emergency were made in France in the eighteenth century, in Britain in the nineteenth, and in Germany around the turn of the twentieth. Each of these attempts ended in failure, and the restrictive measures were eventually repealed or allowed to die of nonenforcement—the reason, it appears in retrospect, being that short selling, whatever its evils, is a mechanically essential element in the fair and orderly operation of any stock exchange. And so it was with the original Dutch effort to do away with the *windhandel*. The 1610 edict soon came to be ignored. When, in 1621, a new wave of speculation, including much wind trading, followed the formation of the Dutch West India Company and the first issue of its shares, short selling was again officially prohibited—and again apparently continued to be practiced with gusto. After one more unsuccessful try in 1677, the municipality gave up on eliminating the *windhandel*, and in 1689 the city magistrate issued a decree levying a special tax on it—a measure that, while intended to discourage it, seemed to concede its legitimacy.

Soon even the tax fell into disuse, and the *windhandel* continued to flourish. Moreover, the trend toward less government supervision of stock trading in Amsterdam continued thereafter. In the mid-nineteenth century, the government formally withdrew as owner and proprietor of the Stock Exchange, which thereupon built its own building and took to managing its own affairs with practically no interference. In 1914, a national stock-exchange law was passed that gave the Minister of Finance theoretical power to stipulate how negotiations should be conducted on all Netherlands stock exchanges (in addition to Amsterdam's, there were at the time of my visit much less important exchanges in Rotterdam and The Hague), but it quickly became the custom for

Ministers of Finance to adopt a hands-off attitude and leave the policing of stock trading to the exchanges themselves. The Amsterdam exchange is proud of its resultant self-discipline, Mr. de Graaff told me, and went on to point out that it is so meticulous in the requirements it imposes on companies before their shares may be listed that it even specifies the quality of paper and printer's ink to be used for stock certificates. As to the conduct of its members, it has an elaborate set of rules stipulating what they ought and ought not to do, and an escalating series of penalties for offenders, as follows: first offense, a private warning; second offense, a published reprimand; third offense, a fine of up to ten thousand guilders (about twenty-eight hundred dollars); fourth offense, suspension of membership; fifth offense, expulsion. The members are evidently well behaved, because the Exchange seldom has had occasion to mete out any penalties beyond perhaps one or two private warnings a year, and at the time of my visit not one member had been consigned to the fifth level of damnation in years. Meanwhile, the Minister of Finance lets the 1914 statute languish on the books, and devotes himself to other matters.

By contrast, of course, the New York Stock Exchange, having long since been expelled from its jungle Eden of nonregulation, now functions under the usually severe and vigilant surveillance of the Securities and Exchange Commission, which for almost half a century has been carrying out what is generally recognized as the world's only successful program of federal regulation of modern securities markets. To make the contrast more specific, take the matter of how short selling is treated on the two exchanges. In New York, it is hedged in by a whole constellation of restrictions, of which perhaps the most telling are the federal law prohibiting short selling by corporate insiders and the rule against selling short on a downtick—that is, at a price lower than that of the last previous trade. (Ironically, the downtick rule was initiated not by the S.E.C. but by the Stock Exchange itself in 1931, three years before the birth of the S.E.C., precisely in hopes of preventing such a birth.) In Amsterdam, where the *windhandel* still blows freely, it blows unhindered by any restriction on corporate insiders, any downtick rule, or even any special tax like that of 1689.

To be sure, de Graaff told me, there are some Dutchmen, Socialists and others, who feel that the Amsterdam Exchange needs a much heavier government hand on it than it has now. But by and large, most people concerned with Stock Exchange doings, members and investors alike, are well satisfied with the present arrangement on the ground that it seems to work. I asked de Graaff just why, in his opinion, the brokers and traders of Amsterdam seem able to police themselves so much better than those elsewhere —certainly than those in New York. "Well, we're traditionally a trading nation, and have been for many centuries," he replied. "People here instinctively know the rules of the trading game, and abide by them because they know that without them the game can't go on." In any case, I found myself reflecting, any American who boasts to a Dutchman of the American free-enterprise system is, as far as securities trading is concerned, just making a fool of himself.

FROM his office, Mr. de Graaff led me to a balcony overlooking the floor, where trading was in progress. Although considerably smaller than the New York Exchange's main trading room, this one has a feeling of capaciousness, perhaps because of the exceptional height of the barrel vault that serves as a ceiling. There were some two hundred members and clerks on the floor, most of whom were, as promised, arranged into groups around central spots, with one or two men the centers of attention in each group —clearly enough, the *hoeken* and their *hoekmen*. Most of the groups were made up of five to ten men, but here and there I noticed a lone member standing, feet planted and arms crossed, with no one paying any attention to him—*a hoekman* at his *hoek*, de Graaff explained, waiting for business while his particular stocks went through a moment of unpopularity. (At 11 Wall Street, on a slow day a specialist can at least lean on his post.) At the other extreme, there was a particularly large and spirited group comprising some two dozen, which de Graaff identified as the *hoek* of Royal Dutch Petroleum, the most traded stock on the Amsterdam exchange in each year for as far back as anyone could remember, and the company that with its associate, Shell Transport & Trading, made up the largest industrial firm anywhere outside the United States. Trading in Royal Dutch was lively, as I could tell by interpreting with de Graaff's help the symbols and numbers representing the prices of current transactions that were being printed on a lighted screen above the central desk. The screen was just like the New York Exchange's, only smaller; in fact, de Graaff said, the ticker that activated the screen was an old New York model.

Despite this and other evidence of transatlantic similarity, I noted several ways in which the manners of the Beursplein differ rather strikingly from those of 11 Wall. For one thing, the sounds rising from the floor were different. The Amsterdam brokers and traders tended to emit loud, discrete cries, some of them unmistakable bellows of pain or ecstasy (the Dutch equivalent of the American term "bull," or stock-market optimist, is *liebhefer,* or lover), while the sound that most characteristically comes from the floor of the New York Stock Exchange is a steady hum, denoting efficiency rather than emotion. Again, everywhere on the Amsterdam floor there were members scuttling, loping, even trotting as they hastened from the *hoeken* to their firms' telephones at the side of the floor and back again. On the New York Exchange floor, all forms of running are forbidden, and the rule is seldom violated. In general, to one accustomed to the vast, largely automated machine that constitutes the United States stock market, that of Amsterdam seemed refreshingly informal and personal, and I was not surprised to learn that the Amsterdam Exchange used no computers in any part of its operations except for personnel administration.

"A quiet morning," Mr. de Graaff remarked as we left the gallery. He excused himself, saying he had to get back to his office. With his permission, I hung around the Stock Exchange until after closing time, and found that, in contrast to the early days' rules that I'd read about, members are not now required to get off the premises promptly upon closing—on the contrary, the closing bell had hardly rung when a group of eight or nine traders set up a table right on the now otherwise deserted floor, and began a game of poker. An Exchange aide whom I questioned about this explained that a certain amount of unofficial trading is carried on after hours, with official consent, and that the poker players were brokers who were ready to handle such business should it come along.

On my way out, I stopped in to see Mr. de Graaff and thank him for his help, and took the opportunity to ask him whether there was anyone connected with the Exchange who took a particular interest in its history.

"The man you want to see is Baron Schimmelpenninck," he replied.

"The cigar man?"

No, said Mr. de Graaff, the Baron was C. J. Schimmelpenninck van der Oije, head of his own Stock Exchange firm, and a member of an entirely different family from that of the celebrated cigar manufacturer. He was also a former president of the International Federation of Stock Exchanges, a former vice-president of the Amsterdam Stock Exchange, and a member of its board of directors for more than thirty years until his recent retirement. As a matter of fact, Mr. de Graaff added, he had the impression that the Baron was tired of having my question put to him, and thought perhaps it might be tactful of me not to mention cigars if I were to meet him. In any case, Mr. de Graaff went on, the Baron was universally considered the leading resident authority on the Exchange's history, and he'd be glad to try to arrange an appointment for me. He picked up his telephone, engaged in a brief, brisk conversation in Dutch, and then reported that Baron Schimmelpenninck would meet me in the Stock Exchange boardroom the next morning at ten o'clock.

I FOUND the Baron at the appointed place and time, leafing through some old books that he had spread out on the boardroom table. He was a smiling, white-haired man. After we had been introduced by the man in the tailcoat, he said that if he seemed unnaturally elated, it was because he had just become a grandfather for the second time.

I told him that I had been told he was considered the Stock Exchange's history authority.

"Pooh-pooh," said the Baron.

Nevertheless, he set about giving me a brief, roughly chronological, and very informal history of the Exchange through the centuries, illustrating it with prints from the books he had laid out on the boardroom table and those hung on the room's walls. Exactly what physical evidence of their ownership in the Dutch East India Company the shareholders had during the company's first four years is not known, he said, because no stock certificates issued between 1602 and 1605 are extant. The Amsterdam Stock Exchange does have a 1606 certificate in its vaults, though, and the Baron showed me a copy of it. It was a far cry from the gloriously embossed stock certificates of today—just a businesslike printed form like a standard contract, with blank spaces for the name of the stockholder, the amount paid, and the date. The Baron translated the certificate, the blanks of which were filled in handwriting, as follows:

We the undersigned on behalf of the "Camere der Oost-Indische Compagnie" at Hoorn, acknowledge to have received from (Mr. Dirck Pietersz, Straetmaker) the amount of (fifty guilders) being the remainder of (six hundred guilders) for which amount forementioned (Dirck Pietersz) has been registered by the "Compaignie" to inherit from the Great Book of the "Camere" folio (10). Being brought in and paid in full the amount of (six hundred guilders) for which the said (Dirck Pietersz) participates in the First Ten Years Account of the "Compaigne." Being cancelled and annulled all receipts Actum (December 8, 1606).

ON the back of the certificate, in handwriting, was an accounting of dividends paid on the investment, including, on November 7, 1611, slightly more than forty-four guilders in cash and three hundred and seventy-nine pounds of peppers. In those days, the

Baron explained, a stockholder could take his dividends in either cash or goods, or, like Pietersz, in both. Stock and commodity trading were not yet clearly separated, and commodities were traded daily on the Stock Exchange, along with Dutch East India Company shares. The great tulipomania of 1636, which caused the prices of the most esteemed varieties of tulip bulb to shoot up in a few months from a few guilders each to over twenty-five hundred each before plummeting down again—and which is still cited regularly as the all-time classic case of a speculative mania—took place on the Amsterdam Stock Exchange. In the latter half of the seventeenth century, Baron Schimmelpenninck went on, the various cities of the Netherlands provided the Amsterdam traders with a new kind of security to traffic in when they took to issuing bonds. There was an active municipal bond trade by 1675, and it was to be followed, in due course, by great booms in the bonds of European nations during the eighteenth century and by those of American railroads during the nineteenth. In 1683, the Dutch East India Company delighted stockholders and traders, as subsequent companies have so often delighted stockholders and traders of *their* times, by announcing the first corporate stock split—in this case, ten new shares in exchange for each old one. Showing me prints of the Stock Exchange at about this time, Baron Schimmelpenninck pointed out that many shops had sprung up in the vicinity of the Exchange, some of them in its very arcade. Most of these seemed to be bookshops, suggesting an early affinity of stock traders for literature. If such an affinity existed, it cannot be accounted among the traditions of early Amsterdam that have been carried on into world stock trading in modern times.

Moving on to the eighteenth century, the Baron showed me a cartoon of the seventeen-twenties, when John Law's Mississippi Bubble in France—another of the great speculative disasters of financial history, which, nevertheless, some modern economists credit with having brought about the rise of paper money—had repercussions in the Netherlands, bringing about another stock-market boom and bust there. The cartoon showed anguished-looking brokers carrying placards bearing such messages as "Losses for sale," "I can't sleep," and "To hell with the wind trade!" "Charming, isn't it?" said the Baron. "And here," he went on, directing my attention to more pictures, some in books and some on the boardroom walls, "is a beautiful watercolor of 1756, showing the Exchange from the Rokin. Here's the same thing in winter, with people skating on the canals. And now we move on to the nineteenth century, when they finally tore down the original building, in 1835. It's a shame they did, because it was a beautiful building."

I suggested that maybe, after more than two centuries, the traders were tired of having no roof over their heads.

"Unfortunately for that theory, the new building they put up had no roof either," he said. "It was beautiful, too, though—in neoclassical style, with a three-column façade. It stood right at the end of the Damrak, across Dam Square from the previous building, and it wasn't finished until 1845, so there was a ten-year interval during which the Stock Exchange had no permanent home. They put up a temporary wooden exchange right in front of the Royal Palace, but that caused eyebrows to be raised, and they were kicked out. They moved to another temporary building, but I've never found a print or a description of it. A roof was finally put on the new building in the eighteen-seventies—a great break with tradition, of course. By the turn of the century, though, everybody had decided that the building was old-fashioned, so they tore it down and put up a new one. It still stands, next door to us, and is now used as the Commodity Exchange. It was decided in 1912 that stock and commodity trading should be separated, and the Stock Exchange built its own building, the one we're in now, which is practical but nothing special architecturally." The Baron sighed. "I will say that when it comes to preserving its own architectural heritage, the Stock Exchange has a poor record," he said.

Indeed, from what I had seen and heard, it seemed to me that apart from Baron Schimmelpenninck himself and the custom of drumming on September 10th, the Amsterdam Stock Exchange was remarkably lacking in antiquarian spirit—that it seemed to behave almost as if its unique past had never been. I said as much to Baron Schimmelpenninck, and he replied, with a little chuckle, "It *is* astonishing, but I seem to be just about the only one who's interested."

On further reflection, though, I concluded that perhaps it isn't so astonishing, after all. The Dutch are still a trading nation. Dutchmen still have the trading instinct in their bones, and traders, close students that they are of every nuance of the immediate moment, characteristically turn their backs on the past as good gamblers avoid post-mortems of the last hand.

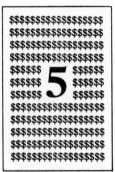

Spanish Privateer

I

ON FEBRUARY 5, 1970, in the Great Hall of Justice of the Peace Palace, in The Hague, sixteen judges of the International Court of Justice, scores of lawyers, representing the governments of Belgium and Spain, and a couple of hundred spectators and reporters gathered to hear, at long last, the Court's judgment on the Case Concerning the Barcelona Traction, Light & Power Company,

Ltd. The case was the biggest as to length of time under consideration, and the second biggest as to quantity of testimony, ever
heard by the Court since it had been constituted under the United
Nations Charter in 1945. Originally brought in 1958, the case had
been withdrawn in 1961 and submitted again in 1962, and over
the intervening years the testimony and written submissions on it
had. come to fill eleven fat printed volumes, totalling some seven
thousand seven hundred pages, along with a whole shelf of sup-
porting documents. But it was of unusual interest to those concerned with international law, and particularly with international
trade, for reasons more relative than that. At issue was whether or
not the Belgian nationals who owned most of Barcelona Traction's
once valuable and now worthless shares had been given adequate protection by the Spanish government and courts while the
company was in the process of being seized, by startling and unprecedented means, between 1948 and 1952, by a group of private Spanish financiers. The matter was complicated (and, in the
Belgian view, explained) by the fact that the only important member of the Spanish takeover group, a former tobacco smuggler
named Juan March, had, through financial aid during the Spanish
Civil War of 1936–39, been to some extent responsible for the
ascent to power of the Spanish regime—that of Francisco Franco
—which still ruled Spain during the years when the takeover was
being effected.

Following customary procedure, the judgment, some fifty pages
long, was read by the President of the Court—José Luis Bustamante y Rivero, of Peru—from his seat at the center of the judges'
curved table at the front of the hall. At the moment Judge Bustamante began to read, two printed copies of the judgment were
placed in front of the chief lawyers who had argued the case for
Belgium and for Spain. Again following custom at The Hague—a
particularly austere custom in some cases—the lawyers refrained
from peeking at the last page to learn the outcome. On this occasion, they had little temptation to do so: Over the preceding two
days, first the Spanish side and then the Belgian had learned
through mysterious leaks that Spain had won. Thus the lawyers,

on hand merely for reasons of ceremony and decorum, were not surprised when the crucial passage came: "The Court rejects the Belgian government's claim by fifteen votes to one."

Thus ended a case characterized by lawyers on the Belgian side as "almost unique in judicial annals" and "without precedent not only in Spain but abroad as well." It ended in what many authorities on international law regard as the successful legalized theft from its foreign owners of a company that supplied twenty per cent of all electric power produced in Spain—a far higher percentage than is supplied by any single company in the United States, private or governmental—and that would have been one of Spain's largest companies but for the fact that it wasn't a Spanish company at all. Its charter and headquarters were in Canada and the owners of nearly all its stock were in Belgium. The theft, if such it was, had been accomplished by a series of maneuvers perhaps as reticulated and Machiavellian as anything in the whole checkered history of world finance. These began in February, 1948, when, despite the fact that Barcelona Traction had shown net profits of about three million seven hundred thousand dollars the previous year and had in its possession enough cash to pay off instantly all its obligations, a court in a provincial Catalan town declared it "bankrupt," in an action in which, as later evidence strongly suggested, the complainants, the trustees in bankruptcy, and the judge himself were all allies of the man seeking to seize the company, Juan March. The maneuvers had continued with the physical seizure of Barcelona Traction's assets by the March-dominated trustees and then with a series of March-engineered blocking tactics, timed as exquisitely as a master's chess moves, that effectively prevented Barcelona Traction's owners from taking self-protective action under Spanish law. The whole affair had come to a head in 1952, when the trustees—emboldened by strange and, some thought, suspicious encouragement from the British Treasury, which was nominally acting to protect Barcelona Traction's British bondholders—declared the old foreign-held shares representing Barcelona's assets to be void; issued an entirely new set of shares, which were variously called "duplicate" and "bogus"; and sold those shares at a ridiculously low price to Juan March, thus establishing him as the new owner. Before the matter was brought to The Hague court, it was the subject of repeated diplomatic protests by the governments of Belgium, Great Britain, Canada, and the United States, and on one occasion was the subject of a face-to-face plea by a Barcelona Traction representative, accompanied by the American lawyer and diplomat Arthur H. Dean, to Generalissimo Franco himself.

JUAN MARCH ORDINAS, by his own accounting the seventh-richest man in the world, was eight years in his grave—he had died following an automobile accident in 1962 at the age of eighty-one—when he achieved his greatest triumph. He had long since been canonized in Spain as "the last pirate of the Mediterranean"; more recently, he has been described by a young Spanish economic historian of the post-Franco era as "Spain's greatest capitalist and perhaps Spain's only capitalist." All but unknown in the United States, he was certainly the only Spaniard, and almost the only European, of this century to fit the description "robber baron," applied by Matthew Josephson and others to certain nineteenth-century Americans. The social climate of Europe has generally been far less favorable than that of the United States to individual rise by skill, guile, and ruthlessness from poverty to great wealth and power—and perhaps the temperament of European entrepreneurs has, too. March is an exception; but his career, the details of which are only now becoming known as post-Franco Spain opens up, does not exactly fit the American model, either. It is an example of the predatory capitalist (fired by a touch of financial genius) operating in a relatively unindustrialized nation and, in the case of Barcelona Traction, preying upon victims beyond his own nation's borders—the citizens of industrial countries, themselves so often thought of as predatory—who invest for profit in countries poorer than their own. No doubt more Juan Marches will be seen in the future. In the meantime, March stands as one who in some ways outdid all our Carnegies, Rockefellers, and Vanderbilts: He was bolder, more guileful, and less inhibited by restraints of either prudence or conscience.

March's outstanding characteristics as a financier were patience, nerve, subtlety at negotiation, crude skill at bribery, and prodigious political adaptability. Over some fifty years, he put together deals that bore his unmistakable stamp as surely as a canvas of an accomplished artist bears *his* stamp; often March's financial victims could detect his hand in machinations against them from the style alone, long before they heard his name spoken as their enemy. He took corruption for granted, and used it casually and openly. Once when he was entertaining a foreign businessman at his Madrid palace, where a footman stood behind each guest's chair, the foreigner found himself seated next to a high Spanish tax official. "Don't offer him anything," March told the foreigner, indicating the tax man. "He's already been taken care of." March's one weakness seems to have been an irresistible propensity for boasting about his financial prowess, even to his own disadvantage. Early in the Barcelona Traction affair, for example, he equably told a key Barcelona Traction man that he was going to take over the company and make a hundred and fifty million dollars on the deal. (In fact, he probably did make nearly that much.) As for adaptability, he managed not just to survive but to increase his fortune progressively under a string of radically different political structures, such as no American entrepreneur ever dreamed of encountering: The old monarchy of Alfonso XIII, under which, between 1903 and 1923, March made his first pile, chiefly by smuggling tobacco from North Africa to Spain; then, from 1923 to 1930, the Directory of Miguel Primo de Rivera, who began by driving March into exile but later welcomed him back, granted him a state monopoly worth millions, and honored him as a philanthropist; from 1931 to 1939, the ill-fated Spanish Republic, which sent March to prison and later, following Primo de Rivera's example, let him return and pursue his private interests unobstructed; and, beginning in 1939, the dictatorship of Franco, which, perhaps in return for March's timely bankrolling of the Nationalist uprising, seems at times to have granted him a kind of latter-day letter of marque authorizing him to plunder foreign economic targets of opportunity.

As a man past sixty—the time when he scored his greatest coup and when his fortune probably grew fastest—March was, by all accounts, anything but a prepossessing figure. The Spanish artist Ignacio Zuloaga depicted him in a 1941 portrait as tall and languorous, with an aristocratic air of command; but, in fact, as photographs and March's acquaintances of that time and later attest, he was rather short, bald, fragile-looking, and extremely pale, with very thick spectacles and a puttylike complexion that gave him the aspect of a puppet. An English businessman who had dealings with him in the years after the Second World War describes him as "a hideous old chap" with a bent, crooked walk, which March attributed to "all those years in prison." (The reference was evidently to seventeen months that he spent in 1932 and 1933 in Cárcel Modelo, in Madrid, and the prison of Alcalá de Henares, a short distance from that city, when he was charged with but not yet tried for bribery of government officials. Whatever hardships he endured must have been made more bearable by the fact that in the first prison he had what was called an "officer" cell, with cognac and liqueurs always handy to serve visitors, and two full-time secretaries and two full-time orderlies, while in the second he had, along with the secretaries and orderlies, a well-furnished suite consisting of a bedroom and a sitting room, and was able to assure himself of excellent meals by tipping one of the head cooks more than a hundred dollars a month and each of two assistant cooks half that much.) His manner of life was in keeping with his appearance. A bodyguard-valet—a thickset and determined but not really menacing looking fellow named Bernardo—went with him everywhere in public, making arrangements and handing out tips. Women who had the bad luck to sit next to him at dinner have described him as having no conversation with them at all, and as seeming to feel that no effort at conversation was required of him. (Apart from Spanish, he spoke only halting French.) At the palace he maintained in Madrid, the many servants were well liveried but not polished or gracious. On some occasions, when a visitor arrived and told the footman who greeted him that he wished to see Señor March, the footman, instead of leading the way to the master of the house, would brusquely indicate the proper direction for the visitor to go with a pointed finger or a jerk of the thumb. Indeed, it might appear in retrospect that March in his later years had a disposition to exaggerate his physical unattractiveness, his lack of culture, and his lack of social graces, as if he were consciously playing *L'Avare*. Perhaps— although on the basis of other evidence it is an unlikely surmise— he shared with other celebrated rich men a craving for pity.

March's reputation with his countrymen had wild ups and downs during his lifetime, but now it is well settled. He is thought of as a villain by almost everyone, though from different points of view. To the Right he represents an aberration of capitalism, one whose misdeeds gave it a bad name; to the Left he represents capitalism's epitome; to both he is a symbol of an iridescently wicked, irresistibly fascinating past. (The shelves of the leading bookstores of early post-Franco Madrid were lined with inside accounts—unpublishable during Franco's rule—of Spanish social, economic, and political life during the Civil War and under Franco, among them books about March.) Only outright Francoists continue to revere March—for the aid he gave their hero in 1936. The visible traces of him in Madrid now, more than a decade and a half after his death, are suggestive. There are the local headquarters and eight local branch offices of Banca March, a banking institution he founded in 1926, which these days generally tends to national business and avoids the foreign connections that were its founder's specialty. There is his former home on the Calle Núñez de Balboa, a six-story nineteenth-century structure with a huge, lush garden, which nevertheless lacks privacy, being overlooked by the balconies of a middle-class apartment house next door. March's house, when seen in 1977, stood empty and was dilapidated to a degree; pieces of masonry had fallen off, and on the walls facing the street were scrawled pro-Francoist graffiti —ironic reminders of the old man and his most useful political connection. Quite different in aspect is the Juan March Foundation, a few blocks away, at the corner of Castelló and Padillà. March established the Foundation in 1955, with an initial gift of three hundred million pesetas (the peseta was then worth about two and one-third cents) and one million two hundred thousand dollars, to make grants and awards in the arts, the natural sciences, and the social sciences. He subsequently gave it much larger sums. The reputation of the March Foundation was insubstantial at first —particularly after some early grants to people who appeared to be in a position to help March's business interests—but it has risen since his death, and the Foundation is now without question the largest and most influential institution of its kind in Spain. (In this regard, March comes off as more public-spirited than Henry Ford, who left it to his successors to establish the Ford Foundation in its present form.) The March Foundation's building is six stories of immaculate, if undistinguished, modern design, with alternating horizontal strips of gleaming glass and white marble, and smoothly curved corners. Its well-kept garden features modern Spanish sculptures, all briskly abstract, and a wall plaque bearing the Foundation motto, *"Ad maius Hispaniae lumen."* Inside, a showcase on the second floor displays the fruits of typical grantee projects—books and papers with such titles as "William Dean Howells and Armando Palacio Valdés: A Literary Friendship," "Pre-Hispanic Palma," "Architecture and Repression," "Spain à Go-Go," and "Private Life and Information: A Permanent Conflict." On the ground floor is a spacious art gallery, in which in the autumn of 1977 was shown a handsome exhibition of thirty oils and one gouache, mostly borrowed from abroad, by Pablo Picasso —Picasso, who had long since become the living symbol of opposition to March's beneficiary Franco, and would not set foot on his native soil while Franco ruled it. One wonders what he would have thought of the exhibition; in any case, its reception in the transitional Spain of 1977 was well summed up in an observation by the newspaper *Arriba*'s critic, who called Picasso's "reencounter" with Spain "a symbol." (Or it could have been Spain's reencounter with Picasso.) But perhaps even more clearly than by the Picasso exhibition the mood of the March Foundation in the nineteen-seventies is conveyed by the life-size bronze sculpture of the founder, which stands in the lobby. Done in 1974 (twelve years after its subject's death), by Pablo Serrano, it shows March leaning forward in a chair, his chest hollow as if caved in, horny hands gripping the chair's arms, and with the face of a rapacious old bird of prey. The piece is the antithesis of Zuloaga's blandly flattering portrait; its comment is so savage as to make it almost a gargoyle. The implication can hardly be missed that the Juan March Foundation, like so many institutional monuments to the founders of fortunes in other countries, is now disposed to put a distance between itself and the source of its wealth.

In Palma, the capital city of March's home island of Majorca, his residual presence has more broadly symbolic overtones. In the old part of the city, near the waterfront, there stand, in an almost equilateral triangle around the Plaza Almoina, three of the local architectural monuments: the Almudaina Palace, which was built by the Moors in the twelfth century, was later the home of the kings of Majorca, and is now occupied by the local Civil Guard, or national police; the great, soaring Gothic Cathedral of Palma; and the porticoed medieval palace, its façade painted with cupids and draperies, that about half a century ago became Juan March's Palma residence. (He also maintained a vast estate, containing a complete village, in the southeastern part of the island.) If the Almudaina and the cathedral represent traditional secular and religious authority, the March residence may be taken to represent a third, more recent force—the power of the individual, based on money—which has arisen in Spain, as in other European societies, since the Renaissance. As exemplified by March, it is a force that should perhaps not be too quickly accepted as more liberal than the other two. The three forces were joined both physically and metaphorically in the great wedding, shortly before March's death, of one of his granddaughters: After the religious ceremony in the cathedral, the bride, the bridegroom, and fifteen hundred-odd guests proceeded, under the protective eyes of the Civil Guard, along a red carpet laid across the Plaza Almoina to March's house, where a splendid reception was held. Today, the house still belongs to members of the March family, though none of them are there often. A sign on an accessible side door suggests, through a vivid pictograph, that anyone tampering with the door will be

struck dead by electricity. In 1945, one wing of the building became the B. March Servera Library, named for one of Juan
March's sons and open to the people of Majorca (but apparently
not always to strangers, for I twice presented myself at its door
during the announced open hours, asked a guard for admittance,
and was refused).* Finally, Juan March's burial place, in the
Municipal Cemetery, on the outskirts of Palma, is one of the
minor sights of the city. Flanked by the headstones and small
sepulchres of ordinary Palmans, which are arranged in rows, like
streets of modest town houses, and many of which are decorated
not only with flowers but with photographs of the deceased, it
stands like a walled city of massive granite, with its own cypress
garden surrounding it. Its most striking feature, though, is not its
size or impressiveness but the fact that, in contrast to all the surrounding graves, in the stones of which are carved names and,
often, sentimental or religious inscriptions, it nowhere on the outside bears the name of March or any other writing. Its inhabitant,
after all, was a secretive man, who shunned the limelight; but,
what is perhaps more to the point, any Majorcan knows without
being told that this tomb could belong to no one but Juan March.

If there were an inscription on his sepulchre, perhaps none
could be more fitting than the half-loathing, half-admiring words
spoken in June, 1932, to the Spanish Cortes, or parliament, by
Jaime Carner, who was then Minister of Finance of the Spanish
Republic. "March is an extraordinary case," said Carner, a businessman ordinarily given to careful speech rather than to political
rhetoric. "March is not an enemy of the Republic, any more than
he is a friend of the Republic; March was neither friend nor
enemy of the Directory; March was neither friend nor enemy of
the Monarchy; March is neither friend nor enemy of anyone;
March is March; March is an exceptional man, and to judge by his
intelligence and his perspicacity, it is perhaps necessary, gentlemen, to go back to certain types and certain personalities of the
Middle Ages; this is a man of the Middle Ages, with modern

---

* I have since learned that the March Library has welcomed many strangers,
and that I probably approached the wrong door.

means and instruments. March is one of those men who, centuries ago, cruised the Mediterranean in search of their destiny, seeking to realize their will, who considered as enemies only those who crimped or attempted to halt the course of that will. . . . This is a man possessed; he believes himself the master of truth. . . . Either the Republic will submit to him or he will submit to the Republic."

The comparison between March's early career and that of the pirates of past times was apt, and especially apt in terms of geography. The Mediterranean was for centuries the particular province of pirates. As early as the first century B.C., Rome was sometimes almost starved by pirates' interceptions of grain convoys; Pompey succeeded in putting an end to Mediterranean piracy for a time, but it revived with the decline of the Roman Empire, and thereafter continued almost up to modern times. During most of the period, in consequence of the undeveloped state of maritime law, there was not even any great stigma attached to it. Merchant ships took their chances equally with storms and with freebooters. Similarly, the Spanish authorities of the early twentieth century often adopted a lax attitude toward Mediterranean tobacco smuggling, partly because of the generous bribes that smugglers were accustomed to giving revenue officials, and partly because the tax-paying tobacco-importing trade was unpopular anyway. A Spanish newspaper noted in 1916, "Up to a point, the smuggling of tobacco has been viewed with sympathy. It is a protest against an odious monopoly." The Muslim Mediterranean pirates of the sixteenth, seventeenth, and eighteenth centuries operated from the Barbary Coast of northwest Africa—the terrain, perhaps the very coves and cays, that March made the bases of his smuggling operations. All the major European powers, though they made attempts to destroy the Barbary pirates, generally found it more convenient to pay tribute—just as the Spanish government, repeatedly outwitted by March, eventually found it convenient to award him the government tobacco monopoly for Spanish Morocco. In the late eighteenth century, Mediterranean piracy declined—or, rather, it transformed itself gradually into privateering. A pirate is a free-lance thief, holding no commission and protected by no national flag; a privateer, on the other hand, is a privately owned vessel, or its commander, formally commissioned by its owner's government to plunder, for his benefit and that government's, the ships of rival nations. Privateering in the Mediterranean, primarily by ships of the Barbary States, reached its peak around 1800, then declined rapidly under vastly increased pressure from the growing European and American navies. The last privateers in history sailed for the Confederacy in the American Civil War. True enough, smuggling is neither piracy nor privateering; smugglers, preoccupied with avoiding seizure themselves, do not ordinarily attack or seize other ships—although March, who succeeded in manipulating the German submarine fleet during the First World War, was probably able to bring about such attacks. The analogy is nevertheless a striking one, even down to the detail that March, in the manner of the Muslim corsairs, was eventually able to graduate from what might be called civil piracy to what might be called civil privateering.

II

MARCH was born in Santa Margarita, a village in north-central Majorca, on October 4, 1880. (Inexplicably for a man with a genius for figures and no apparent physical vanity, in later years he gave his birth year on various affidavits as 1881, and his foundation now gives it as 1882.) According to one of his posthumous biographers—Ramón Garriga, the author of *Juan March and His Time,* who interviewed people close to March—he was the son of a laborer who late in life was able to become a pig farmer, and the father, noting the son's unusual mathematical ability, made sacrifices in order to send him to the Franciscan school in Pont d'Inca, on the outskirts of Palma. There, though a later legend had it that he remained illiterate until the age of forty, March learned what most Majorcan peasants of the time, and more than forty-five per cent of all Spaniards of the time, never learned at all—reading, writing, and arithmetic. Later, his parents arranged for him to become a messenger in the offices of a Majorcan businessman. No documents concerning March's first twenty years survive, but Garriga says that he "had scarcely come of age when he left his parents' house and struck out on his own" as a pig dealer, a buyer of land, and a financier of contraband. Much of the information about March's life in his early twenties comes from an autobiographical speech he made in the Cortes in 1931, defending himself against charges of bribery brought by various leaders of the newly fledged Republican government. By 1903, March said, he was engaged in Majorcan real-estate operations, his capital being "solely and exclusively . . . the credit that my capacity for trade inspired in the Majorcan banking industry." In Majorca, which had lived formally under a feudal system until early in the nineteenth century, for a peasant to become a landowner at the beginning of the twentieth was in itself a remarkable achievement. Getting into the smuggling trade was a less remarkable one. Many seagoing residents of the Balearic Islands, of which Majorca is the largest, had dealt for centuries in contraband—particularly tobacco, which was brought from Morocco and stored in Majorcan caves, pending its distribution to the Iberian mainland. March, although he soon became part owner of a schooner, did not himself sail on the risky voyages necessary to his enterprise; his contribution was to study the sea routes and the government's surveillance methods, and, from a desk onshore, to organize the smuggling trade into what a Spanish Finance Minister later called, with grudging respect, "modern, technical" smuggling.

As March told the Cortes in 1931, to deny that he had "dealt more or less indirectly in contraband" would be "puerile." In mitigation of his having done so, it is only fair to point out that for an ambitious young Spaniard with a talent for business and industry but without higher education or social standing there were few opportunities in Spain in the time of March's youth and young manhood. It was in that period that large-scale industry in Spain was being organized for the first time, mostly by foreigners. (To name an instance that was to play a large part in March's career,

Barcelona Traction, the great hydroelectric power company of Catalonia, was organized by an American, with mainly British backing, in 1911.) Those Spaniards who were able to make fortunes out of companies like these were usually men of inherited means and professional training. Even in the case of Spanish-owned industries, the government was in the habit of granting official monopolies to people with the proper social or political credentials. The North African tobacco trade, which March made his field of endeavor, was a rigid government monopoly. There was virtually no way for an outsider to enter it as an entrepreneur except by becoming a smuggler.

In any case, March's statement that he had "dealt more or less indirectly in contraband" was a wild understatement. In 1906, according to his account to the Cortes, he used the first profits from the land business to invest in an Algerian tobacco factory. This foothold in North Africa marked the beginning of an enormous expansion of his business interests. Soon he was making investments in real estate and hydroelectric power in Majorca. A whole fleet of launches, faster than those used by the Spanish revenue authorities, came into play to carry his tobacco from North Africa to Spain, and from point to point along the Mediterranean African coast. Meanwhile, March provided himself with astute and politically influential legal counsel in the dapper, mustachioed person of Emiliano Iglesias, a journalist, politician, and lawyer, two years older than March, who in the first years of the century was deputy to Alejandro Lerroux as head of the so-called Radical (which later came to mean centrist) Party. Sometime after 1910, Iglesias became March's principal lawyer. He was, in Garriga's words, "a man who would be skillful in buying witnesses and convincing judges of the innocence of his clients, arts that are not learned in law school." Should one of March's launches carrying contraband somehow be overtaken by a lumbering revenue boat, there was always Iglesias to persuade the authorities that the event had been misinterpreted—or that it had never occurred.

By one means and another, March went on to become by 1911 the dominant factor in a good part of the North African tobacco trade and eventually, as Finance Minister Carner put it in 1932, the founder and proprietor of "an invisible and mysterious city that sprawls from Tangier to Cape Creus," at the eastern end of the Pyrenees. In 1911, the Spanish government of King Alfonso XIII formally allowed March to buy from a French concern a monopoly on tobacco sales in the entire Spanish North African zone, excluding the ports of Ceuta and Melilla. This was an important exclusion, since Ceuta and Melilla were among the leading tobacco-exporting ports of the region, but it was nevertheless an outstanding victory for March, in that it represented an outright capitulation of the government to him and his organization. March explained to the Cortes in 1931 that the grant of monopoly had been made "because of my knowledge of the tobacco business, because of my credit from my Moroccan manufacturing, and because of exclusively personal measures." Whatever these last may have been, evidence presented before the Cortes in 1932 suggested that the reason for the grant was that the Spanish authorities, having found tobacco-tax revenues to be dropping precipitously as a result of March's increasingly effective smuggling operations, had decided that it would be cheaper to join him than to fight him. If so, they yielded in vain, because March, the new monopolist, cheerfully continued smuggling, now cheating not only the government but also his own officially sanctioned company.

The First World War provided March his first major opportunity to develop what later proved to be his greatest talent—the ability to exploit conflicting forces to his personal double advantage. Toward the end of his thirties—by that time married and with two sons—he was, according to a contemporary account by a lawyer with whom he had dealings, "agile and decisive, with a cropped head of hair and a birdlike face." The lawyer's description continued, "He had a slightly squinting look, which became more penetrating through his glasses. His gestures were grave and rapid, and he was master of a language that cut like a razor." And he chain-smoked thick cigars, leaving behind in rooms where he had been a cloud of smoke that seemed to the lawyer to be physical evidence of "a force of nature." The principal source on March's activities during the war is a book by Manuel Dominguez Benavides entitled *The Last Pirate of the Mediterranean,* which is in some ways as interesting for its publishing history as for its contents. First brought out in Barcelona in 1934, it was so effectively suppressed —presumably through purchases of all available copies by March, his family, and his business associates—that it quickly became, for all practical purposes, unobtainable. In 1953, it was republished in Moscow, with a Russian introduction; then, in 1977, a Mexican edition was issued, of which some copies have found their way back to Spain. *The Last Pirate* is the story of the early career of March, who is thinly disguised as "Juan Albert," apparently to ward off lawsuits or more forthright forms of reprisal. A young Spanish Socialist, Bernardo Díaz Nosty, whose careful biography *The Irresistible Rise of Juan March* was published in Madrid in 1977, calls the Benavides book "outstanding, and not precisely for its worth," but nevertheless finds that it "corresponds in its major parts to true documentation." According to Benavides, March early in the war negotiated an agreement with the British Admiralty under which the Admiralty would use its influence to persuade the French to authorize the export of tobacco from Algiers, to March's advantage, and March, for his part, would supply intelligence on Mediterranean ship movements to the Allies. (This may have been the first agreement between March and British officials who were willing to sacrifice commercial ethics to realpolitik or other considerations; if circumstantial evidence is to be credited, more such agreements followed, extending well into the post-Second World War period.) That some accommodation between March and the French actually came about is suggested by Paris press comments of the time to the effect that a certain "Señor M . . . a contrabander celebrated in all Spain" was engaged in activities "on the one hand to cheat the [French] State, and on the other to favor the government that rules it." A bit later in the war, a French paper went so far as to call March a "lover of France." According to Benavides, though, March, based in Gibraltar, was at the same time energetically dealing with the Germans.

German submarines dominated the Mediterranean but were always short of supplies; March offered them fuel and food in exchange for free passage of his smuggling ships. Obscure Spanish-shore havens became the loading and fuelling points; Benavides names specific places where the March organization kept caches for delivery by appointment to submarines. As for the Germans, Benavides says, they were only too happy to cooperate with March in a baroque arrangement designed to allow them to acquire goods and capture or destroy Allied ships without putting March in the Allies' disfavor. An Allied ship consigned to Marseilles would be loaded with gasoline at one of March's North African hideaways; then, en route to Marseilles, it would be intercepted by a German sub, which would seize it and its cargo. The captain of the captured ship would, of course, be unaware that March had notified the Germans of the victim's cargo and route, and March could say to his trusting friends the Allied authorities, "What bad luck! But such are the fortunes of war." However, he had indirectly delivered to the Germans a ship and a load of fuel, for which he would presumably be paid. The evidence that this form of transaction, and variations on it, took place repeatedly is circumstantial but convincing. For example, according to a story still told in Majorca—from whose coast submarine attacks on Allied and neutral ships were often plainly visible—one Mediterranean sea captain who had several times lost his ships and their cargo to submarines en route from Africa to France finally became exasperated and took a devious, evasive course without telling anyone, even his principals. Having arrived safely in Marseilles, he found himself dismissed, without explanation, by the company manager. It seemed to be his skill in evading the German submarines that had earned him dismissal. Another captain who escaped ambush and got through safely found when he arrived with his cargo at Marseilles that there was no one there to deliver it to; apparently, March had thriftily decided that to set up a dummy receiving station would be a waste of money.

These coolly contrived arrangements are early, and rather crude, examples of the characteristic March transaction. Later in his career, when he was dealing in national currencies and in large companies rather than in ships and their cargoes, he would add many refinements. Indeed, as the war dragged on, some refinements began to appear. According to an article that appeared in the American magazine *Current History* in 1936, March eventually took to selling "insurance policies" against German attack to the owners of neutral ships plying the Mediterranean; those who refused to buy the policies were pinpointed for attack, whereupon March would claim what amounted to a finder's fee, instead of an insurance premium, from the Germans.

By 1916, March had done so well that he was able to command his own shipping line, the Transmediterranean Company, with initial capital of a hundred million pesetas, or almost twenty million dollars. Already, his activities were being whispered about, and more than whispered about, throughout Spain; a Madrid newspaper had referred to him as a smuggler as early as 1914, and in 1916 he was publicly attacked in the Cortes, where a senator said of his smuggling operation, "The whole Coast knows about it." March and his activities even became the subject of a verse by the Spanish poet Luis de Tapia:

> A little ship of mine
> Sails without fear,
> So if you lack fuel
> I will give you in Santa Pola
> Spanish petrol through the hands of some traitor.

ALSO in 1916, in connection with what was eventually known as the "Garau affair," March came under a cloud of suspicion which hung over him for most of his life. On September 29th of that year, on the Camino del Grao, in Valencia, Rafael Garau, a young member of a family from March's home town of Santa Margarita, with which March had for more than a decade been in partnership in the North African tobacco business, was murdered —by a paid assassin, it was generally agreed. Suspicion immediately fell on March as the hirer of the assassin. As the conservative journal *La Acción* summed up the situation years later, "the whole of public opinion in Palma as in Valencia pointed to March as being interested in the tragedy for many reasons." For one thing, subsequent testimony indicated that Garau had been lured to the place of assassination on the pretext that he would meet there a Spanish tax official willing to make a smuggling deal. For another, a witness to the killing, a local guard, testified that the victim had gasped out just before he died, "I've been killed by bad friends!" Finally, March's own actions before and immediately after the assassination did little, in the general opinion, to clear his name. A couple of weeks earlier, he had summoned Rafael Garau to Palma for a conference, the subject of which is unknown. Immediately after the murder, he sent to the victim's father, José Garau, in North Africa, a chillingly abrupt telegram, reading, in full, "YOUR SON HAS BEEN HORRIBLY ASSASSINATED. JUAN." He then embarked on a whirlwind of travel: first to Valencia; then to Palma, where he arranged a huge funeral for his former associate; then back to Valencia; and then, successively, to Barcelona, Alicante, and Madrid. On his second stop in Valencia, March presented himself voluntarily before Antonio Delgado Curto, the judge who was handling the case. As Judge Delgado Curto later told it, March said, "I've read in the papers the reports about the event in the Camino del Grao, in which the victim was the son of my partner. It is said that high personalities and powerful persons are implicated in this event. Does suspicion fall on me? . . . You need proof for a trial, right?" Delgado Curto replied, "The judge, whenever he tries a case, must have proof," whereupon March replied quickly, "Well, then, it's going to be very difficult to prosecute me." There is no more than a hint that in this case March resorted to his lifelong favorite expedient for getting his way—that of offering a bribe. Fifteen years later the Attorney General of the Spanish Republic remarked to the Cortes that "a summary exists showing that the judge was forced to eject one of Mr. March's representatives from his chambers for having alluded to the figure of five thousand pesetas." The "summary" appears never to have been presented as evidence. In fact, the Valencia judge, in contrast to the local police, appears to have been a man of duty and diligence. No documents recording a police investigation of any sort ever appeared, even though José Garau immediately offered a reward of fifty thousand pesetas, or over ten thousand dollars, for information leading to the arrest of those responsible for his son's death. Frustrated, Judge Delgado Curto drew up an order asking the police for their cooperation, but it was apparently not forthcoming. A small section of the Spanish press ventured to take up the case, denouncing the pervasive passivity of the Spanish administration—and, consequently, of the local Spanish police—in regard to tobacco smuggling. In particular, one journal, *España Nueva*, conducted a crusade for justice in the Garau case, publishing over a period of several months more than fifty articles dealing with it and with the government authorities' seeming indifference to it. In Valencia, Delgado Curto conducted a series of hearings in which the name of Juan March was repeatedly mentioned but no proof of his involvement was produced. In the course of the investigation, March himself gave testimony, and other witnesses suggested motives that March might have had for doing away with his associate—that Rafael Garau had been independently establishing a rival smuggling connection through Gibraltar, that March had been drawing improperly on their company's funds, and so on. A rumor even arose, perhaps inevitably, that Rafael Garau had been having an affair with March's wife. But nothing was proved.

Chronology suggests that *España Nueva*'s energetic campaign to get to the bottom of the matter brought a sudden end, inadvertently, to Delgado Curto's investigation. Early in November, the paper, which was known to be working in close cooperation with him, spoke pointedly of "insuperable difficulties that the investigators of this case encounter because it is related to the smuggling of tobacco." A few hours after that was published, government authorities in Madrid abruptly relieved Delgado Curto of his duties as a judge in Valencia and reassigned him elsewhere. His successor let the investigation drop, and took no action on the case. Even *España Nueva*, after reacting with surprising temperance to news of Delgado Curto's replacement ("In the history of judicial proceedings, this is really a remarkable case," the newspaper noted. "We find ourselves a little perplexed."), gradually gave up, continuing its own series until the end of the year and then dropping it. So the Garau affair faded into the limbo of unsolved crimes.

Díaz Nosty points out that at the time the order transferring Delgado Curto came from Madrid, March was in that city, and had been there for several days. More than thirty years later, the sudden replacement of a judge who was acting inconveniently for March would play a key role in the Barcelona Traction case. As time went on, José Garau became firmly convinced that March was responsible for his son's death, and said so publicly. In 1917, the March-Garau joint company was liquidated. Thereafter, if the opinion of a French court in Algiers is to be credited, March took reprisals against the elder Garau for denouncing him: In 1918, as a result of the appearance of two letters apparently incriminating him as a paid German agent, José Garau was sent to military prison, only to be exonerated and released when the Algiers court came to the conclusion that the letters had been forged and given to the French vice-consul in Valencia by Juan March.

As far as March's career is concerned, this lurid, operatic tangle, taking place almost within hearing of the guns of war, is nothing but a shadow, for which there may or may not have been substance. Díaz Nosty grants, as one possible hypothesis, that March may have had nothing to do with the murder. At all events, March emerged from the First World War greatly enriched. Different sources have estimated his personal fortune in 1916 at between twenty and thirty million pesetas, or, roughly, between four and six million dollars; and it was rapidly increasing—a reflection of the continued expansion of both his legitimate business interests and his smuggling organization. The latter, however, suffered a temporary setback in 1921 and 1922, as a result of March's first serious brush with government authority—a brush that made J. Pierpont Morgan's differences with President Theodore Roosevelt seem like a tea party. In 1921, Francisco Cambó, a prominent

Catalan lawyer who had recently made a fortune—honestly enough—in connection with the formation of the Spain-based international firm Compañía Hispano-Americana de Electricidad, or CHADE, became Minister of Finance. Soon after taking office, Cambó was startled to learn that tobacco smuggling was operating so effectively that for the year 1920 the treasury revenues on legally imported tobacco had come only to the equivalent of about twenty-six thousand four hundred dollars—a pitifully tiny fraction of what might reasonably have been expected. Accordingly, he proceeded to launch a full-scale attack on smuggling—and, in particular, on his less reputable fellow-millionaire March. Cambó's opening salvo, which made front pages all over Spain, spoke of "a modern, technical contraband operation, built by a man of exceptional quality who has proclaimed himself, with pride, the last pirate of the Mediterranean." Apart from Cambó's assertion, there is no evidence that March had ever called himself that, or that Cambó did not invent the phrase. But there is no reason, either, to believe that March was not proud of the designation; and, one way or another, it stuck with him thereafter.

Cambó followed up his denunciation of March with decisive action. Having discovered that March had many officers of the Customs Guard on regular salaries—augmented by fringe benefits in the form of insurance against their dismissal for bribe-taking—he announced bluntly, "This can't go on. Either we nail March's operation or I dissolve the corps entirely." Three officers convicted of being on the March payroll were imprisoned. The Spanish Navy, too, was found to be involved in condoning and covering up smuggling; when a Navy emissary came to Cambó to complain about the uneasiness that his crackdown was causing, Cambó said, "Tell the admirals, the vice-admirals, and the rear admirals to shut up, because if they don't I'm going to start talking." Thereafter, the Navy cooperated with a will; its chief minister, the Marquis of Cortina, held a press conference in which he said, "Our vigilance must be carried to an extreme. . . . The disposition of captured boats has been modified. Previously . . . they went on public auction, selling cheap right back into the hands of the smugglers. From now on, if the boats aren't suitable to the Navy, they will be burned." Over the succeeding weeks, the authorities seized and confiscated along Spain's Mediterranean coast huge amounts of contraband tobacco—in one case, after being offered fifty thousand pesetas to allow the importation of six hundred sacks, and, in another case, after a gunfight that resulted in one smuggler's death.

To top all this off, Cambó had March followed. "Two police-men slept in rooms adjoining his at his hotel," Cambó explained years later. "They had their morning coffee at the table next to his, they sat close by him in restaurants, they placed his house under surveillance." Not even Cambó can have been so quixotic as to suppose that the last pirate of the Mediterranean did not take note of the presence of these scarcely subtle tails and conduct himself accordingly; in any event, no direct evidence against March was obtained. And March—although his organization undoubtedly had a poor year, like a United States toy company, say, in a year when the government is loudly insisting that its products are un-safe—survived the Cambó movement the way private entrepreneurs usually survive reform waves: by hanging on and waiting for a change of government. In March, 1922, the government that had appointed Cambó fell, and he left office with the tobacco smuggling problem still unsolved.

III

THE lesson that March took from the Cambó affair seems to have been that government can be troublesome and that one way to minimize the trouble is to become part of government. He had been interested in Majorcan politics since 1913 or 1914, and in 1923 he decided to stand for a Majorcan seat in the Cortes. To outward appearances, March conducted a typical island campaign, exceptional only for its lavishness: On the Saturday night before Election Day he threw a huge outdoor party, open to all, in a Palma square, and served four lambs, ten suckling pigs, and a hundred or so chickens. When the votes were counted, he was found to have received more votes than the half a dozen rival candidates (four of whom were also elected), among them no lesser figure that the pride of Majorca, Antonio Maura, who had previously brought honor to the island by becoming Spanish head of state. But immediately there were cries of corruption. One of the defeated Majorcan candidates accused March of outright vote buying, and the successful candidate from Ibiza, Carlos Román, went before the Cortes in Madrid to repeat denunciations by others of March as a leading smuggler; to point out that the government authorities had in their possession at that very moment many crates of confiscated contraband on which the name of the manufacturer, Juan March, was insolently stamped in large letters; and to question on ethical grounds whether he should be allowed to take his seat as a delegate. After some political skirmishes, the motion was overwhelmingly defeated, even though none of Román's charges had been refuted. March had scarcely won this vindication, and taken his seat in the Cortes, when political fortune turned against him. Four months later, Miguel Primo de Rivera, a volatile, rather garrulous military officer, brought off a coup d'état that ended with his becoming Spain's Director, or chairman of a board of dictators, with the full assent of King Alfonso, and announcing that it was his intention to clean up the decadence and corruption of the previous regime.

March's relations with Primo de Rivera over the succeeding seven years, as Garriga describes them, were a sort of vaudeville skit, with the following plot: Director in an initial fit of moral indignation drives financier into exile; financier returns, and woos Director with favors; Director is gratified, and meanwhile discovers that he needs financier's help anyway; Director ends up wooing and flattering financier. At the outset, March was quick to read the new handwriting on the wall. For one thing, an influential Catalan friend of his had warned him of danger and advised him to head for the border; for another, Primo de Rivera himself had spoken sharply in public about contraband, and many felt that the allusion was to March. Within three weeks of Primo de Rivera's coming to power, March was reported in the Spanish press to have disappeared, and a few days later he turned up in France. According to Garriga, most probably he crossed the border by automobile from Barcelona, accompanied by his friend, lawyer, and fellow-delegate to the Cortes, Emiliano Iglesias; the popularly accepted detail that both were disguised in priests' robes is, Garriga says, pure embroidery.

Some weeks later, March was back in Madrid, where he appeared before the Directory to plead for an investigation of his personal and business affairs to clear his name, and, seizing the offensive, launched into a denunciation of Francisco Bastos, the Cambó-appointed managing director of the Tobacco Leasing Company, the Spanish government supermonopoly, which doled out lesser monopolies, such as the one on Moroccan tobacco that had been granted to March in 1911. Primo de Rivera took no action to drive March back into exile, or to investigate him, either; on the other hand, he assumed a protective attitude toward Bastos, the man March wanted prosecuted. In a note leaked to the press, Primo de Rivera said in part, in his characteristic chatty, reasonable-parent style, "The Directory has yet to receive one single, personal, concrete accusation [against Bastos], although thousands of administrators and legal people are at work on this. All in all, one cannot help but pity a man surrounded up to this minute with great prestige . . . who now finds himself toppled by the unproven accusations made by an adversary. . . . We don't want anybody—and this includes the press—to lose his head in these difficult moments. To act beneficially, one must be serene and just. As far as the Directory is concerned, there must be only one proper course of action, and that is duty. We shall not be pushed into persecuting anybody."

In light of the fact that Bastos was subsequently cleared completely, it is perhaps surprising that no measures were taken against his accuser. But, on reflection, perhaps not. March, for one thing, was becoming a power of the press that Primo de Rivera was so anxious to have keep its head. In the middle nineteen-twenties, March bought two influential Madrid dailies, *Informaciones* and *La Libertad*. *Informaciones*, the new owner instructed its editors, was to lean to the right politically, while, for the sake of balance, or, possibly, prudence, *La Libertad* was to lean to the left. Around the same time, it seems to have dawned on Primo de Rivera by degrees that March had what the financially strapped government needed most—ready cash. In the first few months after March returned from France, the Director treated him with elegant disdain. But a gradual thaw ensued. In December, 1924, Primo de Rivera, hard pressed to put down military rebels in Morocco, swallowed his scruples and asked March to authorize tobacco distribution among Spanish troops there without invoking his rights as concessionaire of the tobacco monopoly. March was only too happy to comply, even though the move cost him about half a million pesetas a year, and he was rewarded with a personal expression of gratitude from the Director.

Having once accepted a favor from March, Primo de Rivera found the practice addictive. On one occasion, he wrote March asking for financial help for the *Military Mail,* a publication distributed to Spanish troops, which had been generally friendly to the Directory. March found himself able to help and Primo de Rivera wrote him a short time later, "Very grateful for your earlier favors. The situation is still worrisome, and I beg you to consider giving more money." Whether or not March responded to this follow-up solicitation is unknown. It is clear, though, that on another occasion he buttressed his position as a philanthropist by giving six million pesetas, or about nine hundred thousand dollars, to the Queen of Spain for the construction of a children's hospital. Later evidence suggests that the money was used to redeem some jewels that the Spanish Royal Family had pawned in Paris. That neither Primo de Rivera nor March was party to this intrigue is suggested by a later dialogue in which the Director complained to March that the hospital had not yet been built (it never was), and March, equally mystified, replied, "I have no idea what's become of the six million pesetas."

The good turn of March's that first brought a public expression of gratitude and praise from the Director concerned a business arrangement in Tangier, where the Spanish government was in need of a sharp trader familiar with North African commercial customs to acquire on Spain's behalf a large block of real estate there, which was privately held, and thus strengthen Spain's hand in North African commerce by establishing its possession of important African free-zone property. This was child's play for March. Having been called upon, he went to Tangier and, apparently using his own money, closed a deal highly favorable to Spain within twenty-four hours. This time, Primo de Rivera gave a dinner in March's honor, and the next day, when leaving King Alfonso's chambers, Primo de Rivera said, in the presence of various leading noblemen of Spain, "I have just given His Majesty good news about Spanish influence in Tangier. A great patriot has put his money to work for his country. All of us should learn from his example." The last pirate, clearly enough, had come a long way. Yet another long-desired plum fell to him in July, 1927, when the government, in exchange for certain financial concessions, at last authorized March to sell tobacco without competition in the key Spanish North African ports of Ceuta and Melilla. This grant, which completed March's conquest of the Spanish tobacco trade in North Africa, was made—as Primo de Rivera explicitly stated in another of his unbuttoned explanations—in appreciation of yet another act of patriotism and philanthropy on March's part; a promise to finance large-scale Spanish colonization in Spanish Morocco.

With the Ceuta-Melilla grant, March had moved out of the smuggler class at last. What with the African monopoly, his shipping line, his real-estate interests, his newspapers, his utilities, his concurrent investments in petroleum, agriculture, textiles, and potash, and his Banca March, which he had founded in 1926, he could now make profits beyond the dreams of avarice without bothering to break the law. In a decade during which Primo de Rivera's policy of granting monopolies rather than encouraging competition led, as the British writer Gerald Brenan has pointed out, to large increases in consumer costs throughout Spain and to a Madrid "full of adventurers," March was an exemplary adventurer, holding court every afternoon in the grand salon of the Palace Hotel, where he was customarily surrounded by an admiring group of journalists, bankers, sycophants, and would-be adventurers. His problems with Primo de Rivera belonged to the

past. The reverse, however, was not true. For two years after the
1927 tobacco grant, the relationship between the Director and the
financier was the subject of such constant joking throughout Spain
that finally, in July, 1929, the Director was goaded into issuing
one more official note for public consumption, this one entitled
"The Case of Mr. March." It read, in part:

It is insistently said in reference to Mr. March, "The initial source of
this man's fortune could have been anything." But we do know that,
since it has been in existence, the Directory has been free to make use
of it for whatever patriotic or charitable ends we wished. And Mr. March
has been very much at our disposal and has met our requirements will-
ingly, with what must have been great sacrifice. Some [of his grants]
have been purely charitable, while others have been needed for the
public welfare, which could only have meant some personal loss for him;
but he acted always for the benefit of the national interest. Undoubtedly,
March's name was much discussed in Spain when the Directory came to
power, and at that time he still had cases pending in the courts, from
which he emerged *absolutely free and with a clean bill of health.* This
regime has kept no one from attempting to restore his good name—less
still if (in order to leave that name to his sons wiped clean of all
scandal) he makes great sacrifices for the public good to compensate for
possible past deeds. This is the case with Mr. March, with whom this
was our only possible course of action: to declare him *urbi et orbi* a man
above all suspicion and a man whom public justice has acquitted and
to whom is given the right to purify whatever he touches. . . . Spain's
each day more fervently acclaimed regime cannot stop to examine each
new mud puddle with which slanderers would wish to distract it.

Thus, the vaudeville skit ended with March's straw hat transformed
into a halo.

IV

IN the nineteen-thirties—the decade when the amiable farce that
Primo de Rivera had made of Spanish political life changed first to

chaos and then to tragedy—March's political role deepened and
became more sinister. But even in this decade it began with a sort
of comedy. In January, 1930, Primo de Rivera, increasingly unable to deal with Spain's economic troubles, was forced to resign;
broken in health and spirits, he left Spain, and died within a few
months in a second-class hotel in Paris—according to the British
historian Hugh Thomas, "his last hours divided between brothel
and confessional." Then, in April, 1931, following a nationwide
election in which supporters of the monarchy were heavily defeated
in the cities and large towns, King Alfonso left Spain without
formally abdicating, and the Spanish Republic was proclaimed.
These events followed more than a year of plotting and political
agitation by a coalition of politicians, representing various shades
of anti-monarchist opinion, who were to be the first leaders of the
Republican government. One of their maneuvers during the stage
preparatory to their takeover was an attempt to enlist March as
the revolution's banker. (The political, as well as the moral, risks
of dealing with a former smuggler and darling of a dictator appear
not to have greatly worried the revolutionists. Manuel Azaña,
who came to be the leading political figure of Republican Spain,
wrote later that "in those anguished times, one gave little thought
to consequences.") In August, 1930, three of the revolutionary
leaders—Azaña, Miguel Maura, and Indalecio Prieto, all destined
to be prominent officials of the Republic—happened to have
dinner in a restaurant in San Sebastián when March was there. As
Azaña recalled the incident, he noticed a man he did not know
dining with "one of the loveliest women I have ever seen." Azaña
asked his companions who the man was, and one of them replied,
"It is March." (March was well known at the time for his public
appearances with beautiful young women.) After the meal, according to Azaña, Prieto, who knew March, and who was never
noted for discretion, jokingly called over to him, "You could drop
a couple of million to get on the right side of the revolution and
you'd never feel it," to which remark March's reaction was to
"smile like a rabbit." Prieto, for his part, reported later that March
had replied, "You will understand that with my social position and

my interests I am not going to put myself in that position," and
that some more joking had followed. In subsequent weeks, the
joking was replaced by apparently serious negotiations between
the revolutionary committee and March. In exchange for his financial support, the committee offered March a guarantee that he
would not be held accountable for profits made during the Directory period, or for his relations with the Director; as a financial
guarantee to go along with that political one, Maura offered to
pledge as collateral his town and country houses, and another
committee member, Alejandro Lerroux, said he would pledge his
real estate, too—an offer that appears less heroic in light of the
fact that Lerroux's property was already mortgaged.

Despite all these inducements, March remained aloof and noncommittal, to the point where the committee members finally
came to believe that he was stringing them along—with no intention of financing their enterprise—merely to gain information
about their resources and pass it along to their enemies. Accordingly, they broke off the negotiations, and, to what proved to be
March's great disadvantage, the Republic came into being with no
debts to him. The new Republican government was eager to have
symbols of the wicked past to hold up as examples, and March,
especially now that he had declined to bank the revolution, was
one who filled the bill admirably. The new attorney general,
Ángel Galarza, issued warrants for the arrest of various prominent figures of the Primo de Rivera regime, and on April 29,
1931, when the Republic was a mere fifteen days old, March
attempted to repeat the first step of his dance with Primo de Rivera
by again crossing the border into France. This time, however,
the guards were either more adept or less corruptible: March was
detained at Irún and returned to Madrid under guard.

In the skirmishing over what to do with him which occupied
much of the Cabinet's and the Cortes' time and energy over the
next thirteen and a half months, March had powerful allies. The
Radical Party, headed by his friends Lerroux and Iglesias, had
ninety delegates in the Cortes, and was thus the second most important minority after the Socialists, with a hundred and sixteen;

moreover, the Radicals were proportionately represented in the Cabinet. These friends, however, were powerless to prevent the new Finance Minister, the Socialist Prieto, from stripping March of his African tobacco monopoly that June. In August, the Cortes formed an Accountability Commission, made up of representatives of all political parties and charged with ferreting out the misdeeds of the Primo de Rivera regime, with particular reference to persons now serving as Cortes delegates. Naturally enough, its attention soon turned to March—and his to it. Sometime not long after the commission was created, Iglesias, representing March, went to one of its members, a Catalan delegate named Jaime Simó Bofarull, to say that "political persecution" of March would be "frankly inhuman and intolerable," and to offer a payment of twenty-five thousand pesetas, which Simó Bofarull refused. (According to Garriga, when March later learned the amount that Iglesias had offered, he was furious; the agreed-upon sum had been *two hundred* thousand. As for Iglesias, after Simó Bofarull told the Cabinet about the offer, he rose to praise the Catalan delegate in courtly language, but also to make a correction: The money had been offered as a "donation for a social function.") Following this, Attorney General Galarza sent agents to Calle Núñez de Balboa, where, after taking more than an hour to break down the door of March's house, they found him in his bedroom. When he asked what their orders were, they replied that their mission was already accomplished: The Attorney General had simply wanted to be sure that March was still in Madrid, and had not slipped out the door and back to the border.

In November, the Cabinet—which was supposed to be busy drafting a constitution for the Republic—debated the question of March at length and with heat. March, at his own request, appeared to plead his case. He was, he said, a man of the people; his arrival at his present fortunate financial status was the result of twenty-five years of ceaseless labor; although it would be "puerile" to deny that he had once dealt in contraband, to call him a contrabandist was an "error"; he had not made deals to aid Primo de Rivera; and, finally, the Republic should on principle respect wealth earned through labor rather than acquired through inheritance. The subsequent debate, continuing through three sessions, quickly degenerated into a shouting match, during which the Cortes' president repeatedly had to call for order. When Galarza brought up the Garau affair, March replied icily that there was no proof of his complicity in it, and added that he hadn't believed that men as reckless as Galarza existed. He went on to maintain that during the period of the revolution Galarza had sent word to him that he had better change his attitude toward it or "a few gunmen would show up to kill him." (Galarza later admitted that this was substantially true.) At one point, Prieto—who had clearly undergone a change of heart toward March since the dinner meeting in San Sebastián the previous year—shouted from the government bench, "Mr. March should have been hanged by the Republic in the Puerta del Sol—and I would have pulled on his feet!" As Azaña, who had been a writer before he became a political leader, noted later, "March looked like an old, plucked rooster, set upon by enemies, but furious. I had the impression that I was seeing a man about to suffer a violent death. Trepidation and rage."

The debate came to little. Iglesias was declared "incompatible" with the Cortes but continued to sit in it anyway, while the Accountability Commission recommended the same fate for March, but the Cortes took no immediate action on the proposal. So March walked out still a delegate and still not formally charged with anything. The following February, by which time March's friends, the Radicals, had been purged from the government, the Cabinet met in secret session to decide whether or not to bring March to trial, and ended up voting the proposal down—partly because at that time Prime Minister Azaña was cautiously negotiating to get March to finance a Portuguese revolt against the dictator António de Oliveira Salazar. But time was running out for March. On June 8, 1932, the Portuguese intrigue having failed, the full Cortes again took up the matter of March—this time more resolutely, in a secret night session. March, defending himself against the principal charge—that he had obtained the 1927 tobacco concession from Primo de Rivera through bribery—was remarkably categorical. He had, he said, made a loan of twenty thousand pesetas to a Madrid printing house, at Primo de Rivera's request; he had credited the *Military Mail* with a hundred thousand pesetas, at the government's request; and, as a result of urging from the same quarter, he had put up a hundred and twenty-five thousand pesetas each for a cancer institute and a church in Tetuán, and six million for the never-built children's hospital. "This is what my accusers consider bribery," March summed up, with what he evidently intended as triumphant irony. But the irony seems to have been lost on many delegates; just before adjourning, at four-fifteen in the morning, they voted, a hundred and forty-seven to seventy-four, to evict March from the Cortes and thereby deprive him of immunity from arrest.

Even so, the case might have ended up buried in parliamentary dithering but for the Ciceronian intervention of Finance Minister Carner during a public session of the Cortes held on June 14th to decide whether or not to have March arrested. Carner, who had been expected to speak in a dry, legalistic way, took the delegates by surprise by leaving behind the apparently endless wranglings and accusations of petty corruption, and putting March into the broad sweep of history by depicting him as one of those cold, wholly amoral, preternaturally forceful persons so rare that centuries may pass between the appearance of one and the next in any given place. When Carner ended with "Either the Republic will submit to him or he will submit to the Republic," the Cortes was in an uproar. There was another vote, this one unanimous, and the following day March was arrested and taken to Cárcel Modelo.

IT is possible to argue that one element of March's perverse genius was his ability to pick enemies who deserved him; in any event, the Republican parliament, by arrogating to itself the right to imprison a citizen without a proper indictment by the courts, exhibited a most un-Republican governmental tendency. Its permissive treatment of March in prison may have reflected a measure of

guilt. Not only was he allowed to live there in comparative com-
fort, at his own considerable expense in tips and salaries, but he
was also allowed to make gifts to his fellow prisoners. Each hall-
way at Modelo received its own football with his compliments,
and he habitually kept his pockets full of five-peseta chits for the
prison canteen, which he handed out at every opportunity, thereby
becoming Modelo's own John D. Rockefeller—and a far more
munificent one at that, since each of his chits was worth not a
dime but something like forty-seven cents. On Christmas Eve,
1932, a van arrived from the Palace Hotel loaded with food and
wine for a seasonal feast for all the prisoners. The order to the
hotel appeared to have been sent and personally signed by March.
Afterward, he insisted that he had never given the order and that
his signature on it had been forged by a trickster seeking to get
him in trouble; on Christmas Eve, however, he blandly accepted
thanks, and general approbation, as the benefactor.

To his far greater advantage (and, as things turned out, to the
Republic's disadvantage), March in prison was allowed unrestricted access to visitors, including political figures, and—even
more surprising—to his vast financial resources outside. In August, 1932, José Sanjurjo, a hard-drinking, philandering general
whose exploits against the Moroccan rebels had made him mo-
mentarily Spain's most famous soldier, attempted a coup d'état
against the Republic. It was a total fiasco; most of the rebels were
captured after some skirmishing in the Plaza de la Cibeles, in
Madrid—right under the offices of the Ministry of War, from the
balcony of which Prime Minister Azaña nonchalantly watched, a
cigarette dangling from his lips—and Sanjurjo went to prison. It
was later maintained that March, in collaboration with Lerroux,
had planned to finance the Sanjurjo uprising but had then helped
bring about its downfall by withdrawing his support at the last
minute; his ally Lerroux may have been one of several early supporters of the conspiracy who betrayed it by tipping off the government in advance.

Thereafter, March pinned his political hopes on Lerroux. "The
government of the Republic has been committing an iniquity and

an infamy against a citizen," the Radical leader said publicly, in reference to March, going on to speak of "the envy that settles so easily in the soul of the multitude." (A respected Madrid lawyer stated, and Lerroux denied, that March had bribed Lerroux with a gift of sixty-three thousand pesetas, or about five thousand dollars.) Early in May, 1933, when March had been in prison almost eleven months, the director of prisons decided that things had gone far enough. He notified Azaña that March was engaged in "dangerous political maneuvers" involving "direct contact" with politicians of various stripes, including Anarchists, and even Communists, and ought to be moved to some prison outside Madrid, where such contacts would presumably be less convenient. Acting on the suggestion, Azaña had March moved to the prison of Alcalá de Henares, the ancient university town, some thirty kilometers to the northeast, which is famous as the birthplace of Catherine of Aragon and of Miguel de Cervantes. But at Alcalá de Henares, March, instead of reducing his political activity, raised it to a new pitch. A member of the Garau family of Algiers, March's enemies since 1916, maintained that during the summer of 1933, March attempted unsuccessfully to hatch a plot to have Azaña and Prieto murdered. What is certain is that during July, March gained control, by one means or another and to one extent or another, of three more Madrid newspapers—*El Sol, La Voz,* and *Luz*—which had previously been supporters of the government. Together with the two papers he already owned, that gave him virtual mastery of the city's press. March then offered "his press" to the government in exchange for his freedom, but the offer was refused. March's press retaliated with even more virulent attacks on the government. Azaña noted plaintively in his diary, "In *Luz,* they call me stupid where once they called me a genius. In *El Sol,* they speak of my mind as of a madman's or a brute's."

Early in September, 1933, the people of Majorca, still loyal to their beleaguered fellow-islander, defiantly elected March to, of all things, the Tribunal of Constitutional Guarantees, one of the Republic's highest political bodies, whose duty was to judge the actions of the sitting government on such matters as abuse of power and safeguarding the rights of individuals. His election was quickly annulled, but his prestige and influence continued to grow. The unceasing barrage of the March press against the government helped bring on a Cabinet crisis and the fall of the Azaña regime. "Either this Republic swings conservative or there will be no republic," March, airily paraphrasing his condemner Carner, said to a *New York Times* reporter on September 9th. The same day, Lerroux, March's choice, was called upon to form a new government. March, *The Times* reported, was "the man behind the crisis." From a prison cell—or, rather, a prison suite—he had brought about a change of national leadership. Anti-Lerroux mobs rioted in Madrid on the eleventh, and the Radical leader was barely able to form a government, which in any case fell three weeks later, without having mustered the strength or the daring to release its principal sponsor from prison. Thus power reverted to March's enemies. By October 27th, when an indictment of March was finally filed in a Madrid paramilitary court, he had evidently decided to take matters into his own hands. Six days later, he made one of the more sensational prison escapes of modern history.

His absence from Alcalá de Henares prison was "discovered" on the morning of November 3rd, when his personal servants arrived, as usual, from Madrid. What had happened soon became clear from the graphic accounts of those concerned. The previous day, March had dropped by the office of Martín Arnáiz Moreno, a warden of the prison, which was conveniently next to March's quarters. As Arnáiz explained later, "he told me that he was the victim of a runaround and that he had been unjustly imprisoned. . . . He was very anxious and particularly susceptible, because of the delicate condition of his health. He was afraid he would die if he remained in prison much longer. Because Mr. March's declarations were of a highly reasonable and justified nature, I promised to grant him his freedom." Shortly after ten o'clock that night, Arnáiz unlocked March's door. March walked out, and was immediately met by another prison official—his personal guard,

Eugenio Vargas Rodríguez—who escorted him to his chauffeured limousine, waiting nearby. March—and Vargas, too—climbed in, and the car roared away, headed for Gibraltar. During the twelve-hour trip to the border, there was a change of cars and an addition to the company of passengers; the new passenger was Raimundo Burguera, a trusted March employee and manager of El Tesorillo, a March estate barely on the Spanish side of the Gibraltar border. At the border, the party smoothly passed through both Spanish and British customs without March's being so much as asked to get out of the car, allegedly because over the previous weeks Burguera had been making the same passage in the same vehicle over and over again, thereby inducing the customs men to think of him as an innocent commuter. March stayed in Gibraltar four days, and then sailed, unchallenged, to Marseilles—still accompanied by Vargas, the compassionate jailer, who cheerfully told reporters there that he had decided to retire and live in Greece.

The escape projected March, generally known for secretiveness, into a state of voluble euphoria. Quantities of prose, rich in righteous indignation and patriotism, flowed from his tongue and pen for several days. In a series of press conferences held in Gibraltar soon after his arrival there, he attacked the Accountability Commission for having kept him locked up for so long without trial; quoted a Socialist member of the commission as having said that he should remain imprisoned, if only "for the evil he had done to the Socialist Party"; and ended up with his own analysis: "They did it with the hope of taking from me my patrimony with the least excuse." On the telephone to the *Daily Telegraph* in London, he explained that at Alcalá de Henares the jailer Vargas "helped me to my car, as I was feeble almost to death from my long confinement and ill treatment in prison." (March's doctor was quoted in Gibraltar as having said that he was suffering from a "nervous breakdown" but that his condition was "not considered serious." Apart from that, no professional opinions on the state of his health were published.) "The jailer offered to come with me," March continued chattily. "The prison adjutant might have come, too, for he believes my escape was justified. But he stayed behind to vindicate his action in the light of reason and equity." March then went on to remark that it was a good thing the border guards had not required him to get out of the car, because at the time of crossing he had still been wearing his prison trousers.

March's most fulsome exposition of his thoughts and feelings, though, was contained in a letter addressed to his lawyer, José Antonio Canals, dated "Dawn, November 3, 1933" but evidently written earlier, in prison, since at that hour he was en route to the border. Clearly intended for publication—and, in fact, published in *La Libertad* the next day—the letter was, if nothing else, happily free of the bloodless, tongue-tied, lawyer-ridden prose style so characteristic of United States businessmen, past and present. Certainly to some extent striving consciously for comic effect, it showed the kind of cheerful cynicism—like that of *The Three-penny Opera* in Germany—that often appears shortly before the coming of Fascism. The letter read, in part:

If my decision to escape has had a successful outcome, I will be far from my homeland by the time these lines are in your hands. Those of you who know my love of Spain will understand how profoundly bitter I am to leave her and how powerful the reasons must be which have led me to take this step. I can bear no more, dear friend . . . after seventeen months of captivity, I am in such a weakened state that, if I were to allow it to continue, the homicidal intention of those who want to do away with me would be fully realized. I want to spare them a guilty conscience. . . .

Maintaining my hopes, I spent a year and a half in prison. My soul was burdened with pain. I knew that, outside my cell, a savage horde of demagogues, sectarians, heartless opportunists, mercenaries, and traitors were giving poor Spain the same treatment they were giving me. . . . I kept waiting for relief, and relief did not come. . . . No use the fervent protests by writers of every stripe, no use—in short—the reaction of all noble spirits to the iniquity which was being perpetrated against me. The Accountability Commission imprisoned me without right or reason. Its design was that I should perish in prison or go mad. . . . I was convinced that a few more days of captivity would have meant death. . . .

I cannot close this letter without humbly begging all who had stood by me in the past to forgive me. . . . I trust you will take into account that my physical resistance was running out, and forgive my rebellious gesture. Your forgiveness will assure my peace of mind. The judgment of the others does not concern me: I know that they will howl like starving dogs deprived of a coveted bone. I know many are afraid that with my freedom their shameless behavior will be revealed. I don't care. They did not complete their task. When the coming elections are over and Spain is a country where one can live, in which the personal rights of citizens are more than a myth, I won't be able to return to her fast enough, in order to take you into my open arms.

Meanwhile, to a remarkable extent, Spain was taking March into *its* arms. The police, immediately after hearing about the escape, held for questioning a number of obvious associates of March, including his son Juan; the secretary of his shipping line; officials of *La Libertad* and *Informaciones*; and the lawyer Canals. None of them could be implicated in his escape, and they were released. Thereafter, the government vacillated about whether or not to ask for March's extradition, and ended up doing nothing. This inaction may have been in part a response to a big upsurge of public sentiment in favor of March's escape, which was widely perceived as being in the great, ancient tradition of Spanish picaresque, in which the rogue-hero survives by defeating authority with his wits. Like the midget on J. P. Morgan's knee, the escape had precipitated an overnight reversal of public opinion about a previously hated rich man. "All Spain was chuckling" over the event, according to a report by Claude G. Bowers, the United States Ambassador to Spain at the time. "In the cynical, ribald laughter of the cafés, men told this story and roared with the joy of it." Most of the press—not only the "March press"—seemed to feel about the same way. "IF ONLY THERE WERE MORE VARGAS," read a banner headline in one Madrid daily. The Spanish Leftist press, of course, took the occasion to renew its attacks on March and all that he represented, but in London—where, as would become evident later, March in 1933 already had a strong financial foothold—the *Daily Telegraph* and the *Daily Mail* took his side, on the premise, demonstrably false, that his opponents in government had been

Communists. As if all that were not enough response to his plea for forgiveness, in the general election of November 19th, which resulted in a sweeping triumph of the Right and Center and the reinstallation of Lerroux as Prime Minister, March was reelected to the Cortes as a Majorcan delegate.

After remaining prudently, and quietly, in France for four and a half months, March, fulfilling the promise made in his letter to Canals, returned to Majorca, where he was ceremonially welcomed home at the Transmediterranean dock—his dock—by his father, his son, and local officials of the Banca March. No move to reimprison him was made then, or would ever be made.

V

"AGAIN the mean, meagre figure of Juan March was seen lounging in the lobby of the Palace Hotel," Bowers wrote later. March's activities during the almost two years between his return from France and the election of February, 1936, are comparatively obscure, and perhaps not by chance. Hugh Thomas believes that March was then devoting himself to speculation against the Spanish currency for the purpose of sabotaging the Republic; if so, his efforts were unsuccessful, because the peseta remained remarkably stable against other currencies during most of the period, which was marked by rapid disintegration of the Republic in other respects. Bowers relates that early in 1936, after the Sub-Minister of Finance had ventured to interfere with an attempt by March to get a government refund of eighteen million pesetas to his Spanish Porto Pi Oil Company, March "crowded the corridors of the Ministry of Finance with agents, armed with bribe money." The agents were ejected, and the refund was not paid; what the episode makes clear is that March "the last pirate" (who would reappear in a new guise in the postwar world) had not in 1936 given way entirely to March the embattled statesman. But the fact is that later evidence strongly suggests that March's principal preoccupation in 1935 and early 1936 was secret political intrigue—specifically, the financing of the Nationalist coalition that in July, 1936, would launch the Spanish Civil War.

The result of the general election of February, 1936—a sweeping victory for the new coalition of Leftist parties called the Popular Front—was anticipated, with trepidation, by many Spaniards identified as enemies of the Left, March among them. By the day after the election, as an aura of impending class war filled the Spanish air, the two country clubs near Madrid were deserted, society functions in that city were cancelled, train reservations out of it were unobtainable, and The Rock hotel in Gibraltar was packed with members of the Spanish nobility and aristocracy who had made their escapes in the previous days. As for March, at ten-thirty on the morning of election day he crossed the border into France, accompanied by his family, thereby accomplishing his third successful flight into exile out of four attempts. (That same day, the voters of Majorca reelected him, as usual, as one of their deputies in the Cortes.) In the following months—while the government was busy with such undertakings as forcing employers to rehire employees they had sacked after the strikes of 1934, and settling tens of thousands of peasants on land seized from large holders—March, in France, was, Thomas says, "in close touch with the military conspirators." March is generally known outside Spain, to the extent that he is known at all, as the man who financed Franco's rise to power. The precise extent to which he did will not be known until all Spanish documents on the subject are opened to scrutiny. However, much information has come to light, some of it quite recently.

To begin with, March and the Nationalist coalition were by no means natural allies. As Carner noted in his famous speech, March was the least ideological of men, ordinarily deriving his principles—if they can be given that name—from his personal financial interest. (Indeed, in studying March closely over a long period one comes gradually to think of him as some strange human mutant—a disembodied mind, detached from all emotions but acquisitiveness. It is not just that one misses idealism, affection, hope, or fear; finally, one asks, where is jealousy? Where, despite March's occasional bluster, are real malice, pettiness, even vengeance?) Moreover, each of the various elements in the coalition had reason to oppose or dislike March, and vice versa. The Falange, the Spanish Fascist Party, founded in 1933 by Miguel Primo de Rivera's son José Antonio, was categorically opposed to individualistic capitalism, while March, for his part, was disturbed from the first about the possible effect on his fortunes of the Falange programs for agrarian reform and the nationalization of banks. The landed and titled gentry tended to regard March with the disdain that aristocrats in all times and places reserve for the upstart rich; for example, the aristocrats of Majorca had for years excluded him from their private club in Palma. The military officers who would lead the revolt tended to share the aristocrats' prejudice. As for the Catholic politicians, led by José María Gil Robles, if they were serious about their faith they could scarcely condone March's notorious business methods and practices. Two powerful bonds remained: mutual opposition to the Republic, and the fact that March had money when the Nationalists needed it.

Those were bonds enough. In June, 1936, the month before the uprising began, March sent messages to Franco—himself in semi-exile at Tenerife, in the Canary Islands, where he had been sent by the Ministry of War to keep him at a safe distance from mainland Spain—expressing his predisposition toward the counter-revolutionary cause and promising financial help to the conspirators in case of its failure. "It appears that March guaranteed the safety of all the principal figures involved in planning the insurrection," Díaz Nosty says. "It appears that this special 'insurance policy' amounted to one million pesetas per capita. The safety of the plotters' families was also guaranteed as completely as possible."

The most publicized, and probably the most spectacular, assistance that March gave was his paying for the aircraft that carried Franco from the Canaries to Spanish Morocco to take command of the Nationalist Army. Franco, having been chosen almost at the last minute by the junta of rebellious generals to be their leader, showed a tendency to procrastinate, whereupon a group of his fellow-conspirators decided to force his hand by arranging without his knowledge to have a plane go and call for him. In the first week of July, one of these men approached March in Biarritz, and he agreed immediately to finance the plane-sending operation, whereupon the London correspondent of the Monarchist daily *ABC*, Luis Bolín, was instructed by his editor, the Marquis Luca de Tena, who was a strong Nationalist sympathizer, to procure a plane capable of flying directly from the Canary Islands to Morocco. The money, Luca de Tena explained, was to be provided by the London merchant banking firm of Kleinwort, Sons & Company, Ltd.—of which, according to a later affidavit of Cyril H. Kleinwort, of that firm, March had been a client since December, 1930. Bolín then chartered from the Olley Airways Company, of Croydon, on the outskirts of London, a transport-bomber called a Dragon Rapide. (Or else, as Díaz Nosty insists, the plane was bought outright; whichever was the case, the money came from March's sterling account at the Kleinwort bank.) On July 11th, the Dragon Rapide flew from Croydon to Lisbon with a British pilot and with a passenger complement consisting of Bolín, a retired British major, and two young women, one of them the major's daughter and the other a friend of hers. Neither the pilot nor any of the passengers except Bolín knew the purpose of the journey; the pilot was a hired hand, and the British passengers, arranged for as decoys by English sympathizers with the Nationalist side, believed that they were on a joyride. Four days later, the Dragon Rapide—this time without the British passengers, who were left to enjoy themselves in Lisbon—flew to Las Palmas, on Grand Canary Island, to fulfill its mission of picking up Franco and delivering him to Spanish Morocco.

There remained the somewhat awkward problem of getting Franco from his station at Tenerife, separated from Grand Canary by about forty miles of water, to Las Palmas, where the Dragon Rapide was waiting for him. An excuse was tragicomically provided when, on the day after the plane's arrival, the military governor of Las Palmas accidentally killed himself at target practice, and Franco got permission from the Ministry of War in

Madrid to go to Las Palmas for his colleague's funeral. This he did, by boat, on the night of July 16th–17th. By evening of the eighteenth, the Spanish African ports of Ceuta, Tetuán, and Melilla had been seized by the Nationalists, with the help of the Spanish Foreign Legion. On the morning of that day, Franco, after first issuing a manifesto from Las Palmas, left in the Dragon Rapide bound for Tetuán, making unscheduled landings at Agadir and Casablanca, perhaps to telephone ahead and make sure that his friends were firmly in charge of things at his destination. The same day, fighting began on the Spanish mainland, and the terrible war that both exemplified and exaggerated all the social and ideological conflicts of its time was begun.

In the early days of the war, March, travelling frequently between Biarritz, Rome, London, and Lisbon, played a crucial role in obtaining Italian military help for the Spanish Nationalists. On July 22nd—the same day that in Madrid, now ruled by the Socialist Trade Union, March's mansion was being seized by the Socialist-Communist Youth to serve as its headquarters—March was reported by French Communist sources to be in Biarritz engaged in nothing less than plotting the course of the revolt, along with Gil Robles and the Falangist José Antonio Primo de Rivera. What is certain is that on the twenty-third he met in Biarritz with several of the leading conspirators to help prepare a request for Italian aid; and on the twenty-fifth the conspirators proceeded to Rome (perhaps accompanied by March) to ask the Italian Foreign Minister, Count Ciano, for twelve combat aircraft for shipment to North Africa. Ciano apparently demanded payment in advance, and March apparently met the demand without question. According to one account, the sum was one million pounds sterling; according to another, March simplified matters by buying control of the Savoia Corporation, manufacturers of the aircraft. Confirmation of sorts of some transaction along these lines came on July 30th, when six Italian aviators landed at Berkane, French Morocco, where they were detained by French authorities and, through their attorney, told a local court that they were on their way to join the Franco forces in planes paid for by March.

At almost exactly the same time, according to what Garriga

was told by the secretary to General Emilio Mola, Franco's second-in-command until his death the following year, March turned up at Mola's headquarters in Pamplona and handed over a document listing securities worth almost six hundred million pesetas, or around eighty-two million dollars, that he was putting at Mola's disposal should he need it to raise funds. One of Mola's aides was "overcome with emotion," Garriga says, adding that "March's financial intervention in Pamplona was one of the decisive factors that allowed the generals to continue to fight." (Díaz Nosty, in repeating the story, expresses doubt that March came to Pamplona in person; and, indeed, apart from the risk involved, his known travel schedule that week makes it seem unlikely that he did.)

In August, the month after the government had confiscated March's Transmediterranean shipping line—at little personal cost to him, inasmuch as on July 11th he had forehandedly withdrawn all the company's liquid funds and ordered its newest and best ships to safe areas—March used his expertise and his connections to make purchases of foreign exchange for the Nationalists, whose desperate need for it is dramatized by evidence that at one point their foreign currency reserves had dwindled to the equivalent of fourteen hundred dollars. (The Nationalists, in mid-March of 1937, issued a decree requiring all citizens and organizations within territory they had captured to surrender their foreign currency, foreign securities, and gold in exchange for Nationalist pesetas. There is some evidence that March profited, and cheated the Nationalists, by amassing such assets for himself and taking them abroad shortly before the decree.) What virtually all authorities are agreed on is that March personally financed in large part the Italian intervention that secured Majorca for the Nationalists in the latter half of August. The island had fallen to them without a struggle at the start of the war, but on August 16th a Republican force made up of Catalans, and numbering perhaps twelve thousand five hundred, landed and established a beachhead on its eastern coast. Shortly afterward, the beachhead was attacked by three March-financed Savoia bombers with Italian crews, accompanied by an Italian fighter squadron—and attacked so relentlessly and effectively that within a matter of days the few surviving Republican troops had been thrown back into the sea. The Italian attack was soon followed by the arrival, as effective Majorcan dictator, of a farcical yet unbelievably fanatical and cruel Italian Fascist named Arconovaldo Bonaccorsi, who called himself Count Rossi. Driving a red racing car, wearing a black Fascist uniform and a large white cross on his chest, and carrying on his person a one-man arsenal consisting of pistols, knives, daggers, cartridge belts, and grenade belts, for four months he roamed the island spreading casual death. The French writer Georges Bernanos, a Catholic monarchist who was living on Majorca at the time, and who originally sympathized with the counter-revolution, recorded later that by the spring of 1937 there had been some three thousand assassinations on Majorca, among the victims being whole families wiped out on the basis of hearsay evidence that they had ventured to cheer Catalan planes flying overhead. "In the end, they ceased to horrify," Bernanos wrote of the Fascist murders. March cannot be held personally responsible for them, or for Bonaccorsi—only for the Italian attack that prepared the way for Bonaccorsi's regime in his homeland and that probably would not have occurred on the tactically unimportant island without his intervention.

That March may have been involved in financing the counter-revolution well before the start of the war; that his credits in Britain played a huge role in the financing; and that his relations with the Nationalists were anything but smooth—all these things are suggested by evidence that has recently come to light in a surprising way. Not long before Franco's death, in November, 1975, a young economic historian, Angel Viñas, of the University of Valencia, was commissioned by the Franco Ministry of Finance to do a book on a question to which the Ministry had never known the precise answer: What happened to the Spanish gold reserve, which at the beginning of the Civil War was the fourth-largest national gold reserve in the world and by its end had all but disappeared? Viñas was given free access to certain relevant and previously secret documents. His book, *Spanish Gold in the Civil War*, revealed that most of the national treasure had been sold in 1936 and 1937 to the Soviet Union and the Bank of France to finance the Republican side in the war. Published in the autumn of 1976, a year after Franco's death, the book was suddenly suppressed after Viñas, doing a publicity appearance on television—the not always happy lot of eager modern authors in many countries—made some remarks that apparently miffed government officials. It was rereleased, just as suddenly, the following August—as a result, Viñas believes, of a government reshuffle—and Viñas was allowed even wider access to secret files, to do further research, for a new edition. While doing this research, Viñas came upon various documents relating to March's dealings with the Nationalists, and in November, 1977, he told me of his new findings.

According to Viñas' sources, as early as April, 1936—three months before the outbreak of the insurrection—a contract was made under which the Kleinwort bank in London would supply credit to the Nationalists, to be drawn on as needed, and personally guaranteed by March. The limit of credits, originally five hundred thousand pounds, was raised in August and September to eight hundred thousand pounds, and in December it reached a peak of nine hundred and forty-two thousand, or more than four and a half million dollars. But what was abundantly clear from the documents he found, Viñas says, was that March, in so liberally putting his resources at the counter-revolutionists' disposal, was careful to insist on a sound commercial basis—and, indeed, sometimes drove such a hard bargain that the generals were greatly annoyed. A Nationalist agent's report in the Spanish military archives, dated July 25th, states pointedly that in agreeing to pay for the first Italian military aircraft March requested a formal order and a receipt signed by a representative of the Nationalist leadership. The tone of the report suggests that the request was resented. That attitude becomes explicit in another document—an agent's report made in August, in which the agent quotes March as complaining that the military junta was no longer paying much attention to him. "I inspired Juan March to put his credit to the service of the fatherland, and begged him to approach the junta in a way that wouldn't be so commercial," the agent reported.

Whether or not March accepted the plea not to be so commercial, and whether or not the junta resumed paying attention to him, his financial operations in the second half of 1936 were on a gigantic scale. Other papers found by Viñas show that on September 3rd March deposited forty-nine and a half metric tons of gold in the Bank of Italy, and that on September 9th he deposited seventy-two metric tons more. In 1936, a metric ton of gold was worth about one million two hundred and thirty-five thousand dollars. The source and ownership of the gold that March deposited and the purpose for which he deposited it are not known; surely it is a reasonable speculation that he had acquired much if not all of it for his own benefit, in exchange for pesetas, by exploiting the privileged trading position that the Nationalists had given him, and that he chose the Bank of Italy, which at that time functioned as a private bank as well as a government one, as the safest available depository. Whatever the case, the fact that one man could within a week make gold deposits greater than the national gold reserves of any but a few of the world's nations vividly shows the financial power he was then able to command.

As the Nationalists prospered militarily, Italy decided to support them at its own expense, as a political matter, and credits from British and American banks and corporations became more readily available to them. (In particular, The Texas Company—later called Texaco, Inc.—made vast shipments of oil to Franco between late 1936 and early 1939; as to payments, Franco's negotiator wrote later, "we paid what we could pay, when we could pay it.") Consequently, Franco became less dependent upon March. Late in 1936, rumors spread that March had refused to continue financing the war and was demanding repayment of sums due him. Even one Republican journal wrote of "the traitorous and miserly Majorcan's urgent demands," and implied that the Franco regime's pillaging of the treasure of the famous Virgin of the Cathedral of Nuestra Señora del Pilar, in Zaragoza—the jewels were reported to have brought some fifty million dollars in London and other cities—had been made necessary by March's tightfistedness. Nevertheless, through the first half of 1937 he continued to serve Franco regularly as a financial diplomat and purchasing agent. On April 11th, with the insurgents pressing Bilbao, March arrived by ship in Naples, and announced that he was headed for Rome to join his family, some of whom were then living there. In Rome, he refused to see newsmen, and they reported that his purpose there was believed to be to confer with Italian officials and to purchase supplies for the Nationalists. In late May, at another critical point in the war, March again sailed for Italy, this time from Gibraltar, and this time accompanied by a delegation of Spanish notables, including the Duke of Alba, a jaunty, scholarly man—at one time or another director of the Royal Academy of History and president of the board of governors of the Prado, and the author of several books—who had become Franco's chief link with the Spanish nobility. In Naples, again en route to Rome, March told reporters that he was in Italy as a tourist. Some of his countrymen in Gibraltar, however, which at that time was still a nesting place for Spanish aristocrats sympathetic to Franco but waiting out the war at a safe distance, said that March's and Alba's mission was to dissuade Premier Mussolini from withdrawing the thousands of Italian "volunteer" troops fighting for the Nationalists in Spain. Then, in early July, March was reported on his way to Italy yet again, this time from Algeciras.

Opinions and calculations as to the extent and value of March's over-all financial contribution to Franco's victory vary widely. One Nationalist official declared, with what was certainly Latin exaggeration, that March had offered his personal fortune down to the last centavo. A future Franco Cabinet officer called his support "the sole decisive factor in Spain's triumph over Communism." Viñas, however, feels that while March's contribution was crucial tactically, especially at the beginning of the war, when Franco had virtually no other sources to draw upon, it did not determine the war's outcome. Díaz Nosty, accepting as a "working figure" an estimate by *El Pueblo,* of Valencia, in 1937 that March had "donated one billion pesetas for the purchase of fratricidal weapons," points out that on the basis of an authoritative estimate that the war cost the Nationalists about ten billion pesetas, "we can tentatively state that one of every ten pesetas spent on the war had been advanced by March."

Thus, with the Republican surrender on April 1, 1939, and Franco's accession to the position of dictator, Carner's 1932 prediction—that either the Republic would submit to him or he to it—in a fashion came true. Now, of course, March's personal financial prospects were bright indeed. For the first time, a man in his personal debt for past services had become head of state—and head of state without democratic checks on his power. March now enjoyed a kind of advantage that no financier in even the most complaisant or corrupt representatively governed state—not a Jay Gould under a Grant Administration, for example—ever had available to him. He was quick to use the advantage. His confiscated properties were promptly restored to him. In February, 1939—by which time the British government was waiting only for the Republicans' surrender before recognizing the Franco regime—the firm of J. March & Company, Ltd., was formed in London, its formally announced purpose being "to facilitate the entry of British products and capital into Spain in order to collaborate in the reconstruction necessary owing to the havoc wrought by war." However, the impression gained by Thomas J. Hamilton, of *The New York Times,* was that the firm's ambitions were a good deal higher, wider, and less purely humanitarian than that. "Deep within the financial district I found the new company's modest office," Hamilton wrote later. "March . . . was not in London. The manager was more than willing to explain his chief's aims. The new company intended to take over Spain's trade with the entire world."

VI

NEITHER J. March & Company nor March himself succeeded in doing that. The period just before and during the Second World War was nevertheless a golden age for him. The currency tangles created by such a war, imposed for the first time on a sophisticated modern economy involving many interdependent nations, were just March's meat. Through the middle months of 1939 and into the early months of the war, J. March & Company exploited its privilege of acting as a middleman in the Spanish export-import trade. Maintaining a separate account with each country, it collected foreign currency generated by Spanish exports, reimbursing the exporter in pesetas; then it either held the foreign currency in banks outside Spain or sold it to the Spanish government at a profit. This amiable rake-off system ended shortly after the outbreak of war when conscientious officials hostile to March and his methods came to the Spanish Ministry of Industry and Commerce. For the first time in his career, March then turned to large-scale dealings with the United States. A Majorcan story has it that early in the war a priest from Pennsylvania, visiting relatives in Majorca, expressed a wish to help out Spanish priests there with money but was refused permission by the United States to bring dollars into Spain. Presented with the problem, March is supposed to have said, "Tell the good father I'll pay for Spanish Masses in Majorca if he'll buy cigarettes for me in Kentucky." The deal fell through, so the story goes, when a Louisville firm reported to Washington a priest's order for millions of cigarettes for Spain.

But March, of course, had other, and bigger, fish to fry in the United States and elsewhere. Using neutral Spain and Portugal as convenient platforms, he attempted to return to his old wartime game of playing off the belligerents against each other. At the end of 1941, he went to bomb-devastated London, where, using the office facilities of the Franco government's press attaché there (his friend the Duke of Alba, now Spanish Ambassador to Britain, had the grace or the caution to refuse him use of the Embassy), he reestablished old contacts with important figures in the City of London. It seems clear that he also had conversations with representatives of the British government, promising it information obtained from his shipping operations, and threatening it with the use of his influence to reduce or cut off the shipment of Spanish iron ore to Britain. At about the same time, March made earnest efforts through the German Navy Secret Service to treat with the

Nazi side. That these efforts were largely unsuccessful may have been in part due to the fact that March was alleged to have Jewish ancestry; like many Majorcans, he was thought to be descended from Jews who had been converted to Christianity during the Inquisition. At all events, he seems to have emerged from his various negotiations with a limited but valuable British license to ply his trade, nefarious or otherwise, in exchange for his cooperation with the British as to information and supplies.

The results of this arrangement surfaced spectacularly in December, 1941, when the *Isla de Tenerife*, a freighter of March's Transmediterranean line, bound for Lisbon, was seized at a Staten Island pier by order of the Secretary of the Treasury, and five men associated with the ship—her captain and chief radio operator, two representatives of Transmediterranean, and a Spanish-born shipping broker with a British passport—were taken into federal custody, charged with attempting to export prohibited commodities and with violating the Trading with the Enemy Act. As to the former offense, the *Isla* was caught red-handed, inasmuch as the federal authorities had found aboard her large quantities of radio parts, parachute silk, and lubricating oil, and, on the pier alongside, apparently waiting to be loaded, thirty thousand dollars' worth of additional silk and more than a hundred fifty-five-gallon drums of oil. These materials were blandly listed on the ship's manifest as "ship's stores"; the authorities believed they were war matériel destined for Germany. The incident caused an international uproar, and the Spanish government felt obliged to issue a statement reasserting its nonbelligerent status. Nevertheless, in New York the matter was quickly disposed of. Charges were dismissed against the two Transmediterranean representatives, who subsequently complained through their lawyer that the accusation alone caused them to lose a South American connection that had "netted them two hundred and fifty thousand dollars annually." The *Isla*'s captain and the shipping broker were allowed to plead *nolo contendere* to the charge of exporting prohibited matériel, and were fined a thousand dollars each. Transmediterranean pleaded guilty to the same charge, paid twenty thousand dollars in fines and costs, and forfeited some of the cargo; and on January

12, 1942, the *Isla* was released, to steam away unhampered. The United States Attorney said that the government's investigation had failed to prove that the cargo was to end up in Nazi hands, and the shipping broker's lawyer praised the Department of Justice for its fairness in the case. Well he may have, if one is to credit later reports from United States Treasury sources that the investigation had shown the Lisbon consignee of the *Isla*'s cargo to be a veteran smuggler with diplomatic connections, that the investigators had recommended the blacklisting of March's ships for United States trade, and that the lenient handling of the accused and the refusal to blacklist March had been the result of British intercession.

For whatever reason, the British government—which in the postwar period would find itself able and willing to give March's business career a couple of huge and unaccountable boosts—seemed willing during wartime to go far out of its way to help him. At one point, an American Treasury agent, commenting on a hundred tons of Mexican sisal shipped to March under British certification, said, "This authority, granted by the British Economic Warfare Ministry, is only given when [the] ultimate consignee is known and considered friendly to British interests." In 1943, according to the memoirs of Gil Robles, the British government confirmed its soft spot for March by putting him on a list of six Spaniards who were to be granted asylum in the British Embassy in Madrid if they should ever find themselves in trouble there.

Indeed, for a time during the latter stages of the war there were serious risks of such trouble for March. In 1939, he is supposed to have boasted, "Franco can refuse me nothing." Within a year or so, however, Franco's ministers were refusing him as much as they could, on the ground that his operations were depriving the government of foreign currency and causing domestic inflation. There even came to be some question of March's personal safety in Spain. In January, 1943, he became officially a resident of Lisbon, where, in fact, he had spent much of his time over the previous three years. In good March style, this move served several purposes: Besides getting him formally away from the political shoals of Madrid, it made legal his maintenance of foreign-currency accounts outside Spain (for which, as a resident Spaniard, he had earlier been theoretically subject to the death penalty), and it put him in his natural milieu—Lisbon in wartime being the European center of both espionage and black-market activities. Nor, once safely established there, could March restrain himself from mixing in anti-Franco politics. Even as he was raking in new fortunes from speculating in wolfram and trading with the Americas (and also "losing his hair," while his complexion took on a "strange rubbery appearance," as Upton Sinclair had Lanny Budd note in the novel *Presidential Mission*), he found time for a flirtation with the Lisbon-based Spanish monarchist movement, which now sought to overthrow Franco and place on the vacant throne Juan de Borbón, the heir to Alfonso XIII. The Allied powers openly supported Juan and the monarchists, and March was clearly coming to believe that in the event of an Allied victory Franco would be deposed and the Spanish monarchy restored. In Lisbon in July, 1943, March rashly let it be known that he believed the crown might be restored under certain conditions, even though four months earlier he had been warned by the Spanish government not to "get entangled in political activities." Then, in a strange episode in mid-1944, he apparently offered a blank check to the National Alliance of Democratic Organizations, an anti-Franco coalition, and, in the process, referred to Franco as "that dog." As the story was later told to Díaz Nosty by Régulo Martínez, the head of the National Alliance, March and one of his men, Tomás Peire, met with the National Alliance leaders at the house of a female friend of March's, and March said, "I would give half of my fortune and then some . . . if you got that dog out of there." When Régulo Martínez reminded him that he had supported Franco, March replied, "For that very reason, because I've helped him, I know him inside out." And Régulo Martínez says that March had the gall to add, "Besides, I'm a Republican. Tomás, get the checks." Tomás Peire then placed a blank check in front of Régulo Martínez, who refused it, on the ground that it would not be proper for the Alliance to accept March's support.

It all led to nothing. With the end of the Second World War, in 1945, the Allied powers at first continued to support Juan de Borbón and to oppose Franco, whose government was refused representation in the United Nations; but with the start of the Cold War, soon afterward, they came generally to see Franco as a bulwark against Communism and stopped seriously trying to promote his overthrow. As for March, he emerged from his wartime political indiscretions unscathed. Franco, whether or not he ever heard in any detail about March's meeting with the National Alliance, was willing in the new, more stable condition of his dictatorship after 1945 to welcome March back into his good graces. As early as July, 1945, an old admirer of March's, Juan Antonio Suances, was made Minister of Industry and Commerce—an unmistakable signal that Franco was ready to forgive and forget, and that his former benefactor was free to come home and claim what was due him.

Franco had reasons for his magnanimity. A number of the leading business enterprises in Spain, among them Barcelona Traction, were owned principally or wholly by foreigners. It was the postwar policy of the Franco government to help bring these enterprises under Spanish ownership, when possible, without incurring the compensation costs or the international opprobrium, or both, ordinarily attendant upon outright government expropriation of foreign property. By allowing or encouraging March to seize such an enterprise, Franco could now in one stroke use March and reward him for past services. Thus, March was at last in a position to benefit both his country and his bank accounts by becoming an economic privateer.

VII

FINANCIAL maneuvering is a form of endeavor favorable to old men: The financial brain, unlike brains adept in various other areas—for example, mathematics, physics, chess, and, quite possibly, armed bank robbery—apparently deteriorates very little, if at all, with the passage of time, even in the eighth and ninth decades of life. (Women, even geniuses at financial speculation like Hetty Green, seem never to have entered the arena of large-scale financial predation.) March's greatest single undertaking, the conquest of Barcelona Traction, Light & Power Company, Ltd., was his chief occupation from the age of sixty until his death, in 1962, at eighty-one. The master of a perverse and unlovable yet somehow appealing craft, he clearly meant to make this his masterpiece.

Barcelona Traction, certainly one of the most attractive industrial plums in Spain in the nineteen-forties, was founded in 1911 by Fred Stark Pearson, an American engineer who had previously been responsible for the installation of huge hydroelectric plants in Brazil and Mexico. In 1911, so the legend goes, he was taken by a young Spanish engineer, Carlos Montañés, to the Catalan peak of Tibidabo—the place, a much older Spanish legend insists, where Satan tempted Christ by offering him the rule of the world. Montañés had prepared a plan for the electrification of Catalonia by water power, and counted on Pearson's skill to execute the project. Looking out over the Barcelona plain, Pearson—flouting, perhaps rashly, Tibidabo's renunciatory tradition—said, "There are few pearls like this left in the world today. I'll take on the business." Initial financing having been obtained, work on the vast project began, but it was brought almost to a standstill by the economic pinch that came with the First World War; and in May, 1915, when Pearson was en route to Britain from the United States, the British liner he was aboard, the *Lusitania*, went down under torpedo attack by a German submarine off the Irish coast. Pearson was among the nearly twelve hundred persons who died. So great was the impression that he and his enterprise had made on the city of Barcelona even then that a few days later its council passed a resolution ordering that a Barcelona street of the future be named for him.

The subsequent history of Barcelona Traction up to 1948 was marked by fairly consistent success and increasing international complexity of structure. From the beginning, it was a venture in economic colonialism; its original shareholders were almost exclusively non-Spanish, and, by charter, its headquarters and official home were not in Spain but in Canada, a country that offered tax advantages to such companies at the time. Construction in Catalonia resumed after the end of the war. By the mid-nineteen-twenties, the enterprise was producing enough hydroelectric power to be solidly profitable, and a controlling interest in it had been bought by a combination of Belgian companies headed by an American-born engineer, Dannie N. Heineman.

Heineman, the key man of Barcelona Traction over the next twenty-five years, is one of the less remembered, perhaps because one of the sounder, of the crop of international utilities magnates who got their start at the turn of the century, when electrification was the rage in many countries. Born in North Carolina in 1872, of German ancestry, he grew up in Germany, having moved there with his mother after his father's early death, in 1880. After studying the then avant-garde science of electrical engineering at the University of Hanover, he joined Union-Elektrizitäts-Gesellschaft, a Berlin company affiliated with General Electric, and within a few years had made a name for himself by directing the conversion from horse to electric power of the tramways of Naples, Koblenz, Liège, and Brussels. In 1905, on the strength of that, he joined as managing director a Belgian-based firm, then a fledgling, which he was to rule with an iron hand for half a century—the Société Financière de Transports et d'Entreprises Industrielles, or SOFINA. When Heineman joined SOFINA, it had on its payroll only two other employees; just before the Second World War, having either built or taken charge of the tramways and electrical systems of Bilbao, Buenos Aires, Constantinople, Bangkok, Barcelona, and Lisbon, among other places, SOFINA, along with its subsidiaries, employed forty thousand people and was one of the world's largest companies of its kind. Heineman, meanwhile, had won distinction as a diplomat and a humanitarian by helping to found the Commission for Relief in Belgium, the institution that launched Herbert Hoover on a political career that culminated in the White House.

At heart, Heineman was clearly a builder rather than a finan-

cial manipulator. His surviving colleagues say that he was actually
uninterested in money, although he did leave several million dollars when he died, in 1962, at the age of eighty-nine. Soft-spoken
and publicity-shy, he was a businessman in the high European
style, collecting books and manuscripts (as, indeed, March did,
too), cultivating the friendship of European heads of state, operating SOFINA along conservative, debt-free lines, and liking to discuss politics, writing, or music in his office before getting down to
business. In his later years, he bore, and seemed to be amused by,
a rather striking physical resemblance to J. Pierpont Morgan. His
connection with Barcelona Traction began in 1924. In 1923, the
flamboyant yet secretive Belgian financier Alfred Loewenstein
had formed a company called Société Internationale d'Energie
Hydro-Électrique, or SIDRO, and bought for its account, along
with holdings in various other companies, most of the shares of
Barcelona Traction. The following year, Loewenstein, finding
himself in temporary financial straits, sold to SOFINA a block of
SIDRO shares large enough to insure control of its operations.
(Loewenstein died in 1928, in what *The Times* called "one of the
strangest fatalities in the history of commercial aviation." Crossing the English Channel from Croyden to Brussels in his private
aircraft, at an altitude of four thousand feet, he apparently fell out,
unnoticed by his pilot, his mechanic, two stenographers, and a
valet, all of whom were aboard. His death caused a wave of jitters
on European stock markets—a foreboding of the panic that attended the catastrophic international market crash of the following year.)

Thus SOFINA, and Heineman, gained control of Barcelona Traction. The company flourished under their management. By 1935,
its annual net profit was almost three and a half million dollars.
During the Spanish Civil War, the company's physical property
and its bank accounts were taken over by the Republican government, which held parts of Catalonia until shortly before the Republican surrender. After Franco's victory, however, the company
reverted to its previous owners. It did well through the Second
World War; and in the early postwar years, when it was supplying

four-fifths of Catalonia's electricity and one-fifth of all of Spain's, its profits were back to, and even slightly above, the 1935 level.

In structure and ownership, Barcelona Traction was a fairly typical example of a much-deplored corporate genre—the enterprise owned by absentee foreigners, with their ownership organized in a totem pole of holding companies. Barcelona Traction, indeed, was a holding company itself, without so much as an office in Spain; it existed merely to hold all the stock of various operating subsidiaries, of which the principal one was the Ebro Irrigation & Power Company, Ltd., with its head office in Barcelona. In early 1948, SIDRO owned three-quarters of all Barcelona Traction's shares, while SOFINA, in turn, owned about one-third of SIDRO's shares, or enough to be able to control SIDRO's activities. Barcelona Traction's management was first British and later Belgian, but its employees were mainly Spanish. In such circumstances, it was obviously difficult for an Ebro operating man, responsible for maintaining the turbines that produced Catalonia's electricity, to know how his company was being run, or for whose benefit. Someone far away in Brussels, or perhaps in Canada, was calling the tune. In addition to this structural vulnerability to criticism, Barcelona Traction had at one time or another since 1911 been accused of most of the several sins to which what are now called multinational corporations are notoriously prone. It had conducted intricate maneuvers for the apparent purpose of avoiding Spanish taxes. It had violated Spanish exchange-control regulations on occasion, especially during the Second World War —when, to be sure, it had done so for the benefit of and at the request of the British government. It had reorganized itself repeatedly—according to later Spanish accusations, in order to deprive its bondholders to the advantage of its stockholders. And in the nineteen-thirties it had contrived by various means, bribery among them, to destroy Catalonian electricity cooperatives that had arisen to compete with it.

Thus, Barcelona Traction was a company by no means above criticism, particularly in Spain. A British lawyer for the Spanish government, Sir Humphrey Waldock, later put the matter more picturesquely: The company's history, he said, showed repeated traces of "the cloven hoof." From a postwar Spanish point of view, the very fact of any company's being a foreign-owned enterprise operating in Spain endowed that company with cloven hooves. In choosing Barcelona Traction as an object for seizure, March had again—as he had with the Spanish Republican government of 1932—selected an adversary that to some extent had at least the appearance of deserving him. But along with this moral weakness the company had what was quite likely of even greater appeal to March—a material weakness not directly of its own making—an Achilles' heel. In 1911 and 1915, to attract badly needed British and other European funds, Barcelona Traction had sold two issues of bonds that were due fifty years later and had a total value of slightly less than eight million pounds sterling. The buyers of these bonds were entitled to be paid interest in pounds sterling, which Barcelona Traction expected to acquire in exchange for the pesetas that its subsidiaries earned from operations. This arrangement ran like clockwork until 1936. During the Civil War, however, the payment of such interest had to be suspended because of the seizure of the company's properties in Spain, and in the years afterward, when Barcelona Traction had in hand at all times plenty of pesetas to finance the payment of the interest, it could not pay it because the Spanish authorities resolutely refused to let the company trade in its pesetas for the required pounds sterling. Thus, by the start of 1948 the holders of the bonds, even though the company to which they had lent their money was sound and flourishing and anxious to pay them, had not received a single interest payment in eleven years.

This was the Achilles' heel of Barcelona Traction that March spotted and decided to exploit. (As Thorstein Veblen noted in 1918, "the typical American businessman watches the industrial process from ambush, with a view to the seizure of any item of value that may be left at loose ends." He need not have included the qualification "American.") March knew that he would need additional help from the Spanish government, if only in the form of its looking the other way as he went about his predation. And he was evidently confident that he would get that help, as recompense for his past services to Franco.

VIII

THE first, indirect approach of March to Barcelona Traction was made by none other than Carlos Montañés, the man who had supposedly stood on the mountaintop with Pearson three decades earlier, and who had subsequently been an Ebro employee for many years. Sometime before October, 1940, Montañés sent a message to a former Barcelona Traction engineer who was an old acquaintance and colleague of his, making an offer, on behalf of what he described as a "solid European financial group," to buy Barcelona Traction lock, stock, and barrel for one million seven hundred thousand pounds. The offer was accompanied by a hint of threat. Montañés by implication called attention to the fact that German troops were at the Pyrenees, a few miles from the Catalonian border, and he wrote ominously, "I am certain that in a few months a similar offer will be impossible." The engineer forwarded the message to the Barcelona Traction directors, who were in New York as refugees from Nazi-occupied Belgium. The directors cabled back asking the names of the financial group's members, whereupon Montañés replied that, while he absolutely guaranteed the group's solvency, to disclose the members' names would be "delicate." This secrecy had more form than substance, since in 1940 Montañés was widely known to be, and to have been for some years, a close associate and agent of Juan March. Despite another attempt by Montañés to press the case in December, the Barcelona Traction directors continued to spurn the offer.

In 1944, March, after having bided his time for four years—evidence of a longer attention span than most financiers possess, but only a minor feat of patience for him—decided to throw aside the veil and manifest himself directly to his intended victims. Meeting in Spain with Heineman, he said that he had been buying up the company's sterling bonds and was interested in getting control of the company, not only as an investment but out of a concern to increase his "personal prestige." Heineman said later, "He also tried to impress me with his financial ability in telling me that he had bought U.S. dollars at the price of two Swiss francs per dollar and resold them at four Swiss francs per dollar, realizing a profit of eight million francs." Heineman was unimpressed, however—at least to the extent that he coolly replied that the Barcelona Traction shares were not for sale.

When the end of the European war, the following year, failed to bring a change of Spanish government policy which would permit interest payments to resume on the Barcelona Traction sterling bonds, the bondholders, who were mostly British, began casting about for some alternative way to get the money that was due them. Meeting in London, they concocted, with the cooperation of SOFINA-SIDRO, what came to be called a Plan of Compromise. It provided that all holders of Barcelona Traction sterling bonds were to be paid all or a substantial portion of the face value of their bonds plus interest—including the eleven years' arrears—mostly in pounds and the balance in common stock of Barcelona Traction. The problem was that the plan called for Barcelona Traction to pay out three and a half million pounds sterling—then equivalent to fourteen million dollars—which the Spanish government's Institute of Foreign Exchange declined to let the company have in exchange for its amplitude of pesetas, on the ground that Spain was still suffering from a foreign-exchange shortage. To meet this difficulty, it was eventually arranged that the sterling would be collected entirely from companies in the SOFINA-SIDRO group that operated outside Spain: one million pounds from SOFINA; seven hundred and fifty thousand from SIDRO; and the balance, of one million seven hundred and fifty thousand pounds, from a Panamanian company called La Sovalles, which was tied to SOFINA and SIDRO in a labyrinthine way. Under this arrangement, the bondholders would get their money out; Spain would not have to provide any sterling, and thus the apparent basis of its objection to the plan was eliminated; and Barcelona

Traction, freed of the burden of obligations that could not be satisfied, would have clear sailing ahead. The Plan of Compromise was approved in October, 1945, by a majority of the bondholders in London and, in December of the same year, by the Supreme Court of Ontario, Barcelona Traction's home province.

There remained, for the Plan of Compromise to become effective, only the need to get the approval of the Spanish Ministry of Industry and Commerce, which was in a position to veto it by technical means. Inasmuch as Spain was seeking to be accepted as a postwar trading partner by the rest of Europe, and so was anxious not to offend Britain, such approval depended, to one extent or another, on the attitude of the British Treasury and Foreign Office, in their capacity as government representatives of most of the sterling bondholders. It appears in retrospect that a favorable British attitude, and consequent Spanish approval of the Plan of Compromise, might have been forthcoming except for the opposition of Juan March—acting, as he so often did, as a sort of government of his own.

March was adamantly against implementation of the plan, for reasons that were obscure at the time. His opposition became evident at the October, 1945, bondholders' meeting in London, at which, while the plan was being approved by an overwhelming margin, more than ninety per cent of the minority vote against it was cast by Fenchurch Nominees, Ltd.—a front for March which had been set up by his London bankers, Kleinwort, Sons & Company, Ltd. March's role in the ensuing negotiations over the plan, which continued for more than a year, is entirely implicit. What is explicit is that he had friends in the right places. Suances, who, as Spanish Minister of Industry and Commerce, was now the key man in the matter, was a veteran March admirer, and had said of him publicly after the end of the Civil War, "Europe, the West, and—why not say it!—Christianity are in that fabulous man's debt for the support he gave at certain crucial moments. His support was the sole decisive factor in Spain's triumph over Communism." At the same time, Suances was not exactly in March's pocket, much as March might have liked to have him there. That

March at some time considered attempting to bribe the Minister, and decided that it would be impossible, is drolly suggested by an offhand remark he made later to a third party: "Suances is an impossible man. Why, there's hardly a stick of furniture in his house!" Suances' public style is well suggested by a statement he once made to the Cortes in answer to a deputy's protest against government actions: "In all questions submitted to its vigilant attention, the government, under the directon of the Caudillo, is always required to act with the most scrupulous honesty, without other concern than to serve successfully the prestige and the decorum of the nation and the legitimate interests of Spaniards. I have spoken!" A man with flamboyant Latin notions of propriety and probity, Suances probably needed more than his admiration for March, or even his patriotic wish to deliver an enterprise in Spain into Spanish hands, to induce him to decide the matter in March's favor. What else was needed, perhaps, was the influence of the British government.

That the British rapprochement with March during the Second World War—in particular, as regards the British Embassy in Madrid—went well beyond the normal courtesy of a belligerent nation toward a powerful citizen of a neutral one, and even beyond such matters as the *Isla de Tenerife*, is strongly suggested by various documents on file in the British Public Record Office, in Kew, on the outskirts of London, and at the International Court of Justice, at The Hague. One of these is a later affidavit of Captain Alan H. Hillgarth, who was His Majesty's naval attaché in Madrid from 1939 until 1943—and, the evidence suggests, a British intelligence agent as well. In it, Hillgarth declared that during the war March had "rendered this country services of incalculable value." He went on to cite an example of calculable value: In 1942, when the British were severely strapped for funds in Spain, the Madrid manager of the Anglo-South American Bank, the British bank in Spain, had come to the Embassy to say that the bank was about to be ruined by the sudden withdrawal of a deposit of seventy million pesetas by Ebro, Barcelona Traction's subsidiary. The Embassy pleaded with Barcelona Traction and Ebro not to make the withdrawal, but in vain. At which point, wrote Hillgarth, "I went to Mr. March as a last hope and asked him if he would assist us; he thereupon put on his hat and went down with me to see the manager in Madrid and opened an account in which he lodged the necessary millions." Former officers of Barcelona Traction say that Ebro's sudden withdrawal was a technical necessity rather than an anti-British move, and that, in fact, the deposit had originally been made specifically to help the British; however that may be, it would appear that the British, in their extremity, gratefully accepted a handout from March, very much as Franco had done six years earlier. (March's move, it may be noted, implied a violation of Spanish foreign-exchange regulations exactly analogous to the violations that Barcelona Traction had previously been committing in favor of the British, only bigger. When Heineman subsequently pointed this out to him, March replied, "Of course. But, unlike you, I don't keep books.")

As for Hillgarth, in 1946, having retired from naval duty, he went on March's payroll, where he remained for years thereafter; what Americans like to call the "revolving door" from government service to private industry seems to have worked in this case in an exceptionally well-oiled, transnational way. In March, 1978, following Hillgarth's death, a British businessman and former government adviser who signed himself J.G.B. wrote a letter to the *Times* of London in which, after noting that Lord Templewood, who, as Sir Samuel Hoare, had been Britain's wartime Ambassador to Spain, had called Hillgarth "the embodiment of drive . . . a veritable sleuth on the track of enemy submarines in Spanish waters, [who had given] us valuable contacts that effectively helped at critical moments." J.G.B. went on to comment, almost in the tone of Suances, "Prominent among those contacts, but always in secrecy, was Don Juan March, the millionaire who having backed Franco in 1936 was wrongly believed in Britain to be anti-British but was, in fact, a sincere admirer of this country and rendered services to the Allied cause unsurpassed in any neutral country."

It is at least possible, then, that in 1946 the British government felt that it owed March a favor or two. At all events, the British attitude toward the Plan of Compromise evolved during the summer and fall of that year—while Minister Suances stalled—principally under the influence of Hugh Ellis-Rees (who was later knighted and made chairman of the Organization for European Economic Cooperation). In the early years of the war, Ellis-Rees, as the British Treasury representative in Madrid, had been a colleague of Hillgarth's and a key participant in the acceptance of March's seventy-million-peseta deposit. The British Treasury and Foreign Office records at Kew show that in July and August, 1946, Barcelona Traction was pressing the Foreign Office to intervene with the Spanish government by urging its approval of the Plan of Compromise. Ellis-Rees, by then with the Treasury in London, was the government's highest official in charge of financial relations with Spain; no one in the Foreign Office or the Treasury cared to differ with him on that subject. During 1946, Ellis-Rees repeatedly and forcefully urged the Foreign Office to leave the matter of the Plan of Compromise alone—an attitude that was particularly mystifying in view of the fact that an incidental effect of the plan would be to funnel into the British Treasury fourteen million United States dollars that it badly needed at the time. On August 19th, Ellis-Rees wrote the Foreign Office, "There is some queer business going on at the other end. . . . It is for the Spanish Government to decide. . . . In our view it would be better not to be associated with a deal of this kind."

The whole matter was reopened briefly at the end of September, when the Treasury Solicitor became convinced by lawyers for Barcelona Traction that by refusing to consider intervening with the Spanish, the British government was "forcing an injustice." On being informed of this development, a Foreign Office official commented in a memo, "This change of attitude makes us look a little silly, but if it would be an injustice to maintain our attitude, we clearly cannot do so." Nevertheless, Ellis-Rees had his way in the end. Barcelona Traction's highly influential friends and associates in the City of London sought in vain to bring their influence to bear on the Treasury. Through the autumn, Ellis-Rees went on stubbornly opposing any British intervention with the Spanish, and the Foreign Office—whose representatives appear never to have quite understood what was at stake—made none. In mid-December, Suances delivered a speech to the Cortes broadly denouncing Barcelona Traction and all its works, and with that the Plan of Compromise was dead. It is fair to say that the absence of British intervention in its favor was what killed it, and that Ellis-Rees, whether out of gratitude for March's wartime help to Britain or for some other reason, had performed with skill and persistence an extraordinary service to March.

AT SOFINA-SIDRO headquarters, in Brussels, there was puzzlement and a certain apprehension. What was clear was that March had pulled every string at his disposal to bring about the defeat of the Plan of Compromise and its intended effect, which was to remove the sterling bonds from Barcelona Traction's books. What was not clear was why. The puzzlement increased when, soon after the defeat of the plan, March, through Fenchurch Nominees, and with the full consent of the British Treasury, made a public offer in London to buy any or all of the Prior Lien bonds, as the more important of the two Barcelona sterling issues was technically called. Within a few months, March held nearly two million pounds' worth of them at face value (as opposed to his cost, which was very much less because of huge discounts occasioned by the interest-paying problem). This gave him a clear majority of the Prior Lien issue. What did he want them for, and why had he wanted the plan defeated? As he had told Heineman in 1944, he wanted to get control of Barcelona Traction. But a bondholder (to recapitulate the first principle of corporate ownership) is a mere creditor of a company; unlike a shareholder, he owns no part of it. Even majority possssion of bonds, unlike majority possession of common stock, does not confer control, except in one circumstance. That circumstance is bankruptcy, in which case the bondholders, not the shareholders, are entitled to the company's assets. And Barcelona Traction in 1947 was quite evidently anything but bankrupt. On the contrary, it was reliably profitable and exuberantly solvent. Its chief subsidiary, Ebro, had in its bank account in cash the peseta equivalent of more than fourteen and a half million dollars—more than enough to meet the entire arrears of interest on Barcelona's sterling bonds, if permission for transfer of funds could be obtained from the Ministry of Industry and Commerce. Ebro's annual report on the fiscal year 1946, issued in October, 1947, spoke of a twenty-three-per-cent rise in profits over the previous year, and then went on to discuss such cozy housekeeping details as the removal of weeds that had been impeding the flow of water in the Gabet Canal. Clear days seemed to be ahead, if only a way could be found to dispel that overhanging cloud—the unpayable and unredeemable bonds.

March had now abandoned his wartime base, Lisbon, and was spending several months of each year in Geneva, which was to become his official residence in June, 1948. (As in wartime, he still went to Madrid and to his various estates in Spain at will.) In Geneva, he lived in a hotel, which also housed his entourage, consisting of a doctor, a business manager, a chauffeur, a valet-bodyguard, and a cook. In 1947, he undertook to buy Goya's "La Tirana" for three million pesetas, or about two hundred and seventy-five thousand dollars; he then managed to convince a Swiss finance inspector that he need not pay a Swiss luxury tax on the purchase, since—as he explained, no doubt truthfully—he wasn't a bit interested in its artistic value, and had bought it solely for resale. As a Genevan, which he formally remained for the rest of his life, March always cut a modest figure. Many years later, at the time of his death, the *Journal de Genève* wrote of him, "The regular clientele of a beer garden in the center of our city will probably remember a small man of sickly aspect, slightly stooped, who played dominoes enthusiastically or took part in lively discussions. He was surrounded by his countrymen and constantly chewed cigars of unusual size." People visiting him at his hotel reported that he liked to sit alone in a corner, smoking cigars and thinking—apparently, about Barcelona Traction. Once, he quoted his cook as having said to him, "I believe I know as much about Barcelona Traction as you do, because you talk about it all the time." And there is other evidence that such was the trend of his thoughts in 1947. Years later, at The Hague, Belgian lawyers produced letters that had been exchanged that May between a March agent and an employee of Ebro, Joaquín Maluquer, whom one of the lawyers described as having been "secretly devoted to the cause of Juan March." In this correspondence, in which March was designated by the scarcely impervious code letters "MJ," the March agent reassured Maluquer that "the [Spanish] government will not play SIDRO's game," and that March had "no intention of . . . accepting any arrangements with the directors of SIDRO."

Certainly he showed no such intention in Basel in November, when he and several of his aides met with Heineman and several other SOFINA-SIDRO men—among them Charles K. Wilmers, a young Englishman whom Heineman, then in his middle seventies, had chosen as one of his chief assistants. According to Wilmers, March got the conversation warmed up, as usual, with a business boast: He had, he said, just bought a quantity of United States war-surplus trucks and sold them to the Spanish government at a huge profit. "I accepted payment in pesetas," March added. "After all, one has to do something for one's country." In the subsequent negotiations, the SOFINA-SIDRO party tried to find out what March would take for his Barcelona bonds, and March made it plain that his price was immediate working control of the company—which, he said, he expected to get in any case, at a personal profit of one and a half billion pesetas. He went on to regale the now speechless Brussels group with a more categorical and perhaps less ironic reference to his patriotic sentiments. By his own later account, he insisted on "the duties and engagements that I have undertaken with regard to the higher interests of the Spanish nation."

Just what that meant, Heineman and his aides could only guess. They returned glumly to Brussels, having accomplished nothing. Three months went by. Then, in February, 1948, the cloud that had been hanging over Barcelona Traction broke into storm with stunning suddenness: Word reached Brussels that a Catalan court had declared Barcelona Traction bankrupt, on the pretext that it could not pay interest on its bonds, and had ordered the immediate seizure of both the shares and the physical assets of its operating subsidiary, Ebro.

IX

THE singular sequence of events that culminated in the "bankruptcy" of Barcelona Traction began on February 10th, when three owners of comparatively small quantities of Barcelona sterling bonds submitted a petition for the company's bankruptcy—based on the company's nonpayment of interest due on their bonds—to the Court of Reus, a provincial town, some seventy-five miles southwest of Barcelona, that is distinguished chiefly for being the birthplace of the celebrated architect Antonio Gaudí. In asking for relief, the petitioners, all of whom were March men, and one of whom was a brother-in-law of one of March's sons, adopted a piteous tone. "Eleven years without payment, it is a case that calls for consequences or else surrender," they wrote. "We will not be accused of a lack of patience. . . . Resignation is a good thing from a moral point of view, but a bad thing in the eyes of the law. It is not out of taste that we attack but out of necessity. We are driven not by ambition but by the fear of our own putrefaction. Persistent absenteeism is banishment. A prolonged coma is death." Now it was clear why March had worked so hard to defeat the Plan of Compromise. If it had gone through, there would have been no Barcelona Traction bonds in default, and thus no pretext for a bankruptcy petition. However, the rhetoric of the petitioners did seem rather to exceed what the circumstances warranted—even to lend an air of farce to the proceedings. Inasmuch as the record of purchase of the bonds owned by the petitioners was dated February 5th of that year, their condition of banishment, coma, and incipient putrefaction, however agonizing it may have been, had apparently existed not for eleven years but for five days.

Why Reus, rather than Barcelona, the headquarters of the company's operating subsidiaries? Because, the petitioners explained, the company supplied electric service and owned property in Reus, among other places. But later comments by a March lawyer and by March himself suggest another reason. Joaquín Dualde, advocate for the petitioners, when asked later by the Barcelona Court of Appeal why he had advised his clients to file for bankruptcy at Reus, replied with admirable candor, "I did that because had I done so at Barcelona, the company's agents would have become aware of it as soon as I had presented the petition and I should not have been able to carry out the whole of my plan. Whereas at Reus nobody became aware of it and nothing was known until all was prepared." As for March, only a few days later he remarked in a man-to-man way (through an interpreter) to J. Donald Duncan, the president of Barcelona Traction, that the bankruptcy had been obtained "in a manner and by a method about which we need say no more." Nevertheless, later in the year—apparently yielding once again to his incorrigible weakness for boasting—March could not resist saying considerably more about it, explaining to Wilmers that, as Wilmers quoted him, "the judge at Reus would do anything that he, March, wanted—and that, in fact, he could control him."

On February 11th, the petition was heard by the court, and on February 12th the Reus judge, Carlos Andreu Domingo, accepted it and declared Barcelona Traction bankrupt. "The Barcelona Traction, Light & Power Company, Ltd., is declared in bankruptcy," Andreu wrote in his decree, "and in consequence there is ordered the seizure of all its goods, shares, and rights, books of account, papers and documents of all sorts. Also to be seized are all shares of the subsidiary company Ebro Irrigation & Power Company, Ltd. . . . all its goods, books, papers and documents of all sorts, it being understood that the seizure implies mediate and most civil possession [*posesión mediata y civilísima*] for all that which concerns the shares of this company. . . . The declaration will be published in the *Official Bulletin of Tarragona,* inasmuch as the domicile of the bankrupt company is unknown."

In conformity with Spanish bankruptcy law, Judge Andreu was

required to appoint two impartial functionaries—a *depositario*, or receiver, and a *comisario*, or temporary trustee. The former role went to Francisco Gambús, and apparently not by chance: Gambús had been a March man as far back as the early thirties, when March was engaged in battles with the Republican Cortes. For the latter role, the judge chose Adolfo Fournier Cuadros. There was a slight hitch here, but it was resourcefully overcome. The law required that the *comisario* be a businessman within the jurisdiction of the court, and Fournier came from Barcelona, so on February 9th Fournier had had it inscribed in the Commercial Register of the Province of Tarragona, in which Reus was situated, that he intended the very next day to open a perfume business there. Although Fournier neglected to record what the address of his establishment would be, his statement was good enough for the judge, who forthwith accepted Fournier as *comisario*.

Over the next twenty-two years, the decree would be the subject of millions of words of earnest and often heated discussion, both oral and written, not only by many of the leading lawyers of Europe but also by representatives of the governments of Spain, Belgium, Great Britain, Canada, and the United States. However —leaving aside the likelihood, later circumstantially apparent, that just about everyone involved in the Reus proceeding had been associated with Juan March—several of its anomalies are immediately evident even to a layman. For one thing, the judge might have learned from the letterhead of some of the very papers he cited in his decree that the domicile of Barcelona Traction was not unknown but was in Toronto, Ontario, Canada. For another, before ordering that the decree be published in the *Official Bulletin of Tarragona*, and nowhere else, he might have been expected to ask himself whether the company's agents in Barcelona—to say nothing of its owners in Belgium and its headquarters staff in Canada—were faithful readers of that publication. Moreover, he might perhaps have been expected to realize that the petitioners were committing, and asking him to commit, one of the more elementary logical mistakes—that of confusing a symptom with a disease. Barcelona Traction was unable to pay interest on its debts; bankrupt companies are unable to pay interest on their debts; therefore, Barcelona Traction must be bankrupt. The fact was, of course, that Barcelona Traction's inability to pay resulted from a situation that was unrelated to bankruptcy—the refusal of the Spanish government to allow it to do so.

Finally, there was the puzzling concept of "mediate and most civil possession." What kind of possession, exactly, was that? Lawyers for Belgium at The Hague described it, with a bemused air, as "miraculous" or "fictive" possession, and pointed out that no such concept existed in *their* law, or in any law they had ever heard of before the Barcelona case. Their Spanish antagonists at The Hague patiently explained that the phrase was "well-rooted in Spanish law," and they referred approvingly to Judge Andreu as a "rigorous jurist." Sir Humphrey Waldock, who was one of two hundred or so lawyers representing Spain, described the bankruptcy decree—gamely, one can't help thinking—as "a competent, persuasive piece of judicial workmanship." Nevertheless, Joaquín Garrigues, a much-revered Spanish lawyer and law professor, used the decision as occasion for a little flight of irony. "In no way do we wish to diminish the merit and the well-established value of the judge of Reus and of the various lawyers who agree with him," Garrigues wrote in 1956. "On the other hand, they do seem to be putting aside the primary and elementary things that the rest of us have learned. . . . Why should not Reus be the home of a new school . . . that discards as useless the books that we have employed up to now, and substitutes for them others which tomorrow will be the flourishing examples of the new School of Reus?" One thing did seem to be clear, at any rate, and that was that the founder of the School of Reus, conceivably with the help of March's lawyers, had invoked the doctrine of *posesión mediata y civilísima* to meet a specific problem: He wanted the shares of Ebro, all of which belonged to Barcelona Traction, to be seized immediately, but those shares were physically lodged in the vaults of the National Trust Company in Toronto, where they were being held as collateral for the Barcelona sterling bonds; there being no likelihood that the bank or the Canadian government would allow them to be released for material seizure, Judge Andreu had, it appeared, found it necessary to order them seized fictively and miraculously.

As for the seizure of Ebro's physical assets, that could and did proceed on a material level. The morning after the decree, and on several subsequent days, Fournier and Gambús, accompanied by officers of the court, presented themselves at the various Ebro offices and declared them seized. This was the first that the Ebro managers had heard of the bankruptcy. (The manager at one of the offices, unable to believe what was happening, but nonetheless faced with a court order, insisted on turning over the keys and then leaving the premises, so that he would not have to watch the seizure. The court officers had trouble making the keys work, and spent several doubtless frustrating hours getting into a cabinet full of records.) Beginning on February 14th, all the principal administrative officers of Ebro and of Barcelonesa Electric Company, another Barcelona Traction subsidiary, were summarily fired; and on March 16th the receiver Gambús, in his new capacity as mediate and most civil possessor of all Ebro's stock, held a one-man shareholders' meeting of that company at which, by unanimous vote, he threw out all the incumbent directors and elected a new board, consisting of March nominees. Gambús as chairman addressing Gambús as sole stockholder then declared the meeting adjourned.

MEANWHILE, the suddenly unemployed managers and directors of Ebro gave SOFINA-SIDRO, by telephone, *its* first notification of what had been going on at Reus and Barcelona during the past few days. The recipients' reaction, one of them said later, was "surprise and stupor." (Indeed, everyone connected with Barcelona Traction seems to have reacted to the Reus judge's decision and to subsequent Spanish court actions in the case with surprise and stupor even more than with anger and indignation. A poleaxed tone pervades their statements. Spanish counsel for Barcelona spoke on one occasion of "systematic and total violation of the most elementary principles of law"; another Spanish counsel, this one for the National Trust Company of Canada, referred at another time to "extremely violent measures, unjustified and without legal base"; and later on, yet another Spanish lawyer for Barcelona declared, with a kind of awe, "The case is so unprecedented that we prefer not to comment, for the commentary would be so harsh that our self-respect forbids it.") As soon as they had recovered enough to act, they began taking steps to appeal the bankruptcy decree. Too late: They had been anticipated, and a deftly designed blocking mechanism had already swung into place. On February 13th, when Barcelona Traction had just received word that it had been declared bankrupt, a certain Francisco García del Cid had filed with the Reus court a *declinatoria*, or denial of the court's jurisdiction in the matter. Nothing could have been more logical, since the court's jurisdiction was, to say the least, open to question. Apparently, Barcelona Traction had found unexpected support from an unknown quarter. But it soon appeared that the support, however well meant, was a mixed blessing, because when Barcelona's lawyers attempted to file their appeal from the bankruptcy on behalf of Ebro, they were informed that they could not do so, inasmuch as all legal proceedings were frozen while García del Cid's *declinatoria* was pending. This situation continued for three weeks, during which time the seizure of Barcelona's Spanish operating companies was accomplished. The day after completion of the seizure, García del Cid suddenly, and at first unaccountably, withdrew his *declinatoria*. Almost immediately—before Barcelona Traction had had a chance to react—the judge declared the bankruptcy final and no longer subject to appeal, on the ground that the time limit for appeal set by Spanish law had run out. In short, when the company's hands were untied by the withdrawal of the *declinatoria*, it was too late for them to use their hands, because of the time limit. Then the role of García del Cid became clear. His *declinatoria* had not been well meant at all. Far from being a disinterested devotee of justice, he was, and had been all along, a March man, whose role had been to block Barcelona Traction's right of appeal until it no longer existed.

A ray of hope for the Belgians appeared in April, when the

Spanish government, goaded by diplomatic pressure from Belgium and Canada, brought about the appointment of a special judge, not controlled by March, to replace Judge Andreu. But it soon developed that the game was not yet over, and could perhaps be prolonged forever. Just before the special judge assumed office, yet another *declinatoria* was filed, this one by a certain Juan Boter Vaquer; one of Judge Andreu's last acts in office was to tie things up for eight more months—and so prevent the special judge from immediately hearing Barcelona's side of the matter—by granting Boter that much time to prepare his case. (The degree of lunacy that by then pervaded the proceedings is indicated by the fact that the petitioners for bankruptcy, whose lawyer had chosen the Reus court's jurisdiction in the first place, and who had had their petition granted in every particular, now cheerfully and without apology joined in Boter's protest against that jurisdiction.) In the legal realm, the owners of Barcelona Traction seemed to face either stalemate or checkmate. One can well imagine that, nightmarishly frustrated in a distant court, where their lawyers were repeatedly blocked by technical means from even appearing, they might have simply decided that the situation was hopeless, and devoted themselves to other matters. On the contrary, by October, 1952, Barcelona Traction, SIDRO, and their bankers had introduced more than four hundred separate legal actions in Spain. Heineman turned seventy-six during the year of the bankruptcy, and thereafter he spent more and more of his time in New York, although he remained active in the affairs of SOFINA until 1955, when he retired and Wilmers took command. Meanwhile, Wilmers, as the man on the spot in Brussels, and as a fluent speaker of Spanish, gradually assumed the role of SOFINA-SIDRO champion in the joust with March over Barcelona Traction.

Thirty-nine years old at the time of the bankruptcy, the son of a London stockjobber, Wilmers had earned a Cambridge degree in modern languages in 1930 and immediately thereafter gone to work for Heineman. Wilmers is a tall, handsome man with a very British air of lordliness, and at the same time a raffish gleam in his eye. Though he had originally planned to become a modern-languages don, he soon found that the world of international finance, with its technical intricacies, its cultural variety, and its opportunities for travel and high living, was his natural arena. Wilmers denies that he enjoyed all of the long battle for Barcelona Traction, but he admits that he enjoys it in retrospect, and that he harbors a sneaking admiration for March. As for March on Wilmers, he once expressed his opinion of the Englishman by pulling one eye wide open with his thumb and forefinger and exclaiming, "Watch out!" The two men met at the Hôtel des Bergues in Geneva in May, 1948, three months after the bankruptcy decree. At that meeting, Wilmers found March rather pleased with himself about the way he had stage-managed the drama at Reus, and apparently looking for Wilmers' approval of his craftsmanship. Wilmers also found March, now that he was far ahead in the courts, in a mood to negotiate. In settlement of the whole affair, March offered SIDRO and the other Barcelona Traction stockholders two million pounds—a little more than eight million dollars—and a twenty-five per cent equity in a new company, which would own all of Barcelona's former properties, and of which March would own the remaining seventy-five per cent. Humiliating as it was to be blandly offered one-fourth of one's own property, along with a cash sweetener, Wilmers was so deeply discouraged by the course of events in Spain that he decided it might be well to take what he could get. By long-distance telephone, he swayed a reluctant Heineman to his point of view. However, as soon as Wilmers told March that SIDRO was disposed to accept his offer, March altered it. As a condition for the Barcelona Traction deal, March now said, he would have to be given the right to name most of the directors of CHADE, the Spanish holding company of the SOFINA group whose operating subsidiaries supplied most of the energy to the city of Buenos Aires. Giving March control of the directors would, of course, mean giving him control of the company. As long as SOFINA-SIDRO was willing to negotiate away one company, March seemed to be saying, Why not two? Wilmers refused, and the whole deal fell through. SOFINA-SIDRO, which subsequently insisted that it was entitled to get back all of Barcelona Traction, rather than just a quarter of it, seemed to have been saved from surrender in its moment of despair by the intransigence of March himself.

March and Wilmers met again later in May, by March's invitation, at his Madrid palace. After employing his habitual gambit of making a financial boast—in this case, that he had just turned down an offer of over nine million dollars (a hundred million pesetas) from the government of Argentina for his Madrid house —March went on to top that off with yet another boast, to the effect that it had indeed been he and he alone who had blocked counterproceedings at Reus through Boter's *declinatoria*. No more negotiating took place on that occasion, and there appeared to be not the slightest indication that March had any intention of acting in what Wilmers would consider a reasonable way. Accordingly, in July a SOFINA-SIDRO delegation made another trip to Madrid, this time to see Minister Suances. When they protested to the Minister, as tactfully as possible, about the nonintervention of the Spanish government at the top level in the activities of the Reus court, Suances—as Wilmers paraphrased him in a later affidavit—"stated that he regarded March as carrying the Spanish flag in the Barcelona affair, and that he would refuse to allow him to put it down." This seemed to be the equivalent of a carbon copy of March's letter of marque—his official authorization to sail as a privateer on the high seas of commerce, under the flag of, and for the benefit of, Spain.

Legal skirmishing went on over the next three years, with the March side generally getting the best of it. In July, 1948, the Supreme Court of Ontario, recognizing de facto the Spanish bankruptcy of Barcelona Traction, though not admitting its validity, appointed a Canadian receiver to administer the company's assets, or those that he could get his hands on. On December 13th, a special stockholders' meeting of Barcelona Traction was held in Toronto, at which nearly all the shares—the seventy-five per cent held by SIDRO, thirteen per cent held by others in Belgium, and those held by still others, in Europe and North America—were represented in person or by proxy. One of these individuals, a

New Yorker named Redvers Opie, remarked at the meeting, to general applause, that the bankruptcy "can only be described as a travesty of justice that is likely to bring the Spanish judicial system into disrepute in economic and finance circles abroad." What could be done about it, though? For the moment, nothing. But two days later, in Reus, Boter's eight-month grace period expired, and two months later, after hearings on the *declinatoria* had been held, the special judge dismissed it, thus apparently freeing the Belgians and the Canadians to make their protests at last. The victory was illusory. Just four days later, Boter gave notice of appeal from the dismissal of the *declinatoria* to the Court of Appeal at Barcelona. It shortly became apparent that Barcelona Traction would have little more luck in that tribunal than in the one at Reus. In April, 1949, the Court of Appeal admitted Boter's appeal from the dismissal of his *declinatoria*, and Barcelona Traction was stymied again. Just to make sure that it stayed that way, a March-controlled company called Genora, S.A., which was based in Switzerland, applied to the Court of Appeal in September for an eight-month delay in the start of hearings on the appeal from the special judge's eight-months-delayed dismissal of Boter's *declinatoria*. The Court of Appeal, presumably with a straight face, granted Genora's request.

The effect of these patter-song machinations—a classic instance, the Belgians believed, of legal complexity serving simple predatory intent—was to bar Barcelona Traction from making its first application to set aside the bankruptcy until late in 1950, almost three years after the decree. Nor was there any reason to believe that when Genora's grace period had run out someone would not protest against *that* and demand another eight months to prepare *his* case. The game could go on indefinitely. Meanwhile, on September 19, 1949, at the order of the Court of Appeal and the special judge, the Barcelona Traction sterling bondholders met in Reus to elect permanent trustees in bankruptcy, who would replace Gambús, the receiver, and Fournier, the temporary trustee. *The New York Times'* account described the meeting as "stormy," but the storm was more noise than force: inasmuch as March owned a majority of the bonds, it was a foregone conclusion that his nominees for the three trusteeships would be elected. And so they were. The newly elected trustees took charge of Ebro and Barcelona's other subsidiaries, keeping in office the pro-March boards of directors that Gambús had so expeditiously elected, and even fixing up Gambús himself—suddenly out of a job, as he was—by appointing him the new general manager of Ebro.

Nevertheless, March did not yet have control of Barcelona Traction—only control of its trustees in a bankruptcy that had not been affirmed in any court except the curious one in Reus—and large obstacles still stood between him and that goal. What had been scarcely more than murmurs of diplomatic protest were becoming something like an uproar. In March, 1948, the month after the bankruptcy decree, Belgium and Canada had entered their protests against it, and these had led to the appointment of the special judge. Then, on July 21, 1949, Great Britain, through its embassy in Madrid, made a formal complaint to the Spanish government at the urgent request of its Commonwealth partner, Canada, which did not maintain an embassy in Madrid. The following day, the United States joined in, with its own note of protest. This was a particularly significant intervention, for two reasons: First, the United States in 1949 ruled the non-Communist economic world as its acknowledged suzerain; second, since United States citizens had very little economic interest in Barcelona Traction, the protest was obviously more a statement of policy than a protection of citizens' interests. Years later, the United States government explained that it had been "motivated to communicate its note of July 22, 1949, to the Government of Spain by considerations of principle relating to the equitable treatment of foreign investment." By early 1950, it was widely believed that the United States government was engaged in implementing its policy by privately advising American investors not to lend or invest in Spain until the Barcelona Traction matter was cleared up.

The Canadian and United States protests—which, since they came on successive days, were unmistakably the outcome of consultations between the two North American nations' governments

—were a serious matter for Spain, which badly needed United States investment to promote its economic growth. Nevertheless, the Spanish government continued to refuse to intervene, chiefly on the basis of its conviction that Barcelona Traction, over its history, had played a predatory role in Spain, sucking huge profits out of the Spanish economy while pumping comparatively trifling sums into it. And one basis for that belief was a report prepared in 1949 by a Spanish accountant, Ángel Andany Sanz, at March's request and expense, which came in no uncertain terms to precisely that conclusion. SOFINA-SIDRO, however, believed that the Andany report was grossly in error—and not by chance, inasmuch as it had been paid for by March. Accordingly, early in 1950 SOFINA-SIDRO persuaded the Belgian government to propose that a commission of accounting experts representing Belgium, Canada, and Spain be appointed to take a fresh, impartial look at the question of whether, over the years since 1911, Barcelona Traction was on balance a creditor or a debtor vis-à-vis the Spanish economy, with the outcome of the investigation determining whether or not Spain was justified in allowing March to carry the Spanish flag by seizing Barcelona Traction.

The Belgians, it turned out, were in for a couple of shocks. Before they could even formally present their proposal, Spain came up with a counterproposal for a Commission of Experts on which Britain would be substituted for Belgium. This seemed illogical, in view of the fact that March's purchases of Barcelona Traction bonds had left comparatively few of them in British hands, and thus had left Britain, in contrast to Belgium, with only a small stake in the whole matter. Nevertheless, Spain, Canada, and Britain constituted the commission that was decided upon. And then the identity of the chief Spanish expert, when he was chosen, gave the Belgians further pause—as well it might have. Britain and Canada appointed accountants of apparent impartiality: for Britain, F. W. Charles, of Peat, Marwick Mitchell & Company's London office; for Canada, H. G. Norman, of Price, Waterhouse & Company's Toronto branch. But Spain, which was to have a two-man delegation, chose for its head none other than

Andany, the former March employee, whose opinion on the matter was already on record. Apparently, all that Andany would need to do as an expert was recast and resubmit his previous, March-commissioned report, calling Barcelona Traction a blatant exploiter. Still, Spain had a right to appoint any experts it chose, and, as for Belgium, there was nothing it could do about the fact that it had been blackballed. In June, the work of the Commission of Experts began.

International commissions of experts, each of whose members is necessarily torn between his expertise and his nationality, have enough trouble agreeing when the subject of their deliberations is some matter as concrete as, say, a national border. When the subject is accounting—a form of inquiry whose practitioners are often accused of being able to arrive by mathematical means at whatever results they seek—the chance of agreement seems at the outset to be all but nil. Sure enough, in due course Charles and Norman arrived at the conclusion that over Barcelona Traction's thirty-seven years up to 1948 its net investment in Spain had been something over nineteen million pounds, whereas the Spanish experts' conclusion was that Barcelona Traction had on balance taken many millions of pounds *out* of Spain. Under the circumstances, neither of these findings could be regarded as remarkable.

The experts' reports left the matter just where it had been; but the aftermath of their activities was the last and probably the most decisive of all the extraordinary and puzzling favors that Britain had done, in peace and war, for Juan March. In the spring of 1951, after the experts had made their self-cancelling reports but before the reports had been made public, came a bizarre sequel. The governments of Spain and Britain, the latter speaking for both itself and Canada, prepared a joint statement, purportedly based on the commission's reports. This document was a strange one in at least two respects. For one thing, it made no reference of any kind to the only matter that the experts had been appointed to investigate—the question of whether or not Barcelona Traction was a net investor in Spain. For another, instead of summarizing the conclusions of all the experts it simply ignored those of the

British and Canadian accountants, and stated flatly that Spain had been "fully justified" in withholding foreign currency from the company in recent years and would be equally justified in continuing to do so, at least "until such time as the position . . . has been regulated." Plainly, the statement did not reflect the reports of the Commission of Experts at all—only the report of the Spanish experts. Suances, having signed it on June 11th, sent it to the British Embassy in Madrid with a request that the Ambassador, Sir John Balfour, sign it on behalf of his government. Later the same day, quite possibly to Suances' astonishment, Balfour did sign it, and six days later Suances, with great fanfare, made it public as an Agreed Minute of the governments of Spain and Great Britain.

The reaction in Brussels and Toronto was near-panic. Barcelona Traction's board of directors issued a statement to the effect that "the most elemental rules of national justice" had been violated. Spanish newspapers refused to publish the statement; it did appear in the *Times* of London, but only as a paid advertisement. The *Times* at first commented cautiously in its editorial columns that the Agreed Minute was "in a sense unexpected"; but a month or so later, after the experts' reports had been released in full, the *Times* changed its tone, and declared that "perusal of the full text of the report of the accountants appointed by the British and Canadian governments on the affair . . . makes it extremely difficult to understand why the British Ambassador to Spain signed [the Agreed Minute]."

Indeed, why *did* he sign it? All the evidence suggests that the act was one of those diplomatic faux pas—minor in immediate political terms but crucial in long-term ways not foreseeable at the time—which are compounded of adherence to tradition, lack of understanding of the subject matter, and mere casualness. Balfour, a career diplomat who was a graduate of Eton and Oxford with a bent for literature and history, and who had just previously served as Ambassador to Argentina, was new to the Madrid post. He shared the distaste for technical financial details that goes with the aristocratic and humanistic British Foreign Service personality. Very likely, he had not read in full the reports of the experts. However, Balfour's own later account makes it clear that, even so, he was reluctant to sign the Agreed Minute, and asked for guidance from the Foreign Office, which referred him to the Treasury, and that it was on the Treasury's explicit recommendation that Balfour signed.

Why, then, did the Treasury take the seemingly unjust and inappropriate position that it did? It had first appeared evident that the Treasury was playing a major role in the Commission-of-Experts operation when Charles and Norman, en route by plane from London to Madrid to meet their Spanish colleagues for the first time, unexpectedly found themselves escorted and introduced to Andany and his Spanish colleague by H. H. Eggers, Ellis-Rees' successor as the British Treasury man in charge of financial relations with Spain. That the Treasury approved, if it did not help write, the Agreed Minute is made explicit by its recommendation to Balfour. Did the Treasury still feel indebted to March, and was it helping play Barcelona Traction into his hands as a last recompense for secret past favors?

Wilmers, speaking from the SOFINA-SIDRO point of view, states it was his conviction that the British Treasury was an integral part of the operation right from the beginning; that "March knew exactly what was going into the Agreed Minute"; and that, in fact, the Agreed Minute may have been planned on March's initiative. But even if that is so, the British Treasury surely had reasons for favoring it other than a desire to repay March. A centuries-old British-government notion—perhaps based in part on the geographical isolation of Britain's prized outpost of Gibraltar—that the Iberian countries and their powerful citizens were to be given special consideration whenever possible had probably filtered into the consciousness of the Treasury men, and of Balfour, too. In 1958, when Balfour was in charge of the British exhibition at the Brussels World's Fair, and Wilmers came at Balfour's invitation to visit it, Balfour said to him, "Awfully decent of you to come, after what I did to you." Whether that constituted an apology or merely a social gesture made no difference in 1951.

The Agreed Minute, by enabling the Spanish government to point out that the British shared its view of the matter, put March in a position to execute checkmate. This he quickly did, with a bold combination of moves. The remaining problem was what to do about the shares of Ebro and the other subsidiaries, in which resided the real value of Barcelona Traction. True enough, the permanent trustees now possessed them mediately and most civilly in Spain. But at the same time the National Trust Company possessed them physically in Canada. The solution the trustees adopted to this dilemma was to declare the shares in Canada null and void, and to issue an entirely new set of shares in Spain. One of the lawyers for Belgium at The Hague, in conformity with the dignity required of international proceedings, later spoke of these as "what may euphemistically be called the duplicate shares." Out of court, however, he and his colleagues called them the "bogus" shares.

Having created the new shares, the emboldened trustees decided that they should promptly be sold at auction. This might have been orthodox enough procedure in a normal bankruptcy, but was hardly orthodox in this case, inasmuch as the company that had been declared bankrupt had still not had a chance to try to prove in court that it was not. The trustees disposed of this difficulty, to their own satisfaction and the Barcelona court's, by declaring that the new shares were "perishable goods," and that, regardless of any legal delays in other aspects of the case, they should be sold before they went rancid. The auction that the trustees arranged bore the unmistakable signature of March, the same man whose most recent previous work of financial conceptual art had been the Reus bankruptcy. The minimum, or upset, price for all of the shares was set at ten million pesetas, or about two hundred and eighty thousand dollars. However, the buyer was to assume the further obligation of paying off within ninety days, in pounds sterling, all the principal and interest on Barcelona Traction's sterling bonds; while a third condition stipulated that even after the sale the trustees would be allowed, if they so chose, to impose various further conditions on the buyer, and unless these were met the sale would be invalid. The effect of all the rules was to create a game that only one player could play. The sterling payment requirement alone effectively eliminated all Spaniards but March. As for Barcelona Traction itself, its owners and directors—even if they could swallow their chagrin and bring themselves to bid on what they considered to be counterfeit copies of their own property—would face the unappetizing prospect of winning the auction and then finding that what victory amounted to was the privilege of meeting any conditions that March's trustees might care to impose upon them. March, with the full consent of the Reus court—which by this time had mysteriously been turned over to a new special judge, entirely favorable to March's interests —had arranged an auction at which there would be no bidder but March.

The auction was set for January 4, 1952. A last-minute snag developed, however, for the British government, as a result of further investigation by a new Government, headed by Winston Churchill, which took office in October, 1951, apparently had a change of heart. On December 22nd, Britain addressed Spain on the matter in harsh terms:

His Majesty's Government wish . . . to draw the attention of the Spanish Government to the unjustifiable use to which the Agreed Minute . . . [has been put] by the trustees to the special judge . . . in which they sought his authorization for the sale of the assets of the subsidiaries of Barcelona Traction. . . . If, as seems possible, the judge's decision to authorize the sale was influenced by [a] distorted interpretation of the Agreed Minute . . . His Majesty's Government desire to express the strong hope that the Spanish Government . . . will take urgent steps to clear up this regrettable misapprehension. . . . In addition, His Majesty's Government consider that in this whole matter there are a number of questions which should be the subject of a careful and impartial enquiry, such as the creation of the duplicate shares. . . . They consider that, if the sale of the assets is carried out on 4 January 1952, this will constitute a grave injustice.

Evidently, that warning, or threat, caused some wavering in Madrid. March's nervousness, at any rate, is indicated by the fact that on December 31st he wrote to the Spanish Foreign Minister, Alberto Martín Artajo, trying to persuade him that the terms of the proposed auction were, if anything, *too* fair to SIDRO. "It seems to me impossible, Mr. Minister, to offer greater facilities to a foreign group," March wrote demurely. Whatever misgivings there may have been in the Spanish halls of state that holiday season had been resolved by January 3rd, when Spain sent Britain a note briskly rejecting the British note of December 22nd. The next day, the auction at Reus went off as scheduled. The only bidder, which thriftily bid the precise minimum price of two hundred and eighty thousand dollars, was a new Spanish company—Fuerzas Eléctricas de Cataluña, S.A., or FECSA—created and owned by March, who thus at last became ostensible sole owner of all the assets of Barcelona Traction. SIDRO and the other old stockholders, in compensation for the loss of their ninety- or one-hundred-million-dollar property in Spain, might have been expected to get FECSA's two hundred and eighty thousand dollars as a consolation prize. But no; that sum, it seemed, was needed in full to pay the March trustees' expenses. The distinguished British solicitor Francis Mann said later of the auction, "Without the Agreed Minute, it wouldn't have been done. They wouldn't have had the nerve."

X

MARCH, whether in Geneva or in Madrid or at one of his various estates, was surely smiling his rabbit smile. For a comparatively trifling sum, he had taken over a company that was now showing an annual net profit of around five million dollars, and it immediately became the center of his industrial empire. He had served his country well as a privateer by converting a prize piece of foreign property in Spain into a prize piece of Spanish property—that is to say, his. On top of that, he had added an avant-garde chapter to the long annals of legal-financial prestidigitation. Bankruptcy when it is used by a slick operator to escape his liabilities by concealing his assets is one of the oldest dodges in that whole book. But March had neatly turned the old dodge on its head: Instead of using bankruptcy to protect his own assets, he had used it to snatch someone else's. Finally, by means that were at least ostensibly legal, he had accomplished what had previously been within the power only of national governments—expropriation of a foreign-owned enterprise. March's was apparently the first private nationalization.

And, in accomplishing all this, March had finally achieved respectability—possibly by virtue of the irony that financial predations become publicly acceptable when they are big enough. (Veblen noted, "The habit of holding private property inviolate is traversed by the other habit of seeking wealth for the sake of the good repute to be gained through its conspicuous consumption. Most offenses against property, especially offenses of an appreciable magnitude, come under this head.") Newspaper accounts now customarily spoke of March as "the billionaire industrialist," seldom as "the former smuggler." Abroad—even in Belgium and Canada—most publications found the whole thing too distant and complicated to be worthy of notice. In Spain, press coverage of the Barcelona Traction affair was brief and bland, and the one editor who presumed to criticize March and the courts, Ekkehard Tertsch, of *The Spanish Economic News,* found himself several times in trouble with the Spanish authorities. As befitted a man of such substance, March was now treated chiefly as a social celebrity. A huge party that he gave in Majorca in 1955 for his granddaughter María Gloria was covered minute by minute by the Spanish-government radio. Even March's old political enemy, Prieto, now in exile in Mexico, seems to have been dazzled at transatlantic range by this affair. "The guests numbered fifteen hundred, and in order to serve them, there arrived from Madrid two hundred waiters and forty cooks," the old Socialist wrote breathlessly, in an account published in the late nineteen-sixties, several years after March's death and his own. It continued:

More than one thousand workers decorated the gardens which were illuminated with two hundred thousand lights. Not a flower was left in

Majorca, for all had been cut. . . . Tons more arrived by plane from southern Spain and Holland. . . . Uniformed guards watched over all. Here were to be found notables from all over the world, diplomats, financiers, aristocrats, artists, military men . . . and the Marchioness of Villa-verde [Franco's daughter]. . . . From foreign lands had come selected persons to animate the party: the Italian singer Eleanora Cerli, the Claude Marchant ballet company from New York. . . . In the palace garden's patio of honor was a flamenco scene, and in one corner a tavern was installed. In one of the esplanades was a buffet offering a choice of Spanish or international cuisine. . . . At daybreak a chocolaterie was opened, and the dancing went on.

A Spanish priest, Father José María Llorens, showed that not everyone had forgotten the past when he noted bitterly, more than a decade later, "The Balearic smuggler Juan March, the day after he had wasted eighty million pesetas on the coming-out party of his granddaughter, sent to the Bishop of Majorca one million pesetas, an attitude . . . worthy of so illustrious a crusader. What seems to us less worthy is that the bishop accepted this sum."

Meanwhile, SIDRO and Barcelona Traction—the former now deprived of a large portion of its worldly goods, the latter deprived of all of its, and both still deprived of a hearing in the Spanish courts—resorted in their desperation to attempts to appeal directly to Franco. Their first move toward that end—a move that was later ridiculed by the March forces—was to retain as Barcelona Traction's counsel Ramón Serrano Suñer, who was married to Franco's wife's sister, and who in the early years of the Second World War had served as Spanish Foreign Minister until he and Franco had had a falling out over Spanish policy toward Germany and Italy. In September, 1953, Serrano Suñer—a practicing lawyer who, though he had long since retired from public life, was a feared and revered figure in Spain, because of his former office and his kinship by marriage with the Caudillo—succeeded in getting a hearing on behalf of Barcelona Traction before a special convocation of the Sala de Justica of Barcelona, an august body that included all the magistrates of the Barcelona Court of Ap-

peal. Serrano Suñer launched into a windy, thirty-page disserta-
tion, studded with learned references to such topics as the ancient
Greeks and Romans, the Wars of the Roses, the Dutch historian
Johan Huizinga, and the unity of Europe. However, between
feints he got in some solid punches. Describing this as the most
important and serious statement he had ever made as a lawyer, he
declared that in the Barcelona Traction matter an insult had been
done to Spanish justice before the world, and added—being careful to exempt specifically his brother-in-law from his criticism—
that various powerful authorities had already attacked him for
daring to criticize the decisions of the various judges in the case.
As to those judges, some of whom were seated before him, Serrano Suñer accused them, in general or in particular, of inconsis-
tency with their usual principles, inordinate speed in making
decisions, inappropriately harsh language, and "lack of serenity."
And what were their motives for this aberrant behavior? Certainly
not corruption, Serrano Suñer said, and he went on to speculate
that one motive might be "erroneous patriotism" and another—a
possible motive so inflammatory, apparently, that it had to be
expressed backward—"the opposite of an aversion to Juan
March." He summed up, "I want to write decently this page in our
judicial history. Let us be worthy of our vocation." And he ended
by asking for the replacement of everyone he had accused—a
category that seemed to include all the judges who had up to then
had anything to do with the case.

Nothing happened as a result of the speech. Serrano Suñer's
learning might be impressive and his opinions daring, but his political power belonged to the past. Accordingly, SOFINA-SIDRO cast
about for another way of getting Franco's ear. In 1954, after
several frustrating failures, two SOFINA-SIDRO men finally managed
to see the Caudillo. One of them was Wilmers himself, and the
other was Arthur H. Dean, a partner in the New York law firm of
Sullivan & Cromwell and a well-known public figure, whose most
celebrated diplomatic mission had been to represent the United
States and sixteen other United Nations members in the 1953

Panmunjom negotiations leading to the end of the Korean War. Soon after the successful completion of that mission, Dean, back in New York, was asked by André Meyer, the senior partner in Lazard Frères & Company, and David Rockefeller, then a senior vice-president of Chase National Bank, to go to Europe and have a look at the Barcelona Traction situation. (Meyer had been a director of SOFINA since 1929, and his firm had a substantial holding in its stock; Rockefeller was acting merely as a friend of Meyer's.) Dean went to Brussels in the summer of 1954, where SIDRO presently retained him as one more legal howitzer to trundle up to the front. In July, Dean went as SIDRO's counsel to Madrid, where he was joined by Wilmers. Through the United States Embassy, Dean applied for an audience with Spanish Foreign Minister Martín Artajo, "for the purpose of greeting him" in the name of his client, SIDRO. The request was quickly granted, and Dean saw Martín Artajo twice within a few days—on one occasion, bringing Wilmers along with him. According to Wilmers, he and Dean found the Foreign Minister sympathetic to their cause. Encouraged, Dean mentioned his recent negotiations with the Communists in Korea, and suggested that perhaps Franco would like to hear about them. He would not, he assured Martín Artajo, bring up the Barcelona Traction dispute, a private matter, in the Generalissimo's presence. To Wilmers' and Dean's astonishment, Martín Artajo replied, "On the contrary, you should bring it up. It should be a public matter."

The big chance appeared to be at hand. An audience with Franco having been arranged for July 21st, Dean and Wilmers set about preparing for it. Dean pronounced it axiomatic that no one in authority will read more than one page on any subject; therefore, he and Wilmers attempted to condense the essence of the whole affair into a document of that length. On the appointed date, Dean and Wilmers set out by automobile for the Pardo Palace, Franco's residence outside Madrid. En route, they were met and escorted by a troop of cavalry that gained a ceremonial glister from the fact that the hooves of the horses were painted gold. At the palace, they were duly received by Franco. About a year later, Dean described the meeting in a letter to Martín Artajo, as follows:

On July 21st, Mr. Wilmers and I had the honor of being most graciously received by his Excellency, the Chief of State. At the conclusion of the audience we left with the official who had acted as interpreter [Dean did not speak or write Spanish] a one-page note summarizing the essential points of our exposé. In this note we pointed out that the value of the assets, adjudicated to FECSA for ten million pesetas plus the face amount of the Barcelona Traction bonds, exceeded the price by thousands of millions of pesetas. [Dean later told a SOFINA man that when Franco had been told how much money March had made on the deal, he had acted startled and had asked for a repetition of the figures.] We repeated our sincere belief that the most just and honorable settlement of this matter could best be achieved with the cooperation and under the auspices of the Spanish State. We expressed our hope that this cooperation toward a settlement would be forthcoming, and stated our willingness, on grounds of equity and national justice, to hold available a part of the enterprise for acquisition by the Spanish State on terms the prime consideration of which would be the interest of the Spanish economy.

In other words, Dean and Wilmers were offering Franco a compromise: If they could have their company back, they would agree to the nationalization of some fraction of it at a bargain compensation price. Dean's letter ended, "His Excellency was kind enough to tell us that the matter would be studied."

Wilmers' account of the meeting supplements Dean's, and on the most essential point—the tone and substance of Franco's reply—differs from it. Wilmers says, "A Franco aide interpreted while Dean talked in English about Panmunjom. The Generalissimo appeared to be interested. Then Dean brought up Barcelona Traction. He summarized the situation, and I added a few words. When we had finished, Franco said quite coldly—as you know, it was said that a visit with him felt like a cold shower—'This is a question between private parties. Unfortunately, the shareholders of Barcelona Traction have not always acted very wisely.' "

And that, it seemed, was that. The following spring, by which time there was no evidence that Franco planned to do anything about the matter, Dean returned to Madrid and saw Martín Artajo again. Once more, he went back to New York empty-handed, this time with the sense that all his client's resources in Spain had been exhausted. But a few months later, just as things looked darkest for Barcelona Traction and its owners, there was a favorable turn of events. In December, 1955, Spain was finally admitted to membership in the United Nations, of which the chief judicial organ is the International Court of Justice, at The Hague, the presumptive Supreme Court of the world, existing to hear and judge disputes among nations which cannot be settled by other means. Under the United Nations Charter, acceptance of the International Court's jurisdiction is optional to members; and Spain, in joining, did not accept its compulsory jurisdiction. (Nor, in the absence of fulfillment of various broad conditions, has the United States accepted it, to this day.) However, Spain and Belgium in 1955 had a commercial treaty dating back to 1927, and that, combined with Spain's new U.N. membership, had in the opinion of international legal authorities the effect of mandating Spain's acceptance of a challenge in the International Court by Belgium. Quickly realizing that in the new situation SOFINA-SIDRO might be able to persuade the Belgian government to take the Barcelona Traction case to the International Court, March's lawyers, led by a formidable advocate named Antonio Rodríguez Sastre, undertook an enterprise that for outrageousness was fully in the March tradition. Travelling individually or as a team to the leading European capitals, they attempted, sometimes with success, to engage the leading international lawyers to write opinions, for an appropriate fee, on the Barcelona Traction case. The resulting opinions, not surprisingly, tended to favor March's side of the question. However, the pearls of legal wisdom contained in the opinions were of only incidental interest to March or his lawyers. What interested them—or so it came to appear—was that the lawyers who had written the opinions were thereby ethically barred from appearing for Belgium before the International Court, if Belgium should decide to bring the case. March, who had so often proved himself adept at preempting property and court proceedings, now seemed to be engaged in trying to preempt the legal talent of Western Europe.

In the meantime, SOFINA and SIDRO were having trouble persuading the Belgian government to take the case to The Hague court. For one thing, that nation's Socialist government had a marked distaste for defending the rights of one private enterprise against another, in Spain or anywhere else; for another, many of the Belgian civil servants simply weren't much interested in the complexities of high finance. March, never one to miss a chance to fish in troubled waters, had some of his agents buy small holdings of SIDRO in the open market and then attend SIDRO's annual meetings in Brussels as stockholders. At the 1956 and 1957 meetings, after it had become public knowledge that SOFINA and SIDRO were trying to persuade the Belgian government to take the Barcelona case to the International Court, a March representative virtually dominated the proceedings, making long speeches, the gist of which was that FECSA had bought Barcelona's assets fair and square at auction, that the Belgian side would have no chance at The Hague, and that therefore the SIDRO management would be wantonly wasting the stockholders' money if it took the case there.

In American corporate affairs, a minority stockholder who attempted thus to dominate an annual meeting would be apt to find his microphone turned off, or find himself bodily removed, before he was fairly started. Wilmers, presiding for SIDRO management, took encouragement from the cries of agony and rage from other stockholders that repeatedly interrupted the March men's filibusters, and evidently decided to let them run on. And he may have been right to do so. In the end, Belgium decided to take the case to The Hague after all. On September 15, 1958, it entered on the roster of the Court a complaint charging that in the matter of Barcelona Traction the Spanish government had, among other things, usurped the rights of the Spanish courts and shown a lack of impartiality, which resulted in a denial of justice to Belgian citizens. As reparations, to be paid by the Spanish government to the Belgian government for distribution by the latter to Barcelona Traction's unhappy stockholders, Belgium suggested that Spain be required to pay eighty-eight per cent of the company's net worth on the day of the bankruptcy decree—eighty-eight per cent being the portion of all Barcelona Traction shares held by Belgians—plus annual interest of six per cent on that sum from 1948 to the date of judgment. If judgment should be pronounced quickly, that would mean a total sum approaching a hundred and forty million dollars; if, on the other hand, the case went on for an extended time, additional interest would keep accruing, at the rate of nearly five million dollars a year.

Two weeks later, the Spanish Ambassador to the Low Countries informed the Belgian government that he had been appointed agent of the Spanish government before the International Court. This act constituted formal Spanish acceptance of the challenge, and the case was on.

XI

INTERNATIONAL LAW, its practitioners point out, is "normative," which is to say that it has no statutes to consult and few sanctions to apply. Parties that are declared to have been wronged can depend for relief on little besides the offender's respect for the court making the judgment. Although attempts to settle international disputes by arbitration go back hundreds of years, the first, halting modern attempt at establishing an international tribunal was the Permanent Court of Arbitration, which was set up by The Hague Peace Conference of 1899 and began operations at The Hague in 1902. It still exists, but, because of various limiting requirements, such as that the two parties to a dispute must agree on who their judges shall be, and, indeed, agree on taking their dispute to the Court at all, it has decided only about twenty cases over its first three-quarters of a century. The Permanent Court of International Justice, set up in 1920 under the Covenant of the League of

Nations, had a considerably more stringent structure, and proved to be a considerably more popular resort for nations with disputes to settle. Sitting in The Hague's Peace Palace—a huge brick Victorian-Romanesque structure built in 1913 by Andrew Carnegie (on a square that is still called the Carnegieplein), to give at least architectural substance to his dreams of world peace—it decided fifty-one contentious cases (as distinguished from matters in which it was merely asked to give its advice) between 1922 and 1939. In 1940, it was driven from The Hague by the German military advance; thereafter, it dragged on in Geneva, where it heard no new cases, until 1946, when it expired along with the League of Nations itself—a victim of world war, the very catastrophe it had been established to help prevent.

The present International Court of Justice, created by the United Nations Charter in 1945, is, with minor structural differences, a copy of its predecessor, except for its founders' prudent omission of the word "permanent" from its name. It occupies the same building, its members use the same reference library, and its rules are essentially the same. Its fifteen judges are each paid fifty thousand dollars per year out of United Nations funds, and are not supposed to have other employment while serving. They are elected for nine-year terms—staggered so that five new judges assume office every three years—by majority vote of the U.N. General Assembly and Security Council. No more than one judge of any particular nationality may sit at any given time. Only nations, as distinguished from persons and corporations, may bring cases, and, with few exceptions, any nation in the world may bring a case, whether or not the nation belongs to the U.N. The law applied by the Court, as is stated in the U.N. Charter, consists of international treaties binding the contesting nations in any given case; "international custom, as evidence of a general practice accepted as law"; "the general principles of law recognized by civilized nations"; and, finally, the judicial decisions and published opinions of the most highly qualified authorities of the various nations. Like all international courts before it, this one makes decisions from which there can be no appeal; but, again like its predecessors, it lacks any real power to enforce those decisions. If a nation that has lost a case refuses to abide by the Court's decision, the offended party's recourse is to refer the matter to the U.N. Security Council, which may, if it chooses, decide on punitive measures; yet, although some of the Court's judgments have indeed been flouted, no nation has ever availed itself of its privilege of complaining to the Security Council.

Along with the sponginess of its subject matter and the frailty of its authority, the Court, by its nature, suffers from the law's delays in almost grotesquely exaggerated form. For a judge merely to ask a question of a litigant nation requires a special session, at which, with due ceremony and simultaneous translation, the judge intones the question, and a representative of the litigant nation responds that the question will be answered in due course. There follows a fury of analysis by all lawyers, sometimes numbering in the hundreds, for the two sides in the case; while one side is deciding how to answer the question, both try to figure which way the tone and content of the question implied that the judge who asked it was leaning. Sometimes a judge's question sends lawyers scurrying to distant countries for the answer, and by the time they return to continue the ponderous colloquy months may have elapsed. Up to now, the average I.C.J. case has lasted two years and three months. In the all-time champion for longevity, however, which was Barcelona Traction, the proceedings dragged on for more than eleven years.

Given all these problems, the new Court—although in the nineteen-seventies its case load became alarmingly light—was fairly effective over its first thirty years. Between 1946 and 1975, it heard forty-four contentious cases, including Portugal v. India, on what rights Portuguese had to cross Indian territory between Portugal's separate enclaves near India's west coast (the Court defined the rights in a 1954 decision), and Cambodia v. Thailand, on whether or not Cambodians could make pilgrimages undisturbed to the ruined Temple of Preah Vihear, the immediate area of which Thailand occupied with troops prior to the Court's decision in favor of Cambodia in 1962. Of the forty-four cases, more than half were decided by judgments of the Court; the rest were either thrown out because the Court believed that it lacked jurisdiction, withdrawn by the applicant before a decision had been reached, settled out of court, or left undecided because during their consideration the disputes were made obsolete by new events. Most of the decisions were complied with by the defeated nation. This, however, was conspicuously not so in the one case before Barcelona Traction which involved a demand for money reparations. In 1946, several British vessels passing through the Corfu Channel, off Albania, suffered loss of life and serious damage from mines that had apparently been laid after Allied postwar mine-clearing operations were completed. Later the same year, Britain brought the matter before the United Nations, which referred it to the Court; and in December, 1949, the Court ordered Albania to pay Britain reparations of eight hundred and forty-four thousand pounds, then worth about two and a third million dollars. Albania simply did not pay, and Britain never pressed the matter in the Security Council.

On the basis of this precedent, in which a Court award of something over two million dollars had been blandly disobeyed, Belgium's chance of recovering many times that sum from Spain in the Barcelona Traction case seemed unpromising indeed. But SOFINA-SIDRO—having assembled, in spite of March's net to catch lawyers, a formidable legal staff, consisting of Belgians, Frenchmen, Englishmen, Spaniards, and a Canadian, to plead Belgium's case—took a quite different view. Wilmers' bullishness on the Court is dramatically illustrated by the fact that in 1956, when a visiting American financial operator with Spanish connections approached him and said he believed that he could put together a syndicate to buy all of SIDRO's Barcelona Traction shares for forty million dollars, Wilmers replied that he wasn't interested. What he didn't say was that Belgium proposed to recover at least three times that amount at The Hague.

March, for his part, pithily summarized his attitude by saying to a Barcelona Traction representative at about this time, "I don't give a fig for The Hague Court." Whether or not it gave a fig for him remained to be seen. At stake, finally, was the question of whether or not international law, with all its abstruse learning, its comfortable fees, its overseas delegations, and its aura of wealth, power, and culture, was any match for the likes of Juan March.

XII

THE first round of pleadings came to an abrupt end—and a quick one, by The Hague court standards—because of a most unexpected development: a sudden decision by Belgium to withdraw its complaint, for the purpose of directly negotiating a settlement with March. This was brought about in large part by a change of management at SOFINA-SIDRO. In the late nineteen-fifties, Wilmers fell victim to corporate infighting there. The infighting was complicated by scandal when, in 1956, Heineman, Wilmers, and a third SOFINA officer were accused of having made improper payments to an official of the Belgian government. The official, at the same time he held the government post, was serving as a director of two of SOFINA's subsidiary companies, and was receiving fees for his services. In 1958, a criminal action brought by the Belgian authorities against Heineman, Wilmers, and the third executive on charges of corrupting a government official came to trial in Brussels. Heineman, in poor health and living in the United States, did not stand trial, and charges against him were eventually dropped. Wilmers and his other colleague were first convicted, then exonerated on appeal. In 1959, Wilmers resigned, and since then he has devoted himself to his own investments. His departure from the stage of the Barcelona Traction drama was to be followed by a curtain call. In 1964, two years after March's death, a Spanish court declared that, of all things, Barcelona Traction's own directors had brought about its "fraudulent bankruptcy," and, accordingly, lodged criminal charges against those persons who had been Barcelona Traction directors in 1948. Wilmers, in particular, was singled out several years later, after he—now acting merely as a shareholder of SIDRO—had spoken up at a SIDRO annual meeting, calling March's takeover of Barcelona Traction "the most extra-

ordinary spoliation that has ever been seen." Soon after that,
Wilmers received in Geneva, where he was then living, the Spanish court's demand for his extradition to face the charges, and a
further demand that he immediately post bond of ninety million
dollars. The sum, implicitly flattering as it was to Wilmers' bank
account, was not even intended to be realistic. In fact, as the
Spanish complaint stated, the figure represented the entire value of
Barcelona Traction's assets in 1948, which *Wilmers* was now alleged to have somehow despoiled. A Geneva magistrate declined
to enforce either demand; but Wilmers—who, if he had learned
anything from almost three decades of jousting with March and
his men, had learned not to underestimate them—thought it prudent not to visit Spain for a number of years after that. The preposterous charge, the demand for extradition, and the preposterous
sum asked as security were no doubt partly tactical moves. But
perhaps they were partly, also, a sort of final salute from the
successors of one financial chieftain to another, who had been a
worthy antagonist.

Wilmers' successor as champion of the Belgian cause was
Maurice Frère, a Belgian banking official of international re-
nown, who had previously served as governor of his nation's
central bank, the National Bank of Belgium, and had in addition
occupied two of the key positions in world finance—membership
on the board of governors of the International Monetary Fund, in
Washington, and the presidency of the Bank for International
Settlements, in Basel. In 1957, upon taking over as president of
SOFINA and SIDRO, he decided to essay again what his predecessors
had found so frustratingly unproductive: direct, out-of-court
negotiations with March. Frère believed that where Heineman
and Wilmers had not only failed but been left fairly reeling from
the intransigence and effrontery of their antagonist, he himself,
with his long experience in international negotiation, could
succeed—especially since, as he put it in 1960, "a wind of conciliation was blowing which it was neither in my nature nor in the
interests of the company to ignore."

To get things started, in October, 1960—by which time the
Barcelona Traction case had been before the International Court

of Justice for two years, and was still in a preliminary stage—
Frère, through a Spanish-speaking colleague of his, José Manuel
Hernández, made an approach to the Count de Motrico, a Spanish diplomat, who had previously served as his nation's Ambassador to Argentina and to the United States, and who in 1960 was
its Ambassador to France. Motrico was a logical choice as intermediary, for several reasons. Frère had known him since 1958,
and was aware that he was an old and close friend of March's.
Indeed, in an affidavit presented later by the Spanish side at The
Hague, Motrico averred that he had known March since 1934,
when the two were introduced by the Count's father, a banker
with whom March had had a long association; since the end of the
Spanish Civil War, in 1939, the Count went on, he had seen
March from time to time, and March had always conferred on
him "an affectionate regard." Moreover, Motrico had previously
been involved in—or, at least, had tried to get involved in—the
Barcelona Traction matter. As early as 1949, when he had been
Ambassador to Argentina, he had tried unsuccessfully to act as
intermediary between SOFINA and the March group; again, in
1955, he and Arthur Dean had met, fruitlessly, in New York to
discuss possible resolution of the matter. Now, approached again
on the same subject, this time by Frère, Motrico was apparently
still anxious to serve as emissary. He promptly notified March that
SOFINA-SIDRO was in a mood for direct talks.

The resulting negotiations—or, more properly, negotiations
leading toward negotiations—were to be March's last big scene.
The month of Frère's approach, he turned eighty. A few years
earlier, he had been through an extended and nearly fatal illness:
In 1954, in Barcelona, he had suffered a massive internal hemorrhage; the following year, when he was in Geneva, another
hemorrhage had occurred; and in 1957, after a third, and even
more serious, episode of bleeding, in Palma, he had undergone
surgery. One of his biographers quotes him as having said before
he entered the operating room, "I feel calm, just as I did when I
escaped from Alcalá de Henares. The hardest thing is to make a
decision. But once I make it I regain my tranquillity."

By the time Frère's message reached him in the fall of 1960,

March had regained not only his tranquillity but, apparently, his health. In fact, he was in fine fettle. (At Basel in 1947, March had told Wilmers, evidently by way of warning him not to expect his early demise, that his grandfather lived to be ninety-six.) His reputation as a philanthropist now rested on far firmer ground than it had in the dear, dead days of Primo de Rivera, the *Military Mail*, and the never-built children's hospital. Now it rested on the Juan March Foundation, which was five years old in 1960, and had been established because, March said, he felt a "profound need" to leave evidence of his "love for Spain, her national culture, and Christian civilization." (To be sure, the charter of the foundation contained an unusual clause to the effect that if the Spanish state or "any other agency" should interfere with or "not respect" the wishes of the founder as to the conduct of the foundation, then the foundation "will be automatically extinguished" and its assets distributed by the directors as they saw fit. But in Spain, as elsewhere, one does not look a gift horse in the mouth.) As for his business acumen, March had clearly kept it intact. His response to Frère's initiative seemed to show that in his old age he had developed an entirely new bargaining method. Shortly after going to March with Frère's suggestion, Motrico forwarded to Frère, through Hernández, a little note—unsigned, and written in Motrico's hand—reporting three conditions that March had set for entering into new negotiations. One was that the negotiations be entered into and conducted "in good faith." Another was that there be no public announcement by either side until a definite accord had been reached. The third, and most important, read as follows: "From a moral point of view, the definitive withdrawal of the [Belgian] complaint [to the International Court of Justice] is a preliminary condition to the opening of the negotiation." As Motrico explained later, March was "extremely proud and sensitive, and strongly resented [the Belgian government's] contemptuous treatment of him" in its complaint to the Court, and, therefore, until the insult had been expunged by an unequivocal withdrawal of the complaint March would not negotiate. Instead of trying to intimidate his opponents by boasting about his financial prowess, March seemed to have decided to seek advantage by standing on his sacred honor.

Frère, taken by surprise by this tactic, hesitated. More than two months went by before he authorized Motrico to arrange a face-to-face meeting between him and March. (Meanwhile, in December, the "wind of conciliation" of which Frère had spoken picked up force, at least as regards Belgian-Spanish relations, when Belgium's King Baudouin and a Spanish aristocrat, Doña Fabiola de Mora y Aragón, were married.) Finally, on January 12, 1961, March and Frère, accompanied by translators, had lunch together with the Count de Motrico at the Count's residence in Paris. The weather of the meeting was sharply changeable. According to Frère's account, March repeated that he could not agree to enter into negotiations as long as the International Court case was pending; and, as Frère paraphrased him, he went on to say, "In his eyes, the case at The Hague had no validity. It would end in the confusion of the Belgian government. And why? He would explain. As for him, March said, he had kept in reserve a series of particularly compromising documents involving the former directors of Barcelona Traction—documents that would stir up a scandal if they were produced before The Hague Court." That sounded more like the old March. Frère then said that March's prior condition of the withdrawal of the Court proceedings constituted a serious obstacle to the start of negotiations—whereupon, according to Frère, March suddenly changed his manner completely, moving from threats to amiability, and assuring Frère that once the condition had been fulfilled he would make an offer of settlement so reasonable that SIDRO would be unable to refuse it. Frère promised to consult his board of directors and "try to find a formula enabling him to satisfy Mr. March's demand on the moral point." The session broke up in an atmosphere of conviviality.

That atmosphere endured for not quite three months. In mid-February, Frère and Motrico met, and the Count expressed confidence that once the Belgian withdrawal had been made one or two weeks should suffice to wind up the whole matter, once and for all. On February 23rd, Frère wrote Motrico that March had now succeeded in convincing him of his good faith. Accordingly, SOFINA-SIDRO asked the Belgian government to discontinue its case at The Hague; on March 23rd, Belgium formally filed notice of discontinuance; and on April 5th, Spain duly gave the Court notice of its acceptance of the discontinuance.

March's "preliminary conditions" having been met, the negotiations could begin, and so they did, at five o'clock on the afternoon of April 8, 1961, in the Paris quarters of the Spanish Ambassador there. Present were Frère, March, various other representatives of the two sides, and—in the role of moderator—Motrico. The March representatives immediately put their proposal on the table, in a memorandum that they read in Spanish: even though the Barcelona Traction shares held by SIDRO had long since been sucked dry by the issuance of "duplicate" shares of Barcelona's subsidiaries in Spain, they would, in order to put the dispute to rest, offer to buy all the old shares from SIDRO. Moreover, they would pay for them the full market price of those shares on the Brussels Bourse. (The minority of Barcelona Traction shares not held by SIDRO had been traded on that exchange since the nineteen-twenties.) The remaining question, of course—since the price of the shares on the Bourse had fluctuated wildly over the years, in response to the company's changing fortunes—was the full market price on what date? And there came the catch to the March offer. The March group offered SIDRO its choice of the average price either during 1948 or during 1952. Frère and his colleagues had no trouble realizing that those years had not been selected at random. As they could not help but recall, 1948 had been the year of the Reus "bankruptcy," while 1952 had been the year of the sale of the "duplicate" shares, and of the complete takeover of Barcelona Traction's assets by FECSA, the new March company. As a result of those events, the price per share of Barcelona Traction, which had reached a high of eighty-five dollars back in 1928, had in those two years been depressed to about three dollars, or five million four hundred thousand dollars for the entire company—a tiny fraction of the true value of the company's goods and installations, whether in 1948, 1952, or 1961. March, then, was generously offering to buy SIDRO's Barcelona Traction shares at ridiculously low prices that he himself had contrived to bring about.

Thus, Frère had his initiation into the unique, if not necessarily pleasant, experience of negotiating with March. Frère may well have felt the same sort of shock that Wilmers had felt in May, 1948, when March, in what had similarly passed for a burst of generosity, had offered SIDRO a quarter interest in what was already its own company. This time, though, the offer was far smaller; the shares at 1948 or 1952 prices would bring hardly more than enough to pay SIDRO's legal expenses on the case up to then. Frère naturally refused. Six days later, Motrico, still nominally playing the intermediary, told Frère placatingly that March was "in principle" disposed to a settlement more favorable to SIDRO than the one he had proposed in Paris. However, no concrete offer followed this hint of conciliation; indeed, as time went on, March seemed more and more inclined to stick to his Paris offer—the very recollection and contemplation of which, with its dumbfounding impertinence fitted into a frame of technical elegance, may be presumed to have brightened the old man's last year. Late in April, addressing the annual meeting of SOFINA, Frère, with the best cheer he could muster, told the company's stockholders of the assurances that Motrico had given him of March's willingness to negotiate in good faith. In June, he wrote Motrico again, reminding him, "If we finally consented to ask the Belgian government to desist from the case, it was solely because Mr. Juan March had made that a condition *sine qua non* of the negotiation, and because the assurances that he gave me, and that you confirmed, convinced me that he had decided to end this litigation through a transaction granting an equitable indemnity to our shareholders."

But a wistful note was creeping into Frère's comments. He was losing heart. That he had cause to do so became amply clear at the next face-to-face meeting of the two sides, which occurred at Biarritz on September 6th—Frère accompanied by Hernández, and March by Antonio Zuloaga, son of the painter who had depicted him regally twenty years earlier. March opened the meeting with a new bombshell: He proposed this time that all those present sign a declaration affirming that throughout the preliminary discussions and the negotiations to date the Count had represented only himself—not the Spanish government, not the Belgian government, and not March. Frère—astonished and dismayed, since if Motrico was not acting as a representative of the Spanish government, then Spain had committed itself to nothing in exchange for Belgium's withdrawal of the case from the International Court—refused. March then modified his proposal. All he asked, he said, was that Frère sign some sort of letter acknowledging the private character of Motrico's intervention; then he would be ready for a secret meeting with Frère, at which no one else would be present except Hernández and Zuloaga, as interpreters, and at which he would make a new and irresistible settlement offer. Again Frère refused, and the meeting ended in stalemate.

Now Frère was thoroughly discouraged. Each meeting he had with March seemed to bring forth new demands for "preliminary conditions" that could not be met without improving March's position and weakening his own. Three days later, he wrote to March expressing his objections to the new demand. The letter, addressed to Biarritz, came back marked "Departed Without Leaving an Address," but later in the month Frère tracked March down in San Sebastián and got the letter to him there. March replied, stating again that although he was anxious to work out a settlement, he had been "injured and insulted morally" in the Belgian complaint at The Hague, and concluding, "Where I was, I am." And then, at last, Frère gave up; he informed Motrico that he was now convinced that March had no intention of negotiating seriously.

The episode ended with a round of epistolary bickering. On October 3, 1961, Frère wrote to March saying, "Your new protestations of good faith and affirmation of your desire to find a solution have no more than a Platonic character. They are contradicted by your attitude. This forces me to state that it is vain to pursue this negotiation. I consider it terminated." March, on October 25th, replied with a twenty-page letter in which he fulsomely reiterated his stand, and on November 24th, Frère wound up the correspondence by writing to March, "I desire above all . . . to tell you my regret to state that . . . to accredit a version of history of these negotiations that coincides with your interests, you do not hesitate to do violence to facts, to words, and to documents."

It was an admission of defeat. Frère, who as governor of the National Bank of Belgium had managed the monetary affairs of a major industrial nation, and who in his posts with the International Monetary Fund and the Bank for International Settlements had held major responsibility for safeguarding the financial system of the whole Free World, had found it beyond his powers to make a deal with March. Belgian counsel at The Hague, where the Belgian complaint was in due course reintroduced, later insisted that March had tricked Frère. If he had done so, it may well have been not so much to bring about the Belgian withdrawal of the case from the Court, for which he didn't give a fig, as to enjoy a satisfaction he had never experienced before—that of getting the better, in face-to-face dealings, of a certified leader of the respectable European financial establishment.

In any case, if a trick, it was his last. On February 25, 1962, March was riding in his Cadillac with his chauffeur and valet a few miles north of Madrid, en route to visit Rodríguez Sastre in Torrelodones, when the car skidded on a wet road in making a ninety-degree turn, and collided head-on with a Chevrolet coming the other way. Miraculously, the chauffeur and the valet were not hurt (subsequent published accounts of the accident do not mention the fate of the Chevrolet's occupant), but March suffered fractures of his right arm, thigh, and shinbone. He was rushed to a Madrid clinic, where he underwent a two-hour operation, and afterward was at first reported to be doing well. However, he himself apparently understood at once that his injuries were mortal. The day after the accident, he arranged from his hospital bed to give his foundation an additional one billion pesetas (then worth between sixteen and seventeen million dollars), saying that he had been planning for some time to make this additional endowment but had not got around to it. Father Félix García, the priest who attended March in the hospital, later described him

during his last two weeks: " 'I am dying,' he told me with the
sobriety and precision that characterized his words. 'But it is most
important to die properly, in God's forgiveness. There is no time
to lose.' With his admirably organized mind's singular clarity,
without a stammer or a moment's hesitation, he summed up his
intense and varied life. He expressed it all by saying, 'My Jesus,
have mercy!' " He died early on the morning of March 10th. His
body, after having been viewed by a procession of Spanish dignitaries at his Madrid mansion, was taken to Valencia and thence,
aboard one of the boats of his Transmediterranean Company, to
Palma. There the Bishop of Majorca conducted March's funeral,
in the cathedral; then a hearse carrying his coffin proceeded in the
cool of evening through the streets of Palma between rows of
torches held by an endless line of March family retainers, and the
coffin was lowered into the great, nameless family mausoleum,
which March had ordered built after the death of his wife, Leonor,
in 1957.

March obituaries, both domestic and foreign, were generally
scanty. The Spanish press, which was subject to Franco's censor-
ship, seemed to adopt the attitude of least said, least risked; it
relied mainly on sanctioned biographical data. The *Times* of London treated March respectfully and at some length—his last tribute
from his British friends—and *The New York Times* at equal
length but less respectfully. In most foreign places, though, his
name was so little known that his death rated no more than a few
lines. The field of historical parallels and poetic appraisals was left
to Spanish notables of the time, and they made the most of it. In
the view of the writer Ernesto Giménez Caballero, a longtime
March booster, March's death meant the end of "our Picasso or
Rubens of the financial art." Giménez Caballero went on, "He
worked gold the way these others worked color, design, and
rhythm. Superhumanly, as Nietzsche would say. Sportingly, in
Ortega's philosophy." The Monarchist poet José María Pemán,
echoing the theme of Finance Minister Jaime Carner's speech before the Cortes in 1932 but reversing its judgment, said, "One
cannot understand Juan March without the Mediterranean. The

shores of this sea spawn men like this, who confront the sea and its dangers only to donate their fortunes, in the end, to the service of Culture and the [human] Spirit. The Medici came of this lineage. . . . The entire Renaissance was a historical transaction conducted by bankers and humanists." The president of the Cortes at the time of March's death, Esteban Bilbao, reached back even further into history—and perhaps tortured it more cruelly—to find parallels. "Don Juan March Ordinas' death is a national tragedy," he said in a long eulogy. "In our age, we have few Virgils to guide us and even fewer Maecenases to serve as patrons. . . . May God repay him!"

In the narrower but perhaps more apposite context of modern international financial swashbucklers, March stands out not only for the distinctive Mediterranean style noted by Carner and Pemán but also for the fact that his personal drama ended in triumph. As a cautious man, ever reluctant to gamble on borrowed money—indeed, within the terms he set he was a paragon of financial soundness—he stands in marked contrast to his contemporary Ivar Kreuger, and to such others as Samuel Insull. And, in even sharper contrast to Kreuger, he ended his life a billionaire and a philanthropist, not a bankrupt and a suicide. In classic moral drama, he might have died ruined or in prison, or perhaps murdered by a Garau or some other ancient enemy. He did not. If, in keeping with his name, he was a Don Juan of money—a man always ready to risk everything to get his financial, rather than his sexual, will—his life did not pursue the Spanish legend to the end: In the last scene, there was no statue of a duelling victim to drag him off to Hell.

XIII

FRERE AND SOFINA-SIDRO, however, continued to wish as much as ever to drag off the March interests to a secular hell at The Hague. At the moment of March's death, they were already making plans

—over the strenuous objections of the Spaniards, who contended that Belgium's "definitive withdrawal" of the case was irreversible —to submit it again to the Court. On June 19, 1962, the Case Concerning the Barcelona Traction, Light & Power Company, Ltd., this time designated "New Application: 1962," was entered on the Court's General List. As to reparations demanded, this time Belgium raised the ante. In addition to the Belgian stockholders' eighty-eight-per-cent share of Barcelona Traction's net value in February, 1948, plus the ever-mounting annual interest at six per cent from 1948 on, Belgium now asked for almost four million dollars to compensate its nationals for their legal expenses on the case over the years, and, on top of that, about three million, plus interest, for the Belgian former sterling bondholders of Barcelona Traction, to make up for losses they had suffered as a result of March's various maneuvers and the Spanish authorities' laissez-faire attitude toward them. All told, the demand came, at a minimum, to well over a hundred and fifty million dollars; and, as a final touch, Belgium asked that, in the event of a favorable judgment, Spain be required to pay interest on *that* sum from the date of judgment to the date of payment. Since such interest would probably come to about twenty-five thousand dollars a day, it would, the Belgians apparently felt, offer ample inducement for quick payment.

Spain then entered four "preliminary objections": first, that the discontinuance of the previous proceedings disentitled Belgium to bring new ones; second, that the Court was not competent, because Spain was not required to submit to its jurisdiction; third, that because Barcelona Traction was by charter a Canadian company, Belgium lacked judicial standing to bring the case; and, fourth, that even if Belgium did have judicial standing the claim was inadmissible because Barcelona Traction had failed to exhaust the legal remedies available to it in Spain. In July, 1964, after hearing extensive arguments on Spain's objections, the Court ruled on them. It rejected the first two outright, and, as for the other two, it neither accepted nor rejected them; instead, it decided to join them to the merits of the case, to hear further arguments on them along with arguments on the merits, and, finally, to pronounce a single judgment based on the merits or on the remaining Spanish objections or on all three.

The March interests anticipated this development, which clearly meant that the Court wanted to hear the merits of the case in full, in a way that might have made the old man feel proud. At the annual meeting of FECSA in Barcelona that June, the company's secretary-general, Rodríguez Sastre, abruptly declared, "The Hague court can never cause FECSA to pay any indemnification." What was implied was that if Spain should lose the case, that would be the Spanish government's problem, not FECSA's. The Spanish government, however, let his declaration pass without comment, and FECSA seems to have continued both to direct the Spanish pleadings and to pay for them.

Glacially, but this time resolutely, the proceedings at The Hague moved forward. Summers and winters came and went in the Carnegieplein, and the case went on. Spain, in seven hundred and fifty-four closely printed pages, presented its Counter-Memorial, answering the Belgian complaint; Belgium, at slightly greater length, gave its Reply; then Spain came through with a two-volume Rejoinder; and at last, in sixty-four separate sessions in 1969, the Court heard oral arguments by both sides. Meanwhile, presidents of the Court came and went—Bohdan Winiarski, of Poland, from 1961 to 1964; Sir Percy Spender, of Australia, from 1964 to 1967; then José Luis Bustamante y Rivero, of Peru—and the rest of its membership kept changing as members' terms expired and new members were elected to replace them. (Under the Court's rules, a judge, to be qualified to vote on a case, is expected to have read the written submissions of both sides, and to have attended the essential parts of the oral proceedings. He need not have been on the Court when the case was first submitted, and in fact when the Barcelona Traction case was finally decided, in 1970, not a single one of the judges who had attended the first proceedings, in 1958, participated in the decision.) Through it all, lawyers, many of them of international reputation—all told, more than a hundred of them for Spain, including March's old political ally Gil Robles, and several dozen for the Belgians—swarmed over the Peace Palace. The nominal leader of the Spanish horde was J. M. Castro-Rial, legal counsellor to the Spanish Ministry of Foreign Affairs, but March's favorite counsellor, Rodríguez Sastre, although he was never seen at the Peace Palace, was generally considered to be the behind-the-scenes mastermind. For Belgium, the lead arguments were made by Henri Rolin, a Socialist senator much celebrated in his country as one of the men chiefly responsible for Belgium's extrication of itself from the Congo. Some of the former participants recall that an atmosphere of diffidence, or even hostility, unusual in the brotherhood of the bar, prevailed between the adversary advocates throughout the case. Even the various Englishmen retained by the two sides—men who were accustomed to cordial relations with one another in the vicinity of the Temple or the Old Bailey—found themselves barely speaking in The Hague. "Everybody was continually afraid of dirty work," Francis Mann, one of the Englishmen who argued for Belgium, says.

The ghost of Juan March, who in his lifetime had never deigned to come to The Hague, now lurked in the Peace Palace. Although his name was only occasionally brought up in the proceedings, his presence was inescapable. Was it not a foregone conclusion, the Belgian representatives asked themselves, that lawyers indirectly representing March, whether he was alive or dead, would sooner or later resort to some kind of Mediterranean trickery—even when among those lawyers were such un-Mediterranean personages as M. Bos, professor of international law at the University of Utrecht, and Sir Humphrey Waldock, C.M.G., O.B.E., Q.C., professor of international law at Oxford? Conversely, the members of the Spanish team asked themselves, was not fast footwork of one kind or another to be fully expected of the representatives of an international financial octopus that, from their perspective, had long been engaged in ruthlessly exploiting the resources of Spain? These suspicions were faithfully reproduced in the emphases of the two sides' arguments. Belgium insisted on the injustices to its nationals and the outrages to the principles of justice which, its advocates said, had resulted from the various steps in March's conquest of Barcelona Traction—the defeat of the Plan of Compromise, the Reus bankruptcy, the Agreed Minute, and the sale of "duplicate" shares—and charged the Spanish courts and government with complicity in allowing those injustices and outrages to occur and to stand. Spain's lawyers brushed aside all those events as deftly as possible—Barcelona Traction in 1948, the Spanish lawyers were driven to argue at some length, had been in a "permanent state of *latent* bankruptcy"—and came down heavily on Barcelona Traction's alleged misdeeds and depredations in Spain in the past. One of the Spanish lawyers declared categorically that the "lack of clean hands" of Barcelona Traction and its owners "should now defeat their claim for an indemnity in this Court." Belgium argued that whether or not its nationals' hands had been unclean in the past, such uncleanliness was irrelevant to the question at hand; that is, whether or not justice had been denied to Barcelona Traction's Belgian stockholders between 1948 and 1952. On the contrary, Spain seemed to be arguing, *that* question was irrelevant: If Barcelona Traction had been denied justice, it had got what it deserved.

At last, in the summer of 1969, the arguments and counterarguments had all been heard, the memorials, countermemorials, replies, rejoinders, annexes, and documents had all been filed, and the judges retired to the Salle Bol, a room in the Peace Palace named for three huge works of the Dutch painter Ferdinand Bol that hang there, to conduct their deliberations. On February 5, 1970—at the very last minute, since it was the final day in office of no fewer than five of the judges—they delivered their Judgment, in a fittingly ponderous document, consisting, what with the separate opinions of eight judges and the dissenting opinion of one, of a volume of three hundred and fifty-seven pages. It began, neutrally, with a detailed summary of the agreed-upon facts (including only the briefest of passing references to Juan March, who as far as the Judgment was concerned might have been a minor figure in the case) and the arguments of the two sides. Then, in a leisurely way, it went on to discuss the law involved. At first, this discussion was bland and inscrutable, but gradually the Court's preoccupation narrowed down to Spain's third preliminary objection—the question of whether the Belgian government was a party at interest and thus had the right to make a claim before the Court on behalf of a Canadian company. "It is common ground that from the economic viewpoint the company has been entirely paralyzed," the Court pointed out. But the question it put to itself was, "Has a right of Belgium been violated on account of its nationals' having suffered infringement of their rights as shareholders in a company not of Belgian nationality?"

Insistently—and, for the Belgian side, ominously—the Court proceeded to worry this question. In a previous case—Liechtenstein v. Guatemala in the matter of Nottebohm—Liechtenstein had complained that one of its citizens long resident in Guatemala had been deprived of his rights there under international law, and the Court had ruled in 1955 that, inasmuch as Nottebohm had been a German national for most of his life and had obtained Liechtenstein nationality late in 1939 simply to acquire the status of a neutral national in wartime, Liechtenstein was not entitled to make an international claim on his behalf. To that extent, there was a precedent for denying Belgium's right to make a claim against Spain on behalf of Barcelona Traction. But the Court was not disposed to decide the case on the basis of the Nottebohm precedent. There was also, it felt, a question of human rights to be considered. Such rights as they were recognized by the Court, it pointed out, included protection against denial of justice; however, "the instruments which embody human rights do not confer on States the capacity to protect the victims of infringements of such rights irrespective of their nationality." And the nationality of Barcelona Traction was, at least nominally, Canadian. That disposed of human rights. As to the question of ordinary fairness, as opposed to technical law, the Court declared, "The incorporation of the company under the law of Canada was an act of free choice. . . . When establishing a company in a foreign country, its promoters are normally impelled by particular considerations; it is often a question of tax or other advantages offered by the host state. It does not seem to be in any way inequitable that the advantages thus obtained should be balanced by the risks arising from the fact that the protection of the company and hence of its shareholders is thus entrusted to a State other than the national State of the shareholders. . . . The Court is not of the opinion that . . . *jus standi* is conferred on the Belgian government by considerations of equity." In other words, Barcelona Traction could be thought of as hoist on its own petard; it had made its big mistake back in 1911, when it incorporated itself in Canada to get a tax break. Then on to public policy as regards international affairs: "The Court considers that the adoption of the theory of diplomatic protection of shareholders as such . . . could create an atmosphere of confusion and insecurity in international economic relations."

All in all, a gloomy text for the Belgians, rolling on from argument to argument against their standing before the Court—a question that seemed to them to have been implicitly answered long since by the very willingness of the Court to take up its time through so many weary years with hearing arguments and reading submissions. Was it really possible to believe that the Supreme Court of the world, made up of leading jurists of many nations, could bring itself to deny a litigant's right to be heard before it, after it had heard that litigant and its opponent over the course of more than eleven years? At last, in Paragraph 102 of the Judgment, came a sudden note of encouragement for Belgium:

It has been argued on one side that unlawful acts had been committed by the Spanish judicial and administrative authorities, and that as a result of those acts Spain has incurred international responsibility. On the other side it has been argued that the activities of Barcelona Traction and its subsidiaries were conducted in violation of Spanish law and caused damage to the Spanish economy. If both contentions were substantiated, the truth of the latter would in no way provide justification in respect of the former.

That was to say that the gravamen of the Spanish case—that Barcelona Traction's past bad conduct in Spain disentitled it to protection against recent actions to its detriment there—was irrelevant, just as Belgium had contended all along.

It was a doomed man's last meal. A sentence later came the Court's death blow:

However, the possession by the Belgian Government of a right of protection is a prerequisite for the examination of these problems. Since no *jus standi* before the Court has been established, it is not for the Court in its Judgment to pronounce upon any other aspect of the case. . . . Accordingly, the Court rejects the Belgian Government's claim.

The vote was fifteen to one, and even the single pro-Belgian vote was a special case, almost a foregone conclusion. Under the Court's rules, in cases in which one side or the other (or both) has no judge of its own nationality on the bench, that side is entitled to appoint a judge ad hoc, to sit in that case only. Belgium, availing itself of this right, had appointed Willem Riphagen, legal adviser to the Ministry of Foreign Affairs of the Netherlands, Belgium's close neighbor, and a former member of the Netherlands' delegation to the U.N. General Assembly. And it was Judge Riphagen who had cast the single dissenting vote. (Spain had had its own judge ad hoc—Enrique C. Armand-Ugon, of Uruguay—and he, obviously, had voted Spain's way.) To be sure, several of the other judges, concurring in the Court's decision in separate opinions, had given radically different reasons for doing so. For example, Judge Gaetano Morelli, of Italy, had gone further than the other judges, flatly expressing the view that international law does not protect the interests of corporate stockholders in any circumstance; Judge André Gros, of France, had based his opinion on Spain's fourth objection rather than on its third; and Judge Kotaro Tanaka, of Japan, alone among the judges, had rejected all of Spain's objections and decided in Spain's favor on the merits of the case. The fact remained, though, that the Court, by unanimous vote of its regular members, had done what the Belgian side had thought impossible. It had been caught in the clownish act of having spent eleven years on a case that, according to its own belated decision, the complainant had not been entitled to bring before it in the first place.

XIV

THE Barcelona Traction decision caused an uproar, and not only among the lawyers for Belgium and their clients but in international law circles in various countries. United States Secretary of State William P. Rogers, addressing the American Society of International Law in April, 1970, said that the Court's finding "has further eroded confidence in the Court." Detlev F. Vagts, a professor at the Harvard Law School, wrote in *Worldwide Projects & Industry Planning*, a journal for managers of international corporations, "The result in this case is somewhat depressing. Those who would like to see the I.C.J. become a stronger institution are disappointed." Francis Mann, the English solicitor who had done much of the pleading for Belgium since the new submission of the case in 1962, went beyond disappointment to downright depression. In an article in *The American Journal of International Law*, he spoke of "the truly astonishing fact that the unique and outstanding event that was at the root of the whole case"—the bankruptcy of Barcelona Traction at Reus in 1948—had not even been mentioned in the part of the Judgment in which the Court gave its reasoning. "The Judgment . . . has carried a new note into international law," Mann went on. "The idea and the ideals of international law have in the past not been circumscribed by legalism. The practice of international tribunals has, on the whole, been characterized by careful analysis of the facts against the background of broad principles of law. Does the Judgment in *Barcelona Traction* inaugurate a new trend? . . . The Court [showed] disinclination to attend to the facts of the case. It must have thought them wholly irrelevant. . . . The Court subordinated facts to formal law. Legal conceptualism prevailed over realism."

And, of course, March had, as usual, prevailed over his opponents. Eight years dead, and scarcely considered more worthy of mention in commentaries on the case than the Reus bankruptcy had been in the Judgment, he had this time beaten nothing less than the international corporate and legal complex that more and more people have of late come to believe rules the Western world. Perhaps the best clues to the real meaning of the case are to be found in the remarks of some of the judges in their separate opinions. The American judge, Philip C. Jessup, quoted a legal-journal article as saying, "It is small wonder that difficulties arise when nineteenth-century precedents about outrageous behavior towards aliens residing in outlandish parts are sought to be pressed into service to yield principles apposite to . . . international investment," and stated that the case could not be looked upon as pitting rich against poor, in the nineteenth-century style. On the contrary, Jessup said, "Basically the conflict was between a powerful Spanish financial group and a comparable non-Spanish group. This case cannot be said to evoke problems of 'neo-colonialism.' " But Judge Fouad Ammoun, of Lebanon, from his perspective as a citizen of a poor country, tended toward an almost opposite view. In considering the case, Judge Ammoun wrote, "One cannot help thinking . . . of the large companies which continue to undertake the exploitation of the natural resources of the less developed countries, including their agricultural, timber and mineral wealth, their oil production, and also their transport and other public or municipal services." And he added, "An equitable sharing of the profits is mandatory."

If an implied moral right of citizens of poor nations to rob those of rich nations was a hidden motif of the decision, a more overt one was the simple inadequacy of international law in its present state of development to deal with the issue of whether or not such a right exists. Judge Sir Gerald Gray Fitzmaurice, of Britain, stated in his separate opinion that he had voted with the majority of the

Court "with some reluctance," and went on to explain, "I . . . hold it to be an unsatisfactory state of the law that obliges the Court to refrain from pronouncing on the substantive merits of the Belgian claim, on the basis of what is really . . . somewhat of a technicality. . . . International law must . . . be regarded as deficient and underdeveloped in this field." President Bustamante, in his separate opinion, spoke of "the insufficient development of the law in its present stage of evolution." And Judge Ammoun, even though he voted in favor of Spain with what seemed to be enthusiasm, mentioned "the overall problem of the development of modern international law in the face of recent transformations in international life."

The International Court existed, and exists, in part to repair such insufficient development by developing new law to meet new situations. However, it does not always do so. In the Barcelona Traction case, it failed—just as maritime courts for many centuries, up to the middle of the nineteenth, had failed, because the underdevelopment of maritime law in those times made it powerless to deal with the realities of piracy and privateering. The International Court had said, in effect, that only Canada would have been competent to bring the Barcelona Traction case—and Canada, since its citizens had virtually no economic stake in that company, had little interest in the whole matter and, understandably, felt disinclined to bring the case. The inevitable conclusion is that, as the Court interpreted international law, for practical purposes no nation was competent to bring the Barcelona Traction case before it. The many other international corporations that, like Barcelona Traction, have their headquarters and their charter in one country, the majority of their stockholders in another or others, and their business in still others were thus served notice that, again for practical purposes, recourse to the International Court when a company is damaged in any country other than that of its charter is not available. And, as Arthur Dean has pointed out, with international corporations getting bigger and bigger and their ownership more and more dispersed, this situation is becoming increasingly common. It constitutes, Dean said in 1978, "a real vacuum in international law." More Juan Marches—and, if there are to be more, the next will be African or Latin American —may be expected to notice the opportunity thus offered, and to seize it. If, as René Dubos has contended, human health does not steadily improve—if, instead, vanished diseases are merely replaced by new, emerging ones—it may be that, similarly, international social aggression is not conquered or eliminated but merely changes forms and methods, and that the onetime pirates and privateers have their counterparts in modern international financiers. The lesson of the Barcelona Traction case is that an economic privateer in the nineteen-seventies may sail and ply his trade on seas of paper with little fear of intervention by international law.

IN the autumn of 1977, I went to London and talked to Francis Mann. Originally German, he came to London in 1933 as a refugee from Hitler, and there established himself as a member of the solicitors' firm of Herbert Smith & Company—of which he became senior partner—and as one of the world's leading authorities on international law. I found him in his room in his firm's quarters, at 62 London Wall—a modest room, in the style of tradition-minded London solicitors, with an electric heater, leather chairs, and shelves of worn law books reaching to the ceiling. Mann himself I found to be a pleasant man of seventy, with an air of mildness which I quickly learned could change in an instant to one of fierceness. "We lost," he said reflectively when I brought up the Barcelona Traction case. Perhaps a half minute went by while he stared at the ceiling with the tips of his fingers together, evidently thinking back. Then he suddenly fixed me with a stare so intense as to be disconcerting. "We lost," he repeated, and then said again, this time just above a whisper, *"We lost!* I could not believe it was possible that we would—certainly not on those grounds. And the whole thing is a monstrous situation. That the merits of such a case as that could simply be brushed aside by the

Court in favor of a technicality! Let's be realistic: We are not entitled to expect decency from a national government—any national government. But let us suppose that there *were* such decency. What would happen? A government that had won a case on such grounds as Spain won the Barcelona Traction case would come forward and say, 'All right, now let the merits of this matter be submitted to a new tribunal. Let it not be decided permanently on technical subterfuges.' " After a gloomy pause, Mann added, in a flat voice, "Law is words. It's only a question of finding the right words."

Listening to Mann's words—coming, as they were, from one long known as a dreamer of a world peacefully ordered by international law and, at the same time, as a hardheaded man of affairs, who had devoted himself to such practical tasks as being lifelong legal counsellor to the oil heir Nubar Gulbenkian—I found that I, too, was profoundly depressed. Seven years after the end of the Barcelona Traction case, Mann still seemed to be suffering something like shock about the state of international law that it had revealed. Thinking about that shock, I found I could not feel that it had been produced entirely by the decision of The Hague court or the subsequent failure of the Spanish government to suggest some sort of rehearing. It seemed to have something in common with the shock that had been felt, at various times over the preceding three-quarters of a century, by such antagonists of March's as the Garaus of Algiers, Cambó, Primo de Rivera, the Spanish Republic itself, Heineman, Wilmers, and Frère. Even though Mann had never met March, and March had died at almost exactly the time when Mann first became involved in the Barcelona Traction case, Mann's shock seemed to be very much akin to that experienced by all those who had ever ventured to stand in the way of the last—or perhaps not the last—pirate of the Mediterranean.

The obsequies for March's greatest victim, Barcelona Traction, had been pronounced more than two years before I talked with Mann in June, 1975, when Frans H. Terlinck, the nominal president of the empty shell of a company, issued its first annual report to stockholders since 1946—the year when all the trouble began with the failure of the Plan of Compromise. Terlinck reported that the original shares of Ebro and of Barcelona Traction's other operating subsidiaries—the shares that had been declared void by March's men and the Spanish courts in 1951—had on June 18, 1974, been sold by the National Trust Company of Toronto, which then still held them as trustee, to SIDRO for the sum of $1,897,643, which was precisely the amount that SIDRO had already advanced to the Canadian trustee and receiver for fees and expenses in the twenty-six years between 1948 and 1974. SIDRO had then sold these shares through a London bank, for the same sum, to "an undisclosed principal." (That principal was later reported to have been none other than FECSA, the Spanish holder of the "duplicate" shares that had been created for its and March's pleasure. FECSA had apparently bought the original shares, worthless though they seemed to be, as insurance against any future legal trouble.) After reviewing the events since 1948—the bankruptcy, the creation of the duplicate shares and their sale, the application to the International Court of Justice, the withdrawal for the purpose of negotiating, the failure of the negotiations, the reapplication, the eight-year Court debate, and, finally, the Judgment—Terlinck concluded his death certificate for Barcelona Traction. He wrote, simply:

There are no funds available for the shareholders. . . . The shareholders of this Company have been deprived of their entire investment. . . .

Thus, your board of directors regrets to state that, despite immense efforts, it has been impossible to obtain any judgment on the merits in any forum of competent jurisdiction in which the Company was or should have been afforded the opportunity to be heard on the merits. Left saddled with liabilities and with no assets, the Company is henceforth unable to seek in any forum the redress which it equitably deserves.

Although there are no present favourable indications whatsoever, one may not altogether exclude all hope that responsible persons in authority may one day recognize that this Company and its shareholders should obtain compensation.

We cannot terminate this summary recital of a lost struggle which has extended over a period of twenty-eight years, without acknowledging a debt of gratitude to the Governments of Canada, Belgium and the United Kingdom for their support.

No reports to the shareholders have since been issued, and none are ever likely to be.

PART THREE

U. S.—the Sixties

$$\text{6}$$

The Gentlemanly Junket

WHEN THE PARTNERS of Brown Brothers Harriman & Co., of 59 Wall Street, the only major private bank in the United States, decided to put on a celebration in September, 1968, in observance of their firm's hundred-and-fiftieth anniversary, they resolved that they would do it up—well, brown. Specifically, they decided to invite about a hundred of the bank's "good and long-standing friends"—chief executives of leading American companies, and chief executives of banks abroad—along with their wives, to come to a four-day party, beginning with a visit to Seattle and its leading industry, the Boeing Company; continuing with a twenty-two-hour ride on a super-special, dome-car Union Pacific train from Seattle to Sun Valley, Idaho; and winding up there with a symposium on worldwide capital problems, an afternoon of sport and recreation, and a formal banquet.

All this was quite uncharacteristic. When you come right down to it, the celebration was to be a combination of two low-down modern business institutions, the junket and the convention, and Brown Brothers is hardly known for being either low-down or modern. On the contrary, it is known for paneled walls, portraits of ancestors, roll-top desks, and conservative methods; it manages to come across as the *crème-de-la-crème* bank in a way that Morgan's and Kuhn Loeb, even in their heyday, never quite could, because of being so big. Its partners—there were twenty-one of them at the time—prefer, and are able, to appear on most occasions to treat banking as if it were an amusing amateur sport, like croquet. "If this sort of business isn't fun, it isn't worth doing," Robert A. Lovett, a Brown Brothers partner, remarked shortly before the big party. The firm's lineal ancestor, John A. Brown & Co., of Philadelphia, was founded in 1818 to import Irish linens and, incidentally, to finance transatlantic trade in them. (The Rothschilds, the Morgans, and the Seligmans got their start in dry goods, too.) A private bank might sound to the layman like one that wouldn't accept his money, and Brown Brothers probably wouldn't; as its partners explained forthrightly in a publication of theirs, they prefer to concentrate on "wholesale banking—giving top-level personal attention to the special financial needs of corporations, other banks, institutions, and individuals of substantial means." However, what defines Brown Brothers as a private bank is not its exclusiveness but the fact that it is a partnership wholly owned and managed by its members, rather than a corporation owned by stockholders and run by professional managers. This means that in the event of its failure the partners individually would be accountable to the depositors down to the last dollar of their personal assets, and the Brown Brothers partners feel, understandably, that having their own property on the line makes for a certain intimacy with their clients that the managers of public banks don't enjoy.

Up to the nineteen-thirties, there were many private banks in the country, but most of them became casualties either of New Deal legislation, which nudged them into stock-and-bond underwriting, or of estate taxes. The greatest of them, J. P. Morgan & Co., incorporated, and sold public stock, in 1940. Brown Brothers survived the legislation, and has the estate-tax problem all figured out—quite legally—so it confidently expects to be able to remain a private bank permanently. In its earlier days, the firm played a key role in financing the nation's first large railroad, the Baltimore & Ohio; supplied letters of credit to Americans travelling abroad; became the leading foreign-exchange authority in nineteenth-century Wall Street; and as early as the middle of the century—as John A. Kouwenhoven relates in his history of Brown Brothers, *Partners in Banking*—was considered so reliable that the Reverend Henry Ward Beecher once felt called upon to urge the members of his congregation to grant God the same confidence they freely accorded to Brown Brothers. The firm in its present state was created by the merger, in 1931, of Brown Brothers and another private bank, Harriman Brothers & Co. Why the merger took place is a question the present partners answer in different ways, according to what mood they are in. One day they will say that the Brown firm was in dire financial straits and Harriman Brothers bailed it out; another day they will say that the whole thing happened simply because the partners of the two firms were such good friends. Some of them were undeniably good friends; for example, Lovett, first made a Brown Brothers partner in 1926, and E. Roland Harriman, one of the two Harriman brothers, had been friends since their boyhood, when Lovett's father worked for Harriman's father, the railroad entrepreneur E. H. Harriman, and the two sons went to Yale together. (Until a few years earlier, almost all Brown Brothers partners were Yale graduates; by 1968 merely a working majority were.) Whether Yale men or not, the 1968 partners bore names familiar in American history, long past and present. In addition to a vintage Brown—Moreau Delano Brown, a great-grandson of the founder's brother—and Lovett, a former Assistant Secretary of War for Air, Under-Secretary of State, and Secretary of Defense, they included Prescott Bush, a former United States senator from Connecticut; Elbridge T. Gerry, a descendant and namesake of the onetime governor of Massachusetts who became vice-president of the United States and was the source of the word "gerrymander"; R. L. Ireland III, a grand-nephew of Mark Hanna; Robert V. Roosa, Under-Secretary of the Treasury for Monetary Affairs in the Kennedy Administration; and, of course, the elder Harriman brother, W. Averell, the life-long diplomat and former governor of New York.

The partners chose the particular sesquicentennial program they did because, in the words of one of them, Thomas McCance, "E. H. Harriman reorganized the Union Pacific at the end of the last century, Averell started Sun Valley in 1936, and Boeing is an old friend and client of ours." Moreover, they thought that Boeing had much of special interest to show the foreign bankers, and the train that the party would ride to Sun Valley they resolved, as veteran railroad bankers, to make a paragon—perhaps the last great luxury train. As to the combination of United States indus-trialists and foreign bankers, this involved excluding domestic bankers, a slightly sticky business. But the risk was worth taking, the partners reasoned, inasmuch as the encounter they planned might help break down the artificial barriers, social as well as pro-fessional, that normally separate the two groups they planned to invite; as Roosa put it, most American businessmen think of an international banker as something between a devil and a gnome, while the international bankers cheerfully dismiss American busi-nessmen as rich Babbitts.

Eventually, and rather astonishingly, ninety-two bankers and industrialists—eighty-five of whom were accompanied by their wives, and fifty-five of whom were from abroad—came to Seattle and Sun Valley to help the partners amuse themselves. Among the good and long-standing friends present were the governors or deputy governors of the central, or government, banks of Germany, Denmark, Norway, Iceland, and the United States, and their wives; Dr. Marcus Wallenberg, a member of the leading banking and industrial family of Sweden—a sort of combination of the Morgan bank and the Rockefeller fortune—and Mrs. Wallenberg; Kiichiro Satoh, the acknowledged dean of Japanese bankers, and Mrs. Satoh; Conrad Hentsch, the acknowledged dean of Genevan private bankers; John Thomson, of Barclays Bank, who was often called the outstanding British banker, and Mrs. Thomson; three knighted British bankers, Sir Cuthbert Clegg, of Martins Bank, Sir John Stevens, of Morgan Grenfell, and Sir Cyril Hawker, of the Standard Bank, with Ladies Clegg, Stevens, and Hawker; and, among the Americans, to name just a handful, Roger M. Blough, of United States Steel, William S. Paley, of the Columbia Broadcasting System, John T. Connor, of Allied Chemical, George Russell, of General Motors, Charles B. (Tex) Thornton, of Litton Industries, and Juan T. Trippe, of Pan American World Airways, with their wives. One of the guests, Luc Wauters, of the Belgian Kredietbank, later said that it had been the most representative group of bankers ever assembled anywhere, and estimated that those who were present handled about sixty per cent of world trade—the balance of the world, in the phrase Byron used about Rothschild and Baring. As for American business, fourteen of the hundred largest companies on *Fortune's* most recent list were represented by their chief executives. When the partners invited me to come along, I eagerly accepted the chance to get an outside-the-boardroom look at all the balance holders, and, incidentally, to see how Brown Brothers' traditional, reticent style would work out when applied to the lavish sort of affair they planned.

ONE of the prospective guests, asked by a porter at Kennedy Airport, as he was preparing to board a plane for Seattle, if he was part of "the Brown Brothers' convention," was so outraged by the expression that he firmly said no, at the cost of having his luggage lost for a day or so. Guests arriving at Seattle–Tacoma International Airport on the celebration's opening day—a Sunday—

found two junior Brown Brothers men, one of them wearing on his lapel tag the reverberating name John J. McCloy II, posted there to greet them, round up their luggage, and steer them into limousines assigned to take them to the Olympic Hotel. Having myself arrived and been duly greeted and steered, I stood awhile looking at the bankers and industrialists and their wives, not yet identifiable, as they soon would be, by name tags. Old acquaintances were being renewed and new ones made. Was that, perhaps, the power behind the City of London meeting the power behind General Motors? Could that mysterious-looking lady be the wife of a gnome of Zurich? Everything seemed to be going smoothly. I learned later that there had been one snag at the airport, which had been swiftly and efficiently overcome. Brown Brothers had almost lost a guest to an interloper host. Dr. Wallenberg, who had dozens of business responsibilities, was chairman of the board of Scandinavian Airlines System, and the moment he and Mrs. Wallenberg alighted from their plane a group of local S.A.S. officials had tried to whisk them off to an S.A.S. affair—to borrow them from Brown Brothers for a time, so to speak. But Mr. McCloy had firmly refused the loan, and the Wallenbergs had gone with the Brown Brothers group to the Olympic.

The limousines were long, black, and carefully polished. "This car is so shiny it reminds me that *our* car is dirty, darling," an English lady sitting next to me said to her husband. (Later, I learned that she was Mrs. C. K. R. Nunneley, wife of the general manager of Robert Fleming & Co., Ltd., of London, a merchant bank with vast worldwide interests.) "We must remember to get it washed as soon as we get back." Her husband nodded in agreement. Mrs. Nunneley made the dirty car seem only a few blocks away and the momentary preoccupation of these particular balance holders engagingly down-to-earth. There were no snags visible at the hotel, where a platoon of Brown Brothers secretaries— assigned to do everything for everyone, decked out in white hats for easy identification, and immediately nicknamed the Brown Sisters—were efficiently checking people in and putting the proper tags on their luggage and their persons. I heard one of the Brown

Sisters telling Mrs. Wauters, wife of the Kredietbank man, that there would be an armored-car luggage pickup. The following evening, she explained, when it was time for the guests' luggage to be transferred from the hotel to the train that would take the party to Sun Valley, ordinary luggage would be picked up in the ordinary way and delivered to the guests' train compartments, but any items that were to be given special treatment would be picked up in the hotel rooms by armed guards, who would deliver them to the train in an armored car.

"How wonderful!" Mrs. Wauters exclaimed. "If only I had brought something worthy of being moved in the armored car!"

Cocktails and dinner that night, the first events of the celebration, were at the Eye of the Needle Restaurant, at the top of the Space Needle Tower, which was a survival of the 1962 Seattle Exposition and had become Seattle's chief landmark. Some six hundred feet in the air, balanced on narrow struts, and reached by an elevator that looks like a cable car, the restaurant is circular, with walls almost entirely of glass, and it revolves at a barely perceptible rate—one complete revolution per hour—thus affording the diner an almost decadently accessible three-hundred-and-sixty-degree view of Seattle, the dramatic mountains around it, and Puget Sound. I was told that the Union Pacific Railroad, which was host for the dinner, had scored a social coup by being the first organization ever to succeed in preempting the entire Eye of the Needle for a private occasion. The centerpiece of the canapé table was a huge locomotive of ice. A window-washer's cab that hung, apparently permanently, just outside the window had been decorated with a bank of flowers and a sign reading "WELCOME— UNION PACIFIC RAILROAD." It was a nice stroke of creative hostmanship, I thought, though less spectacular than the first notion the Brown Brothers and Union Pacific planners had had, which one of them told me about; that had been to seat E. Roland Harriman, who was chairman of the railroad's board of directors, out in the cab and have him sit there all through dinner, waving. (As it happened, E. Roland Harriman had to miss the whole celebration, because of a death in his family, and Averell Harriman,

whose presence had been doubtful all along, because of his responsibilities at the Paris peace talks on Vietnam, had to miss it,
too. All nineteen of the other Brown Brothers partners were on
hand, nearly all with their wives.)

The cocktail hour was deafening, the noise presumably representing the shattering of stereotypes about gnomes, devils, and
Babbitts. The few sentences audible to me, however, were not
particularly encouraging on that score.

Mrs. Johannes Nordal, wife of the governor of the Central
Bank of Iceland, said politely to one of the American wives that
the terrain around Seattle reminded her of Scandinavia.

W. G. Pullen, chairman of the Chartered Bank, the only British
bank to have a branch inside Communist China, told a Brown
Brothers man that his bank was having a bit of trouble there—
that one of its men had been accused by the Chinese government
of spying.

Lady Clegg, a lively lady with a mischievous expression, said
upon being asked why she had come, "When my husband told me
about the invitation, I asked, 'Who is Brown Brothers?' He replied, 'The most gentlemanly bankers in New York.' That made
me want to come. Besides, I love America. Before I was married,
my name was Jefferson—I am descended from Thomas Jefferson,
and, more directly, from Joe Jefferson, the actor who made the
American stage respectable. When I came to this country for the
first time, on a business trip with my husband in 1951, a most
unpleasant thing happened almost immediately. As we were riding
up in an elevator at the St. Moritz Hotel, in New York, a man
looked at us and said, 'What do these limeys think they're doing,
coming over here and crawling on their bellies to get some
money?' I was most upset. But I still love America."

Mrs. Alfred Hayes—whose husband, then president of the Federal Reserve Bank of New York and the key man in the recent
three-year battle to save the pound from devaluation, had made
the Brown Brothers invitation list because his was a central rather
than a commercial bank—said that she loved being there, for
when her husband and the other leading central bankers went to

their regular monthly meetings, in Basel, Switzerland, they left their wives behind, except once in a great while.

W. Graham Claytor, Jr., president of the Southern Railway System, explained himself to me, after we had been introduced, by saying, in a marked drawl, "I've just got this little railroad; we try to hold our own with the city slickers." I asked Mr. Claytor if he was meeting a lot of foreign bankers. "No, but I'm meeting a lot of domestic shippers," he replied, with a gleam in his eye.

Mr. Hentsch, the dean of Genevan private bankers, who proved to be a smallish man of seventy or so with a look of inscrutability that seemed appropriate to his station, expressed the gloomy view that the interchange between American industrialists and foreign bankers would be minimal. The Americans, he said, do things so big, and operate in such a big country relative to European countries, that they think they can borrow whatever they want whenever and wherever they want it, and therefore have little interest in meeting foreign bankers.

Dinner was king crab, filet mignon, and Beaulieu Vineyard Georges de Latour Private Reserve Cabernet Sauvignon '60, the first of seven California vintages that Brown Brothers had thought the foreign visitors might like to sample in the course of the celebration. Of this one, a booklet distributed to the guests said, "A wine of good color, very clear with brilliant finish. The nose is considerable, comparable to that found anywhere. This is a big wine with true Cabernet flavor and good body." I watched one of the Frenchmen—Jacques Merlin, president of the Credit Commercial de France—inhale the regional product and taste it, but his expression yielded no comment on its nose or flavor. One of the Brown Sisters, Miss Mary Bayone, told me that a computer had been engaged to help with the seating arrangements at the various meals during the affair but that the computer's suggestions had been unsatisfactory and that the job had finally had to be done by people. Looking around the restaurant, I saw apparently amiable table combinations such as Sir Cuthbert and Lady Clegg with William S. Beinecke, chairman of the board of Sperry & Hutchinson, and Mrs. Beinecke; Jacques Ferronière, president of the Société Générale, of Paris, and Mrs. Ferronière with Lang-bourne M. Williams, chairman of Freeport Sulphur, and Mrs. Williams; and Mr. and Mrs. Trippe with Sven Viig, managing director of the Christiania Bank Og Kreditkasse, of Oslo, and Mrs. Viig. It was nice to know that the computer hadn't matched them up.

Toward the end of dinner, I noticed that a small ledge between the windows and the windowside tables had suddenly become littered with place cards. It is the Space Needle's core, containing the tables, that revolves, while the ledge and the windows are stationary, so the cards were slowly going the rounds of the tables, and as they went they were attracting hilarious attention from the occupants of the tables. The foreign bankers, it turned out, were indulging an irresistible propensity to play games; this game consisted of sending each other messages via the ledge. The game had taken ingenuity to invent, and it took patience to play, since logistically an answer to a note could not be received for a full hour. But then, I thought, inventing and playing ingenious and patience-demanding games is what international bankers do. Evidently, they were feeling at home.

"High spirits for the first night, wouldn't you say?" a Belgian banker commented as everyone was preparing to plummet to earth through the dark in the cable-car elevator.

BACK in my room at the Olympic, I found that the following mimeographed message had been pushed under the door in my absence:

BROWN BROTHERS HARRIMAN GUESTS

May we take this opportunity to urge you to be in the Georgian Room for breakfast tomorrow morning by 7:30. The . . . program booklet, which we hope you have read carefully, indicates that buffet breakfast will be served from 6:45 to 8:00 A.M. in the Georgian Room. The important thing, however, is to be there by 7:30 because Mr. Malcolm T. Stamper, who is the Vice President in charge of the Boeing 747 program, is going to tell us about the genesis of the 747, for which he has a major responsibility. He will speak to us for about twenty minutes and with the benefit of this background, you will get even more enjoyment out of the tour of Boeing.

I had read the program booklet carefully, and knew that the next day was going to be Boeing Day from start almost to finish: a morning visit to the plant at Everett, twenty-eight miles north of Seattle, where the 747 superjet, the fastest and by far the largest airliner ever designed, at that time widely heralded but not yet ready to fly, was under construction; an afternoon visit to Renton, twelve miles *south* of Seattle, where the guests were to be introduced to the Boeing Space Division and its works; and dinner at the home of William M. Allen, Boeing's chief executive of many years' standing, and Mrs. Allen. Back in July, when I first heard about the plans for the celebration, I had wondered why a firm as much interested in a railroad as Brown Brothers is in the Union Pacific would devote a whole day of its sesquicentennial blowout to celebrating a competing form of transportation, and, having raised the question, I had been invited to lunch at 59 Wall with E. Roland Harriman and Lovett, two of the three Brown Brothers partners who were Union Pacific directors. I had found the two men to be the sort of old friends who enjoy being together so much that they put on what amounts to an involuntary running act—both of them just past seventy, Lovett a tall man with a long, greyhound face, and Harriman shorter, and crisp and twinkly.

"In the first place, Bill Allen and Boeing are *very* good and long-standing friends of Brown Brothers, and I think they deserve a lot of the credit for winning the Second World War," Mr. Lovett had said. "Why, I remember how, as Assistant Secretary of War for Air, I bought the B–29 from just a blueprint, in a lousy little greasy-spoon restaurant in Dayton, Ohio. In and out of government, I've been close to Bill and Boeing ever since those days."

"Bob Lovett always says Boeing won the war," Mr. Harriman had said, "but I say Boeing didn't win the war. Bob Lovett's ulcer did. Now, about competition between airlines and railroads. Soon after the war, a friend said to me, 'The airlines are going to take away ninety-five per cent of your passenger business.' I said, 'I wish they'd take away a hundred per cent of it.' As you know, it isn't profitable."

"We all love trains," Mr. Lovett had explained, "but we don't fight the future. Long-distance passenger travel by rail isn't the future, as we see it."

So the conclusion left with me was that in planning its outing Brown Brothers had not meant to emphasize—and certainly had not meant to do anything so crass as promote—either rail travel or air travel. The firm had aimed at a lofty impartiality.

Somewhat bleary-eyed, I made it to breakfast at seven-thirty. To my astonishment, the Georgian Room, a large one, was almost full. After all, both the program and the mimeographed message had made the point that breakfast would be available until eight o'clock; hadn't that been a broad hint that it would be at least acceptable conduct to slip in at the last minute, at the cost of missing the briefing? That had been the well-understood implication of similar communications to the guests at nearly all business parties I had ever attended before. But such was the devotion to Brown Brothers of its good and long-standing friends, if not their preoccupation with the Boeing 747, that apparently almost every one of them, ladies included, had dutifully fallen out for the reveille briefing. Mr. Stamper, the Boeing man, ran through a bewildering string of fiscal and physical statistics about the 747. The first production model, which we were to see later, was almost finished; in a few days it would be rolled out of the hangar where it was being assembled, and then it would be ground-tested for a couple of months, and, after that, test-flown. The plane's development had cost Boeing so many millions of dollars; its sale price would be so many millions each; sales to foreign airlines were expected to be so large as to have an instant, significantly favorable effect on the United States balance of international payments. ("I'm not remembering a thing," whispered Lady Clegg, at whose table I found myself.) As to payload, the plane would have a maximum capacity of four hundred and ninety passengers, most of them sitting ten abreast, but airlines were considered more likely to use an arrangement providing for a capacity of a mere three hundred and sixty, nine abreast, with two aisles. As to size, the 747 was twice as large as any airliner ever built before; just standing on the ground, it was both longer and higher than the first *flight* of the Wright Brothers at Kitty Hawk. ("That's my favorite statistic," said Lady Clegg.) It would fly at or near the speed of sound, and its jet engines would not leave trails of black smoke behind them, as other jet engines do. "Why not?" Lady Clegg demanded, sharply if rhetorically.

After Mr. Stamper had finished, someone at our table asked dreamily, "What did he say that aircraft costs?" Nothing but silence came from the several bankers present, and at last Sir Cuthbert said, "I didn't catch that figger," and I guessed it was, after all, pretty early in the morning to think about sums in the multibillions, even for them.

Buses took us to Everett, where we trooped into the hangar, a vast, cavernous room, its ceiling covered with steel beams and scaffolding illuminated by row upon row of lights, giving a sort of tracery effect. Everyone gasped. Rune Höglund, president of the Svenska Handelsbanken, of Stockholm, remarked that it reminded him of St. Peter's in Rome. In the middle stood the first 747—not yet a bird but, rather, a great aluminum-colored winged whale, swarmed over by men on ladders and scaffolds. The plane, the hangar, the assembly equipment, the very workers themselves conveyed an impression of almost antiseptic cleanliness, and this, along with the enormousness of everything, gave the scene a feeling of unreality.

As we walked, gaping, past the 747, I felt a hand on my shoulder, and turned to see a tall man with a lined face. He was Mr. Blough, chairman of United States Steel, whom I happened to have met once or twice before. "Let's have some fun," said Mr. Blough. He introduced a man walking with him as "my friend Jacques Merlin, of Paris," and went on, "Jacques, I want to ask you a question. What do you think the author of *Le Défi Américain* would say if he could see this?"

(I knew that *Le Défi Américain* was the French title of *The American Challenge*, the best-selling book by the French journal-

ist Jean-Jacques Servan-Schreiber, which extolls American production methods, among other things, and chides the French,
under de Gaulle's leadership, for being so backward in their approach to industrial progress.)

"He would say it proves him right," said Mr. Merlin.

Mr. Blough asked him how he felt himself.

"I have only one thing to say," said Mr. Merlin. "How can
anyone see this and still want one's country to remain small?"

Mr. Blough looked at Mr. Merlin and nodded with evident
satisfaction.

Most of the other foreigners in the Brown Brothers party had
even less to say than Mr. Merlin. They seemed to be struck dumb
with wonder, or incomprehension, or indifference. Those I asked
for their impressions mostly replied with polite, routine expressions of admiration. Later, at Renton, we were taken through a
mockup of the finished interior of a 747. (The interior work on
the real one hadn't been done yet.) It was a first, and startling,
glimpse of a scene later familiar to air travellers: the first-class
compartment with seats six abreast, two aisles, lots of legroom and
other free space, and a spiral staircase leading up to a small
lounge that would convert into sleeping quarters (but unlikely to
be converted very often, since it apparently accommodated only
two single beds); the tourist compartment with nine seats abreast,
divided by two aisles; a wide movie screen at the front; and considerably more legroom and headroom than current airliners. Indeed, the effect of the whole interior was of a small, well-appointed
art-film theatre.

Also at Renton, after a lunch of local salmon, George Stoner,
who was introduced as "Mr. Space at Boeing," gave the party a
slide-and-film presentation of the company's space activities. On
color film, rockets went up with an ear-splitting roar. On slides,
the practical, earthly applications of space exploration in such
fields as meteorology, medicine, and natural-resources development were demonstrated. At one point, Mr. Stoner put on the
screen a slide showing in radiant color a large pile of United States
bills and coins. At first, the point seemed to be that this was as

remarkable an American product as the interplanetary rocket, but as Mr. Stoner went on talking, with the money still resplendent on the screen, it gradually became clear that what he meant was that space exploration could pay off. When he had finished, most of the foreigners seemed to be as dumbfounded as they had been by the 747, but Mr. Merlin, continuing to be the perfect Boeing audience, expressed himself again—this time silently, by bringing the heel of his hand to his forehead in the familiar but still eloquent Gallic gesture of *bouleversement.*

Late that afternoon, as we were boarding buses at the Olympic to ride to the Allens', from which we were to go directly to the train, I spotted the promised armored car, into which, sure enough, armed guards were loading several innocent-looking pieces of hand luggage while several of the guests—the owners of the luggage, I supposed—looked on contentedly. In the bus, I landed next to Conrad Hentsch, who was looking unapproachable as well as inscrutable. He turned out to be neither, and amiably chatted about his life and ideas all the way to the Allens'. "I'm the seventh-generation Hentsch to head my firm, Hentsch & Compagnie," he said. "We Swiss are always thought of as the world's experts on foreign exchange. Perhaps we are, but we weren't the first. In the early nineteen-twenties, at the time of the German inflation, we learned it all from the Chileans. They had been through the whole thing. Having watched the world economic crises over the past fifty years, I can say this: Today everyone thinks everything will always go up, up, up. Everyone has forgotten 1929 and 1931, not to mention 1922. A day of reckoning will come. However, I am a pessimist by nature. Allow for that, please. My firm is conservative—perhaps too much. We hesitate to take chances with our clients' money. If you can tell them that your own son's money is invested in the same thing, you feel better, hmm? Not so much so in Zurich. Banking in Geneva is more conservative and less intense than in Zurich. There the general manager gets up and is driven to his bank in his car at seven-thirty in the morning. I don't mean that the general manager in Geneva has no car. He has a car, but he is driven to his bank at nine-thirty or ten-thirty. I, personally, am driven there at seven-thirty, but in Geneva that is exceptional."

By this time, we were at the Allens', an estate among great Northwestern evergreens in the highlands, on the northern outskirts of Seattle. There was a reception on the lawn, on which, here and there, log fires were blazing for warmth against the evening, for it was nippy. Earlier, there had been ominous black clouds and a splatter of rain, but now a dazzling late sun had broken through, set off by dramatic, racing clouds. On one corner of the lawn stood a replica of a Wright Brothers' biplane; our host averred that it was equipped with a more or less modern engine and would fly. Conversation around the lawn was spirited. J. A. H. Saunders, an ebullient Briton who is head of the Hongkong & Shanghai Banking Corporation, said that anyone interested in people ought logically to come to the Orient; there might not be more important people out there than anywhere else, he said, but there were more people. Mrs. Allard Jiskoot, wife of a partner in Pierson, Helding & Pierson, a leading Dutch private bank, said that in Amsterdam the hippies had got together and elected one of their number to the city council. "How organized of them," said Mr. Roosa, of Brown Brothers. The Belgian Mr. Wauters explained to me how anomalous all this amiable socializing among the European bankers was. At home and under normal circumstances, he said, the central bankers snub the commercial bankers as moneygrubbers and therefore avoid having anything to do with them, while the commercial bankers are usually at each other's throats as a result of business competition and therefore seldom have anything very pleasant to do with each other.

The climax of the reception was a "flyover" by an antique flying machine that looked a good deal like the Wright Brothers'—a replica of the B & W, the first airplane ever made by Boeing, in 1916. Playing in the stiff wind like a gull, the bizarre craft would hover, almost stationary, over the woods beyond the lawn, then peel off downward and sidewise, then climb and attack the wind again. Mr. Allen said that the pilot was Clayton Scott, a veteran Boeing test pilot, now in his sixties, who had taken Allen himself on his first flight, in 1929; he was at the controls of the B & W replica tonight because he was just about the only living pilot who both was competent to fly it and cared to. Everyone was squinting up into the sunset and saying what a charming contrast the B & W presented to the 747.

"Only the Americans do things like this!" exclaimed Mr. Saunders, surveying the whole scene. "What energy! What initiative!"

Dinner was in a huge orange-and-white striped tent, with a red-carpeted floor, that had been set up on the lawn; the meal was accompanied by music from a dance band and followed by entertainment provided by a group of local high-school students—"real kids," as the Boeing man who introduced them said. "We didn't import them from Chicago or anything." The boys and girls were all fresh-faced, white, wholesome-looking, well groomed, and constantly smiling; their act consisted of dances in the style of nineteen-twenties musical comedy and renditions of such songs as "The Simple Life" and "Buttons and Bows," and was climaxed by a song-and-dance interpretation of "The Battle Hymn of the Republic." The students seemed to exude sincerity, but at the same time it occurred to me that the only high-school students in my experience who resembled them were ones who had contrived to adopt unfamiliar attitudes in order to please older people. A British banker, asked for his reaction, hesitantly admitted that he had been faintly put in mind of the Russians, but the act seemed to make a great hit with most of the guests, foreign and American; someone said afterward that the real product of Seattle and Boeing wasn't the 747, it was kids like those.

THE group moved by bus to the Seattle Union Station shortly before midnight. The station was preternaturally clean, and seemed like no railroad station on earth. It was entirely empty of any irrelevant travellers and loiterers unacquainted with Brown Brothers. (I was somewhat relieved to learn later that they had not been banished, and regular train service suspended, to give us exclusive use of the station; rather, the place normally closes for

the night shortly after five-thirty, when the last train goes out.)
Now we proceeded on a ribbon of red carpet through the echoing,
weirdly gleaming concourse to an escalator leading down to the
waiting train. At the head of the escalator, the top officers of the
Union Pacific Railroad—its president, the chairman of its executive committee, its Northwestern general manager—and their
wives were deployed in a receiving line to greet the guests.

The train would depart shortly after midnight, its eight-hundred-and-sixty-mile route taking it first south to Portland; then east,
through the Columbia River Gorge, to Pendleton, Oregon; then
southeast, reversing the old route of the fur traders and homesteaders, through the Blue Mountains and along the Snake River, to
Boise, Idaho; on to Shoshone; and then north on a spur to
Ketchum, the station for Sun Valley, where it was scheduled to
arrive at ten o'clock the following evening. The train consisted of
two sections of twenty cars each; counting locomotives, glass-enclosed dome lounges (there were two on each section), dome
diners (one per section), and regular diners, the ratio of Brown
Brothers guests and their hosts to cars figured out to around five to
one. A doctor would be on each section, and I learned (accidentally—no one was supposed to know) that a small plane would
circle above the train all along the route, ready to swoop down in
case a heart attack should necessitate fast transport to a hospital.
Security guards would discreetly watch over us at crossings. All
railroad stations along the route had been freshly painted—even
the stations we would pass during the hours of darkness, a Union
Pacific man told me. (He added dryly that some of the stations
had been painted only on the three sides that would be visible
from the train.) One out-of-use station had been considered beyond visual reclamation, and the only possible course had been
followed. It had been razed.

Metal name plaques on the doors identified the guests' compartments. Inside, they found, along with their ordinary luggage and
their armored-car-pickup luggage, a booklet with color illustrations describing the route and entitled "From Your Train Window," which the Union Pacific had prepared for the occasion. I

resolved to read mine later; the last thing I was aware of that night was the gentle jolt as the train left Seattle.

We went through the famous Gorge ahead of schedule—around seven in the morning instead of seven-thirty, as announced in the program—and, accordingly, I, along with almost everybody else except trainmen and porters, missed it; for what consolation it could bring us, the porters said that, owing to the early hour and an overcast sky at the Gorge, it had been almost entirely dark there anyway. When I did get to breakfast, and subsequently to the dome lounges, we had left the Columbia River and were following the smaller Umatilla through prairies and farmlands, with brief showers intermittently spattering the cars' domes and brilliant sunlight illuminating them in the intervals.

Everyone in the lounges was very relaxed, revelling in the enforced idleness, which most of Brown Brothers' good and long-standing friends probably don't get very often. I spent the morning enjoying the classic, and perhaps soon to be extinct, train-ride privilege of striking up idle, expansive conversations with strangers.

Mr. Trippe, of Pan Am, had chosen a seat right in the front of a dome car, and was taking in the scenery with the enthusiasm of a novice traveller; as a matter of fact, he said, although he had crossed and recrossed this part of the country hundreds of times, he had never crossed it by train before.

Farther back in the same car was Hans J. Baer, of Julius Baer & Cie., a private bank of Zurich, who was about forty and who once attended Horace Mann School and subsequently took an M.A. at New York University. Mr. Baer was wearing a bright-blue turtleneck shirt and was sitting with Mrs. Baer, a dazzling blonde, who was wearing a bright-green turtleneck shirt. I reported to Mr. Baer what Mr. Hentsch had told me the previous evening about Zurich banking in contrast to Geneva banking. "Yes, we have to admit Geneva is more French and relaxed, in banking and in everything else," Mr. Baer said. "We're more stiff and German, even in our furniture styles."

Mrs. Baer, looking out, remarked that the Union Pacific's

sprucing up in preparation for our passage seemed to have extended beyond the stations; even the crossbars of the telegraph poles along the roadway had evidently been freshly touched up with orange paint. "Those shiny bars—isn't that funny?" she said, with a silvery laugh.

"Whaddya mean, funny?" said Mr. Baer, in impeccable Horace Mann School mock outrage.

"I've never seen the Swiss bankers like this before!" Frank Hoch, the Brown Brothers partner—of Swiss parents himself—who had the most dealings with them, remarked to me a bit later in the morning, with astonishment in his eyes. "So positively exuberant! And, you know, I doubt that I'll ever see them this way again, either."

In another dome lounge, another exuberant, ungnomelike Swiss banker—Alfred E. Sarasin, of Basel—told me that, in 1948, as a young man, he had spent six months at Brown Brothers as a trainee. He had enjoyed the stay, he said—even his constant arguments with the landlady of his sublet apartment, in the East Eighties, who had been something of a Nazi. "They were comic arguments, if you can believe it," he said. Mr. Sarasin went on to say that he was going to have to leave the Brown Brothers party early, so as to get back to Basel in time to preside at a meeting of the Swiss Bankers Association. The minute that was over, he intended to go with his family to his private game preserve, across the French border, and spend the weekend shooting partridge, pheasant, deer, and white boar.

J. Howard Rambin, Jr., originally of Stonewall, Louisiana, who was chairman of Texaco, Inc., and a director of Lincoln Center for the Performing Arts, sat by himself, staring contentedly out of the window. He did not seem to mind when I interrupted his reverie, though, and as Rieth, Pendleton, Cayuse, Gibbon, and a great deal of sagebrush shot by, he told me that in his opinion the United States must end the Vietnam war, cut down on Great Society programs, further reduce foreign aid, and continue to be wary of the Russians.

Nicolas M. Salgo, a native of Hungary, who was chairman of

the Bangor Punta Corporation, of New York City, which consisted of a railroad and concerns that manufactured lifesaving flares, boats, jewelry, and firearms, among other things, told me that his company was always being tagged with the fashionable term "conglomerate" but that he objected to the designation, on the ground that it connoted a misleading vulgarization of the specialized art he practiced—that of assembling and managing such a company. If Tex Thornton wants to let his Litton Industries be called a conglomerate, said Mr. Salgo, that was all right with him (Mr. Thornton, being on the train but out of hearing, couldn't testify whether he did or didn't), but, for his part, he wasn't going to have people calling Bangor Punta that if he could avoid it. I asked Mr. Salgo what railroads, jewelry, boats, and so on have to do with each other. "Nothing," he said. "Except that we hope that they all prove to be profitable. When Bangor Punta takes over a company, the head of the company says to me, 'What do you want me to do tomorrow?' I say, 'What did you do yesterday? If it worked, go on doing it.' If it doesn't work, of course, he's out."

Dr. Wallenberg, the financially and industrially mighty Swede, a tall, handsome man of around seventy, with chiselled features and silver hair, said that he had just seen one of the other guests—Charles S. Garland, of Alex Brown & Sons, Brown Brothers' banking cousins in Baltimore—for almost the first time since they encountered each other in an early round of the 1920 English Championships, at Wimbledon, when both men had been internationally ranked players. Who won? I asked. "I don't remember," said Dr. Wallenberg. "Everybody here says that means he won, but I think it's the other way around. I think the matches you lose are the ones you remember. Tennis is like banking in one respect: You have to have a good, hard drive and a good, soft lob. Remember that—hard drive and soft lob."

At about noon, the train stopped at La Grande, a small town in eastern Oregon, southwest of Troy, Promise, and Paradise and a bit northwest of Halfway and Cornucopia. The main purpose of the stop, apparently, was to have the outside of the glass of the dome cars hosed down and scrubbed, and during the five or ten minutes that this operation took many of the guests got off. They saw the huge prairie sky stretching to bare hills, and, since the sun was out strongly now, got a whiff of furnacelike intermountain heat. In front of the incongruously gleaming clapboard station, a few rail-road men eyed them with faint curiosity. Unseen and unheard, somewhere overhead, the heart-attack plane presumably circled.

Back aboard, I had lunch with Frank E. Barnett, the Union Pacific's chief executive officer, Mrs. Barnett, and J. O. Blair–Cunynghame, chairman of the Royal Bank of Scotland. Mr. Blair–Cunynghame said that he was one member of the party—and, apparently, except for Union Pacific people, one of the few members—who had travelled this route by train before. It had been twenty years ago, he said, when he was a junior member of a British Overseas Airways Corporation purchasing team that came to Seattle to buy Boeings. "We weren't satisfied with the price, so we decided to go away for a little while," said Mr. Blair–Cunyng-hame. "A nice, leisurely train trip to the Midwest and back seemed appropriate. Several days later, when we got back to Seat-tle, it was all right."

Mr. Barnett said he had been doing some scratching in the company archives, and had figured out that the foreign banks represented on the train—and, in many cases, the previous gener-ations of the families represented on the train—had at the turn of the century raised a hundred and seventy-five million dollars to finance an expansion of the Union Pacific, including the laying of part of the roadway we were travelling. "Last night, I inspected this train before you got aboard," Mr. Barnett said, "and after-ward my wife and I turned to each other with tears in our eyes, and I said to her, 'This is the last great train.' "

On my way back to my compartment for a rest after lunch, I encountered Mr. Garland, who said, "I don't remember how that match came out, either. Wonderful fellow, Wallenberg, isn't he?"

Outside my compartment were more parched fields, sparsely cultivated, and here and there a farmhouse and a battered car, miles from any other sign of habitation. On a barn I saw a sign: "DR. PIERCE'S GOLDEN TONIC A MEDICAL DISCOVERY." The 747 suddenly seemed remote and unreal, and even the train itself a bit ahead of its time. Indeed, everything about the trip suddenly seemed unreal. It struck me that in its sesquicentennial program Brown Brothers was—unconsciously, as far as I knew—showing its foreign guests the surviving American past and the emerging American future to the exclusion of a more immediate and perhaps painful subject, the American present. And the guests appeared to be avoiding that subject, too, presumably out of tact. The manners so prized by Brown Brothers as an institution and so well exemplified in its partners and guests were getting in the way of reality. Later that afternoon, in one of the lounges again, I did hear one Scandinavian banker speaking, with a kind of sympathetic regret, of "your unfortunate war," and saying that in his observation, rightly or wrongly, anti-American sentiment in his country seemed to have waned since the Russian invasion of Czechoslovakia. The banker's American listeners were noncommittal. Otherwise, for all the talk I heard, the nation a part of which we were crossing might have been a strange combination of, on the one hand, space vehicles and superjets and lavish restaurants revolving in the sky and, on the other, lonely farmers nursing themselves with patent medicines—and nothing in between.

We reached Boise at about five-thirty, and stopped to take aboard several late-arriving guests, among them William McChesney Martin, Jr., chairman of the Federal Reserve Board, who was to be the speaker at the formal dinner at Sun Valley. Many of the passengers climbed off for another stretch. One of these was Lady Clegg, who said to someone on the platform that she understood that this was Bwahz and was informed that, on the contrary, it was Boysey. Boise seemed to take our passage in stride, except that, I was told, a local funeral had had to be postponed an hour so that the only available limousine could be used to bring the dignitaries who were joining the Brown Brothers party from the airport to the train.

At dinner, and after it, in the last hours of the train ride, the guests made themselves at home in various ways, according to their tastes. The heads of Celanese and Union Carbide played a joking, or possibly not so joking, game of pretending to trade off their unprofitable subsidiaries. Jean Frère, of the Banque Lambert, in Brussels, and Mrs. Frère played a card game called Crazy Bridge (games, again) with Fritz Schoeller, of Schoeller & Co., Vienna, and Mrs. Schoeller. George A. Stinson, president of National Steel, got permission to go up to the cab of the first locomotive, and there he put on an engineer's cap and held the controls for a while. ("Did you notice that time when the train went faster?" he asked friends afterward.) The representatives of General Motors, United States Steel, the Federal Reserve Board, and the Federal Reserve Bank of New York got off in a corner and had a long, earnest conversation. Later, I asked Mr. Hayes, the Federal Reserve Bank man, what it had been about. "Oh, the national economy—things like that," he said offhandedly.

At Ketchum, the guests left the train and boarded buses for the short ride to Sun Valley. "Goodbye, train!" Mrs. Nunneley called, blowing it a kiss from her bus window.

NEXT morning—Wednesday—in Sun Valley, the hosts and guests "got down to work," as a Brown Brothers partner put it. The work consisted of engaging in a morning's symposium on the problems attendant upon the world shortage of capital. It was a chilly, changeable morning, Sun Valley's enclosing mountains alternately basking in brilliant sunshine and assuming a forbidding gray cast. Sir Cuthbert Clegg said that he had been torn between dressing for London and dressing for Barbados; he had decided, correctly, on London tweeds. The crowd that gathered for the symposium—at the Sun Valley Opera House, a timber-and-stucco auditorium used more often for movies, religious services, and symposia than for opera—appeared to include the Brown Brothers partners and their male guests to a man, and I counted more than fifty dutiful wives, too.

During the symposium, which went on from nine-thirty until twelve, with a half-hour coffee break in the middle, the participants freely bandied terms like "gross-capital formation," "new capital flow," "Eurocurrency market," and "propensity to save," which describe the various aspects of the game of Crazy Bridge that the international bankers and businessmen of the rich countries incessantly play with one another. Dr. Wallenberg asserted—presumably not just out of courtesy—that, in spite of all its troubles, the dollar was still the world's soundest currency. The group manfully tackled what no one denied was the greatest capital shortage of all—that felt by the poor countries. "With eighty per cent of the world's people attempting to exist on twenty per cent of the world's product, it is in everyone's self-interest to act, in order to avert an explosion that could destroy much of the productive wealth that has been built over these two remarkable postwar decades," Mr. Roosa said bluntly. Mr. Roosa's proposal for action was to replace unilateral foreign-aid programs with an arrangement under which the developed countries, acting in concert, would keep funds constantly flowing to the underdeveloped countries, the amount supplied by each developed country in any given year to be determined in part by the current position of its balance of international payments. Dr. Otmar Emminger, a director of the Deutsche Bundesbank, the central bank of West Germany—a country with a large balance-of-payments surplus just then, in contrast to the United States' large deficit—couldn't find himself in agreement with that criterion; he suggested that the amount of the payments by each rich country should be tied instead to its gross national product, in which respect, of course, the United States vastly exceeded West Germany in all years.

The symposium didn't resolve this easily understandable controversy, or any other, but it did raise a lot of pertinent questions, and undoubtedly set a lot of influential people thinking about them. The following morning, Thursday, the group went back into session for another two-hour stint, making a total of four hours' formal deliberations during the four days' program—bankers' hours, I supposed.

Wednesday afternoon was recreation and sports time, with a choice of golf, tennis, skeet, fly-fishing, horse-back riding, swimming, or riding the chair lift up Mount Baldy, Sun Valley's highest peak. A hard-core big-business group, including the Allens, the Connors, and the Trippes, chose golf. The Baers, Mr. Pullen, and Sir Cuthbert chose skeet, the Schoellers and Mr. Salgo chose riding, while Mr. Blair–Cunynghame, Mr. Blough, Dr. Emminger, Mr. Hentsch, and the Paleys were among the fly-fishing enthusiasts. I joined the largest contingent, the Baldy expedition, which proceeded to the base of the mountain in two buses and then, two guests at a time, mounted the moving double chairs, with the help of some coaching from the lift operators. The chairs on the Baldy lift ride some twenty feet above the ground and sway considerably in a brisk breeze, which we had then, and since they are without protective crossbars, the twenty-minute lift ride provides a stimulating experience. But our adventure was to be one that outdistanced even Brown Brothers' thoughtful planning.

From the peak—ninety-two hundred feet above sea level, and bare not only of trees, as its name suggests, but of everything else as well—the prospect was dramatic, even daunting. Several large thunderstorms had suddenly formed, and the deep-blue-green lower mountains surrounding Baldy were obscured here and there by dense black clouds, out of which lightning now and again streaked down into the valley. Just as the couple of dozen of us at the summit—Europeans except for Mrs. Lovett, Mr. and Mrs. Hayes, and me—were deciding that we had better cut short our sightseeing and climb into downward-bound chairs before we got drenched, the lift stopped working. The operator at the summit learned by telephone from the bottom that the storms had knocked out electric power all over Sun Valley, and no one could say when it would be restored. So there we were, on top of Baldy, without shelter, and with a few stray drops of rain beginning to fall, taking consolation in the thought that we were better off than a handful of unfortunate guests who had been caught en route when the power failed, and were now stranded in midair in their chairs.

Mrs. Lovett, who is a vintage Brown—the daughter of James Brown, who was a partner in the firm from 1901 until 1934—told Mrs. Hayes a motto that she said she had learned many years ago from the mother of a friend of hers and liked to remember in moments like this: "Never reflect difficulties." Mrs. Hayes smiled, and so did several of us other summit strandees. Meanwhile, the rain held off, and within a few minutes, after several unsuccessful attempts, the lift operators got a standby diesel generator going, and the lift started moving again. All the way down Baldy, while the wind kept the chairs swinging and the lightning continued to flash, Mrs. Lovett talked equably about old New York.

Back at Sun Valley, later in the afternoon, with the threat of rain past, I learned that the golfing party had been soaked by a sudden shower. "It didn't matter, though, because the rain ended quickly and the wind soon dried us off," said Mrs. Connor. I went to the tennis courts, hoping to see a return match between Dr. Wallenberg and Mr. Garland, and saw, instead, a set of doubles in which Dr. Wallenberg and Mr. Martin stood two Europeans whom I couldn't identify. Mr. Martin, who was renowned for his tennis ability in Washington government circles, showed a strong service, and Dr. Wallenberg made up in guile what he lacked in speed; when I left, their team was leading, 5–4, with Mr. Martin's service coming up.

At the banquet that evening at the Lodge, where most of the guests were staying, Mr. Martin spoke, as he had often spoken before, of the dangers of overspeculation in the stock market, and made specific pejorative references to the activities of overaggressive mutual funds, banks that set up holding companies to enable them to venture into nonbanking businesses, and conglomerates. After his speech, there was dancing on the Lodge Terrace and entertainment by a singing group from the University of Utah. Again, as in Seattle, the young performers were all fresh-faced, white, wholesome looking, well groomed, and constantly smiling; after they had finished, someone remarked that young people like those are the answer to hippies.

AT Thursday lunch, the last meal of the celebration, I sat with a mixed group of Americans and Europeans on the Terrace. Before it was over, a telegram was brought to one of the Americans. His private plane, the telegram informed him, was on its way to pick him up at the little airport at Ketchum; weather conditions were reported as favorable over the Midwest and East for his flight home. I had a vision of dozens of company planes converging on Ketchum to retrieve chief executives and their wives. Most of the European bankers, lacking such facilities, were planning to take an overnight train to Salt Lake City, and there to board regular airline flights the next morning.

At our table, the Amsterdamer Mr. Jiskoot remarked that he could do business with Americans because, unlike many European bankers, he wasn't afraid of them. Mr. Salgo, of Bangor Punta, reported triumphantly that after Mr. Martin's remarks the previous evening he had confronted the Federal Reserve chairman, challenged him on the word "conglomerate," and got him to admit that he shouldn't have used it.

Our group fell into a philosophical mood about the Brown Brothers celebration itself. Someone said again that only Americans do this kind of thing, and someone else asked: Why do they do it? What is accomplished? Well, Mr. Jiskoot said, to take one example, he had met Conrad Hentsch in person for the first time there, after doing business with him by mail and telephone for some years. Mr. Salgo said he had been especially pleased to "establish a dialogue" with the leading Japanese bankers, because his firm might be wanting a Japanese "partner" soon. And then, others pointed out, there were all the incidental conversations that had taken place, part social and part business, lubricated by relaxed conditions such as so seldom obtained at regular bankers' or businessmen's meetings. Who knew what had been accomplished by them—what implications they might have for future world monetary cooperation, investment in underdeveloped countries, and the like? The really astonishing thing, they all agreed, was that everyone who was there *was* there. What on earth had induced all these busy people to take time off from carrying the world's commerce on their shoulders? Obviously, respect, admiration, and affection for Brown Brothers. But which was the real point—establishing dialogues or contributing to the greater glory of Brown Brothers? Both. Paradoxically, the event had been one devoted to the furtherance of commerce at which no faintly commercial note had been struck, unless you considered the 747 presentation a sales pitch, and one of the Europeans remarked that maybe part of the American business genius was a knack for somehow managing to have things both ways.

As for the hosts, whatever intellectual or professional benefits the celebration had conferred upon their guests, socially it had been a triumph. A week or so later, back in Wall Street, they would be enjoying the successful party-giver's time-honored satisfaction of having his party earnestly discussed by those who had not been there. Indeed, David Rockefeller himself—a good and long-standing friend of Brown Brothers whom its partners would surely have leaped to invite but for their blanket ban on domestic commercial bankers—would be heard to complain mildly that for three lunches in succession he had listened to nothing but talk about the Brown Brothers party, and to ask whether there wasn't some other topic of conversation.

After lunch, Juan O. Monasterio, director of the Banco Commercial Mexicano, S.A.—a portly man who looked like Santa Claus with a clipped mustache instead of a beard—made a funny speech of thanks to the hosts on behalf of the guests. He said that he had been made to feel so much at home that he expected to be named a Brown Brothers partner shortly, and therefore felt qualified to invite everyone present to the firm's two-hundredth-anniversary celebration. Of course, he added, it wasn't surprising that the party had been a success, since any party is a success if you invite people for a free four days. Mr. Monasterio sat down amid loud laughter and applause, and was followed by Mr. Hentsch, who made a more traditional speech of gratitude. Mr. Hentsch thanked the Brown Brothers partners, their staff, Mr. and Mrs. Allen, and the Union Pacific Railroad, complimented the wives on their charm, and complimented the partners on their distinction, intelligence, and ability. Then he said, "And now, ladies and gentlemen, I will please ask you to stand." After just a second's confusion, everyone did, whereupon Mr. Hentsch asked for a moment of special thought for Americans fighting in Vietnam, and went on to say, "May I ask the partners of Brown Brothers Harriman & Company to extend our best regards to their partner, Mr. Ambassador Averell Harriman. As you all know, he is in charge of a very difficult and important negotiation concerning the United States. Please sit down."

It was a breathtakingly high-handed gesture, asking the group to stand without telling them why in advance, especially when the purpose was controversial; but old-fashioned European bankers are high-handed, just as cats are independent, and if anybody could have brought it off, it was Mr. Hentsch, and it seemed to me he did. After everyone was seated again, Moreau Delano Brown rose and said, "I am not going to say 'Goodbye' but only 'Au revoir,' and the Brown Brothers sesquicentennial symposium is now adjourned."

Confrontation

I

SPRING OF 1969—a time that now seems in some ways part of another, and a more romantic, era—was in the business world a time of Davids and Goliaths, of threatened takeovers of venerable Pan American World Airways by upstart Resorts International, for example, and of venerable Goodrich Tire and Rubber by upstart Northwest Industries. Such brazen challenges to the long-established and mighty by the newly arrived and aggressive were made possible by a vast, if temporary, popularity in the stock market of the shares of young and fast-growing companies; whether such threatened takeovers represent, on the one hand, constructive efforts to bring legitimacy to vested power, or, on the other, irresponsible acts of unprovoked assault by ravenous treasury raiders, is still being debated a decade later. Undoubtedly, though, the David-and-Goliath act of early 1969 that most caught the popular imagination was an attempt upon the century-and-a-half-old Chemical Bank New York Trust Company (assets a grand nine billion dollars) by the eight-year-old Leasco Data Processing Equipment Corporation of Great Neck, Long Island (assets a mere four hundred million dollars), a company entirely unknown to almost everyone in the larger business community without a special interest in either computer leasing, Leasco's principal business until 1968, or in the securities market, in which its stock was a star performer. In that takeover contest, the roles of Goliath and David were played, with exceptional spirit, by William Shryock Renchard of the Chemical and Saul Phillip Steinberg of Leasco. It would be excessive to call their short, intense confrontation the stuff of classic tragedy. But enough of the famous Aristotelian elements of tragedy were there, along with certain elements of farce, to show that Wall Street could still fill its old role of stage and proscenium for interesting and moving human drama: not just life, but something rather larger than life.

II

WILLIAM RENCHARD, the leader of Chemical, grew up in Trenton, New Jersey, where his father served as an agency manager for the New York Life Insurance Company. Trenton in the nineteen-twenties, when Renchard was in his teens, was a characteristic old city of the Eastern Seaboard, already dominated in numbers by recent immigrants and light industry, yet in power and influence still controlled by an American squirearchy looking backward with nostalgia and pride to a historic past (Washington's crossing of the Delaware; the rout of the Hessians at the Battle of Trenton; the march to Princeton). The city's backward-looking aspect manifested itself in monuments and museums and stately old brick row houses; its forward-looking aspect, in brisk new plants and skyscrapers and freeways. It was a John O'Hara town, its privileged given to the starchy celebrations of country-club life. Above all, perhaps, its quality was provinciality: Trenton was constantly derided for the huge sign on the Delaware River bridge, TRENTON MAKES THE WORLD TAKES—but with stubborn pride it kept the sign in place year after year. Chief among the things it made and the world took were fine china and rubber contraceptives. Even on West State Street, where stood the town houses of the well-to-do and long-established, as well as on Gouverneur Avenue where the Renchards lived in more modest respectability, milk was still delivered every morning by a horse-drawn wagon. After graduating from Trenton High School, Bill Renchard, like most reasonably well-off Trenton boys, aspired to go to Princeton, the famous university lying on the Jersey horizon twelve miles to the northeast; unlike many high-school boys in the days when Princeton still leaned strongly toward preparatory-school graduates, he made it. At Princeton he shared a room on campus with his brother John, quietly did his academic work, joined one of the many eating clubs, and took no part in the extracurricular activities—athletics, the *Daily Princetonian*, the Triangle Club, the humor magazine *The Tiger*—that were the recognized pathways to standing on campus. In his senior classbook it was recorded that "Renchard is undecided as to his future occupation."

Perhaps the Renchard brothers felt somewhat disadvantaged at Princeton and consequently withdrew into themselves. Indeed, they *were* disadvantaged, in spite of being presentable and Protestant, first by their high-school background and secondly by the fact that they came from nearby Trenton, which in those days was generally regarded by Princeton students as a town good chiefly for getting drunk in. At any rate, by all accounts Renchard at

Princeton was the sort of self-contained student whose peers, if they thought about it at all, probably considered him unlikely to amount to much, then or in the future.

If they so thought, they were wrong. However self-contained, Renchard was a tall, alert young man with an emergent air of command, and he was among those late bloomers who in adult life humbled the social winnowers of their undergraduate classes. After graduation in 1928, he went to New York City and landed a job as clerk with the National Bank of Commerce. In 1930, he moved to the Chemical Bank and Trust Company, as it was then called, where he served successively as a clerk, an assistant secretary, and an assistant vice-president. By 1946, when he was thirty-eight, he was a full-fledged vice-president; in 1955 he became executive vice-president; in 1960 he was made president, and in 1966 chairman of the board of the same institution, which was by this time called the Chemical Bank New York Trust Company. Name changes resulting from mergers did not alter the institution's prestige or venerability; founded in 1824, it had been a national banking leader by the time of the Civil War (and in the years soon after, it was Hetty Green's bank, where she had a room assigned for her private use in which she liked to sprawl on the floor surrounded by her mortgages and certificates; later she moved on after she became convinced, erroneously, that someone at the Chemical was attempting to poison her). In 1966, when Renchard became Chemical's chairman, the bank had nine billion dollars in assets—one of the nation's largest capital pools—and was the nation's sixth largest commercial bank.

Renchard's rise to this pinnacle of American banking had been accompanied by marriage to a pretty and sociable woman; a move to New York banking's favorite living quarters, the north shore of Long Island; directorships in half a dozen large corporations; trusteeships of various hospitals and civic groups; and membership in a substantial list of metropolitan and country clubs, including the famous Creek Club in Locust Valley, of which he became president. In 1969, at sixty-one, Renchard was a large, handsome, well-set-up man with iron-gray hair, regular features, and candid eyes that suggested both flinty authority and a certain fatherly capacity for kindness. He carried with him a whiff of the outdoors —the scrubbed outdoors of well-kept lawns and clipped privet; he laughed easily and naturally and he had a penchant for brief, rather intimidating jokes. He seemed entirely at peace with himself—not in the least apologetic about enjoying, and joshing complacently about, his wealth and success at a time of violent social change. Once, he not only appeared with his wife at an epitome of the ancien régime, the annual Diamond Ball for a well-chosen four hundred at the Plaza Hotel (a benefit, of course—for the Institute for International Education), but, according to *The New York Times*, won "the honors in the glitter competition" by wearing as shirt studs three diamond stickpins as big as quarters— all of them obviously fake. A rather heavy joke, perhaps? But if anyone could carry it off, Bill Renchard could. He seemed to have become the prototypical old-style Princetonian, radiating the essence of gentlemanly aggressiveness, of polite personal and professional leverage.

Saul Phillip Steinberg, no relation to the celebrated Roumanian-born American artist Saul Steinberg, came from a background similar to Renchard's in only one respect—the families of both were firmly entrenched members of the American petit bourgeoisie. To begin with, Steinberg was a full generation Renchard's junior. Born in Brooklyn in August, 1939, the son of Julius Steinberg, proprietor of Ideal Rubber Products, a small-scale manufacturer of such objects as kitchen dishracks, Steinberg, at high school in Lawrence, Long Island, was an unexceptional boy—an average student, an enthusiastic dater of girls, a competent but less than dedicated athlete—who was set apart from his classmates chiefly by the fact that he was a precocious subscriber to and regular reader of the *Wall Street Journal*. After high school, he went to the Wharton School of Finance and Commerce at the University of Pennsylvania. At Wharton—a senior at nineteen, precocious, brash, with a round babyface—Steinberg experienced a species of commercial epiphany. One of his instructors suggested that he write his senior thesis on "The Decline and Fall of I.B.M."

—about as maverick an idea as might be imagined, because, by 1959, I.B.M. had already become the corporate Apollo of the modern business pantheon, generally regarded by friend and competitor alike as an organizational masterpiece. "My instructor was sure I.B.M. was some kind of fandangle," Steinberg told a journalist a decade and many millions of dollars later. "And he wanted me to go out and prove it. I was the kind of student who was prepared to believe anything was bad, so I accepted the assignment. After I had gotten into it and done a lot of research, I discovered that . . . I.B.M. was an incredible, fantastic, brilliantly conceived company with a very rosy future. But when I told him this, he wouldn't believe me. He wouldn't even look at my research. So I ended up having to write on another subject."

Steinberg's scorned and discarded research left him with the conviction that I.B.M.'s method of doing business allowed a shining opportunity for a bright, ambitious young man to make a lot of money, and that he was the young man. The basic question involved was the effective life of industrial computers before they became obsolete, and the opportunity lay somewhere in the fact that nobody precisely knew the answer. I.B.M., which dominated the computer-making business, took the sort of conservative view that is characteristic of giant corporations riding the crest of a wave. Assuming that any given computer would become obsolete sooner rather than later, it offered its customers short-term leases, usually cancellable on short notice, for high rental rates. Steinberg proposed to offer computer-using corporations the opportunity to save money by gambling that I.B.M.'s equipment would have a longer useful life than I.B.M. itself appeared to assume. He would borrow money and buy I.B.M.'s immensely expensive computers outright; he would then lease them out—long-term and uncancellable—at rates that would be substantially below I.B.M.'s own rental charges, but still high enough so that he would recover most or all of the cost of the computer during the longer, uncancellable term of its initial lease. Thus, in the simplest terms, Steinberg would have got his purchase money back and still have the purchased computer itself left over to sell or lease again.

As simple as that, and as ingenious. With his bright idea conceived at Wharton, Steinberg gave birth to a new industry, independent computer leasing—an industry that produced no product; one that I.B.M. could kill at its pleasure by changing its leasing policies; one that the leading investment analyst John Westergaard would later dismiss as mostly "an accounting gimmick"; and one of which its founder himself, Saul Steinberg, would later say only half-jokingly, "Computer leasing? It's just a way of getting free computers"—yet still an industry that, before the end of the decade, would shake American finance and banking to its foundations.

After graduating from Wharton in 1959, Steinberg spent a couple of years working for his father; meanwhile, he put in further study on the computer-leasing idea, and conducted a small side business in streetcorner newsstands. Then in 1961, with twenty-five thousand dollars supplied by his father, he started his computer-leasing business in a Brooklyn loft, with his father and his uncle as nominal partners, and his company name—Ideal Leasing Company—cribbed from his father's rubber-goods business. Banks, however wary of his extreme youth and his too-bright-schoolboy manner, liked his scheme and were willing to advance him money to buy computers provided he had leasing customers for them. Finding the customers was another matter. It took him three months to get his first lease; he interrupted his honeymoon to come home and sign it. Ideal Leasing was incorporated in 1962; at the end of its first corporate year it had net income of fifty-five thousand dollars on revenues of one million eight hundred thousand dollars. In 1964, when earnings were up to two hundred fifty-five thousand dollars and revenues to eight million dollars, Steinberg decided to go public. In June, 1965, the company's name was changed to Leasco Data Processing Equipment Corporation and a public sale of Leasco stock brought in seven hundred and fifty thousand dollars.

The computer business was booming, I.B.M. continued charging high rates for cancellable leases, and Leasco's assets leaped from eight million dollars in 1965 to twenty-one million dollars in

1966, while profits in 1967 were more than eight times those for 1966. Meanwhile, the stock, traded first over the counter and later on the Amex, soared upward. Leasco began to be talked about in Wall Street as one of those interesting little situations. As might be expected of a young company with ambition, a voracious need for cash, and a high price-to-earnings multiple, Leasco became acquisition-minded. In 1966, Steinberg hired Michael A. Gibbs, a young whiz from the management-consulting firm of Booz, Allen and Hamilton, as vice-president for corporate planning, and gave him the specific assignment of hunting up candidates for merger. In 1966 and 1967, Leasco increased its corporate muscle by buying several small companies in fields more or less related to computers or to leasing: Carter Auto Transport and Service Corporation; Documentation, Inc.; and Fox Computer Services. These acquisitions left the company with seventy-four million dollars in assets, more than eight hundred employees, larger new headquarters in Great Neck, Long Island, and a vast appetite for further growth through mergers.

The events leading to the merger that put Leasco firmly on the national corporate map, and that made the Goliaths of industry begin to take notice of a Brooklyn David with an air of supreme confidence, began in August, 1967, when Edward Netter, of the deal-making brokerage firm of Carter, Berlind and Weill, came out with a report entitled "Financial Services Holding Company," in which he set forth the rosy possibilities available to both sides in mergers between companies engaged in financial services, such as Leasco, and fire-and-casualty insurance companies. The nub of Netter's argument was that the ultraconservative financial policies of fire-and-casualty companies had in many cases resulted in cash-heavy reserves far in excess of those required by law to cover policy risks. To these excess reserves, Netter gave the picturesque names "redundant capital" or "surplus surplus." State regulations restricted the free use of such reserves so long as they belonged to a fire-and-casualty company; but, Netter pointed out, the regulations could be circumvented, and the redundant capital freed for other uses, if the insurance company were to merge with an unregulated holding company. By implication Netter was pointing out—in the hope of earning finder's fees and brokerage commissions for his own firm—that ambitious diversified companies were missing a chance to better their circumstances by marrying fire-and-casualty companies for their redundant capital—or, more bluntly, for their money. Many diversified companies were to acquire insurance companies over the following years, the greatest such merger (and indeed, the greatest merger in corporate history up to then) being the celebrated and controversial wedding between International Telephone and Telegraph and Hartford Fire in 1970.

One of the numerous desks the Netter report crossed, not by chance, was in the offices of Leasco, and near the end of 1967, Netter met with Gibbs to discuss the views expressed in it. Netter evidently got an enthusiastic reception, because, early in January, 1968, Gibbs sent a memo to Steinberg setting forth in detail the considerable advantages to Leasco of acquiring a fire-and-casualty company—no specific company was mentioned—and the same day Arthur Carter of Carter, Berlind and Weill wrote to Leasco setting forth the brokerage firm's terms for handling the acquisition of such a company (still not named) through a tender offer to the insurance company's stockholders. The terms stated included a finder's fee to Carter, Berlind of seven hundred and fifty thousand dollars, making abundantly clear why Carter, Berlind was going to so much trouble to serve as marriage broker.

It subsequently became clear that the unnamed firm Carter, Berlind had in mind was Reliance Insurance Company, a staid old Philadelphia-based fire-and-casualty underwriter with more than five thousand employees, almost three hundred and fifty million dollars in annual revenues, and a fund of more than one hundred million dollars in redundant capital. At the time, though, there was an urgent need for secrecy, to avoid disturbing Reliance's stock price and thereby stimulating its management to take defensive measures. To preserve this secrecy—and, just possibly, to enjoy some of the fun of cloak-and-dagger proceedings—Leasco men in their interoffice correspondence began referring to Reliance under the code name "Raquel." (The code name, Steinberg later told a Congressional committee, had been borrowed from the actress Raquel Welch.)

In March, 1968, preserving security by trading through a numbered bank account at the First National Bank of Jersey City, Leasco began buying Reliance stock on the open market in daily quantities of anywhere from one hundred to more than seven thousand shares. By early April, Leasco held 132,600 Reliance shares, or about three per cent of all shares outstanding, and had completed Phase One of the takeover. Phase Two consisted of preparing a tender offer to Reliance shareholders, and contriving to overcome any resistance that the Reliance management might mount. In May, Leasco prepared a registration statement for its tender offer—a move that brought matters out into the open: since the statement was necessarily a public document, the public, and Reliance management, now knew at last what Leasco had in mind. Reliance's first action was to announce that the company was engaged in merger talks with another computer-leasing firm, Data Processing Financial and General—this presumably to let Leasco know that it had competition, and thus induce it either to desist from its takeover attempt or to make a better offer. On June 13th, Steinberg and A. Addison Roberts, president of Reliance, met for the first time, and Roberts stated in the clearest possible terms that Reliance would be unreceptive to a Leasco takeover attempt. Nevertheless, on June 21st Leasco went ahead with its tender offer, writing Reliance stockholders and offering them Leasco convertible debentures and warrants—a classic bundle of those often dubious securities that were sometimes derogated as "corporate underwear," but still a bundle that, because of the high price of all Leasco securities, had a current market value well above the current price per share of unswinging Reliance—in exchange for their Reliance stock. Three days later, Roberts, still defiant, wrote to Reliance stockholders strongly urging them "to take no hasty action with respect to your stock," and a month later he capped that action by filing a lawsuit (later withdrawn) against Leasco and its brokers, charging them with violations of the securities laws.

On the surface, it looked to be total corporate war. In retrospect, however, it appears that Roberts, for all his crustiness toward Leasco, was never entirely averse to a merger, and that what passed for furious self-defense was really something more akin to hard bargaining. Roberts, like Netter and Leasco, seems to have fully grasped the advantages of releasing all that redundant capital from the bondage of legal restrictions through a merger. Indeed, he had met with Netter to discuss that very subject as far back as December, 1967, just about the time Netter was making his first contact with Leasco. Then, Netter had informed Roberts that he believed he could get him forty-five dollars a share in securities in exchange for Reliance stock, which was selling at about thirty dollars, through a merger with some other firm—with a conglomerate, perhaps, like Gulf and Western. (Leasco was not mentioned specifically at that meeting.) Despite the tempting 1967 valuation, Roberts was unenthusiastic about the prospect of seeing his solid old company engulfed by some corporate upstart. It was not, then, that he was flatly against any merger; it was just that he thought Reliance ought to be the acquirer rather than the acquired.

Now, with Leasco apparently ready to make a takeover attempt whether its intended partner was willing or not, Roberts realized that the stock market's overwhelming preference for Leasco's shares as opposed to Reliance's made his desire to be the acquirer an idle dream. As to whether or not to be hostile, all through July he wavered. Reliance stockholders who wondered whether or not to accept the Leasco offer got little enough advice from him. Then, on August 1, Roberts declared himself. Leasco, he wrote the stockholders (whose heads must have been spinning by now), had sweetened the terms of its offer greatly, and Reliance management had "agreed to discontinue taking any action to impede." It was a surrender to *force majeure*; a majority of Reliance stockholders were in the act of accepting the tender offer anyway, and Leasco was going to gain control of Reliance whatever management decided. By mid-September Leasco had over eighty per cent of Reliance; by mid-November it had over ninety-six per cent. The takeover was complete.

Truly—to change the metaphor—it was a case of the minnow

swallowing the whale; Reliance was nearly ten times Leasco's size, and Leasco, as the surviving company, found itself suddenly more than eighty per cent in the insurance business and less than twenty per cent in the computer-leasing business. Nor did the whale seem to have been hurt by the ingestion; indeed, at first glance everyone concerned seemed to be decidedly better off. Roberts, still boss of Reliance although now under Leasco's control, came out with a fresh five-year employment contract at his old salary of eighty thousand dollars for the first four years and a raise to one hundred thousand dollars in the fifth, plus a generous portion of potentially lucrative Leasco stock options. Saul Steinberg came out a multimillionaire at twenty-nine, said by *Forbes* magazine to have made more money on his own—over fifty million dollars, on paper—than any other U.S. citizen under thirty. His father and original backer, Julius, and his uncle, Meyer, were themselves worth millions from their Leasco stockholdings, as was his twenty-six-year-old brother Robert, the company's secretary. Carter, Berlind and Weill, in addition to its seven-hundred-and-fifty-thousand-dollar finder's fee, had brokerage fees of almost fifty thousand dollars on the purchase of Reliance shares for Leasco, and dealer's fees of two hundred and thirty thousand dollars on the tender offer, for a total of more than a million dollars on the whole go-round. The Reliance stockholders had their Leasco corporate underwear, which, provided they divested themselves of it immediately, left them (however naked in a corporate-securities sense) well clothed financially. As for Leasco, as a result of its extraordinary feat it suddenly had assets of four hundred million dollars instead of seventy-four million dollars, net annual income of twenty-seven million dollars instead of one million four hundred thousand dollars, and eight thousand five hundred employees doing business in fifty countries instead of eight hundred doing business in only three. In stock-market terms, as of December 31, 1968, the price of Leasco stock had, over the five years preceding, appreciated by five thousand four hundred ten per cent, making it the greatest percentage gainer of all the five hundred largest publicly owned companies during that period—in sum, the undisputed king of all the go-go stocks. But our tale of financial derring-do is not yet ended; rather, it is only begun. Adventurous Leasco was now poised for the decade's greatest, and to defenders of the status quo most disturbing, venture in corporate conquest.

III

AS early as December, 1967, Leasco began looking into the possibility of acquiring a large bank. The stocks of banks, like those of insurance companies, often sold at low price-to-earnings multiples, giving a stock-market high-flyer like Leasco the leverage it needed to take over companies larger than itself. Moreover, Steinberg felt, as a business principle, that it would be advantageous to anchor Leasco's diversified financial services to a New York money-center bank with international connections. It appears that during 1968, at the very time when the Reliance takeover was in process, Gibbs' corporate planning department at Leasco was picking out a banking target as carefully as a bomber command draws a bead on any enemy ammunition dump. Nor was any particular diffidence being shown about the size and strength of targets. Bankers Trust, Irving Trust, Chase Manhattan, Manufacturers Hanover, Morgan Guaranty—the whole array of national banking power seems to have come under Leasco's impudent, although secret, scrutiny as possible candidates for assimilation.

By the fall, when the Reliance acquisition was all but wrapped up, the gaze at Great Neck had come to light on Renchard's nine-billion-dollar Chemical Bank. As with Reliance, a code name was assigned for interoffice use—in this case, "Faye," as in Faye Dunaway. As a first step in Leasco's campaign, an elaborate dossier on the history and operations of the prospective target was prepared: "Faye was originally the banking arm of New York Faye Manufacturing Company," and so on. (Any outsider who might have seen the memo and who knew anything about banking could easily have deduced from the context that "Faye" was Chemical—

again suggesting that the code names Leasco used in its corporate assaults were at least as much for *brio* as for concealment.) *Who's Who* entries of "Faye" directors were reproduced for ready reference, along with annotations. Among those directors were such eminences of American business as H. I. Romnes, chairman of American Telephone and Telegraph; Lammot du Pont Copeland, president of E. I. du Pont de Nemours; Robert C. Tyson, finance chairman of United States Steel; Augustus C. Long, director and member of the executive committee of Texaco, Inc.; T. Vincent Learson, president of I.B.M.; and Keith Funston, former president of the New York Stock Exchange. It was convenient for Leasco—and it tells something about the two firms—that practically all of Faye's directors had long entries in *Who's Who*, while no directors of Leasco at the time were listed there at all. In a kind of unintended irony, the standard checklist of the American ruling class was proving useful as a kind of sighting device to a band of outside insurgents.

The scenario that had been so effective in the case of Reliance was followed as closely as possible. In November, Leasco began buying Chemical stock—again, through the First Jersey National. Within a few days, fifty thousand shares were quietly bought at a cost of more than three and a half million dollars, without giving rise to untoward rumors or market disruptions. Meanwhile, Reliance, now a Leasco subsidiary, held more than one hundred thousand additional shares, giving Leasco control of well over one per cent of all Chemical shares outstanding. In January, 1969—still maintaining strict security, and still, of course, with no contact established between the executives of Leasco and those at Chemical—Leasco proceeded to prepare a hypothetical tender offer to Chemical stockholders. As with Reliance, it involved offering warrants and convertible debentures worth at then-current prices substantially more than the market for Chemical stock. What had worked once would, presumably, work again. Still, Leasco had not yet decided to go ahead with the offer when, on the last day of January, Chemical through its regular intelligence channels finally got firm word that Leasco was preparing a takeover attempt.

The news did not catch Renchard completely by surprise. As early as December, 1967, Chemical had begun following Leasco's acquisition activities in a wary, if desultory, way, and that following autumn Renchard had begun to hear rumors that "a leasing company" was interested in acquiring the bank. Rather astonishingly, the November purchases of Chemical stock went entirely unnoticed, no one at Chemical caught so much as a whisper of the code name "Faye," and the rumors seem to have died down. However, on getting the first firm information on January 31st, Renchard was in no doubt as to Chemical's response. He and his bank were going to fight Leasco with all their strength. True enough, a merger, as in the Reliance case, would result in immediate financial benefit to the stockholders of both companies. But it seemed to Renchard and his colleagues that more than immediate stockholder profit was involved. The century-and-a-half-old Chemical Bank a mere division of an unseasoned upstart called Leasco? H. I. Romnes, Lammot du Pont Copeland, Robert C. Tyson, Augustus C. Long, T. Vincent Learson, and Keith Funston as members of a board of directors headed by twenty-nine-year-old Saul P. Steinberg? In established banking circles the thought bordered on sacrilege, and Renchard, on getting the word, reacted predictably by calling a fellow banker, the one most likely to be able to enlighten him further: Thomas J. Stanton, Jr., who besides being president of the First Jersey National was a director of Leasco. What was going on, Renchard wanted to know. "I'll call you back," Stanton replied. Presumably he then cleared with Steinberg as to what he should tell Renchard. When he called back, it was to inform the Chemical's boss, not too cryptically, that one of the items Leasco had on the agenda for its next board meeting, to precede the company's annual stockholders' meeting on February 11th, was discussion of the possible acquisition of "a major commercial bank."

Thus alerted, Renchard went into vigorous if belated action. He set up an eleven-man task force to devise strategy for fighting off any such takeover attempt, under the direction of the Chemical's chief loan officer, J. A. McFadden—"a bright fellow, good at figures," as Renchard described him later, "not exactly a tough guy, but no pushover, either." He assigned another bank officer, Robert I. Lipp, to prepare a memo outlining all of the possible defensive strategies available to Chemical, and on February 3rd Lipp came through with a list of seven different courses of action. (Out in Great Neck, almost at the same moment, Leasco was putting the finishing touches on its proposed tender offer, and was making further extensive purchases of Chemical stock—to be precise, nineteen thousand seven hundred more shares at a cost of one million four hundred twenty-two thousand two hundred seven dollars.) Renchard said long afterward, "At that time we didn't know how much of our stock they had, or what kind of a package of wallpaper they were going to throw at our stockholders in their tender offer. We were guessing that they would offer stuff with a market value of around one hundred ten dollars for each share of our stock, which was then selling at seventy-two. So we knew well enough it would be tough going persuading our stockholders not to accept."

On February 5th, Renchard made his move, and a drastic and risky one it was. He decided to force Leasco out into the open by giving a story to the press. That afternoon, H. Erich Heinemann, banking specialist on *The New York Times'* financial reporting staff, telephoned him to say that he had heard rumors of an impending takeover attempt and to inquire whether there was anything in them. Rather than make the routine denial that he would have made under ordinary circumstances, Renchard replied that there was, indeed, something in the rumors. He went on to give a few details and some pointed comments, and the following morning the *Times* carried a piece, under the by-line of Heinemann's colleague Robert Metz, who had developed his story independently:

Can a Johnny-come-lately on the business scene move in on the Establishment and knock off one of the biggest prizes in sight?

That, it appears, is what the Leasco Data Processing Equipment Corporation hopes to do next in its dynamic acquisition program. The rumored target is one of the nation's most prestigious banks, the Chemical Bank New York Trust Company, founded in 1824. . . .

Try and get confirmation that something is going on . . . and you get nothing. In fact, Leasco's public relations people called to get a statement from the reporter.

Is Chemical in the bag? Hardly. William S. Renchard, chairman of the Chemical Bank, sounded like a Marine Corps colonel in presenting his battle plan for what he believes may well develop. . . . He said, "We intend to resist this with all the means at our command, and these might turn out to be considerable."

Understandably, the article was the talk of the banking world that day. Renchard went on with his planning, holding new strategy sessions at which one of the possibilities discussed, as phrased in a memo prepared for one of the meetings by McFadden, was the following:

There is some question about the breadth of the market on the Leasco stock and it might be possible to attack its value if need be.

Such an "attack"—carried out by making sales or short sales of Leasco stock over an extended period—would hit Leasco where it lived, since its high stock price was the source of its power and, above all, of the possibility of its taking over a firm like Chemical that was many times Leasco's size. The difficulty lay in the fact that such an attack—a bear raid—would constitute stock manipulation and would be a violation of the securities laws punishable by fines and imprisonment. For obvious reasons, no one has ever been willing to say that at Chemical's February 6th strategy meeting that particular recommendation was adopted for action. The striking and undeniable fact is, however, that on that very day, Leasco stock, which had been hovering in the stratosphere at around one hundred forty, abruptly began to fall in price on large trading volume. By the close the following day Leasco was down almost seven points, and over the following three weeks it would drop inexorably below one hundred. Rumors of impending mergers, particularly between titans, customarily drive a com-

pany's stock price *up*, not down. Long afterward, Steinberg said of
the curious coincidence in timing as to the proposed Chemical
takeover and the beginning of the Leasco slide, "It *is* odd—so odd
that Congressman Wright Patman asked me the same question.
But we've never been able to pin anything down." As for Renchard, he later told a Congressional committee that he thought the
stock drop was simply the result of institutional holders beginning
to lose confidence in Leasco; but still later than that, he pointed
out, without elaboration, that one of the defensive techniques discussed in the Chemical strategy meetings had been drawn from a
Harvard Business Review article on "multiple flogging." "Multiple
flogging," in the context, was a fancy new name for an old-fashioned bear raid. By using various concealment devices, it is theoretically possible to carry out a bear raid without detection by
the authorities. The evidence suggests, at least, that on February
6th somebody, identity unknown, started lowering a very heavy
boom on Leasco.

IV

STEINBERG reacted to the *Times* article exactly as Renchard had
planned that he should. Although Steinberg was not ready to
make his tender offer and, in fact, was considering waiting several
months before doing so, he decided that now he had no choice but
to go ahead immediately—and from his point of view, prematurely—and, as a first step, he resolved to have an exploratory talk
with Renchard early the following week.

On Friday, February 7th, the day after the *Times* article, Steinberg had lunch with Heinemann. By Steinberg's account the timing was pure coincidence, since the lunch had been arranged
weeks before; it was, however, an obvious windfall for Heinemann
as a reporter to be seeing Steinberg at the very moment when the
meteorically successful boy wonder was at the center of the biggest financial story in the nation. At the lunch, Steinberg insists

that it was understood by both sides that everything was off the record; then he proceeded to discuss Leasco's plans freely, not to say indiscreetly. When he had finished, he asked Heinemann, as a man knowledgeable about banking, for his impressions. According to Steinberg, Heinemann replied that in believing for a moment that he could get away with taking over Chemical Steinberg showed himself to be "an innocent." At any rate, Steinberg later decided that he had been an innocent about Heinemann. That afternoon, Heinemann called up the Chemical Bank and talked to a public-relations officer there, to whom he reported in detail what he had heard from Steinberg. That same afternoon, the public-relations officer sent Renchard a memo that read, in part:

Heinemann just came back from lunch with Steinberg, and passed on the following results.

They said they are beginning to feel the pressure. They knew there would be absolute opposition, and they fully believe that when they come in with their proposal it will be rejected. . . .

Erich was told that it is a better than fifty–fifty chance that Leasco will announce their intentions and plan at the annual meeting next week. Steinberg took the position that their offer will be most beneficial for us. . . . Steinberg said flatly that the way we handle international business . . . is wrong and will be changed.

(Heinemann's version of the episode differs from Steinberg's in several crucial respects. In the first place, he said later that his luncheon with Steinberg had not been arranged weeks previously but only four days before—at the urgent request of Steinberg's public-relations counselor. Moreover—and more crucially— Heinemann avows that at the luncheon he was not asked for and did not give any assurance that what was said be held confidential, and that he subsequently called Chemical, as a conscientious reporter, in an attempt to elicit additional information for a possible new story.)

Steinberg said later that the memo gave a generally accurate account of what he had said at the lunch, with the notable exception that he had said nothing about pressure—that, indeed, he had felt no pressure from banks at that time, although he was to feel plenty of it later on. The nearest thing to pressure on Leasco as of February 7th was a conversation Steinberg had that day with Donald M. Graham, chairman of Continental Illinois Bank and Trust Company, a leading Leasco creditor, in which Graham expressed the view that a Leasco attempt to take over Chemical would not be a good thing for banking—and added, most unthreateningly, that his bank highly valued its association with Leasco and expected it to continue. (Renchard, in fact, had talked to Graham and urged him to discourage Steinberg.) The memo seemed to give Chemical a momentary edge; and, seizing the initiative, the bank took the comparatively drastic step of planning a full-scale strategy meeting at 20 Pine Street the following morning, even though the day would be Saturday.

It turned out to be a wild weekend of feints and counterfeints. Steinberg was busy with a semiannual conference of Leasco district managers, and on that account, he stayed in town at the Regency Hotel. By another coincidence, that same weekend was the occasion of the American Bankers Association's annual trust conference, and consequently New York City was swarming with hundreds of important bankers from all over the country. At the Chemical strategy meeting—which was attended, this time, not only by Chemical's in-house task force, but by invitees from other powerful Wall Street institutions sympathetic to the Chemical cause, including First Boston, Kuhn Loeb, and Hornblower Weeks—a whole array of defensive measures were taken up and thrashed out, among them the organizing of telephone teams to contact Chemical stockholders; the retaining of the leading proxy-soliciting firms solely to deny their services to Leasco; the possibility of Chemical's making a quick merger of its own with some other computer-leasing company, to raise an antitrust obstacle for Leasco; and the possibility of getting state and federal legislation introduced through the bankers' friends in Albany and Washington in order to make a Leasco takeover of Chemical illegal. Despite the availability of such weapons, the opinion of those present seemed to be that Leasco's venture had an excellent chance of success. There was a sense of backs to the wall, of the barbarians at the gates, of time running out. Reports of the meeting filtered out that evening to the bankers assembled around town at their cocktail parties, receptions, and dinners. One such report had it that a participant at the session had finally thrown up his hands and said, "Oh, let the kid have the bank. We'll start a new one!" Levity, it seemed, with an edge of hysteria.

On Sunday, New York City was hit by a fifteen-inch snowstorm, the worst in seven years, and as a result, airports were closed, roads were clogged, rail service was disrupted, and the bankers in town were trapped. There was nothing for them to do but stay and talk—largely about Leasco and Chemical. The bankers, and the subject, were caught in a kind of pressure cooker. That evening, Chemical held a large reception for the visiting bankers at the Plaza. (Steinberg, the subject of all the discussion, stayed at the Regency four blocks away; not being a banker, he wasn't invited.) At the reception Renchard took considerable kidding; the prevailing attitude among the bankers he talked to seemed to be that the whole thing was ridiculous, an attitude that Renchard felt he had little reason to share. "Don't joke," he would say. "If this is successful, the next target may be you."

On Monday, with the city still snowbound, Renchard and Steinberg, who had previously never so much as talked on the telephone, met at last. That morning Steinberg, carrying out his plan, called Renchard at his office and asked if they could get together. Renchard said, "Sure. I'll buy you lunch, but I have to go to a meeting right afterward. Do you have transportation?" Steinberg said he hadn't. "I'll send my car to get you," Renchard replied. So Renchard sent his car to the Regency, Steinberg got in and sloshed comfortably downtown, and the lunch that Renchard "bought" him took place that noon in the Chemical Bank's private dining room. One may imagine the first reactions of the antagonists to each other. One was lean, iron-gray, of distinctly military bearing; a North Shore estate owner, very conscious of the entrenched power of the nation standing behind him, very much a man of few and incisive words. The other was round-faced, easy-smiling, a man of many words who looked preposterously younger than his already preposterous twenty-nine years, and given, as he talked, to making windmill gestures with his arms and suddenly jumping galvanically up from his chair; a *South* Shore estate owner (twenty-nine rooms, tennis court, two saunas, Picassos and Kandinskys—as Steinberg himself characteristically described it, "a modern mansion just like that of any other successful kid of twenty-nine"); a young man bubbling with energy and joy in living. (Contrary to repeated press reports, he was not fat, only chunky; photographs of his jowly face deceived people.) Now he seemed to be, in the tragicomic fashion of that year, the corporate version of a campus radical informing the university president, with a mixture of amusement and pity, that the times had changed and the freshmen were taking over.

The two men's accounts of the ensuing meeting, as told to me several years later, differ to some extent as to content, but to a greater and perhaps more interesting extent as to style and emphasis.

RENCHARD: "Steinberg, at some length, gave his ideas on how commercial banking was going to be revolutionized over the next few years. Mostly I just listened, and so did my colleagues [President Howard] McCall and [Vice-Chairman Hulbert] Aldrich, who joined us toward the end of the session. The whole industry was to benefit greatly, Steinberg said. I asked him why he had singled out Chemical. He said he liked our philosophy, that is, we were in the process of forming a one-bank holding company that would enable us to diversify, thereby showing that we believed in the principle of bank diversification. He had evidently ruled out Citibank and Chase as too big. Bankers Trust and Irving were out for technical reasons, and Morgan probably because it was strictly a wholesale business. He seemed to like us better than Manufacturers Hanover.

"I said I wasn't sure he appreciated what might happen to our business when someone with no banking experience moved in on a takeover basis. Directors and officers might leave. I made it clear that I didn't think *I'd* be around. In the trust area, for people to leave their estates with a bank you need confidence built up over many years. Will appointments would leave in droves, I said, not because of anything about him but because it was a takeover. Then there was the worry about somebody acquisition-minded having access to our stockholder lists. The confidential relationship of banker to client might be endangered.

"I think it impressed him a little bit. Steinberg said he had no intention of making an unfriendly takeover—that is, that he didn't want to, but might. There was the hint of a threat. I said, 'If you want to get into a fight, I'm a pretty good gutter fighter.' He said, 'I've already found that out.' He said he wanted to make a full presentation of Leasco's plans the next afternoon, after his company's annual meeting, in the hope that Chemical would change its mind and want to cooperate, after all. I enjoyed the luncheon. There was some kidding around, too."

STEINBERG: "When I got to 20 Pine Street that morning, I got out of Renchard's car and walked into the bank. It was a day when not many people were there, because of the snowstorm. Renchard's secretary was very friendly—'Oh, hello, Mr. Steinberg, I'm so glad to see you.' Renchard came out and shook my hand and said, 'Hello, Saul. Call me Bill. Can I take you around and show you the place?' Well, I wasn't terribly interested in looking at the real estate right then. So we went and talked, first in his office and later in the bank's dining room.

"We did some kidding at first. He asked me why I wanted to become a banker and I said, 'God looks after drunks and bankers, and I don't want to be a drunk.' Then I started in giving the facts. I told him how many Chemical shares Leasco had—more than three hundred thousand. I said we weren't going to accumulate much more because it was getting too expensive. I told him frankly that the *Times* piece had disrupted Leasco's plans; we had wanted to wait until the forthcoming new law regulating bank holding companies was passed, and that might be six months or a year. Now our hand was forced, and I volunteered that for us it was premature.

"I went into my philosophy of how Chemical's management,

and all commercial-bank managements, should be more respon-
sive to stockholders and customers, and how I thought we could
make it that way. I said I thought that adding a broad range of
services to a bank's regular functions would add to the intrinsic
value of its money, and on that he expressed absolute agreement in
principle. He began to talk about the possible detriments to the
bank's business from a hostile takeover. He said top management
would probably resign. He mentioned losing customers, and I said
they would hardly leave in a hurry at a tight-money time like that.
He talked about damage to the trust business. I asked, 'Does it
make money?' He laughed, and said he wasn't sure. He said if I
wanted a fight he was a pretty good gutter fighter, and I said my
record as a gutter fighter was considered to be pretty good, too, at
least for my age. But then I said I wasn't planning a hostile takeover, although I wasn't ruling one out. I told him that in four days
I was going to Puerto Rico on vacation with my wife and kids—it
was the kids' winter semester break—and that I was professional
enough not to be planning such a thing as that if I were thinking
of attempting a hostile takeover. He looked surprised and asked,
'Are you really going to Puerto Rico?' I said yes. He was obviously relieved. Everything became very relaxed. I thought it was a
rather constructive meeting. Everything was friendly and affable.
The atmosphere was dampened at the end, though, when McCall
and Aldrich came in—McCall for lunch with us, and Aldrich at
the end of lunch. McCall just didn't seem to want to have anything to do with me one way or the other, and Aldrich seemed
downright hostile. But Renchard interrupted them to say, 'Look,
Saul has stated that he has no intention of a hostile takeover.'
McCall's face lit up, and he said, 'Well, when can we meet again?'
I suggested after my trip to Puerto Rico, and he and Renchard
said, 'Oh, let's do it before that,' and we arranged for the following afternoon, after our stockholders' meeting. I came out in a
positive frame of mind. The only thing was that Aldrich was still
cold. But wait—come to think of it, he wasn't any too cordial to
Renchard, either.''

So the first meeting of the rival chieftains was a standoff. That afternoon, Renchard heard from Roberts of Reliance Insurance. The apparently satisfied subject of Leasco's previous conquest said he thought a merger of Leasco and Chemical would be a fine thing for the bank. "I told him he was off his rocker," Renchard said later. "I said computer leasing has nothing to do with banking. He said the Leasco–Reliance merger hadn't hurt Reliance. I was disappointed in him." Also that afternoon, McCall had someone at Chemical prepare for him a list of Leasco's creditor banks, and when the list later came to the attention of a Congressional committee, it was found that checkmarks had been made beside the names of certain of the banks; the purpose of the list, and the meaning of the checkmarks, is not known, but the fact is that on that very afternoon Steinberg began to feel "pressure" from the banking business in the form of calls from Leasco's two investment bankers, White, Weld and Lehman Brothers, informing him that they would refuse to participate in any Leasco tender offer for Chemical.

That evening, there was more socializing among the bankers. Renchard went to a dinner of the Reserve City Bankers Association at which, he said later, he may have spoken to three hundred bankers. "I have no recollection of anything except general conversation about this development," he recounts, denying that he used the event as an opportunity to spread anti-Leasco propaganda or solicit support for Chemical. (He had not, however, shown such restraint during working hours; the anti-Leasco announcements of White, Weld and Lehman had followed urgent appeals from Chemical.)

At Leasco's annual stockholders' meeting, held the following afternoon in the auditorium of the Chase Manhattan Bank Building, matters proceeded smoothly enough, with no mention of the subject that was in everyone's mind, until Steinberg observed that Leasco's commitment to becoming a comprehensive financial-services organization included the objective of entering the field of banking. "The realization of so large a plan," he went on, "requires the exercise of careful and deliberate judgment. At the present time, we have not made a decision as to a particular bank."

A hush filled the room; Steinberg broke it by asking for questions. A stockholder asked flatly whether Leasco was planning to acquire the Chemical Bank. Steinberg replied that Leasco had made no statement regarding that bank or any other. Then, a bit later, another stockholder asked whether Leasco had already had merger discussions with Chemical.

Steinberg was on the spot; over the weekend he had planned to announce his tender offer on this occasion, but now, with the door still open to possible agreement with Chemical officers at the meeting to be held in only a couple of hours, he had decided to hold off. For diplomatic reasons, it would be best to evade the question, but he rejected that course. "I said to myself, 'Heck, I'm not going to lie,' " he recounted later. He answered, "Yes, we have met with the Chemical"—thereby publicly confirming for the first time what up to then had been in the realm of rumor and conjecture.

v

BUT later that afternoon, at the private meeting between Leasco and Chemical officers, the crack in the door that Steinberg had discerned at the previous day's luncheon seems to have narrowed perceptibly. The defense was gaining confidence. This time, the rival generals were accompanied by their chief aides; Steinberg came with three, including Roberts and Counsel Robert Hodes, and Renchard with four, including McCall, Aldrich, and Task Force Generalissimo McFadden. Steinberg went over much of the ground he had covered in the previous day's luncheon with Renchard, this time putting more emphasis on his friendly intentions and his disinclination to threaten. (Aldrich's personal notes on the meeting say: "Tender route loathesome to Leasco—but might have to go it to accomplish ends.") Steinberg also made a further concession. He said he was prepared not to be chief executive officer of the merged company, and that all of his Leasco colleagues would be willing to put their jobs at risk on the basis of the merged company's profit record. When Renchard said that he was unwilling to negotiate with "a gun at my head," Steinberg insisted that no gun was intended, that this "wasn't war." Both sides later characterized the meeting as cordial, although Steinberg felt that it had been "not overly friendly." According to Aldrich's notes, it concluded with Renchard saying, in effect, "We have lots to consider. Will do so. They will hear from us—maybe end of week, maybe middle of next week."

In fact, Steinberg would hear from Renchard again that Friday, February 14th, but in the meantime the Chemical defense battalion was far from idle; on the contrary, it was now trundling up its big guns, those "resources" that Renchard had described at the outset as "considerable." Chemical held another full-scale battle meeting at which the discussion centered on the possibility of changing Chemical's charter in such a way as to make a Leasco takeover legally difficult if not impossible. There was also talk about perhaps buying a fire-and-casualty company to create an antitrust conflict with Leasco's ownership of Reliance, or even, as a last resort, of arranging to have some giant insurance company take over *Chemical*—suggesting a positively Oriental preference for suicide rather than surrender.

As it happened, none of these schemes was carried out; certainly, though, the last one reflects the bankers' mood of grim intransigence. As planned, the bank retained the two leading proxy-soliciting firms, Dudley King and Georgeson, to deny their services to Leasco. Renchard called Chairman Martin of the Federal Reserve Board to apprise him of the situation and, hardly incidentally, to try to persuade him that a Leasco takeover would be bad for banking as a whole. (Martin took no action.) And also meanwhile, from whatever cause, Leasco's stock kept dropping; by Friday it was down to one hundred twenty-three and in full retreat. Probably the most effective of Chemical's various salvos was on the legislative front. Beginning on February 14th, Richard Simmons of the Cravath law firm, on retainer from Chemical, began devoting full time to the Leasco affair, concentrating his attention on the drafting of laws specifically designed to prevent or make difficult the takeover of banks similar to Chemical by companies that resembled Leasco, and to getting these drafts introduced as bills in the State Legislature in Albany and the Congress in Washington. Does it seem odd that a proposed new law, hand-tailored by a chief party at interest, should be accepted without question by tribunes of the people in a state or federal legislative body? Whatever the answer, Governor Rockefeller chose that very week to urge the New York Legislature to enact a law enabling the state to stop any takeover of a bank by a non-bank, within its boundaries, in a case where "the exercise of control might impair the safe and sound conduct of the bank." By Friday, precisely such a proposed law (not from Simmons' desk) had been dispatched to Albany, and a national one of similar intent to Senator John J. Sparkman, chairman of the Senate Banking and Currency Committee in Washington. Apparently Chemical had reason to believe that in both cases the drafts would be introduced without significant alteration.

Thus it was with a sense of a turning tide of battle that Renchard telephoned Steinberg again on Friday the fourteenth, to make a new appointment. This time there was no further talk of gutter fighters and the like. Doubtless Renchard no longer felt the need for such talk. Was Steinberg still going on that vacation? Steinberg said he was—leaving the next day, and remaining in Puerto Rico until the following Wednesday, the nineteenth, when he had appointments in Washington. Renchard said amiably, "What's the use of busting up your trip?" and invited Steinberg to come in and see him again on Thursday the twentieth. And so it was agreed.

By the following Monday and Tuesday, the would-be attackers were plainly on the defensive. A *Wall Street Journal* article published on Monday raised questions as to the future earnings prospects for Leasco. Leasco stock dropped eight points that day, to one hundred fifteen, and two and a half points more the following day. The antibank-takeover bill was duly introduced in Albany on Tuesday. (It was subsequently passed, and became law in mid-May.) Leasco suffered a further setback when the company got a letter from the Department of Justice saying it had heard of Leasco's plans to merge with Chemical and commenting, "Although we do not suggest that such a transaction would violate the antitrust laws, questions under these laws are raised thereby, particularly under Section 7 of the Clayton Act." (Section 7 prohibits combinations that may restrain trade by reducing competition; its applicability to a Leasco-Chemical merger, as it was generally interpreted at that time, would appear to be highly questionable. Just how the Justice Department came to send such a letter at that particular moment has never been explained.) While these things were happening, Steinberg was with his family at the Dorado Beach in Puerto Rico, playing tennis, swimming, and, he insisted later, talking on the phone to his office in Great Neck only twice. It is hard, though, to imagine that he did not learn one way or another about the *Journal* article, the continuing Leasco stock drop, the bill introduced in Albany, and the ominous letter from Justice. For all of his impulsiveness, Steinberg is a reflective man, and it seems not impossible that, relaxing by the pool at the Dorado Beach, he reflected with irony that, having conducted his company's annual meeting the previous week at a (David) Rockefeller bank, he was now paying top rates to another (Laurance) Rockefeller hotel for a quick vacation from the battle lines while a third (Nelson) Rockefeller was urging on the State Legislature a law intended specifically to thwart him in what he considered to be a legitimate and even socially beneficial enterprise.

Steinberg's day in Washington—Wednesday the nineteenth— was a depressing one. All occasions now seemed to inform against him. For one thing, the mysterious decline in Leasco's stock price was reducing the company's takeover power day by day. But the situation was not yet hopeless on that front. Steinberg calculated that he could put together a tender offer that would be attractive to Chemical stockholders, and that would not cut Leasco's earnings, down to a Leasco stock price of eighty-five. As of February 19th the price stood at around one hundred ten, so that an interesting offer remained entirely feasible—provided some way could be found to prevent the stock's downward toboggan ride from

continuing. The other pressing concern was the national legislative situation—the matter that had brought Steinberg to Washington—and here he found a bleak picture indeed. The nation's
legislators were in a grimly anticonglomerate, antitakeover mood.
During the day Steinberg talked to half the members of the Senate
Banking and Currency Committee and to several members of the
Federal Reserve Board; without exception, he found his inter-
viewees adamantly opposed to a Leasco takeover of Chemical on
grounds that seemed to him to be entirely unreasonable. Time and
again, he explained that his object was not the destruction of a
bank but its revitalization, and he argued that takeovers of one
company by another, far from being automatically bad, are a
valuable and necessary part of the free-enterprise system, and in
some cases the only way by which backward and outmoded management methods can be replaced by aggressive, forward-looking
ones. Time and again, he found his arguments going unanswered,
and himself being treated as a sort of business pirate bent on
seizing and looting property that did not belong to him. The
climax of these brief and sketchy dialogues was one with the key
man, Senator Sparkman, part of which went, according to Steinberg's account, as follows:

SPARKMAN: A couple of weeks ago I had a fellow in here complaining
that somebody moved in and took over his bank and then fired him.
Now, we can't have things like that.

STEINBERG. But, Senator, the whole economy runs on profit. If a bank
president isn't delivering, he should be replaced just like anyone else.
Unless you want to change the whole system—

SPARKMAN. No, no, I don't want to do that. By the way, have you
seen the bill I'm going to introduce against bank takeovers? (Calling
to his secretary) Miss————, where's that bill the lawyer for Chemical
Bank sent in? I want to show it to Mr. Steinberg.

It was thus that Steinberg learned for the first time of the bill
Simmons had drafted at Chemical's behest and, as Senator Sparkman so candidly put it, "sent in." As it happened, Sparkman introduced the bill in late March; unlike the New York State

legislation, it was never passed; but on March 19th, the knowledge that a lawyer on Chemical retainer was apparently functioning as a sort of unofficial legislative assistant to the chairman of the Senate Banking and Currency Committee served to deepen Steinberg's gathering despair. Only much later did he come to see his conversation with Sparkman as a piece of high Washington comedy.

"I came back to New York that night feeling that I had been given a very clear message," Steinberg said later. In fact, that day, with the realization that the national powers of government as well as those of business were solidly aligned against him, Steinberg decided on surrender. The following morning, he went as scheduled to his third meeting with the Chemical's top officers, at 20 Pine Street. As things turned out, it was to be his last such meeting. Again let us hear two versions:

STEINBERG: "I came into the meeting with a public statement in my pocket—a surrender statement. I told them I'd been in Washington the previous day, and I told them whom I'd met. I said I'd concluded as a result of those conversations that the only way we could proceed with a tender offer was with Chemical's great enthusiasm for the merger, and I wasn't sure even that would help. I waited a few moments. To put it mildly, nobody from Chemical expressed great enthusiasm. Then I said that in half an hour I was going to release a statement of withdrawal. I pulled the statement out of my pocket and read it to the Chemical men. You could sense the relief—almost touch it. There was a kind of quiet pandemonium. Everybody shook hands. I haven't seen any of them since then."

RENCHARD: "Steinberg came in with a couple of henchmen. He said he'd decided it wasn't the time to pursue the matter, and he was going to make an announcement to that effect later that day. It was a very friendly and satisfactory meeting."

The announcement that Steinberg released later—which, in view of the fact that its last part largely negates a philosophy that he had expressed previously and would reaffirm later, suggests that he had been temporarily brainwashed—read as follows:

GREAT NECK, N. Y., February 20, 1969—Saul P. Steinberg, chairman of Leasco Data Processing Equipment Corporation, stated today that he has no plans to acquire control of the Chemical New York Corporation. Without the support and enthusiasm of the management, Leasco has no interest in pressing for an affiliation with Chemical.

Mr. Steinberg observed that hostile takeovers of money-center banks were against the best interest of the economy because of the danger of upsetting the stability and prestige of the banking system and diminishing public confidence in it.

It was presumably with satisfaction that Romnes, Copeland, Tyson, Long, Learson, Funston, and the other Chemical directors that afternoon read the following telegram:

PLEASED TO REPORT LEASCO HAS ANNOUNCED WITHDRAWAL OF PLANS TO PRESS FOR AFFILIATION WITH CHEMICAL.

BILL RENCHARD

VI

So it was over, just two weeks after it had formally begun. "They" —the Chemical Bank, most of the banking business, the Cravath law firm, a cross section of Wall Street power and influence, the leading proxy solicitors, the governor and legislature of New York State, the members of the Federal Reserve Board and the Senate Banking and Currency Committee, and sundry more or less related forces—had combined to beat Saul Steinberg of Leasco, and apparently to cause him to lose his nerve at the last moment. (A further twist of the knife was ahead. Leasco, defeated, was soon to be obliterated as a corporate entity. In the middle nineteen-seventies, when any name identified with the go-go years had come to be anathema in the stock market, the company changed its name from Leasco to Reliance Group, Inc. Steinberg remained as chairman. Having failed to become a banker, he had ended up as what may be the next most God-protected kind of executive, an insurance company head.)

And yet it wasn't really quite over; for American business and society alike, it had reverberations, some perhaps beneficial, others certainly purgative and self-revelatory. Renchard said later, "I took the whole thing very seriously, although a lot of people I know didn't. At the bank we're more on the alert now for that kind of thing. I took a lot of kidding about it. If Steinberg had gone ahead, it could have resulted in quite a fight. I'm not saying we would have been defeated. I still think we could have successfully fought them off. I'm just as glad not to have had to go through the process, though."

What Steinberg, for his part, chiefly remembers about the whole episode is the aura of hysteria that seemed to pervade so many people's reactions to it. "Nobody was objective," he says. "I wanted objective opinions, and I couldn't get them. All through those two weeks, bankers and businessmen I'd never met kept calling up out of the blue and attacking us for merely thinking about taking over a big bank. Some of the attacks were pretty funny—responsible investment bankers talking as if we were using Mafia tactics. And it went on afterwards. Months after we'd abandoned our plans, executives of major corporations were still calling up and ranting, 'I feel it was so *wrong*, what you tried to do—' And yet they could never say why. We'd touched some kind of a nerve center. I still don't know exactly what it was. Once, at a party, the head of a huge corporation asked me if there had been any anti-Semitism in the campaign against us. I said, not that I knew of. There are bankers and businessmen who are anti-Semitic, but it was more than that. I think now it would have been a good thing if we'd done a hostile takeover, and then there had been Congressional hearings, to get all those rancid emotions out in the open air."

Ruefully, Steinberg summed up his emotional reaction when he said, immediately after his surrender, "I always knew there was an Establishment—I just used to think I was a part of it." As for the Establishment, perhaps *its* last word on the affair was the apothegm allegedly pronounced on it by an officer of a lordly commercial bank, who is supposed to have said, with a lordly mixture of misinformation, illogic, and sententiousness, "Never trust a fat man."

PART FOUR

U. S.—the Seventies

$$\$\$\$\$\$\$\$\$\$\$\$\$\$\$\$\$\$\$$$

8

Starting Over

IF IT IS APPOSITE to follow the common practice of comparing a
session of international trade and currency negotiations to a poker
game, then the annual meeting of the governors of the International Monetary Fund, which was held in Washington the last
week of September, 1971, was a game that took place under notably awkward circumstances. The richest and most relied-upon
player, the United States, had just a month earlier committed two
uncharacteristic and almost unforgivable gaucheries. One of

them, the imposition of a flat ten-per-cent import surcharge on all dutiable foreign goods, was a clear violation of the rules of the General Agreement on Tariffs and Trade, which had been signed in 1947 by the leading non-Communist trading nations to promote freer international trade and which, over the subsequent twenty-three years, had generally been effective in achieving that objective. The United States' second action, the sudden move to temporarily stop redeeming dollars with gold, was an equally clear violation of the Articles of Agreement of the International Monetary Fund itself; beyond that, it created conditions that seemed to make it impossible for the I.M.F. to operate or for world trade to continue on its current scale. Both actions were violations of formal international treaties, duly ratified by the parliaments of the participating countries. In terms of the poker analogy, the United States was in the position of a player who, when he sees he is losing, first cheats and then tips over the table; to make matters worse, the offending player had then insolently described his actions as merely strategic moves designed to improve his position. To be sure, such egregious conduct was not unheard of at this particular table; for example, at the same moment, Japan, even after a new liberalization of its trade practices, was adjudged by its fellow-players to be guilty of some forty violations of GATT, and Germany and the Netherlands had broken the I.M.F. rules only last May by ceasing to control the prices of their currencies in terms of the dollar. But the nature of the breaches by the United States and the extent of its influence made those breaches unique. Clearly, if the game was to continue at all—and the alternative might be a paralysis of international trade and a world depression that could result in starvation in many countries—new rules would have to be devised quickly, and under the most trying conditions.

The meeting, which the *Times* described optimistically as "likely to go down in history as the turning point toward the creation of a new world monetary system," actually turned out to be the hopeful yet premonitory first session of an entirely new game, the world monetary game of the nineteen-seventies. Key moves later in that game would be two devaluations of the dollar against other currencies; the establishment of floating rates that would effectively result in much greater dollar devaluations, particularly against the Swiss franc and the Japanese yen; an enormous and almost steady rise in the price of gold against the dollar and all other currencies; and, most important of all, the O.P.E.C. oil embargo in 1973 and subsequent skyrocketing of the world price of oil, which put the United States emphatically in the economic defensive vis-à-vis much of the world for the first time since the First World War. The cheat and table-tipper, that is, was soon to get his comeuppance. The meeting took place at the huge Sheraton–Park Hotel, the corridors of which were crowded with the mighty of world finance, more than fifteen hundred strong. Among the official delegates for their countries were the United States Secretary of the Treasury, John B. Connally; France's Minister of Economy and Finance, Valéry Giscard d'Estaing; Britain's Chancellor of the Exchequer, Anthony Barber; Germany's Minister for Economic Affairs and Finance, Karl Schiller; and Japan's Minister of Finance, Mikio Mizuta. Present as advisers, assistants, or guests were the heads of the central banks of all leading member nations—Arthur F. Burns for the United States, Sir Leslie O'Brien for Britain, Karl Klasen for West Germany, Tadashi Sasaki for Japan—and such eminent private bankers as Baron Lambert, of the Banque Lambert of Brussels; Jerome Istel, of the Banque Rothschild of Paris; and David Rockefeller, of the Chase Manhattan Bank of New York City. In their eagerness to help get the game going again, most delegates were already on hand by Saturday, September 25th, two days before the formal opening of the meeting, and that morning the I.M.F.'s managing director, Pierre-Paul Schweitzer, made some remarks to the press in which he set the key for the week ahead as one of tension and urgency. Pointing out that it had been a tradition of the Fund to remain silent when there was a crisis affecting a leading member nation, he proceeded to break that tradition. He reiterated a view he had expressed previously, to the effect that the United States ought to make a "contribution" to a solution of the current crisis in the form of a small devaluation of the dollar against gold (a move that the United States had firmly announced itself disinclined to make), and he implied that a continuance of the import surcharge and currency instability for any extended period might well result in a disastrous world trade war, in which the worst sufferers would be what he called "innocent victims and helpless bystanders"—the underdeveloped countries.

THE old rules of the game and the steps leading to their collapse can be quickly summarized. When the monetary millennium comes, perhaps there will be one world currency universally honored and freely exchanged across national borders, but meanwhile there is gold, the only world currency that has enjoyed general confidence over a long period, even in times of crisis. To the question "Why should gold, rather than something else, be the basis of money?" perhaps the best answer is "Why shouldn't it be?" But the natural scarcity of gold and the capriciousness of its geographical distribution are weaknesses as well as strengths for a world-currency base, and the rigid gold standard that was the rule among most of the leading trading nations until the Depression of the nineteen-thirties eventually came to be an insupportable burden. After a protracted period of chaos, caused by the Depression and war—and perhaps in part by the gold standard itself—it was replaced, at the United Nations Monetary and Financial Conference at Bretton Woods, New Hampshire, in July, 1944, by a more flexible system, under which gold shared the task of being the world's money base with what was then by far the strongest national currency, the United States dollar. The Bretton Woods agreement, hammered out by an international panel of experts, headed by Harry Dexter White, of the United States, and John Maynard Keynes, of Britain, established the dollar as the *numéraire*, or measuring rod, against which the value of other currencies was set, and also as the principal currency in which the reserves, or national savings accounts, of other nations would be held. Long before 1944, Keynes had pronounced monetary gold to be a "barbarous relic," and now he had taken part in what was at least a lessening of its role. To keep exchange rates relatively stable under the new system, each nation undertook to intervene in the market—buying or selling its own currency—whenever this was necessary in order to hold that currency's dollar price within one per cent of its fixed relation to the dollar. In addition, the International Monetary Fund was established—originally with twenty-nine members, a number that by 1971 had swelled to a hundred and eighteen—to accept deposits from the member nations in amounts relative to their economic size and, as a means of further stabilizing the system, to lend funds from these resources to any member undergoing a crisis that might put it in temporary financial difficulties. The United States was offered the choice of intervening either with foreign currencies or with gold to maintain the value of the dollar; we chose gold, and thus the convertibility of the dollar, and of the dollar alone, at the established price of thirty-five dollars per ounce became the foundation of the system —the basic rule of the game.

It all worked beautifully for a time. Then, beginning in 1950, the United States took to running an annual deficit in its international accounts, as a result of foreign aid, the flocking of American tourists abroad, defense spending abroad and the maintenance of our troops there, overseas investments of American companies, the declining competitive position of American products in world markets, and, finally, the war in Vietnam. Year by year, the deficits grew, and in 1960, for the first time, dollars held abroad— in effect, I.O.U.s issued by the United States against our national reserves of gold, foreign currency, and borrowing power at the I.M.F.—exceeded those reserves. Each year thereafter, the disparity between what we owed and what we could pay increased, until by the beginning of 1971 the cumulative dollar gap amounted to about twenty-five billion dollars, or almost twice our total reserves. The reason this improvidence on the part of the United States was allowed to continue for so long was that it held temporary benefits for our creditors. International trade was expanding during the nineteen-sixties far faster than new gold was coming out of the ground, and the flood of dollars abroad was filling the lack. As long as the dollar continued to be trusted, the United States deficit was serving the useful purpose of supplying the world with the money it needed to conduct its expanding business. The fact that the United States was getting something for nothing was temporarily ignored. A bizarre situation—unprecedented in international finance, if not in poker—had developed in which the game's ever-increasing bets were being financed by the unredeemable chits of one well-dressed, self-assured player, who inspired confidence by his air of affluence but in actuality was known by all, if they stopped to think about it, to be potentially bankrupt.

Of course, this could not go on indefinitely. By early 1971, the United States' stock of gold, which had once amounted to twenty-five billion dollars at the established price of thirty-five dollars per ounce, was down to just over eleven billion. Our international-payments deficit had taken a further large jump and was by now running at the appalling rate of twenty billion dollars a year. In spite of cries of anguish from all over Europe, the United States government adopted an attitude that was described, unofficially but quite accurately, as "benign neglect." In May, a high rate of interest in West Germany brought about such a flood of dollars to Germany in exchange for Deutsche marks that the government there had little choice but to break I.M.F. rules by cutting the price of its currency free from the dollar and letting it float upward under market pressure. Benignity and neglect were abandoned together, belatedly and apocalyptically, on August 15th, when President Nixon announced his new economic program, for this included, along with various measures to spur the national economy and contain domestic inflation, the import surcharge, which suddenly reversed the United States' long-standing commitment to freer world trade, and the gold embargo, which suddenly destroyed the Bretton Woods system.

FOR the first few days after the Nixon announcement, the world's monetary authorities seemed to be in an almost catatonic state of shock and dismay, but then they recovered some of their customary aplomb and were able to devote the weeks before the I.M.F. meeting to setting up the terms of the negotiating that lay ahead. The United States made no bones about describing the import surcharge as a bargaining counter, and made clear that as its price for removal of the surcharge it was demanding a substantial upward revaluation of most other currencies in relation to the dollar. (Such revaluation would tend to give the United States its desired trading advantage by making its goods cheaper abroad.) The other countries replied that the United States ought to devalue the dollar on its own, by raising the dollar price of gold, instead of trying to force *them* to bell the cat. Both upward revaluation and devaluation are politically unpopular in any country, the former because it brings disadvantage in foreign trade and the latter because it is thought to involve loss of national prestige; the Nixon Administration, in particular, seemed to have a terror of the domestic political effects of devaluation. The terms of the contest, then, were: Since everyone agrees that the dollar has to be made worth less in terms of other currencies, who will take the unpopular action required? The I.M.F., nominally neutral in disputes among its members, lost little time in announcing where it stood in this one. Late in August and early in September, Mr. Schweitzer several times stated publicly that the United States ought to devalue the dollar in terms of gold by a modest amount (say, between five and ten per cent), whereupon the rest of the necessary realignment could be made by the other countries. But in mid-September, after a testy and unfruitful private meeting in London of what is called the Group of Ten—a sort of inner club of the I.M.F., consisting of the finance ministers of the United States, Britain, Japan, Canada, Sweden, West Germany, France, Italy, Belgium, and the Netherlands—Secretary Connally was quoted by a high French source as having declared flatly, "I am authorized to say only I will not change our position one iota." A week later, President Georges Pompidou of France pointedly warned the European Economic Community against making "exorbitant concessions" to the United States at the approaching I.M.F. meeting.

While these harsh verbal thrusts were being traded, the foreign-exchange markets were in confusion. With the dollar cut loose from gold, other currencies were cut loose from the dollar, and in trading during late August and early September they moved, or "floated," upward against it, which was exactly what the United States wanted. But the governments of the countries with the upward-floating currencies did not want the floating to go so far as to impair their competitiveness in international dealings, so they restricted artificially the amount of their currencies' rise by intervening in the market to sell them in exchange for dollars and thus create what the United States anathematized as "a dirty float." Indeed, France, perhaps the most intransigent of the nations involved, prevented the franc from floating at all. By the time of the I.M.F. meeting, world currency rates had increased against the dollar on an average of a mere 4.3 per cent—far less than the ten or fifteen per cent that the United States hoped for. Thus, the impasse remained. Meanwhile, because of wildly fluctuating exchange rates, the central banking system and the I.M.F. were all but out of business; the I.M.F.'s resources of more than twenty-five billion dollars were frozen almost as effectively as if the combination to the vault had been lost, and so were almost forty billion dollars' worth of gold held as reserves by various nations, and some twenty billion more in currency ordinarily available in short-term reciprocal-loan agreements between central banks.

So just about everyone came to the Sheraton–Park angry or worried or seized by a sense of urgency, or all three. Here were the top economic authorities of the non-Communist world coming together to engage in discussions that were all but totally incomprehensible not just to the man in the street but to everyone but a tiny fraction of humanity, yet the matters being decided were of vital day-to-day concern to people of almost every station in many countries. No wonder the participants tended to give off whiffs of mystery and self-importance. Such meetings—where big things happening behind closed doors are reflected only dimly in public statements, which have the attenuated quality of the shadows in Plato's cave—are strongly subject to sudden changes in mood. On Saturday, the mood was all hostility and gloom. Early on Sunday morning, the French finance minister, M. Giscard d'Estaing, suggested to a reporter that something had happened overnight to soften the United States' attitude. Whether or not this was true is unknown; the United States swiftly denied it, yet the day's events seemed to confirm it. That morning, the Group of Ten met again, and this meeting, instead of ending in a shouting match, as the one in London had, produced agreement on an agenda for future work: Over the subsequent weeks, the delegates would devote themselves to discussions of a realignment of currencies and removal of the United States import surcharge. It was not agreement on much of substance, but at least it was *agreement*. Then, on Sunday afternoon, it was Secretary Connally's turn to face the press. Generally seeming like a brash freshman among the mandarins of finance, the large Texan nevertheless spoke more moderately than before. He described the atmosphere of the Group of Ten meeting as "very friendly" and "very amiable," and "somewhat more relaxed" than the one in London had been, and he said that "we are talking in a low, quiet voice," though "the position of the United States has not changed at all." On one subject, however, he implied that he meant either more or less than he said. A reporter asked why, in closing its gold window to the world, and thus overthrowing the Bretton Woods system, the United States had kept ten billion dollars' worth of gold in its coffers, especially since Mr. Connally had insisted several times that gold was of only political and symbolic importance in the world monetary scheme and that the United States was determined to lessen the metal's role there. The Secretary replied, "Well, we still have some liabilities that have a call on it. We don't know quite who to give it to. . . . We would like to keep it, under the circumstances." While we had tipped over the table because we said that a whole new game was needed, it seemed that we had been mysteriously careful to salt away a large private supply—a quarter of the world's monetary gold—of the ostensibly discredited blue chips from the old game.

DURING the five days of formal speeches that followed, the representatives of the great monetary powers kept returning to the noble sentiment that the time for recriminations against the United

States was past, that what was done was done, and that the thing now was to get on with the job of rebuilding—and to get on with it quickly, since every week that passed with the import surcharge in effect and the system in chaos made the rebuilding more difficult and the chance for a world trade war greater. Mr. Schweitzer, a suave and studious-looking Frenchman of fifty-nine, with a background in the French Treasury and the wartime Resistance, made these points in his opening address, emphasizing above all the need for a collaborative approach to the common problem, rather than a competitive one, and his views were echoed in one degree or another by the delegates—or, in central-bank language, governors—for West Germany, Britain, and France, and even Japan and Canada, the two countries hardest hit by the import surcharge in terms of volume of exports. It was the governors for the small and underdeveloped countries who seemed to have the hardest time working themselves into a collaborative frame of mind. The governor for New Zealand, for one, pointed out that, much as the large trading countries might worry about unstable currencies, small ones like his had far more reason to be alarmed by the consequent disruption of world trade, since they had, relatively, so much more at stake; for example, exports account for ten per cent of Japan's gross national product and twenty-three per cent of New Zealand's. The governor for Israel, leaving the immediate subject far behind but drawing loud applause nevertheless, took a roundhouse swing at the great powers not as manipulators of money and trade but as physical and spiritual polluters. He said, "One-third of humanity—the developed world—has fallen prey to hedonistic tendencies, worshipping the idol of consumption and status symbols and enslaved to a multiplicity of modern gadgets, turning its back on human and spiritual values. . . . Overconsumption, with its attendant discharge of noxious wastes and its endless accumulation of disused materials, has become a primary source of pollution of water and air, soil and sea, ruining the beauty of the natural environment and perniciously affecting human life in the noisy, grimy megalopolis. . . ." This portmanteau complaint, relevant in spirit if not in letter, seemed to reflect the underdeveloped countries' frustration over their impotence in world monetary affairs. Important decisions in the I.M.F. are taken by weighted vote; it is economic muscle that counts, and in the end, despite the organization's democratic apparatus, the Group of Ten decides while the small countries watch. The governor for Algeria spoke of "the unjust situation of which our countries are victims," and the governor for Trinidad and Tobago spoke of "those of us who now sit on the sidelines and watch with concern the power play in force between the developed countries," while the governor for Tanzania—Amir Jamal, a jovial, witty fellow in corridor conversations—asked his fellow-governors ruefully, "Well, what is one supposed to be able to do here at all?" The big powers' answer to his question was implied in the conduct of Secretary Connally, who sat in his place at the head of the United States delegation during the speeches by representatives of the major nations but was absent during those coming from such nations as New Zealand, Israel, Algeria, Trinidad and Tobago, and Tanzania. A curious sidelight is that in spite of the presence at the meeting of a delegation representing South Vietnam, and in spite of the fact that the Vietnam war was a major cause of the dollar crisis that the meeting was about, the Vietnam war was not mentioned in a single speech.

All the while, however, the governors were biting the bullet and resolutely following Schweitzer's advice to get on with the building of a new international system before the monetary world should come apart entirely. Aside from temporary considerations, like the import surcharge and the matter of United States devaluation, the problem was clear: It was agreed that gold as a basis for money was obsolete and regressive, and that the dollar was a fallen sun, but no other national currency was reliable enough to be considered as a successor. What then? Diamonds? Some other durable metal (like tin, as Tan Siew Sin, the governor for tin-producing Malaysia, shyly suggested)? Rejecting such ideas as impractical, the governors for the great powers turned more and more, as the meeting progressed, to an existing facility of the I.M.F. called Special Drawing Rights, or S.D.R.s.

S.D.R.s had existed for less than two years, and, by an odd irony, had come into being in response to a problem that was essentially the opposite of the present one. In April, 1968, two weeks after the end of a dollar-gold crisis at whose height the United States had been losing gold at a rate of more than a million dollars every four minutes, the Group of Ten, realizing that one source of the trouble was a shortage of money to finance trade, had decided to create a supplement to existing reserve assets which would be periodically allocated to members of the I.M.F. in amounts proportionate to their subscriptions to the Fund, and would, it was hoped, be used freely and trusted just as if it were gold. The notion was to create a trading unit worth one dollar— not even a piece of paper, like a banknote, but merely an entry in the I.M.F.'s books—that, through the alchemy of mutual confidence, would for all practical purposes *become* gold because the members agreed to consider it so. In the early discussions, it had been suggested that the new unit be called a "drawing unit reserve asset," so that it could be reduced to the comforting acronym DURA, but that proposal had been rejected, and the less imaginative term S.D.R. agreed upon, while the far from reassuring phrase "paper gold" became the common nickname for S.D.R.s. Whatever its nomenclatural handicap, the S.D.R. system was ratified by the I.M.F. member nations, and the first allocation of S.D.R.s was made on January 1, 1970. Over the following twenty months, about six billion three hundred million dollars in S.D.R.s was allocated to a hundred and nine I.M.F. members, and in no case were the units dishonored by being treated as anything less than pure gold.

In 1968, the problem had been lack of liquidity. Now it was just the reverse—the world was not merely liquid but awash with unwanted dollars. The governors nevertheless seized on this phantom currency that had been helpful in the old situation to deal with the new one. S.D.R.s were already "in place" and functioning. Why not make *them* the basis of the world's money? On Tuesday, September 28th, the second day of the formal meeting, Britain's governor, Mr. Barber, presented a detailed plan whereby the S.D.R.s, or somewhat modified S.D.R.s, would become not a mere supplement to other reserves but the key reserve, the main asset in which countries would hold their money, and, in addition, would replace the dollar as the *numéraire* for all national currencies; thus an adequate supply of world money could be created at will by the I.M.F.; thus liquidity would be assured without the danger of relying on one country's international deficit. A dollar would be just another white chip. Like most good ideas, it was both a daring and an obvious one. Later that day, it was seconded in general terms, though not in all particulars, by Italy, Japan, and Canada, and even by traditionally gold-loving France.

That evening, there was an air in the Sheraton–Park corridors of shared experience, of excitement at history-making creativity; at the heart of all the talk was the uninspiring expression "S.D.R.s." There was even talk, more or less serious, of valuing gold itself in terms of paper gold, instead of vice versa. But on Wednesday came a letdown. The governor for Australia pointed out in his speech that S.D.R.s, like any other reserve asset, could be discredited by overuse—a point that many of the participants had appeared to overlook in their euphoria of the previous evening. And several underdeveloped countries pointed out that in proposing S.D.R.s as the new main reserve asset the great powers were seeking, in effect, to introduce into the game new blue chips of which they, because of their larger I.M.F. subscriptions, would issue themselves far more than they would anyone else. The solution some of the underdeveloped countries proposed was that allocation of S.D.R.s be determined in the future in part by the amount of a nation's aid to poorer nations—a suggestion that was not picked up by any of the great powers.

Everyone waited to hear from the proprietor of the old *numéraire*, the United States, and on Thursday morning Mr. Connally made his reappearance. His address, the emphasis of which seemed to be largely on economic advantage-seeking rather than on system-building, put a damper on the meeting's spirit of hope and enthusiasm. The United States, he said, would remove the import surcharge when other countries dismantled their own trade barriers and let their currencies float freely upward against the dollar without intervention. On United States devaluation he was coy, saying that "a change in the gold price is of no economic significance and would be patently a retrogressive step in terms of our objective to reduce, if not eliminate, the role of gold in any new monetary system," but he did not entirely rule out such a move. He accepted, by implication, a smaller role for the dollar, but, unlike all the other governors for large trading nations, he didn't mention S.D.R.s at all.

The meeting nonetheless ended on Friday with an apparent consensus that a good start had been made, and that S.D.R.s represented a sort of last, best hope for the restoration of monetary order. A vaguely worded resolution, adopted unanimously on Friday morning, called on the I.M.F.'s executive directors "to make reports to the board of governors without delay on the measures that are necessary or desirable for the improvement or reform of the international monetary system . . . including the role of reserve currencies, gold, and Special Drawing Rights." The executives could go home and make their reports.

The problems of the I.M.F.'s fallen idol, the dollar, and its scapegrace member, the United States, were not solved, and neither were the questions of the import surcharge and United States devaluation. But for one golden moment, it did appear more likely than it had that, for the first time ever, the nations of the world would eventually find themselves trading under a system based essentially on mutual trust rather than on a scarce metal. That likelihood has ironies of its own. At Bretton Woods in 1944, Keynes had backed—and the United States had vetoed—the creation of an arbitrary reserve unit very much like the S.D.R., to be called the "bancor" (literally, "bank gold"). As for the S.D.R.s themselves, although they could not normally be exchanged by their holders for gold, they were officially valued in gold: .888671 gram per S.D.R. Moreover, a little-noted section of the I.M.F.'s Articles of Agreement states that in case a member nation withdraws from the organization while holding S.D.R.s, redemption of the S.D.R.s "shall be made with currency or gold." Even in the new poker game, then, the old, presumably obsolete blue chip would have its possibly sinister place in each player's pile.

THE promise of that euphoric meeting at the start of the decade was, of course, not to be fulfilled. In December, 1971, came the so-called Smithsonian agreement, which Nixon rashly hailed as the greatest such agreement in the history of the world. Under it, the United States lifted its import surcharge, and the dollar was devalued by about eight per cent—the amount Schweitzer had wanted, rather than the "not one iota" that Connally had promised. The "greatest agreement in history" soon sank without a trace. The United States continued to run enormous international payments deficits, and in 1972 was forced to another devaluation. Then the O.P.E.C. embargo and oil price increase changed the whole course of the game. Suddenly, certain underdeveloped countries were holders of the high hand, if not winners on the board. In the resulting world panic, S.D.R.s and their brief promise of monetary salvation were all but forgotten in the general rush for the barbarous relic, gold. As for the United States—a nation that for a generation had been living the life of a Bourbon king largely on the strength of credit and bluff, and that now faced the prospect of gradually coming to face the reality of living something more like the life of a commoner—the plain fact was that its chief remaining blue chip in the game, now that the dollar had been reduced to the status of a very white chip indeed, was the very commodity—gold—that in the nominal idealism of September, 1971, it had declared obsolescent, while holding onto a fat pile, just in case. At that time, the nation's ten billion dollars of gold at thirty-five dollars an ounce had amounted to not quite three hundred million ounces. By late 1978, as one of a series of desperate moves to shore up the ever-sinking dollar, we had sold off more than ten million ounces, and were selling at a rate that would exhaust the whole national supply in about a generation. Meanwhile, at the price of nearly four hundred dollars per ounce prevailing in September, 1979, the remaining U.S. hoard of gold was worth one hundred billion dollars. That sum, despite the dollar's progressive devaluation against other currencies over the intervening years, nevertheless represented in terms of those currencies an enormous increase in the present value of the U.S. gold hoard over its value in 1971.

The table-tipper, it has turned out, before walking away from the table had pocketed the bluest chip of all.

$$$$$$$$$$$$$$$$$$$$
$$$$$$$$$$$$$$$$$$$$
$$$$$$$$$$$$$$$$$$$$$
$$$$$$$$$$$$$$$$$$$$$
$$$$$$ **9** $$$$$$
$$$$$$ $$$$$$
$$$$$$ $$$$$$
$$$$$$$$$$$$$$$$$$$$$
$$$$$$$$$$$$$$$$$$$$$
$$$$$$$$$$$$$$$$$$$$$
$$$$$$$$$$$$$$$$$$$$$
$$$$$$$$$$$$$$$$$$$$

It Will Grow on You

ON NOVEMBER 1, 1972, the second-largest industrial corporation in the world—General Motors was the largest—abandoned the name that it had borne throughout its existence, Standard Oil Company (New Jersey), and adopted instead the rather curious and entirely meaningless designation Exxon Corporation. At about the same time, it dropped for most domestic (though not for foreign) use the trademark Esso, under which it was accustomed to selling, among many other things, millions of gallons of gasoline a day in the United States, and began marketing its products in this country under the new brand name Exxon. Illogical as it may seem, the company name change, as opposed to the change of brand name, had a good deal of precedent in contemporary corporate usage. Companies have been changing their names all the time in recent years, for a variety of reasons—for example, to eliminate product identification that is no longer considered appropriate or desirable (R. J. Reynolds Tobacco Company to R. J. Reynolds Industries, Inc.), to try for zippiness (South Penn Oil Company to Pennzoil Company), to conform to a craze for naming companies by initials (Radio Corporation of America to RCA Corporation), and to recognize diversification of product lines resulting from mergers (Alpha Portland Cement Company to Alpha Portland Industries). Indeed, most successful companies have probably changed their names at one time or another; to cite two spectacularly successful examples, International Business Machines was once called Computing-Tabulating-Recording Company, while Xerox Corporation, before it marketed its first office copier, was known as Haloid Company. Never, though, had the change represented a leading company's relinquishment of its flag at a time when the flag was flying high, and never had it involved the relinquishment of a famous brand name. Jersey Standard's daring and drastic change of company name, and of one of the best-known of all trademarks, was an event unique in corporate history.

The reasons for it involved not a corporate death wish or a corporate identity crisis but legal restrictions, and they went back to 1911, when a Supreme Court ruling resulted in the breakup of the old, and generally infamous, Standard Oil trust into thirty-four competing companies, of which seven retained the name Standard Oil in their titles—among them Standard Oil Company (Ohio), Standard Oil Company (Indiana), and Standard Oil Company (New Jersey). Jersey Standard, the largest of the products of the 1911 split-up, introduced the brand name Esso in 1926, and by 1933 was using it from Maine to Louisiana and hoping eventually to use it in all states. But in 1935 Indiana Standard took court action challenging the use of Esso in its territory, maintaining that the name was derived from the initials "S.O.," meaning "Standard Oil," and that Indiana Standard was Standard Oil just as much as Jersey Standard was. The petition was granted. Jersey Standard was forbidden to call its product Esso in fourteen states, and in a series of subsequent court actions the area in which the trademark might indisputably be used was gradually narrowed to nineteen Eastern and Southern states and the District of Columbia. As a result, in recent years Jersey Standard had marketed its gasoline in the undisputed area as Esso and elsewhere in the nation under two other trademarks—Humble in Ohio, Enco in the remaining states. The resulting anomalies were both frustrating and expensive; for example, customers in the border areas were understandably unable to grasp the fact that Esso gas, Enco gas, and Humble gas were all the same product, and Jersey Standard could not sponsor network television shows without incurring extra costs, running into millions of dollars, for making different versions of the same commercial to be shown in different areas.

Through most of the nineteen-sixties, Jersey Standard's directors had been mulling over the possibility of putting an end to the confusion by adopting an entirely new trademark, which could be used nationally—and, while they were about it, adopting a new company title, which would end the public's chronic confusion of Jersey Standard with the other Standard Oil companies. Then, in 1969, the Supreme Court finally cut off Jersey Standard's lingering hopes of getting the right to use Esso everywhere, and the company's directors were galvanized into action. A special task force, pledged to the strictest secrecy, was appointed to find a new name for both the company and its products, the stipulations being that the name should be short, that it should be easy to pronounce and to remember, that it should have "no adverse connotations" in English or any other language, and that, preferably, it should not be cluttered up with any meaning at all. Naturally, the services of a computer were enlisted, along with those of a team of linguistic experts, a leading design firm, and a battery of lawyers. The computer came through with ten thousand names (eight thousand fewer than the Ford Motor Company's advertising consultants had collected in 1956 in their epic search for a new-car name, which ended catastrophically with Edsel). By slow degrees, the ten thousand were winnowed down to eight—among them the piquant and spiky Exxon. Since there was a possibility that the new name might someday be used overseas, the task force ordered linguistic studies on Exxon and the other surviving names in more than a hundred languages (the experts found that, except in proper names like Foxx and Oxx, the doubled "x" occurs in no language but Maltese), intensive consumer studies in areas where nine different languages are spoken, and interviews with nearly seven thousand persons in the United States and abroad. Did the task force or its consultants, or perhaps the computer, take note of the fact that Exxon is almost an anagram of Xerox, by all odds the most successful new brand name and company name of recent years? No one is saying. At any rate, Exxon passed its tests; it was easy to pronounce in most languages, and apparently did not mean anything vulgar or objectionable—or, indeed, anything at all—in any. Sometime in 1970, the task force picked it as the winner.

A bigger, harder choice then faced Jersey Standard's directors: whether or not to adopt the new name—whether to take arms against a sea of troubles by abandoning an established trademark and company name of inestimable value or to play it safe and muddle along with the status quo. After much soul-searching, they decided to go ahead with the change. Immediately, the company, or those within it who were in on the secret, began girding for a spiritual and perhaps a material crisis. Would employees hate the new name and lose some of their company loyalty? Would stockholders hate it and sell their stock—or vote down the change, as they would be entitled to do? Worst of all, would motorists think that Exxon sounded like funny stuff, and buy Sunoco or Texaco instead? Dozens of executives pondered these questions in secret meetings of ad-hoc committees. Beginning in mid-1971, a number of men in the public-affairs department were assigned full time to communications inside and outside the company on the name change. One of them was David G. Powell, a sharp-featured, soft-spoken suburbanite Princeton graduate of about forty, who had spent his whole working life with Jersey Standard, much of it abroad. Powell's first problem at his new stand was that of being strictly forbidden to communicate at all. Pending a formal announcement by a company spokesman, the choice of the name Exxon was even more secret than the purpose of the task force had been, and for good reason: There are professional pirates who rove the corporate seas seeking to capture new brand names and hold them for ransom, and premature news of a planned replacement for Esso would be the choicest imaginable bit of booty. Company men communicated with each other about the new name in terse notes that were instantly destroyed.

At last, in September of 1971, Humble Oil & Refining Co.—then the name of Jersey Standard's chief domestic affiliate—announced that it had registered the new trademark Exxon and would immediately begin tests of it in service stations in six cities in the United States: Athens, Georgia; Zanesville, Ohio; Manchester, New Hampshire; Battle Creek, Michigan; Nacogdoches, Texas; and San Luis Obispo, California. And now the surprise: From that moment of revelation until November of 1972, when Jersey Standard became Exxon Corporation and Esso gas was well along toward becoming Exxon gas at roadsides from coast to coast, *hardly anything went wrong*. No corporate identity crisis or customer negative transference developed. The company's fears proved to have been unfounded; indeed, comparatively few people seemed to care much. Sales actually rose at the test service stations, surely in response to special promotions. Employees and stockholders for the most part reacted with indifference, if they reacted at all. In May of 1972, Humble Oil announced that in July Exxon would definitely begin replacing Esso, Enco, and Humble as the company's primary brand name in the domestic market (Esso was retained for use on a few domestic products, in order to protect the trademark), and it was revealed for the first time that plans were also afoot to change the company's name to Exxon Corporation. On June 21st, at a meeting in the Grand

Ballroom of the New York Hilton, J. K. Jamieson, the company's chairman, formally notified the company's twenty-one hundred New York City employees that Jersey Standard was going to become Exxon, provided the stockholders approved. The employees —practically all of whom attended the meeting, leaving the company's executive offices, at 1251 Avenue of the Americas, all but deserted for part of the afternoon—were allowed to submit written questions, and Jamieson and Milo M. Brisco, the company's president, spent more than an hour answering them. Company officials have since said that, to judge from the tone of the meeting, the employees' first reactions were, at best, neutral; people like to work for firms with well-known names, and a substantial number of the Jersey Standard people seemed to feel that working for Exxon Corporation might somehow represent a social demotion. So now there *were* signs of an incipient corporate identity crisis. But over the subsequent weeks the public-affairs department communicated furiously, the plans went forward, and the employees gradually warmed to the new name. "It will grow on you," company officials kept telling them. The nearest thing to a symptom of a developing underground revolt was a brief appearance at various places in the headquarters building of stencilled signs reading "Exxit." In September, an intensive changeover advertising campaign was launched nationally. On October 24th, the Jersey Standard stockholders met at the Roosevelt Hotel to debate the corporate-name change and to vote on it. Of a total of about seven hundred and eighty thousand stockholders, only about a thousand attended the meeting, the rest being represented by proxy. Of the stockholders who spoke up at the Roosevelt, few, even among those who most vociferously opposed the change, seemed to entertain any hope that the corporate juggernaut could be stopped and the change voted down. Some felt that Exxon had unfortunate connotations of poison, detergent, laxatives, or a double cross; one, an Esso service-station owner named Louis E. Cress, said that he had changed his name from Crescenzi some years earlier so that it would go better with Esso, and pointed out that he could hardly be expected now to change it to Crexx. The vote, including proxies, was more than ninety-six per cent in favor of the change. Accordingly, a week later Jersey Standard formally became Exxon Corporation, and on January 1, 1973, Humble and most of the company's other domestic subsidiaries were formally merged into it under new names, which in each case included the word "Exxon."

At the same time, the job of changing the company's twenty-five thousand or so service stations in the United States over to the new, rectangular, red-white-and-blue Exxon insignia was going forward, more or less without incident, and apparently without loss of sales. In most parts of the country, dealers gave a plastic thermal mug free to anyone who had his car's gas tank filled up—as if the change of a company name and trademark called for a formal act of expansiveness, like the distribution of cigars by a new father. The company, however, did not press this analogy; on the contrary, in its advertisements and news releases it deliberately avoided any implication of trying to spring forth newborn or to wipe out the past. Letters about the name change—some two thousand of them, all told—were coming in from stockholders and from the public, and the task of answering most of those from the public fell to Powell. A man in Penllyn, Pennsylvania, seemed to feel that Jersey Standard was trading in its soul, and complained, "The desire for more money seems to destroy everything that is good." In reply, Powell, not denying that the company desired money, suggested that the letter writer's devotion to the name Esso resulted "not only from whatever intrinsic value or beauty may reside in the name itself, but also and perhaps more importantly from what Esso has come to mean and stand for in the way of quality products and services, and general corporate conduct," and he declared, "These elements we do not intend to change." Another letter writer pronounced himself disgusted with the company's creation of a hubbub over a name change in a time of such pressing national problems as war, pollution, unemployment, and racism. "We did think about this one carefully and for a long time and in our judgment the project represents a sound investment," Powell replied, in part. A Connecticut correspondent made his cultural criticism more specific. The choice of a "computer-generated pre- and suffix," he wrote, reflected disregard of "a deep-running cultural change which we encounter daily in our work: to search for human and natural values . . . rather than an anonymous . . . and synthetic construct." Powell replied, "In the final analysis, the name itself is probably less important than what people come to perceive it stands for."

WHEN the last Esso service-station sign in this country was replaced with an Exxon sign, in the spring of 1973, the metamorphosis was complete. Its cost to the company has been officially withheld but has repeatedly been estimated by outsiders at around a hundred million dollars. (This covered, among other things, an average of fifty new signs and insignia for each of the twenty-five thousand stations; new plaques for twenty-two thousand oil wells and eighteen thousand buildings and storage tanks; fifty-five thousand new warning signs announcing the presence of pipelines underground; three hundred million sales slips; eleven million credit cards; and an unannounced but clearly astronomical number of television commercials calculated to implant "Exxon" deep in the nation's psyche.) The cost was amortized over a number of years to avoid causing a sudden drop in the company's earnings. Meanwhile, life in the carpeted offices at 1251 Avenue of the Americas remained calm and orderly. Company sales of gasoline and other products continued to run at the previous year's levels or higher. Powell came through the whole experience without acquiring a single visible gray hair; asked later to name the worst thing that had happened during the name-changing process, all he could recall was the time a vice-president, checking out an Exxon sign beside a highway in North Carolina, had narrowly escaped being bitten by a rattlesnake.

NOT much later, Exxon found itself with problems more substantive than its name to worry about. In the autumn of 1973 came the O.P.E.C. oil embargo, which threw the entire oil business into a kind of convulsion, and the public into a disposition to hate all oil companies, starting with the biggest ones. About two years later came revelations of improper political contributions and other payments abroad, amounting to enormous sums, by Exxon and some of its subsidiaries. In its preoccupation with such matters as those, the company quickly lost its initial self-consciousness about its name. By late 1978, it was feeling so self-assured on the matter that it brought suit against Xonex Synthetic Lubricants, Inc., a small manufacturer of motor oil in Miami, Florida, on grounds that Xonex had deliberately chosen to call itself by an anagram of Exxon, and had thus infringed Exxon's trademark. "The conduct of [Xonex] has damaged [Exxon], and will further impair, if not destroy, the value of [Exxon's] trade name, trademark, and goodwill," Exxon said in its court filing.

Regardless of how the case might come out, Exxon's complaint must be regarded as an instance of exaggeration for emphasis. Pretty clearly, nothing, not even competition from Xonex, can destroy the value of Exxon's trademark, which is now firmly rooted in the national consciousness. The company's rash act of 1972 overthrew one of the oldest axioms of business theory—that a successful trademark is sacrosanct, and that to change it is suicide.

Retaking Pittsburgh

ON SEPTEMBER 2, 1975, Société Imetal, a huge French-based holding company with a variety of mining and mineral-producing interests scattered around the world, publicly announced that it intended to buy all the outstanding stock of the Copperweld Corporation, of Pittsburgh, a sixty-year-old manufacturer of such specialized steel products as tubes and alloy wire, with about thirty-six hundred employees and annual sales of three hundred and twenty million dollars, or just enough to put it near the bottom of

Fortune's list of the nation's five hundred largest industrial companies. A substantial number of American companies (Brown & Williamson, Baskin–Robbins, Stouffer, and Bantam Books, to name a few) had foreign owners at that time, so on the face of the matter there was nothing especially out of the way about Imetal's plans. There were, however, some unusual aspects to the situation. For one thing, Imetal's attempt to buy Copperweld—through direct offer to all of Copperweld's eighty-two hundred stockholders to buy any or all of their two and a half million shares for $42.50 a share in cash—was being made over the emphatic, even passionate opposition of Copperweld's management. The management had first heard of the planned attempt only four days earlier, on August 29th, when a man from Kuhn, Loeb & Company, one of Imetal's two New York banking representatives, telephoned Copperweld's executive vice-president, Howell A. Breedlove, Jr., to say that he represented Imetal, that the company intended to buy all of Copperweld's shares, and that he wanted to arrange a meeting. Breedlove, who was hearing the name Imetal for only the second time in his life, might have felt less threatened if the company had still been called by its former name, Le Nickel. In any case, he went through what he has since described as a few minutes of shock, and later that day he talked with his boss, Phillip H. Smith, Copperweld's forty-eight-year-old chairman and president, who happened to be in Hawaii. Smith hurried home, and at the meeting with Imetal representatives, which took place early on September 2nd, the representatives said that they intended to make the tender offer with or without Copperweld's blessing. The following day, Smith sent a letter to all Copperweld stockholders characterizing the Imetal offer of $42.50 a share as "substantially below the true value" and strongly recommending that they turn it down. Thus, the Imetal–Copperweld affair became the first hostile takeover attempt—in contrast to friendly merger agreement—of a large American company by a foreign one in the whole era of conglomerate mergers, then already more than a decade old. And, of course—particularly in days when European capitalists increasingly feared for the future of their domestic political and monetary stability and when Arab oil producers had vast sums of cash to invest as they pleased—it was certainly not going to be the last.

The other arresting aspect of this development was the identity of the insurgent chieftain, the chairman of the board of Imetal. He was Baron (by courtesy) Guy de Rothschild, a great-great-grandson of the original Meyer Amschel Rothschild and, at the age of sixty-six, the nominal head of the current generation of the most celebrated European banking family in history.

OVER the decade preceding Imetal's assault on Copperweld, the form of combat between attackers and defenders in intra-American corporate-takeover attempts had become as stylized as a medieval tournament. For example, it was now de rigueur for the aggressor, in laying his battle plans, to refer to the target company in internal memorandums by a code name, just as Saul Steinberg had done. Accordingly, Rothschild, apparently well versed in the parochial etiquette of the matter and not above conforming to it, had while en route by airliner from New York to Paris on July 10th, eight weeks before the tender offer was made, written a memo to a subordinate—Bernard de Villeméjane, the managing director of Imetal—in which he referred to Copperweld as Bread. In the same memo, he referred to two other American companies, which Imetal later discarded as takeover targets, and whose identity has never been revealed, as Butter and Garlic. ("I don't *like* garlic," the Baron declared later, in Pittsburgh.) Focusing his attention on Bread, Rothschild commented in the memo, "Bread can easily say, perhaps prove, that the stock is worth more than thirty-five [somewhat more than its market price at the time]. . . . We ought to be able to offer forty-three to forty-five so as not to seem broke." (Since Imetal actually offered $42.50, Rothschild's fear of its seeming broke appears to have receded slightly during August.) Of Smith, his future antagonist, Rothschild wrote with rueful respect, "The personality of the boss . . . hard and capable, seems to preclude agreement, and promises a choice of effective and determined means of defense."

The means of defense that Smith chose after the tender offer had been made were equally conventional, with one exception. A standard move for a corporation under attack is to solicit a better offer from some friendlier aggressor, in order to frustrate the original one. Smith, the son of an Australian sea captain in the South Seas trade whose sternness with dockworkers had earned him the nickname Master Hurry-Up, disdained to do this. Once during the Imetal tender offer, another company head called Smith by radiotelephone from his jet, saying that he was on his way to lunch in New York City and would zoom into Pittsburgh afterward to make a bid for Copperweld stock. Smith replied that he was generally around the office until six o'clock and had no intention of remaining later that day. The airborne executive arrived, as promised, but not until after Smith had gone home, as promised. "I wasn't going to solicit counterbids from some Mickey Mouse outfit just to spite Imetal," Smith told me when I visited him at his office later.

In other respects, Smith went by the book. He flooded Copperweld's stockholders (by letter) and the public (through newspaper advertisements) with arguments to prove that the stockholders would be unwise to tender their shares to Imetal. And, in conformity with custom, his attacks on Imetal's offer were brisk but not savagely ad hominem. A defender in a takeover attempt, like a politician in a primary, must remember that if he loses he will probably end up working for his antagonist—a situation that tends to make for a certain gentlemanliness in the combat statements of corporate defenders. "COPPERWELD SECURITY HOLDERS READ THIS CAREFULLY," Smith headlined a prominent ad in the *Times* and other papers on September 8th. He noted in the ad that Imetal's offer was "inadequate," that Copperweld's sales, earnings, and future prospects were excellent, and that, moreover, the transaction would be fully taxable and might violate various United States laws. No mention at all of the Rothschilds or their possibly sinister intentions. Copperweld did mention the Rothschilds in a subsequent ad, published in various newspapers on October 17th, which read, in part, "The foreign-based holding company is controlled by the Rothschild family. . . . This offer, secretly planned and organized, was presented on a take-it-or-leave-it basis," and went on to cite Smith's argument that "the control of Copperweld by Imetal would not be in the best interests of shareholders, employees, and the communities in which Copperweld plants are located." After the whole thing was over, Smith told me, "I felt deeply committed to Copperweld as an independent company, but I wanted all the blows to land above the belt." As for Imetal, after an initial for-the-record advertisement occupying most of three pages of small type in the *Times* and other papers, in which the tender offer was explained in full, it took no ads except those required by law. Perhaps Imetal, for all its ready adaptability to New World corporate customs, could not quite swallow the notion, generally accepted in the United States, that advertisements in newspapers intended for the general public are essential to persuading a few thousand stockholders, who might more logically be harangued by mail. (American corporations still use the mails, too, but are not convinced that their stockholders read letters from them.) Or perhaps Imetal thought that the offer spoke for itself.

One standard feature of the corporate-takeover game that Imetal had early occasion to learn about is that quarrelling over the rules is apt to play a large role in it. Copperweld launched its first legal fusillade on September 5th, by filing suit in federal district court in Pittsburgh asking for an injunction against Imetal on the grounds that Imetal's offer violated the United States antitrust laws, in part because another American company, Amax, Inc., had a substantial minority interest in Imetal, and violated the United States securities laws, because Imetal had failed to make required disclosures about itself to the Securities and Exchange Commission and to Copperweld stockholders. That day, the federal district judge, John L. Miller, issued a temporary restraining order against Imetal pending a hearing on the matter. A few days later, Copperweld opened a new legal front by pointing out that the Imetal offer might violate the securities laws of Ohio, where Copperweld maintained two plants, and a few days after that the Ohio Department of Commerce obtained an order directing

Imetal to cease and desist from offering to buy Copperweld shares until hearings could be held. So far, everything was according to Hoyle. But early in the game a most unorthodox element was introduced when the Copperweld nonmanagement employees made clear that they not only opposed an Imetal takeover but opposed it a good deal more strongly than their bosses did.

THROUGHOUT the history of American labor, the unions representing workers have seldom, to say the least, shown a passionate wish to support company managements in their internal quarrels or in any of their other enterprises. Rather, unions have usually regarded corporate power struggles with disdain, taking the attitude that they couldn't care less who their bosses were as long as the bosses supplied good wages and fringe benefits. Furthermore, in the nineteen-sixties, when American corporations were furiously engaged in extending their operations abroad, there were loud outcries from labor about the evils of thus "exporting jobs." Since labor opposed foreign investment by American companies, wasn't it logical to suppose that labor would *favor* the exact opposite— investment in the United States by foreign companies?

Apparently not. The first public sign of labor's feelings on the Copperweld matter came on September 5th, when I. W. Abel, the president of the United Steelworkers of America, which represented more than two-thirds of the Copperweld workers, issued a statement that read, in part, "The brazen takeover threat initiated against Copperweld by Société Imetal, a foreign holding company based in Paris, France, is a classic example of what we vigorously oppose. . . . We of Labor are vitally disturbed by the special impact the takeover would have on our members . . . their families, and the communities in which Copperweld does business. . . . Our Union intends to do everything possible to protect the interests of our members and their families in this desperate attempt to take over Copperweld." In a rally on September 7th in Shelby, Ohio, the site of Copperweld's Ohio Steel Tube plant, speakers referred to Rothschild as "the robber baron," and one of them expressed the view that "the Rothschilds make the Rockefellers look like French peasants." The next day, about fifteen busloads of workers and their relatives from Copperweld's plant in Warren, Ohio, went to Washington and demonstrated at the French Embassy, the Federal Trade Commission, and the Capitol, carrying placards with such messages as "Keep Copperweld American" and "Go Home, Frenchie." The people of Copperweld's Bimetallics Division, in Glassport, Pennsylvania, had their turn a couple of days later. On the evening of September 10th, a good part of Glassport's population of eight thousand, including the mayor, representatives of the American Legion and the Sons of Italy, and leading local businessmen, staged an anti-Imetal rally outside the Copperweld plant; there was dancing in the streets, with music by the local high-school band, and a cheerfully militant carnival atmosphere prevailed. At midnight, seven busloads of Glassport Copperweld workers and their wives left for New York City. At Rockefeller Center the following morning, they picketed the New Court Securities Corporation, a Rothschild-affiliated banking firm with offices there, which was helping Kuhn, Loeb manage the Imetal offer, and then—with beyond-the-call-of-duty cooperation from the New York police, who not only gave them a traffic escort but offered incidental instruction in how to attract maximum public attention while picketing—proceeded to 40 Wall Street, where for several hours they good-humoredly picketed the offices of Kuhn, Loeb, attracting public attention by shouting and waving placards. Congressional hearings on the Imetal–Copperweld affair were held at Glassport and Shelby on September 12th and at Warren on the 13th. On the morning before the Warren hearing, the Steelworkers' union there, Local 2243, showed its seriousness by spending its own money on a full-page ad in the Warren *Tribune–Chronicle*, which urged all local citizens to attend the hearing and commented, "You may never spend a more important Saturday morning."

That turned out to be a considerable overstatement, but worker opposition to the takeover continued. As the matter was later explained to me by William Kostyzak, the president of Steelworkers Local 7373, representing clerical and technical employ-

ees at Glassport, the opposition was based principally on fears that
Imetal might eventually close one or more of Copperweld's United
States plants and move some of the company's manufacturing
operations to France, or that Rothschild, having got control of
Copperweld's large cash fund earmarked for expansion, might
"take it for his paper empire." (During the period of the tender
offer, Rothschild repeatedly denied that he had any such intentions.) "In a situation like that, you have to fear the worst,"
Kostyzak said. "We thought this guy was going to rape the company." There were also more emotional fears, based on the fact
that the insurgent was a foreigner; for example, one Copperweld
worker was shown on a Pittsburgh news program saying that he
didn't want his children standing in French breadlines. From
whatever motive, at any rate, sentiment among Copperweld workers was close to unanimous; according to Kostyzak, more than
nine out of ten union members at Glassport vocally opposed a
takeover. As for company management, it viewed this bonanza of
support from an unlikely quarter with wary approval. When Abel
made his statement, the company paid for a new spate of newspaper ads to reprint it in full. Smith, upon hearing of the union
plans to picket and demonstrate, at first refused to give his approval, out of fear that the workers were motivated by xenophobia,
but he changed his mind when he found out how much "momen-
tum" the movement had, and the company ended up paying for
the demonstrators' buses and giving the demonstrating workers an
expense allowance to make up part of the wages they lost on the
days of their trips. This anomalous identity of interest between
management and labor was, of course, less than complete. Management was bargaining for the aggressor to pay a higher price,
and trying to do so with such delicacy that it would avoid bargaining itself out of a job; labor, on the other hand, had no interest
either in the price paid for the stock or in the Baron's sensibilities
but was fighting, or so it felt, for its jobs pure and simple. Still, if
the suddenly cozy state of industrial relations at Copperweld could
not be called touching, it could be called rare. A plaque in Pittsburgh's Point State Park commemorates the conquest at that site

of the French Fort Duquesne by the British in 1758, and calls the victory the moment when "Anglo-Saxon supremacy in the United States" was established. Here was another Frenchman, this time as the invader. Clearly, Copperweld workers felt that it was a time to close ranks.

THE dramatic peak of the contest was Baron Rothschild's appearance in Pittsburgh on September 17th. A few days earlier, he had politely declined an invitation to attend a congressional hearing held on September 12th at the firehouse of the Reliance Hose Company No. 2, in Glassport, but now he turned up in Pittsburgh to testify voluntarily in Judge Miller's court on Copperweld's suit to stop the takeover. White-haired, with the distinguished bearing and ironic expression that the situation seemed to call for, the Baron told the court that in his view "for a company to have an investment in America is an upgrading of that company," and that if Imetal's takeover attempt should succeed, Copperweld's present management would remain in office and its policies would remain unchanged. In the courtroom that day, Rothschild and Smith met for the first time. "I walked up to him during a recess and we talked a little about his nephew, at the University of Southern California," Smith said later. On the sidewalk outside the courthouse, a delegation of Copperweld workers, led by Donald Maffitt, the president of Local 2243—wearing a hard hat, a ferocious expression, and a jacket proclaiming his team as Copperweld bowling champions for 1973–74—attempted to give Rothschild eight duffelbags that Maffitt said contained a hundred thousand signatures on petitions against the takeover. "Thank you and God bless you, but I don't think I could carry them," the Baron said. He added that the bags might be delivered to his local lawyer.

Not long after Rothschild's visit, with the tender offer still formally restrained by the Pittsburgh and Ohio court orders, Copperweld began losing ground in Washington and in the courts. On September 24th, Assistant Secretary of the Treasury Gerald L. Parsky told Congress, which had been toying with the idea of enacting legislation designed to stop Imetal, that in his opinion the government had no basis for intervention, and that several months earlier he had explicitly advised Rothschild that "the policy on foreign investment in the United States is to welcome it." On October 23rd, Judge Miller denied Copperweld's request for an injunction. That left only the Ohio case, and on November 12th the Court of Common Pleas in Columbus, satisfied that Imetal had complied with the local laws, dismissed it. Imetal was then legally free to buy Copperweld shares. Copperweld management, beaten on the rules, went on trying to persuade Imetal to sweeten its offer (which Imetal coolly declined to do) and its stockholders to hang on to their shares. Both Smith and Breedlove have since said that until December 1st they believed they could keep a majority of the Copperweld stock out of Imetal's hands. But they were wrong: The fact was that the holders of considerably more than half of Copperweld's stock liked the deal and took the cash. On December 11th, the day after the offer expired, Imetal announced that it had bought sixty-seven per cent of Copperweld common stock, for about seventy-five million dollars.

That same day, Smith stated—euphemistically, in the circumstances—that "we now welcome Imetal as an important stockholder." A few days later, he went at Imetal's invitation to Paris, where he met his future colleagues and had dinner at Rothschild's house. On the latter occasion, champagne was served before dinner, and Smith, who seldom drinks, demurred when it was offered to him, and asked for orange juice instead. This caused the butler to look outraged. Later, at dinner, wine was served in carafes, and the Baron described it to Smith as a "family wine," murmuring modestly that his family had some vineyards of which it was proud. (The Baron is part owner of Château Lafite–Rothschild.) Thus cozened, Smith choked down a little Rothschild wine. "That was when the healing started," Smith commented later. On December 19th, Copperweld added two Imetal representatives to its board of directors, and at the company's next annual meeting, in Chicago on April 28, 1976, a third Imetal man was elected to fill a vacancy. During the spring, Smith began taking brushup French lessons. In late May and early June, Rothschild visited Pittsburgh a second time; while there, he spoke in an amiable and conciliatory way, in impeccable English, to business leaders at the Duquesne Club and the Fox Chapel Golf Club, established a first-name relationship with Smith, and went to dinner at Smith's house, where the host had raised a French flag along with the American flag. Then, on June 15th, Smith was elected to Imetal's board of directors, and the healing, at least as far as Smith was concerned, appeared to be complete.

DURING the summer of 1976, I went to Pittsburgh to try to find out how Gallic supremacy at Copperweld was working out in practice. On meeting Smith and Breedlove at Copperweld headquarters, in the Frick Building, I found them apparently happy in their jobs and determined to remain there as long as their important transatlantic shareholder wanted them to. Smith and Breedlove pointed out to me that Imetal, even though it held a clear majority of Copperweld stock, had not sought formal control of the company's affairs, since its representatives held only three of the twelve seats on the board of directors; moreover, since a Copperweld bylaw provided that under ordinary circumstances only three directorships could come up for election each year, it would presumably be two more years before Imetal could obtain a clear majority on the board. Of course, they conceded, the bylaw could easily be circumvented if Imetal was determined to seize control of the board right away, but Smith told me he had been assured by Imetal that it had no present plans to seek any more board seats, and, further, that it had abandoned its original idea of buying all the Copperweld shares and had no present intention of trying to buy any of the thirty-three per cent still held by more than five thousand shareholders who had not tendered their shares. As for the degree of control over Copperweld operations now being exercised by Imetal, Smith said that he talked to Villeméjane in Paris once or twice a month, to discuss Copperweld plans; that the French directors of Copperweld, when they came to Pittsburgh for quarterly board meetings, usually stayed around an extra day or two to confer with Copperweld executives and visit plants; and that that is about it. I asked whether any representative of Imetal maintained a permanent office in Pittsburgh. "Just one," Smith replied. "Me. Don't forget, I'm on the Imetal board."

In the days following the successful completion of the takeover, Smith and Breedlove both conceded, an atmosphere of consternation prevailed at Copperweld headquarters. One staff man defected to a company that had offered him a higher salary. Breedlove, a combative Georgian of about forty, was by his own account "slower to turn around" in his attitude toward Imetal than was Smith. "I was amazed that Phil could fly right off to Paris," Breedlove told me. "I'm a real poor loser. It took me quite a few days to get turned around. I don't want to try to psychoanalyze myself, but maybe it was because I was the one who got that first telephone call from Kuhn, Loeb back on August 29, 1975." Realizing that the employees were still highly restive after Copperweld management had formally surrendered, Smith sent them all a reassuring letter and visited most of the company's plants, where he was subjected to what he described to me as "very forensic questioning." He added, "I told them, in effect, 'Take it on trust from me—everything will get back to normal. The French are men of character and decency.'" Then he told me, "No use kidding; if I had had my choice, the company would have remained independent, and I still don't like the way the tender offer was made, without prior consultation with us. It might turn out that I'm wrong now. But, as my father used to say, 'Get happy or get out.' In two or three years, this might turn out to be a bloody disaster. But I don't believe it."

I went out to Glassport, a smoky, mountain-ringed steel-mill town ten miles south of Pittsburgh, with road signs at its entrances reading "We Are Proud of Our Town—You Would Be Too If You Lived Here," and talked to Kostyzak, of the Steelworkers local. He said, "When we heard that Imetal had control of Copperweld, we thought the axe had fallen. But then nothing changed. Mr. Smith never came here to explain to us, as far as I know, but he did write us all a good letter. The union members have a lot of respect for him. This is a small plant, and there has generally been

pretty good rapport between union and management here. We
have the same contract as U.S. Steel, and we don't get pushed
around the way U.S. Steel people do. A few of our members felt
sold out when Mr. Smith went rushing off to Paris, and then again
when he joined the Imetal board. They said, 'So it was all a farce
—he was just fighting them for the record.' The majority of us
don't believe that. We saw him in action during the fighting, and it
seemed to us he got pretty worked up. Things are quiet here now.
We haven't noticed any impact since the takeover. I'd like to believe that Imetal means it when it says we won't be touched.
There's even some optimism that the takeover will mean new orders for us from France. We're hoping against hope. The next
three or four years will tell the story."

Things were quiet, but they were not tranquil. Dark dreams of
foreign devils were disturbing the peace of the steelworkers of
Glassport, as I learned from my talks with Kostyzak and other
workers there. Some felt snubbed, because Rothschild had declined to attend the congressional hearing in Glassport, where, or
near where, a majority of the local Copperweld workers were
born and raised; some resented as patronizing his description of
all Copperweld workers, in a newspaper interview in January of
1976, as "good children" who didn't understand the issues; some
had invented, apparently out of whole cloth, a gothically detailed
plot about an ancient Rothschild family grudge against the
specialty-steel business. But there was, as Kostyzak said, nothing
anyone at Glassport or at the other Copperweld plants could do
but wait and hope—and, perhaps, consider that if the British in
Pittsburgh had been as tactful after 1758 as the French at Copperweld have been since December of 1975, French might be the
language spoken in 1977 at the Duquesne Club and the Fox
Chapel Golf Club, and in the town of Glassport.

In fact, it took less than the three or four years predicted by
Smith for the rest of the story to unfold. When the Copperweld
annual report for the year 1976 was issued the following spring, it
contained only two passing mentions of Imetal's controlling interest in the company, suggesting a certain tendency on Smith's part

to pretend that Imetal wasn't there. Then, in October, 1977—twenty-two months after Imetal had assumed control—Smith suddenly resigned, stating without elaboration that he had "policy differences with the board of directors." Imetal had no comment to make. Smith was replaced by Anthony J. A. Bryan, who had previously been president of Cameron Iron Works, of Houston; Breedlove stayed on as executive vice-president. It must have reassured the Copperweld workers at Glassport and elsewhere that the new president wasn't a Frenchman, much less a Rothschild. Certainly it reassured them even more that by the end of 1978 there were more Copperweld employees at work than there had been in 1975; that no Copperweld operations had been moved to France or anywhere else; and that Imetal representatives still constituted a minority on the Copperweld board of directors. However, what the departure of Smith made clear was that with Imetal and Copperweld, as with so many other corporate takeovers not involving international tensions, from the point of view of the head of the old management the whole thing had turned out to be "a bloody disaster."

The Law School and
the Noodle Factory

OVER THE PAST GENERATION, the New York University School of
Law derived a substantial portion of its income from the sale of
spaghetti, macaroni, egg noodles, and related products. For the
academic year 1975–76, for example, the law school had a budget of nine million dollars, while in 1975 it took in two and a
quarter million from pasta. A man who went to work in an administrative post at the law school a few years ago was surprised to be
told by a colleague on his first day, "You'll have to understand

one thing. You may think you're working for a law school, but you're really working for a noodle factory." True, the law school had managed to scrape by for a long time before it had the benefit of pasta sales. Founded in 1835, it had operated continuously in the Washington Square area for a hundred and twelve years—turning out over that period some thirteen thousand lawyers, among them Samuel J. Tilden, Elihu Root, Jacob Javits, and believe it or not, Howard Cosell—before, in 1947, it became sole beneficiary of the profits of the C. F. Mueller Company, of Jersey City, New Jersey.

This circumstance came about chiefly through the efforts of Arthur T. Vanderbilt, then the law school's dean. At the time, the school's facilities were severely limited—it had no dormitories and its academic quarters were two upper floors of a partly commercial building—and its reputation was that of a commuting institution solely for students from the New York metropolitan area and with limited impact on the national legal profession. Dean Vanderbilt dreamed of making it into a "law center" of national reputation, and the main thing he needed in order to realize his dream was more money. That February, H. Theodore Sorg, a New Jersey lawyer, approached Dean Vanderbilt with a piece of news. Henry Mueller—the majority owner and longtime president of the Mueller Company, which his father had founded in 1867, and which by the eighteen-eighties had become renowned for its egg noodles—had died the previous year, Sorg reported, and in consequence all the shares of the firm might be available for purchase on promising terms. Why shouldn't the law school buy Mueller and grow rich on the proceeds? Due inquiries having been made, it was found that all the shares could be bought for about three and a half million dollars, and, moreover, that the entire sum could be conveniently borrowed for this purpose from the Prudential Insurance Company of America.

Law schools are not generally investment plungers, and, obviously, such a large plunge in a single company, even though it required no immediate cash, involved a substantial risk. (Other universities and charitable enterprises also bought up companies in the nineteen-forties, when the tax laws were favorable for such transactions, though few obtained results remotely comparable to those obtained by N.Y.U.) But Vanderbilt was a dean of pluck as well as vision. In August, 1947, the stock of the C. F. Mueller Company was bought in its entirety with the borrowed money by a new company of the same name, whose charter stated that its principal business (like the old company's) would be "to manufacture, buy, sell, deal in and deal with, import and export macaroni, spaghetti, vermicelli, alphabets, fancy pastas, noodles, egg noodles, biscuits, crackers, cakes, pastry, confections and all like and kindred food products," and that (as was not the case with the old company) "no part of [its] income or property shall inure to the private benefit of any stockholder, director, or officer, or any individual or corporation other than New York University for the exclusive benefit of its School of Law." The new corporation's stock was placed in a voting trust, with the stipulation that upon termination of the trust agreement the ownership of the company would fall to New York University, still for the law school's benefit. In 1948, to wrap up the deal, a new institution, the Law Center Foundation, was created to receive distributions from Mueller and dispense them to the law school.

These intricate arrangements pertained to taxes and the like; in effect, the law school had bought itself a noodle factory on easy credit terms. Partly on the strength of nearly two million dollars contributed by alumni and others, but also partly on the strength of the school's hopes for Mueller, work was begun in 1949 on a new law-school academic building, at the southwest corner of Washington Square. As Vanderbilt described the plans for it in his final report as dean, in 1948—he resigned that fall to become Chief Justice of the Supreme Court of New Jersey—"the Georgian Colonial design and texture of the new building with its red brick walls and its limestone trim will not only seem like an old neighbor to those who cherish Washington Square, but to the legal mind and the historian it will be a constant reminder of the place of the law in the achievement and preservation of Anglo-American freedom." The building, finished in 1951, was and is called Arthur T. Vanderbilt Hall. ("Noodle Hall" would, after all, have lacked juridical tone.) Soon afterward, again on a mixture of contributions and hopes, the Law Center Foundation bought an apartment building on Washington Square West as a dining and residence hall for law-school students. As for the hopes, they were not long in being realized. Mueller, which had distributed about seventy-five thousand dollars to the law school (or, rather, to N.Y.U. for the law school's benefit) in 1948, its first year under the new arrangement, never came through with less than a hundred and fifty thousand in any year after 1951; by the early nineteen-sixties the yield was over three hundred thousand in most years, and by 1970 it was approaching the million-dollar mark. Meanwhile, the loan from Prudential was being systematically paid off out of Mueller earnings, and by the beginning of the nineteen-seventies the trusteeship owned a flourishing and rapidly growing company free and clear—while the law school, in fulfillment of Vanderbilt's dream, had become a nationally known institution, with students from all fifty states.

All this was fine with N.Y.U., the law school's parent institution, until the early nineteen-seventies, when the parent institution found itself in desperate financial straits. If twinges of envy of its offspring's prosperity had been felt from time to time at university headquarters, they had been suppressed. However, in the autumn of 1971 the university opened with its enrollment reduced from the previous year's—about twenty-nine thousand students, rather than thirty thousand—and that December its president, James M. Hester, announced a deficit of almost seven million dollars for the academic year 1970–71 and said that N.Y.U. was in such a critical financial situation that it might have to close as a private university. The crisis was eased in 1973 by N.Y.U.'s sale, for sixty-two million dollars, of its University Heights campus in the Bronx to the City University Construction Fund for use by Bronx Community College. But since the N.Y.U. budget deficit was by then running at around ten million dollars a year, it was clear that the money brought in by the sale would not last long, and law-school people began suspecting that President Hester and the university were casting covetous glances at the Mueller money.

The chief piece of evidence they had was a memorandum writ-

ten in May of 1974 by Miguel de Capriles, the vice-president of
N.Y.U. and its general counsel, who, as such, was a spokesman
for the university—but a man with a foot in the law-school camp,
too, since he had previously been its dean. De Capriles proposed
on behalf of the university that in the future the Mueller distributions, instead of being recorded exclusively on the books of the
Law Center Foundation, be included on the income side of the
university's overall annual operating budget, thereby permitting a
large proportionate increase on the general-expense side. (The
N.Y.U. general-expense budget includes allocations for all
branches of the university—its undergraduate school and also the
various professional schools, such as medicine, education, business, and law.) The reaction at the law school to this proposal was
an outraged cry that it might provide an indirect means of divert-
ing part of the Mueller Company's distributions to the central
university, in disregard of the Mueller charter—and, undoubtedly,
one reason for this suspicion of the university's intentions was the
fact that the memo came only a few months after an announcement that Mueller had sold so much spaghetti, macaroni, noodles,
and like and kindred food products in 1973 that its distribution for
that year amounted to a million seven hundred and fifty thousand
dollars, or twice the previous year's sum.

Through the spring and summer of 1974, no action, was taken
on the university's unified-budget proposal, and the matter sim-
mered. It came to a boil in September, when, at the season's first
meeting of the law-school faculty, there was distributed a memorandum written by the treasurer of the Law Center Foundation
in which he reviewed the Mueller/N.Y.U./law-school relationship
and concluded that, while "the university can quite properly take
the position that it, rather than Law Center Foundation or the
Law School, should determine what is 'for the exclusive use of the
School of Law,' " by that same token the university "cannot divert
the Mueller distributions from the law school to the central university." Others at the law school put their concern in a less
Aesopian way. The following week, one of its professors, Graham
Hughes, wrote in its student newspaper, the *Commentator*, "Be-

hind the intricate façade of discussion about responsibility, is it not plain that in truth simple and crude goals are being pursued? The central administration wants to take some of the money away from the School and to have the power to tell us what to do with the rest." The president of the law school's Student Bar Association joined the fray by declaring, "We, no less than the faculty, will resist attempts to subordinate the Law School's interests—financial and otherwise—to the designs of the university."

On behalf of the central university, Vice-President and General Counsel James C. Kirby, Jr. (who had by that time succeeded de Capriles), replied that N.Y.U. was "highly conscious of its fiduciary obligation with respect to the Mueller money," and offered assurances that "while the university wanted the Mueller income reflected in a unified budget . . . it was never contemplated that this money would become available for general university purposes."

But the law school was not mollified. The situation was complicated by the fact that Robert B. McKay, the law school's dean, had announced his intention of retiring. Some members of the law faculty and student body feared that his successor—appointed by the university trustees on recommendation of the president—might turn out to be a patsy who would negotiate away the law school's pasta fortune. Professor Hughes put the matter bluntly in the same article: "It must be obvious that it would be of the greatest advantage to the central administration to have as the next dean a person who would be complaisant to their desired resolution of the Mueller controversy." Eventually, a committee was selected to search for a new law-school dean who would be satisfactory to all parties.

Over the winter, while the search committee looked for a new dean—and another search committee looked for a new university president, Hester having announced *his* intention of resigning and becoming rector of the newly created United Nations University —dissent at the law school edged toward open revolt. "There were rumblings in the corridors," a law-school administrator of the time recalls. Among the more bizarre of the rumblings was a suggestion that the law school might secede from N.Y.U. entirely and form a new affiliation—with Princeton University, which had no law school but had for some years maintained a program under which the N.Y.U. Law School more or less regularly sent a few students and faculty members to Princeton's Woodrow Wilson School of Public and International Affairs. The suggestion reached print in the *Commentator*'s annual April 1st spoof issue for 1975, in which, under the headline "LAW SCHOOL, PRINCETON TO WED," it was reported, "The Law Center Foundation has purchased Princeton University and will soon move its benefactor, the C. F. Mueller Co., to the historic New Jersey campus." (In reality, there was apparently no way that the law school could secede from N.Y.U. and take the Mueller money with it.) In any event, on April 2, 1975, Norman Redlich was named dean of the law school, to succeed McKay, and nineteen days later John C. Sawhill was named president of N.Y.U., to succeed Hester. Thus, with the Mueller controversy coming to a head at last, the rival forces both had new champions, and champions obviously well qualified for combat at the negotiating table: Redlich, a former practicing lawyer who had been a member of the N.Y.U. law faculty since 1960, had while on leave from the latter position served two years as corporation counsel of New York City, a post known to call for a hard negotiator, and, as for Sawhill, after seven years as a credit-company executive in Baltimore, he had just come from a term of service in Washington as Federal Energy Administrator in a time of national energy crisis. Indeed, it was widely maintained around N.Y.U. that the selection of both the new champions had been influenced to some degree by their evident qualifications not only to run a university and a law school but to haggle over a noodle factory.

WHETHER or not that was true, Sawhill and Redlich lost little time in getting down to the negotiating—and no wonder, since N.Y.U.'s operating deficit for 1974–75, in spite of drastic expense cutbacks, had been four million four hundred thousand dollars, while Mueller's payout to the law school in 1975 was in the process of miraculously escalating by half a million dollars over the 1973 figure—to two and a quarter million. The university seemed to be sinking toward bankruptcy while its fortunate offspring down the block painlessly grew richer and richer. Sawhill appointed a committee of N.Y.U. trustees, headed by Laurence A. Tisch, chairman of the board of the Loews Corporation, to look into the question of what should be done about the Mueller Company. In the fall, the committee reported as its conclusion that the company ought to be sold—probably by public stock offering. Such a sale had been proposed many times before but had always been rejected, on the ground that the proceeds would be less than the company, with its bountiful distributions, was truly worth. Now, however, all concerned parties—the university, the law school and its active alumni, and the Law Center Foundation— seemed to agree that getting rid of the company would be the best way to get rid of controversy while bringing in much-needed cash. The delicate question arose of who would get the proceeds— which, it was then believed in university and law-school circles, might come to something like seventy or seventy-five million dollars.

On the basis of the 1947 Mueller charter, the law school was clearly entitled to them all. However, as Sawhill has since said, "I felt some of the proceeds should go for unrestricted university use." On the other hand, Sawhill concedes that "most people at the law school felt the Mueller charter couldn't be changed, and that the law school was legally entitled to all the money." From the beginning of the negotiations, though, there was much sentiment among the law-school people that the law school ought to give up some of its legal rights for the common good—even for its own good. Redlich says, "We were determined that the law school should achieve national preeminence. It is illusory to think that you could have the greatest law school in the nation at a university that wasn't fiscally strong." Redlich maintains that it was he, rather than Sawhill, who broached the possibility of a split of the proceeds—in exchange, he was careful to insist, for a greater degree of fiscal autonomy for the law school, especially in regard to faculty salaries, for these were so far below the income levels available to practicing lawyers, and even so far below the salaries paid at leading United States law schools, as to make it difficult for the law school to attract and hold first-rate faculty members.

Once the law-school representatives had committed themselves in principle to some sort of split—an act of self-sacrifice (or else of enlightened self-interest) of a sort that in routine corporate dealings might have given rise to questions about the sacrificers' sanity—the negotiations could go forward in earnest. They took place in the spring and summer of 1976 in Sawhill's office, in the Bobst Library, on Washington Square South, a little way down the street from Vanderbilt Hall, and almost all the sessions had the same participants: Sawhill; Redlich; Edward Weinfeld, an N.Y.U. law graduate who was a United States judge for the Southern District of New York, representing the Law Center Foundation; and two other enthusiastic law-school alumni—Martin Lipton, a well-known merger and acquisition lawyer, and Lester Pollack, another highly placed executive of Loews—as liaison between the real world of money and the at least presumptive academic mandarins. From the beginning, the law school's ace, the Mueller charter, was face up on the negotiating table. The university, for its part, had an ace in the hole. It consisted of the right to refuse, for the present, to sell Mueller under any terms. If it followed that course, then, in August, 1977, when the voting-trust agreement expired, clear title to Mueller would fall to the university, and, although it would still be subject to the charter's injunction to use the company's proceeds for the exclusive benefit of the law school, the university would thereafter be free to dispose of the company if and as it chose. Mindful of all that, the law-school representatives put on the table early in the discussions a proposal that Mueller be sold, with seventy per cent of the proceeds to go to the law school and thirty per cent to the university. Sawhill, on behalf of the university, was less than happy with that. It was his notion that, in the first place, there should be a division more favorable to the university, and, in the second, the law school should agree as part of the deal to pay thenceforward for certain university programs and facilities that it hadn't been paying for. After a bit of hand-wringing, Redlich suggested, not expecting to be taken seriously, that the two sides "compromise" by agreeing in advance to split evenly any proceeds of the sale above a hundred million dollars.

Redlich is now inclined to believe that he played that particular card prematurely. He says, "Frankly, I didn't think there were going to *be* any proceeds above a hundred million dollars." Not long after that, however, Lipton, who had been serving as the negotiators' emissary to the financial world, reported to them that his soundings indicated that a hundred million dollars, rather than the seventy or seventy-five that had been discussed earlier, might well be the sum that a public sale would bring. The tone and quality of financial negotiations are apt to undergo a subtle yet abrupt change when the assumed value of their object rises sharply. For one thing, everybody concerned becomes more intensely interested in what is going on. For another, a mood of generosity and a disinclination to quibble, which were previously absent, may appear—or, as Redlich says, "It's easier to get statesmanlike as the pie gets larger." One day in midsummer, Sawhill suggested, "Rather than the law school being responsible for those expensive university programs, let's leave that out and change the split to sixty-forty. In other words, capitalize the programs." Mentally calculating sixty per cent of a hundred million dollars, and finding themselves sufficiently gratified by the resulting sum, the law-school men agreed, and exacted in return a pledge that the university, in recognition and support of the law school's determination to achieve national preeminence, would thenceforward grant to the law school the right to pay faculty and administrative salaries that would compete with law schools of the first rank anywhere in the country. (The salaries still wouldn't compete with the annual take of a partner in a big Wall Street firm, but then neither do the salaries at any other law school.)

At this stage, what Redlich had called the pie—which had for so long been growing steadily and miraculously bigger, as if it had its being not in reality but in the dream of a hungry child—inflated itself by one final, implausible degree. Word came from Wall Street at the end of August that Foremost–McKesson, the conglomerate formed by the merger in 1967 of McKesson & Robbins and Foremost Dairies, was prepared to make a public sale of the Mueller stock unnecessary by privately buying all of it for its own use in a single transaction and for a sum substantially larger than a hundred million dollars. At the Bobst Library, the negotiators were so rattled by this development that their agreement almost broke down. Redlich recounts, "Apart from the question of the degree of fiscal autonomy that the law school would have, the university still wanted a split of the proceeds better than sixty-forty. It was at this stage that we of the law school became what you might describe as intransigent." It was at this stage, too, that Sawhill, perhaps with the faintest trace of a smirk, reminded Redlich of his offer, made several months earlier, to split evenly all proceeds above a hundred million dollars. Redlich tells of that development with a rueful little laugh. Nevertheless, he says, he agreed that he had made the offer, and affirmed that the law school would stick by it; that is, the law school was willing to split the proceeds sixty-forty up to a hundred million dollars, and fifty-fifty on anything beyond that.

The logjam was broken. A few days later, Foremost–McKesson came through with a firm offer of a hundred and fifteen million dollars for Mueller. In Sawhill's office, everybody shook hands. In mid-September, the whole transaction—the complicated money split and the proposed terms for the law school's increased fiscal autonomy—was approved by the N.Y.U. Board of Trustees and the Law Center Foundation's trustees. At about the same time, Redlich explained it all to the faculty and the student leaders of the law school. Both groups raised plenty of questions, as might have been expected, in view of the fact that the law school was signing away almost fifty million dollars that was legally pledged as being for its exclusive benefit. But Redlich was persuasive. For one thing, he could argue that part of the proposed agreement was a promise of higher salaries for the law-school faculty; the law-school faculty voted unanimously to approve the deal, and the student leaders seemed satisfied, too. On September 28th, Foremost–McKesson and N.Y.U. were able to announce that the former had contracted to buy Mueller for a hundred and fifteen million dollars, of which sixty-seven million five hundred thousand —sixty per cent of the first hundred million and half the balance —would go for the use of the law school, and forty-seven million five hundred thousand would go to the university for it to do with as it chose.

NOBODY at N.Y.U. is mad at anybody else anymore about the noodle factory affair. Indeed, just about all concerned had, and have, good reason to be happy about its outcome. Foremost– McKesson, in a company publication issued in December, 1976, spoke proudly and contentedly of its new acquisition as a company that had shown uninterrupted profit growth for the past fifteen years and might be expected to show further growth in the future, in view of the fact that per-capita consumption of pasta products in the United States was in a strong uptrend. (In 1974, it was still only one-sixth that in Italy, though.) Since the entire proceeds of the Mueller sale formally went into N.Y.U.'s endowment, the university came out with its total endowment raised at a stroke from a hundred and twenty-five million dollars to two hundred and forty million, and with its endowment for unrestricted use nearly tripled, from twenty-five million to seventy-two million five hundred thousand. President Sawhill commented that the money would be "a help to the university as we begin to cope with the expected financial strains of the nineteen-eighties," and the university's new vice-president for academic affairs, L. Jay Oliva, called the day when the sale was announced "perhaps the most historic moment since N.Y.U.'s founding." In sum, N.Y.U. was in a position to join the ranks, often thought to be sparse, of those who can say "Thank God for lawyers."

As for the law school, it could still thank God, as fervently as it had been doing over the decades, for noodles and like and kindred products. For one thing, it now had for its exclusive and presumably its permanent benefit a sum almost twenty times as large as its original investment in Mueller. For another, it had its guarantee of increased fiscal autonomy. For a third, it had, or was entitled to have, a glow of generosity. And, for a fourth, it had actually emerged with the prospect of greatly increased annual income; at the current yield, of about six and a half per cent, on N.Y.U. endowment funds—a far higher rate of return than the Mueller investment had yielded—the sixty-seven million five hundred thousand dollars would bring the law school annually about four million four hundred thousand, or almost twice the amount of the most recent Mueller distribution. On top of all that, Redlich feels, the whole experience provides an edifying object lesson for law students, the moral of which is that lawyers shouldn't pursue narrowly legalistic positions to everyone's detriment.

All in all, to anyone who in recent years has watched multi-million-dollar Wall Street negotiations repeatedly lead to costly and acrimonious litigation, or has watched the most sophisticated institutional investors repeatedly fall for the investment equivalent of three-card-monte games, the affair suggests that when it comes to high finance they order things better in academe.

```
$$$$$$$$$$$$$$$$$$$$
$$$$$$$$$$$$$$$$$$$$
$$$$$$$$$$$$$$$$$$$$
$$$$$$$$$$$$$$$$$$$$
$$$$$  12  $$$$$
$$$$$      $$$$$
$$$$$      $$$$$
$$$$$$$$$$$$$$$$$$$$
$$$$$$$$$$$$$$$$$$$$
$$$$$$$$$$$$$$$$$$$$
$$$$$$$$$$$$$$$$$$$$
$$$$$$$$$$$$$$$$$$$$
```

Funds Gray and Black

A NUMBER OF the revelations of large-scale illegal or unethical activity made in the dispiriting years 1973–76 concerned the dealings of government officials or political candidates, both domestic and foreign, with large American corporations. The first such revelation came on July 6, 1973, when the Watergate Special Prosecution Force announced that American Airlines had made a contribution of fifty-five thousand dollars from corporate funds to President Nixon's 1972 reelection campaign. In making the announcement, Archibald Cox, then Special Prosecutor, called upon all corporate officials who knew that their companies had made illegal political contributions to come forward and disclose the facts voluntarily. The response, sluggish at first, was eventually profuse—particularly after the Securities and Exchange Commission, the Internal Revenue Service, Congress, and various private litigants joined the Special Prosecutor in looking into corporate political activities. By the summer of 1976, about a hundred and fifty corporations had admitted that over a period of years they had made contributions at home or abroad to political candidates or their parties; later the count would increase to over three hundred and fifty. Those companies which admitted to domestic political payments included Ashland Oil, Inc., the Firestone Tire & Rubber Co., the Minnesota Mining & Manufacturing Co., the Northrop Corporation, and the Phillips Petroleum Co.; and among those identified as recipients of such payments were forty-five members of Congress. The number and variety of corporations confessing to questionable payments abroad was far greater. This list included the Exxon Corporation, the world's largest industrial company (which conceded that over a decade or so some fifty-six million dollars was somehow siphoned out of the company and its Italian subsidiary, and an unknown part of that sum used for political payments in Italy); the Lockheed Aircraft Corporation (which admitted to more than thirty million dollars in overseas payments, including disbursements of more than twelve and a half million in Japan, the disclosure of which caused a grave government crisis and the arrest of a former prime minister, Kakuei Tanaka); such imperial giants of American industry as the American Home Products Corporation, Merck & Co., and the United Brands Co.; and such lesser firms as Levi Strauss & Co., maker of bluejeans. During the spring and early summer of 1976, new admissions and disclosures of overseas payments came to be so commonplace in the daily press as to virtually force a reader to the conclusion that payments to political figures had become a way of life for American corporations operating abroad; and, by way of confirmation, in May the chairman of the S.E.C., Roderick

M. Hills, told a group of leading businessmen (correctly, as it turned out) that more disclosures could confidently be expected in the future. Since such payments serve no legitimate business purpose and are made in the hope, if not actually with the promise, of favors in return, they may more bluntly, and more precisely, be called bribes.

In the United States, political contributions by a corporation (as distinguished from those by individual executives) are illegal in campaigns for federal office under Section 610 of Title 18 of the United States Code, and have been illegal under that or predecessor statutes since 1907. Section 610 reads, in part, "It is unlawful for . . . any corporation . . . to make a contribution or expenditure in connection with any election . . . at which Presidential and Vice-Presidential electors or a Senator or Representative in . . . Congress are to be voted for, or in connection with any primary election or political convention or caucus held to select candidates for any of the foregoing offices, or for any candidate, political committee, or other person to accept or receive any contribution prohibited by this section." In many states, parallel laws have long forbidden corporate political contributions to state candidates. In other countries, more often than not, political contributions by corporations of any nationality are legal; and at the time in question, the United States had no law categorically forbidding such contributions in foreign countries by American corporations. Whether such contributions made abroad by American corporations were any more ethical than those made at home is perhaps a question worthy of Marlowe's Barabas, who defended himself against the charge of fornication partly on the ground that the offense had been committed in another country. At all events, the fact that the emerging pattern of systematic political bribery by American corporations, mostly abroad but to a lesser extent at home, was not a function of "Watergate morality" but went back long before Watergate—and thus, indeed, may have contributed to Watergate morality—is well established by the admissions and disclosures. In particular, it is well established by the disclosures about the Gulf Oil Corporation, which between 1960 and

1973 distributed political contributions and payments in the United States and abroad aggregating over twelve million dollars.

The public disclosures about Gulf's political activities were made piecemeal, beginning on August 10, 1973, when the corporation issued a press release stating that in 1971 and 1972 it had made an illegal contribution of a hundred thousand dollars to the Finance Committee to Re-Elect the President, an adjunct of the Committee to Re-Elect the President, or CREEP. The announcement was not exactly voluntary, as Cox had asked; rather, Gulf was faced with the threat of disclosure of the gift by the Finance Committee itself, which was under court order as the result of a suit by Common Cause to disclose its receipts between January 1, 1971, and April 6, 1972, and which had returned the hundred thousand dollars to Gulf two weeks earlier. On November 13, 1973, Gulf and its chief Washington lobbyist, Claude C. Wild, Jr., were charged under Section 610 in the U.S. District Court for the District of Columbia. Both Gulf and Wild were charged with the Finance Committee contribution, while Gulf was additionally charged with contributions of ten thousand dollars and fifteen thousand dollars to the 1972 campaigns of Senator Henry M. Jackson and Representative Wilbur Mills, respectively. Both Gulf and Wild immediately pleaded guilty, whereupon Gulf was fined five thousand dollars and Wild a thousand dollars— punishments that in the context may perhaps best be described not as wrist slaps but as eye-winks; but then the whole history of Section 610 has been one of slack enforcement and light sentences.

The following day—November 14, 1973—Wild testified publicly before the Senate Watergate Committee. His testimony was entirely about his relations with the Finance Committee; he said nothing about other political contributions, because he was not asked—a fact that may or may not be related to Wild's subsequent statement to a lawyer at a firm retained by Gulf that he had at one time or another dispensed gifts, either legal or illegal, to "all senators on Watergate except Ervin." In October, 1974, the S.E.C. began to investigate to determine whether or not Gulf had violated the federal securities laws. The investigation and attendant negotiations with Gulf led, on March 11, 1975, to a consent decree under which Gulf agreed to appoint a Special Review Committee with a mandate to get to the bottom of Gulf's political contributions, past and present. The committee—consisting of two members of the Gulf board of directors, Nathan W. Pearson and Beverley Matthews, and one outsider, the New York lawyer John J. McCloy, who served as chairman—reviewed and collated all existing evidence, and also interviewed almost a hundred and fifty witnesses in the United States, Canada, and Europe; it issued its report and recommendations in a volume of more than three hundred pages on December 30, 1975. Meanwhile, more facts and details of the matter had come to light independently. In May, 1975, Gulf's chief executive officer, Bob R. Dorsey, had told the Senate Foreign Relations Subcommittee on Multinational Corporations that in 1966 and 1970 Gulf contributed four million dollars to the Korean Democratic Republican Party; and in November a series of depositions by Gulf executives in a new S.E.C. suit were made public, showing, for the first time, a widespread systematic program of political contributions by Gulf which had been in efficient operation for well over a decade.

The McCloy report (as the report of the Special Review Committee came to be called), along with the other available evidence, gives as detailed an account of the techniques and procedures of corporate political bribery as has so far become available regarding any corporation. Since ethical matters are best examined in detail and in the context of their social and cultural setting, one may logically choose the Gulf situation for a study of the subject without implying that Gulf's activities were more egregious than those of other corporations, even though Gulf's illegal domestic contributions appear to have been unusually extensive. (Lockheed's and Exxon's payments, much larger than Gulf's, were all overseas.) In doing so, however, one must point out the dubious provenance of some of the evidence upon which the story is based. For one thing, the testimony of Joseph E. Bounds, a retired Gulf executive, who was the McCloy committee's chief source of information about the early days of Gulf's political enterprise, was taken when Bounds was seventy years old, in poor health and apparently under constant medication, and, to add to his troubles, was suffering from a rattlesnake bite. A more serious cloud overhangs the testimony of perhaps the key witness in the case—Claude Wild, to whom, as the McCloy committee put it, "all evidence seems to point as the chief distributor of corporate funds and the center of most of the domestic political activity." On advice of counsel, Wild was not available to the committee until the very end of its investigation, and when he finally appeared, he refused to give the names of any of the recipients of Gulf's largesse. (No new details came out in Wild's trial in Washington at the end of July, 1976, on charges of having made an illegal campaign contribution to Senator Daniel K. Inouye, of Hawaii, which ended in dismissal of the charges on a legal technicality.) In 1973, however, in a series of interviews with a young lawyer named Thomas D. Wright, who was with a Pittsburgh law firm that represented Gulf and had been designated by the corporation to investigate its political contributions, Wild did give the names of recipients, along with many other details of his operations. Wright took pencilled notes during these interviews, and in September, 1975, in a deposition taken by the S.E.C., he reconstructed what Wild had told him two years earlier, on the basis of notes that he himself was not always able to decipher. In some cases, what Wild told Wright was corroborated by others, and in some cases it was not. It is on such evidence—hearsay, perhaps of the least unacceptable sort, but hearsay all the same—that part of the story as it is now known is based.

THE Gulf Oil Corporation traces its history back to 1901, when a drilling team, financed by a loan of three hundred thousand dollars from the celebrated Pittsburgh banking firm of T. Mellon & Sons, brought in the biggest oil well ever recorded up to then, at Spindletop, an unimpressive-looking mound near the Gulf Coast of Texas. In 1975, Gulf, with worldwide interests and assets of 12.4 billion dollars, gross revenues of sixteen billion dollars, and net income of seven hundred million dollars, was the fifth-largest United States oil company. Its commitment to a program of political contributions as a means of producing more favorable conditions under which to conduct its business seems to have begun in 1958; in any event, that September the company made a public announcement that "in the future the Corporation will take an increasingly active interest in practical politics," and the following June stockholders and employees were issued a pamphlet entitled "A Political Program for Gulf Oil Corporation," in which the author, a senior vice-president, denounced the "creeping encroachment" of government on industry—particularly the oil industry— and asserted that Gulf and the industry had been "subjected to increasing attack" and "increasingly . . . denied a fair hearing." The "Political Program" encouraged employees to become involved in local politics, and to set up among themselves a network of regional political supervisors—activities that, of course, would be perfectly legal.

Machinery by which corporate funds could be surreptitiously collected and illegal contributions made from them appears to have been set up in 1959. Late that year, Gulf hired Wild as a Washington lobbyist, at an annual salary of twenty-five thousand dollars. According to Wild—a lawyer, then in his middle thirties, who had previously worked for the Mid-Continent Oil & Gas Association and had acquired a reputation as an effective lobbyist— two of the Gulf executives who hired him told him that his mission was to build an organization that would give Gulf more "muscle" in politics, and that for that purpose he would have a budget of about two hundred thousand dollars a year. (Later, the figure was doubled.) Nothing was said about where the funds would come from. Also in 1959, Bounds, then the administrative vice-president of Gulf, learned of plans to establish a political fund, in a series of meetings with William K. Whiteford, then the company's chief executive officer. Whiteford, according to Bounds, was convinced (incorrectly) that if funds for domestic political use were generated outside the United States and were handled by a foreign corporation, with no deductions on Gulf's United States tax returns, the arrangement would be legal. Whiteford also insisted, Bounds said, that he had learned from the top management of some of the other major oil companies that they had already set up schemes similar to the one he had in mind. (No such setup has been shown to have existed at any other major oil company.) Nevertheless, Whiteford made it clear that his plans must be kept from the Mellon family, which held the single largest block of Gulf stock, and from certain other Gulf executives, whom he described as "Boy Scouts"—among them Dorsey, who was then a vice-president and was to become Gulf's chairman and chief executive officer in 1972.

In Bounds' account, Whiteford was the moving spirit in the establishment of means whereby Gulf could make political contributions both at home and abroad and keep them secret, from all but a few even within the company. Born in Los Angeles in 1900, Whiteford had studied at Stanford and subsequently served as a leading executive of two Toronto-based oil concerns—the British American Oil Producing Company and the British American Oil Company, Ltd. Having come to Gulf as executive vice-president in 1951, he became president in 1952 and chief executive officer in 1957, and he served in the latter capacity until his retirement, in 1965. He died in 1968 in a head-on automobile collision a few miles from his home, in Ligonier, Pennsylvania. According to the McCloy committee, Whiteford was "dynamic and colorful." It was presumably under his direction that early in 1960 Gulf began channelling funds for political use through the Bahamas Exploration Company, Ltd., an oil-exploration subsidiary with headquarters in Nassau. Bahamas Ex., as it was called, was ideal for this purpose in several respects. For one, it was relatively dormant, its chief activity in 1960 being to hold licenses against the day when Gulf might decide to undertake oil-exploration work in the Bahamas. For another, it was not consolidated with its parent company, Gulf, for tax purposes, and it existed in a tax-haven country, so it was not required to reveal its annual income and disbursements in income-tax returns anywhere. On January 8, 1960, Gulf opened an account at the Bank of Nova Scotia in

Nassau, in the name of Bahamas Ex., and on January 15th the company made an initial deposit of two hundred and fifty thousand dollars. The account was not recorded on the books of Bahamas Ex.; the Gulf executives authorizing deposits in it did so by handwritten notes, which were customarily destroyed; and the bank's statements and records of deposits and withdrawals were never placed in the files of Bahamas Ex. but, rather, were regularly torn up and flushed down a toilet by William C. Viglia, a former assistant comptroller of Gulf, who in July, 1959, had been assigned to Nassau to maintain the accounts of Bahamas Ex.

The secret Bank of Nova Scotia account was now ready to make disbursements. (Some time later, Whiteford, upon being appointed to a quasi-honorary post as a vice-president of the Bank of Nova Scotia, wrote in jocular vein to a working officer of the bank, "This is good news, especially to me, as the next time I have to make a confidential arrangement to secure political funds I can put the blame on the Bank should this great institution . . . fail to protect my anonymity." The recipient of the letter, who had no idea that the Bahamas Ex. account was for political purposes, assumed that the letter was an example of Whiteford's well-known sense of humor. In hindsight, it may be seen as evidence of a penchant of Whiteford's—quite extraordinary in the chief executive of a great corporation—for deliberately skating on the thinnest of ice, for no purpose other than to dare the Devil.) Late in the winter of 1959–60, on instructions from Bounds, William T. Grummer, Gulf's comptroller, made several trips to Nassau and on each occasion withdrew amounts ranging from twenty thousand dollars to forty thousand dollars in cash from the Bahamas Ex. account and in each case subsequently delivered the money to Gulf executives in Pittsburgh. Such deliveries in the early months of the Bahamas Ex. arrangement were, as Bounds told it, handled as follows: The courier from Nassau would hand Bounds, in Pittsburgh, an envelope containing the cash; Bounds would lock it in a safe that, at Whiteford's request, Bounds had had installed in his own office; whereupon Whiteford would enter Bounds' office in his absence and remove the envelope from the safe, leaving the safe open until the next delivery from Nassau. What possible purpose this routine could have served, other than to gratify Whiteford's taste for the baroque, it is impossible to say. By July 6, 1960, one hundred and fifty thousand dollars had been withdrawn from Nassau and delivered to Pittsburgh, and as early as that April the withdrawals had been large enough to cause a logistical problem: The Bank of Nova Scotia sometimes didn't have enough cash on hand in United States dollars to meet the demand. To solve this problem, another intricate routine was worked out. The Bank of Nova Scotia would systematically collect U.S. dollars, in exchange for local currency, from a local casino where visiting Americans were in the convenient habit of losing them; when a good supply of dollars had been assembled, the Bank would notify Viglia, the Bahamas Ex. man; and Viglia would then withdraw the dollars and put them in a safe-deposit box at another Nassau bank, ready for delivery to the mainland as required.

The ultimate destination of the dollars thus collected came, after the earliest days, to be the province of Wild, the lobbyist, who from 1960 on was generally in charge of selecting recipients of political contributions and making deliveries to them. In one of his first assignments along these lines, Wild, by his own account, delivered fifty thousand dollars in cash over a period of months to Walter Jenkins, an aide to Senator Lyndon B. Johnson. As time went on, an efficient standard operating procedure evolved in Pittsburgh, Nassau, and Washington. A Gulf official in Pittsburgh, usually someone in the comptroller's office, would authorize a transfer, usually of one or two hundred thousand dollars, to the Bahamas Ex. account in Nassau. Viglia, in Nassau, would deposit the money and wait for delivery instructions. When they came—usually from Wild, but occasionally from other Gulf executives—Viglia would put the required sum (usually twenty-five thousand dollars) in an envelope, buy an airline ticket (which he would later destroy), and fly to a prearranged destination in the United States—no longer Bounds' office in Pittsburgh but usually somewhere in Washington, Miami, or Houston. (According to Viglia, he became so friendly with the U.S. customs people that his baggage and his person were never examined.) Upon arriving, he would deliver the cash-filled envelope to Wild or another Gulf officer, and then he would fly right back to Nassau. Wild would pass the envelope on to the intended recipient, in Washington or elsewhere—sometimes in the recipient's office, but on other occasions, at the recipient's request, somewhere else.

By the beginning of 1966, some two and a half million dollars had been transferred from Gulf to the Bahamas Ex. account, of which almost two million had been carried by Viglia in cash to the United States for delivery to political figures—most often to national ones, but sometimes, according to Wild's statement to Wright, officials or candidates at the state and local levels. Most of the political figures who received some of the money, either then or later, have since said that they did not know that the contributions they were receiving were from corporate funds—rather than from Gulf executives as individuals—and were therefore illegal. However, not one recipient has said that he asked questions about where the money came from. It is also worth noting that in almost every instance Gulf's political contributions were made on the request—sometimes the urgent demand—of the recipient. There was never a specific quid pro quo offered; the implied offer was merely a more favorable legislative climate for Gulf, or even the avoidance of a *less* favorable climate. In some cases, Wild was made to feel that his bribes were buying no more than a continuation of the status quo. As Wild later put it in connection with the Nixon Finance Committee case, "If there was not some participation on my part or our part, we may be . . . whether you call it a blacklist or bottom of the totem pole. I would just like [them] to answer my telephone calls once in a while."

The entire arrangement suffered a temporary setback in 1961, when Bounds staged a revolt against it. Sometime that year, by his account, he told Whiteford that he did not like "the Bahamian setup." Whiteford told him he had better like it or he would be fired. The matter came to a head with a confrontation between the two men that October at the Duquesne Club, a favorite gathering place of Pittsburgh's business élite, where, after a violent argument, Bounds, as he put it, "decked" Whiteford. Whether or not, by so doing, Bounds violated the bylaws of the Duquesne Club, he violated those of Whiteford, who got up off the deck and shortly thereafter sent Bounds into a sort of exile by assigning him to run a Gulf property in California. Bounds, nevertheless, continued from exile to write requests for transfers of corporate funds to Bahamas Ex., right up to his early retirement, in 1964. So the revolt was quelled, and the arrangement returned to smooth functioning.

Sometimes, Wild found that he needed help from others in making deliveries of cash to political figures, because, he explained, it was "physically impossible for one man to handle that kind of money." Such a helper was Frederick A. Myers, who had been a Gulf employee for forty-seven years at the time he retired, in 1975, and who for fifteen years had held positions in Gulf's Washington office, reporting to Wild and another Gulf official. In October, 1975, Myers, testifying before the S.E.C. under a promise of immunity from prosecution, related that, on orders from Wild, between March, 1961, and September, 1972, he had made twenty-two separate trips to various places in the United States to deliver sealed envelopes to political figures, and, in addition, had made four to six such deliveries per year in Washington to members of Congress or their staffs.

The picture that emerges from Myers' testimony is one of a man forced by circumstances to reduce himself to pure mechanical function—to do what he was told while asking no questions and, if possible, thinking no thoughts. In Washington, Wild would give him a sealed envelope along with precise instructions about where and to whom it should be delivered. Myers would board an airliner and proceed to the designated place. The designated person would always be there. Myers would greet him, and hand over the envelope. The recipient would say "Thank you," and after an exchange of chitchat Myers would fly back to Washington. Most often, the delivery would be at an airport or at the recipient's office, but occasionally it would be at a place suggestive of a desire for secrecy on the part of either the donor or the recipient. In

October of 1964, for example, Myers went to Albuquerque, New Mexico, to deliver an envelope to Edwin L. Mechem, who was then running for reelection as a senator from that state. At the Albuquerque airport, Myers was met by a man who conveyed him by private plane to a ranch, where Myers delivered the envelope to Mechem behind a barn, saying, as usual, "Mr. Wild asked me to give this to you." Again, in 1970, Myers said, he handed an envelope to Representative Richard L. Roudebush, of Indiana, at the latter's suggestion, in the men's washroom of a motel in Indianapolis.

In no instance did Wild, in giving Myers his instructions and a sealed envelope to deliver, tell Myers what the envelope contained, and in no instance did Myers ask. Nor did Wild ever explain why the delivery was to be made by hand rather than by mail. And in no instance, according to Myers' testimony, did he learn from the recipient what the envelope contained. Or, rather, in hardly any instance. On one of several occasions when he made deliveries to Herbert C. Manning, a Gulf attorney in Pittsburgh—presumably for distribution to local political figures—Manning opened the envelope in Myers' presence, revealing cash. On one other occasion—a 1970 delivery at a bank in a small town in Tennessee—the recipient similarly opened the envelope, and Myers saw that it contained cash. Did these two incidents suggest to Myers that his many other deliveries had also been of cash? Apparently not. Time and again, asked by S.E.C. counsel whether he knew what was in an envelope he had delivered, he replied, "I do not," or "I have no knowledge." A minor figure in the tragedy, Myers was apparently content to spin constantly by airliner above the cities, plains, and mountains of America, not knowing why, not wanting to know why—a man living in a moral void.

GULF's heavy involvement in foreign political contributions appears to have begun in 1966, in that precarious, Western-created nominal democracy the Republic of Korea. The company had made its first commitment there in 1963, when it began building a refinery at Ulsan, which became known as the Pittsburgh of

Korea, to create a new outlet for crude oil from Kuwait, which was then in large supply. The venture quickly became very profitable as Korea's industry flourished while its wages remained low, and within a few years Gulf's investment there mounted to two hundred million dollars or more. In 1966, a high official in the secretariat of President Park Chung Hee went to a top Gulf executive in the Far East and asked for a contribution of one million dollars to Park's political organization, the Democratic Republican Party, for the coming election. The executive immediately passed the request along to Dorsey—then president and second-in-command of the company—in Pittsburgh. Dorsey was persuaded, he later told the McCloy committee, that the Korean request was "a very strong approach, indeed; not threatening . . . but certainly, I was told . . . that there were veiled threats . . . that if you want to survive and do well . . . you had best do this." He was also persuaded that American government officials were strongly pressing the Korean government to conduct Western-style elections, and that large sums of money would be necessary to accomplish this purpose. Accordingly, this man whom Whiteford had considered a "Boy Scout" authorized the million-dollar payment; the sum was sent to Bahamas Ex. and thence transferred to Korea via two Swiss bank accounts.

Then, in 1970, when the Democratic Republican Party of Korea was under a heavier political challenge, came what the McCloy committee called "a much more blunt approach." This time, it was made by S. K. Kim, a Korean political boss who was already known to Gulf officials there as "a rough customer." Kim summoned an official of Gulf's Korean subsidiary to his office and coolly demanded ten million dollars. The official took no action pending the arrival of Dorsey in Korea on a previously scheduled visit. Soon after his arrival, Dorsey and Kim had a meeting at Kim's house, which turned out to be highly acrimonious. In describing the meeting later, Dorsey said, in part, "The question of ten million dollars, there was no way I could do anything like that. . . . It was almost preposterous. And at that point he became exceedingly angry with me and exceedingly irritated and talked to me just about as roughly as he could; in effect saying . . . 'I'm not here to debate matters. You are either going to put up the goddam money or suffer the consequences,' although he said it substantially more roughly than that." Dorsey, very angry and upset, walked out of Kim's house. However, after tempers had cooled and further negotiations had been conducted, Dorsey agreed to three million dollars, and that amount was subsequently paid through the same machinery that had been used in 1966. In explaining the 1970 payment, Dorsey said he had realized that Gulf operated in Korea "at the sufferance of the government," and that Korea was "unlike any Western country" in that the corporation couldn't operate there without the government on its side; therefore, Dorsey thought, what he was doing was "in the best interest of the corporation."

The McCloy committee found itself unable to decide whether the two political contributions had been legal or illegal under Korean law, or whether United States regulatory jurisdiction applied in such cases, although it "assumed that outright bribery would be illegal wherever effected." As for Dorsey, the committee concluded that he seemed not to have given any thought to the legal aspect of the matter. In any event, he had decided not to tell the Gulf board of directors about the payments or the demands for them, because, he said later, such disclosure would have been "embarrassing to Gulf and embarrassing to the party to whom the payment was made." Indeed, it appears in retrospect that the reason a ten-million-dollar payment in 1970 was considered "almost preposterous," while a three-million-dollar payment was not, lay in the fact that the smaller sum could be effectively concealed among Gulf's annual disbursements to its various Caribbean subsidiaries, while the larger sum could not.

The situation of Gulf in Korea—a company tempted by a juicy legitimate business opportunity brought about by high demand and low wages, and then, figuratively, held up at gunpoint by a political party bent on getting a share of the profits—suggests the moral ambiguities involved in payments abroad by American corporations. When it is a choice of pay or lose out, and paying seems to be legal under local law, is not the corporation justified in paying, in the interests of its stockholders? Moreover, as the Gulf evidence shows, there are many subtle variations of the situation—a whole spectrum of ethical nuances to be considered. For example, in Kuwait, between 1968 and 1974, the Kuwait Oil Company, Ltd., which was then owned half by Gulf and half by the British Petroleum Company, on one occasion paid more than two million dollars for construction of a beach club, at the request of the Kuwait government, and over a number of years spent two million eight hundred thousand dollars to put a large aircraft at the disposal of Sheik Abdulla, Ruler of Kuwait. But these payments could scarcely be called political contributions, since the Ruler of Kuwait was virtually an absolute monarch, and therefore the country had no politics in the Western sense. Under such circumstances, Gulf could argue that its favors to the Ruler had, in effect, been payments of rent to a landlord.

Again, there was employed in some instances a method of "payment" far less crass than, say, handing over an envelope behind a barn—that of deliberately driving an easy bargain in a deal. In Korea in the nineteen-sixties, for example, Gulf several times sold oil tankers to Korean nationals favored by the government, under terms by which Gulf took all the risk and furnished all the working capital. In 1972, Gulf, probably to please a new Korean Prime Minister, went as far as to sell a supertanker called the *Chun Woo* to a government favorite in a deal whereby Gulf not only lent the buyer the entire purchase price and advanced all operating funds but sweetened the deal by paying, on demand, a "management fee" of half a million dollars. The McCloy committee decided that the *Chun Woo* transaction "had obvious political overtones." Those who made it could, of course, reply that it had merely been a business arrangement and that you can't win them all.

There were cases in which the pressure appeared to be nothing but the grandiose whim of a single foreign official, and the corporate executives could convince themselves that catering to the whim was not bribery but merely an exasperating form of hand holding. Such a case, apparently, was one that Gulf faced in 1966 in Bolivia, where the corporation over the previous nine years had discovered under government concession, and had put in full operation, eight large oil and natural-gas fields. Early that year, General René Barrientos, the co-dictator of Bolivia and a candidate for its Presidency, demanded a helicopter for use in his campaign. By three separate checks drawn on the Bahamas Ex. bank account—checks rather than cash being acceptable because, apparently, the transaction broke no laws—Gulf paid a total of $45,925 to the Fairchild Hiller Corporation to rent a helicopter for the General, who used it in his campaign. Barrientos, having won election on July 3rd, then refused to return the helicopter, and Gulf officials were notified through an intermediary that possession of it had become a virtual obsession with him. Accordingly, in October a cashier's check drawn on the Bank of Nova Scotia in the amount of sixty-two-thousand dollars—the additional sum needed to convert the rental into a sale—was sent to Fairchild Hiller. General Barrientos had his helicopter (in fact, he donated it to the Bolivian Air Force), and the Gulf had clear sailing in its Bolivian oil and gas operations—or did until the fall of 1969, when all its properties were nationalized by the Bolivian government.

Finally, there is the most troublesome ethical question of all: that of precisely when the political contributions of American corporations in foreign countries represent conformity with the accepted code of the place—the custom of the country—and should therefore be condoned. (So stringent a moralist as St. Augustine quoted with approval the advice of St. Ambrose: "When in Rome, do as the Romans do.") It would be possible to describe the American practice of tipping as a system of extorted bribes; a similar judgment can, and perhaps should, be pronounced on the so-called Gray Fund that Gulf maintained for several years in the Republic of Korea, and the more chromatically downright Fondo Nero, or Black Fund, that it maintained in Italy. Both of these funds were maintained off the company books and consisted of money not sent from the United States and passed through the

Bahamas but locally generated through small windfalls—rebates on insurance premiums and commissions on bank deposits paid as a way of circumventing laws restricting interest rates. A Gulf official in Korea described the Gray Fund as being "like trading stamps." As for their disposition, the Korean Gray Fund was used to pay gratuities, routinely expected and routinely given, to low-level government people whose agencies affected Gulf's operations, and the Fondo Nero in Italy was used for such purposes as to combat, through bribes of not only politicians but newspaper editors and writers, a press campaign for the nationalization of Gulf's concession in Sicily. The Gray Fund operated from 1972 to 1975, and in that time paid out only thirty-three thousand dollars; the Fondo Nero, a more substantial and longer-lasting operation, during its existence, from 1962 to 1974, paid out some four hundred and twenty-two thousand dollars.

The McCloy committee concluded that both the Gray Fund and the Fondo Nero were no worse than expressions of conformity to local ethical standards. Of the former it declared itself "satisfied that the uses to which the fund was put were neither unique with Gulf nor uncommon in Korea"; as for the latter, the committee pointed out that on one occasion the head of Gulf's Italian operations had assured his supervisor in the company that no impropriety attached to such accounts in Italy. The implication —and, indeed, the implication of most American recitals of the political activities of American corporations abroad—would seem to be that the representatives of a country with higher standards were, under pressure of necessity, lowering themselves to conform to the ways of countries with lower ones. A rather different light was thrown on the matter in September, 1975, by Adnan M. Khashoggi, a leading Saudi Arabian businessman who at one time served as an agent for the Northrop Corporation and in that capacity, according to a top Northrop official, acted as an intermediary in Northrop bribes of four hundred and fifty thousand dollars to two Saudi Arabian officials. At a conference in New York, Mr. Khashoggi expressed the opinion that bribes paid by United States businessmen to the agents of Middle Eastern governments were quite unnecessary to accomplish their purposes, and that in accepting such bribes the agents were "just following United States customs."

GULF's financial support of what was to become the Nixon Administration—support that provided the climax and catastrophe of the corporation's career as a political contributor—began in the spring of 1968. At that time, according to Thomas Wright's notes, Wild gave twenty-five thousand dollars in cash to Maurice Stans, then a Nixon fund raiser, in connection with Nixon's effort to get the Republican nomination. That summer, so as not to be partial to any one Presidential aspirant or his party, Wild, according to Wright's notes, gave the same sum—twenty-five thousand dollars —to "a personal confidant" of Senator Hubert Humphrey, who subsequently became the Democratic candidate.

That some Gulf officials were again having qualms about illegal political contributions by the beginning of 1970 is indicated by the fact that in January the corporation established a vehicle for making such contributions legally. Called the Gulf Good Government Fund, it derived its resources from contributions voluntarily made by Gulf employees in their own names, usually in a standard amount of one-half of one per cent of an employee's base salary; disbursements from it were usually made by Wild to recipients of his choosing—that is to say, precisely the same way the illegal payments were made except that Good Government Fund payments were almost always made by check rather than in cash. The fund collected between seventy thousand and eighty thousand dollars for each year from 1970 through 1972. Legal though contributions of corporate executives may be, it would certainly seem that the ethical distinction between such contributions and illegal contributions from corporate funds becomes blurred when the former may have been solicited, or even extorted, by higher executives to whom the donor employees are responsible, and when the recipients are selected not by the donor but by a lobby for the corporation. Moreover, in the very year when Gulf made this gesture toward legality its illegal political activities moved along as briskly as ever. Indeed, they moved toward their peak. In the summer of 1970, according to Wild, he had lunch at the White

House with several Nixon aides, who requested fifty thousand dollars to help in the election of a Republican Senate that November. Wild came across with twenty-five thousand dollars in cash, and that October he personally delivered another twenty-five thousand dollars in cash for Republican campaign use to Attorney General John Mitchell. Other payments from corporate funds between 1969 and 1972 included several ten-thousand-dollar donations to Republican Committee dinners; several five-thousand-dollar contributions to Democratic Committee dinners (which seem to have been regarded as half as worthy); and the periodic cash distributions that had come to be routine from Wild and his associates to various political figures outside Washington.

Early in 1971, a representative of the newly formed Committee to Re-Elect the President called on Wild at his office and asked for a contribution of a hundred thousand dollars. Shortly thereafter, having been assured by Mitchell that CREEP was a legitimate operation, Wild contributed fifty thousand dollars. But CREEP was not satisfied; its representative called on Wild again the following January and asked for another fifty thousand dollars. In February, 1972, Wild says, he went to see Maurice Stans, who was then Secretary of Commerce; Stans said that he knew about the previous fifty-thousand-dollar contribution but that he hoped the sum would be doubled. After thinking the matter over, Wild called Viglia in the Bahamas, ordered up fifty thousand dollars in cash, and, when he got it, turned it over to Stans, who by then had resigned his Cabinet post to devote himself to CREEP. With that, it seems, Wild felt that Gulf had met its quota; in the fall, he told William L. Henry, another Gulf official, in the course of a card game at Reston, Virginia, that if Henry should get a request from Stans for further contributions, he should ignore it. And meanwhile, it appears, Wild was throwing a light anchor to windward; early in 1972, he testified later, he gave ten thousand dollars in cash to an assistant to a Democratic senator, Henry M. Jackson, and fifteen thousand dollars, also in cash, to a close friend of a key Democratic member of the House, Wilbur Mills.

At a Gulf management meeting in the fall of 1972, it was decided that, as a cost-cutting measure, all the company's offshore subsidiaries, including Bahamas Ex., should be consolidated into a single entity, Midcaribbean Investments, Ltd., with headquarters in Nassau. The move was approved by Gulf's corporate financial council early in December, and on the last day of the year the effective liquidation of Bahamas Ex. was completed. Thus the laundry for Gulf's illegal political money was put out of business —almost entirely, it appears, by executives merely anxious to save the company money, and innocent of any knowledge of the purpose that Bahamas Ex. had been so efficiently serving. Early in 1973, Wild began clamoring for more funds in Washington, and Viglia, in Nassau, had to reply that there were none, because the Bahamas Ex. account had been closed. Viglia then got authorization from Fred C. Deering, the Gulf comptroller, in Pittsburgh, to borrow funds temporarily from Midcaribbean to meet Wild's need, and by April a whole new system, using Midcaribbean almost exactly as the previous system had used Bahamas Ex., was established and operating. On March 15, 1973, a new infusion of two hundred thousand dollars went from Pittsburgh to Nassau, and between April 26th and July 19th of that year Viglia made five cash deliveries to Wild totalling a hundred and twenty thousand dollars.

But time was running out. A delivery by Viglia of twenty thousand dollars to Wild on July 19th proved to be his last. A few weeks earlier—the exact date is not known—Wild, realizing that the court order to the Finance Committee of CREEP would force it to disclose Gulf's two fifty-thousand-dollar contributions, told Dorsey, by then the company's chief executive officer, about them. On July 19th (the same day that Wild—rather ruefully, one may imagine—was taking his last cash delivery from Viglia), Gulf engaged the Pittsburgh law firm of Eckert, Seamans, Cherin & Mellott to represent the corporation in the matter; a week later, lawyers of that firm met with lawyers for the Watergate Special Prosecutor's office, and the process of disclosure leading to the McCloy report began.

THE McCloy committee concluded that Gulf's domestic political activities had been "shot through with illegality," and that the

whole program, domestic and foreign, had "raised serious questions as to the policy and management of the company." It recommended, among other things, that off-the-books funds of any
kind, for any purpose, thenceforward be proscribed at Gulf; that
the company's chief legal officer be specifically charged with the
responsibility of informing management of any illegal political
activities that came to his attention; that the company's auditors
institute special procedures to detect unusual expenses; and that in
future any legal political fund similar to the Good Government
Fund be dispensed not by a Washington lobbyist but by "a suitable representative committee." At the same time, the McCloy
committee conceded that new rules and procedures alone could
not do the job of reform, saying that "in the last analysis it will be
in the tone and attitude of top management that the eradication
[of improper political activities] will be ensured in the future."

The personnel, as well as the tone and attitude, of top management was the principal question at issue when the Gulf board of
directors met in Pittsburgh in mid-January of 1976, shortly after it
had received the McCloy report. The meeting turned out to be a
corporate thriller. Nearly all the Gulf executives who had been
mentioned as accomplices in the testimony of Bounds, Wild,
Viglia, and others were by this time either dead, like Whiteford, or
retired, like Bounds, Wild, and Viglia. But a few were not, and
among these was Dorsey, the company's chairman and chief
executive officer. The Gulf board, meeting for a total of more than
twenty-three hours, in two sessions, between the afternoon of January 12th and the early morning of January 14th, devoted its
marathon deliberations almost entirely to the question of whether
Dorsey and three other Gulf executives should be forced to resign.

The McCloy committee's conclusions about Dorsey's involvement had been equivocal. While Dorsey had freely admitted his
personal negotiation and authorization of the two Korean payments, totalling four million dollars, the committee concluded that
he had apparently known nothing of the Bahamas Ex. secret account or its successor, and that the evidence fell short of demonstrating that he had known of Wild's unlawful political activities,

but that concerning the latter he "was not sufficiently alert and should have known," and he "perhaps chose to shut his eyes to what was going on." With that judgment as a starting point, the board settled down, in closed session on the thirty-first floor of the Gulf Building, in Pittsburgh, to decide Dorsey's fate. According to Byron E. Calame, the *Wall Street Journal*'s man on the spot, it quickly developed that five directors who were considered representatives of the Mellons—the economic royalty of Gulf and of Pittsburgh itself—were bent on getting Dorsey's resignation, and were unwilling to have the blow softened by any face-saving compromise such as a "Ford-type pardon." With Dorsey and E. D. Brockett, another board member who had been mentioned by the McCloy committee as having been "involved," not participating in the deliberations for obvious reasons, the board consisted of twelve members, with the result that the Mellon block fell only two votes short of a majority. However, according to Calame, three other directors were equally adamant about keeping Dorsey in office; and Dorsey's lawyers were present to plead his case.

As the hours wore on, in an atmosphere described by participants as "brutal" and like that of a jury room, the Dorsey forces gradually gave ground, suggesting compromise plans under which Dorsey would remain in office with reduced authority until his normal retirement, in 1978. These plans were rejected. In the end, a key vote—if not, indeed, the swing vote—belonged to a director who, it seems safe to say, had been nominated with Dorsey's approval, and elected by Gulf stockholders the previous April, with no thought that nine months later she would all but hold the chairman's fate in her hands. She was Sister Jane Scully, president of Carlow College, a local liberal-arts institution for women, who had been elected in conformity with the current custom in corporate circles of putting a token, and presumably harmless, woman on the board. Sister Jane started out neutral, according to Calame, but eventually swung to the anti-Dorsey side. At last, at 1:15 A.M. on the fourteenth, the meeting was adjourned and the results were announced: Dorsey was to resign that same day as chief executive officer and from the board; William L. Henry and

Fred Deering were to resign their posts as president of Gulf's real-estate subsidiary and Gulf's senior vice-president, respectively; and Herbert C. Manning—a vice-president and the attorney to whom Myers had said he had delivered sealed envelopes—was to resign as an officer but remain as an employee, in a different post.

WITH the forced resignation of Dorsey, and with a statement in March by Dorsey's successor, Jerry McAfee, that set forth a stiff new code of business principles to which "strict adherence" by all employees worldwide was described as "a condition of continued employment," Gulf's symbolic and substantive acts of contrition were accomplished, and there was reason to believe that the tone and attitude of top management would change notably in regard to political contributions. Obviously, though, serious and disturbing questions had yet to be answered about the implications of the things that had been shown to have happened, at Gulf and at many other leading corporations. Among those who had been named by Wild—by themselves or through staffs and associates—as recipients of contributions from Gulf funds were two former Presidents of the United States, a former Presidential candidate, several recent aspirants to the Presidency, and various members of key committees of the Senate and the House of Representatives. To be sure, none of these recipients said that they knew they were taking illegal funds. But, one cannot help wondering, did they not once ask themselves why the funds were delivered by hand and in cash? McCloy, in a *Times* interview, emphasized this question, pointing out that it is just as improper for politicians to accept corporate money illegally as it is for companies to give it, and that "the statement 'I didn't know these were corporate funds' doesn't wash when you're talking about cash in sealed envelopes." As for the United States government's attitude toward corporate contributions abroad, McCloy said his investigation showed that American officials in South Korea had made it generally known that they favored "American-style" politics there. "I don't want to suggest that Gulf was relying on United States government consent," he said. "It was just part of the atmosphere." And in mid-July another corporation that had made foreign political payments, the Aluminum Company of America, suggested that the atmosphere was sometimes not hazy but dazzlingly clear; it filed papers with the S.E.C. stating that in 1971 and 1972 the United States ambassador in an unnamed foreign country had actually solicited from Alcoa at least twenty-five thousand dollars, to be used for payments to officials and political parties in that country for the purpose of setting up a program to explain to local citizens the advantages of permitting United States investments there.

Congress and the executive branch, evidently reluctant to reform themselves, were far more enthusiastic about reforming the corporations. In March, 1976, President Ford announced the creation of a high-level panel, headed by Secretary of Commerce Elliot Richardson, to investigate misconduct by American corporations abroad. That same month, Senator William Proxmire, of Wisconsin, introduced a bill that would make corporate bribery of foreign officials a federal crime; that initiative, however, soon bogged down when Chairman Hills of the S.E.C. said that the Proxmire measure went too far, and then, in June, President Ford declared himself to be in favor of legislation that would merely require the disclosure of questionable payments, with no penalty against the payers. Also in June, the twenty-four leading industrial nations that make up the membership of the Organization for Economic Cooperation and Development and account for three-fourths of world trade adopted a code of conduct for multinational corporations which included a clause declaring that multinational enterprises of the member states should "not render —and they should not be solicited or expected to render—any bribe or other improper benefit, direct or indirect, to any public servant or holder of public office." But the code was unenforceable, since the O.E.C.D. lacked the power to impose sanctions on violators. "It's completely illusory to think anything will change," Jerome Levinson, chief counsel of the Senate Subcommittee on Multinational Corporations, said. "I think that once the publicity has faded, many of these guys will go back to the same old philosophy of 'sell, sell, sell, any way you can.'" As for the offending corporations themselves, their public attitudes varied from contrition and good resolutions to defiance. A few, like Gulf, Lockheed, and Minnesota Mining & Manufacturing, forced their top executives to resign or suffer demotion. But the situation was different at Northrop, which was guilty by its own admission of both illegal payments at home and improper ones abroad, and whose president and chairman, Thomas V. Jones, pleaded guilty in May, 1974, to felony charges in making contributions to President Nixon and in July, 1975, resigned under fire as company chairman—a somewhat tentative act of contrition, since he remained as president and chief executive officer. In February, 1976, the Northrop board reinstated Jones as chairman, and at the annual meeting in May the stockholders, praising Jones for his leadership, voted to ratify his reinstatement.

The disclosures and the attendant brouhaha do not appear to have caused much shock or outrage among investors or their professional advisers. Revelations of corporate bribery threaten a corporation's good name but not, apparently, its good profits or good prospects. The price of Gulf Oil common stock was not significantly depressed by any of the revelations, and in the subsequent months it rose strongly. In early March, 1976, when the Lockheed scandal was at its height, Lockheed stock rose three points, or more than forty per cent, in a week, almost as if the front-page stories about bribery were serving as a publicity windfall for the company.

The new Democratic administration that assumed office in 1977 showed more resolution on the subject than its predecessor. Toward the end of that year, Congress finally passed a new anti-bribery measure, and in December, President Carter signed it into law. The Foreign Corrupt Practices Act of 1977, as it is called, make it illegal for United States corporations or their representatives to give bribes to foreign officials, and requires those corporations to keep their books in such a way that slush funds cannot be concealed. It also empowers the S.E.C. and the Department of Justice to enforce those provisions by seeking injunctions or by bringing criminal proceedings. Enactment of the law was followed quickly by widespread expressions of skepticism as to its enforceability; and after it had been on the books for a year or so, the question remained largely unsettled.

Perhaps, then, the era of overseas bribery by United States corporations ended in 1977, and perhaps it didn't. What is certain is that, prior to that year, the huge corporations through their bribes, big and little, of politicians and their parties corrupted, and thereby materially damaged, not only government but themselves. There are ways of looking at the things revealed about corporate political contributions in which they appear, in the aggregate, a worse national aberration than Watergate itself. Watergate was in essence a series of actions by a single national administration, while corporate bribery, it appears, was for a decade and more a pervasive and accepted norm of conduct among many of the nation's largest and usually most respected enterprises.

Index

ABC (Monarchist daily), 135
Abdulla (Ruler of Kuwait), 352
Abel, I. W., 315, 317
Acción, La, 111
Aldrich, Hulbert, 270, 272, 274
Alfonso XIII, 97, 107, 116, 119, 121, 146
Alleghany Corporation, 4, 9, 12–13, 17, 20, 21, 28
Allen, William M., 229, 233, 234–35, 247
Allied Chemical, 223
Aluminum Company of America, 361
Amax, Inc., 314
American Airlines, 337
American Bankers Association, 268–69
American Home Products Corporation, 338
American Journal of International Law, 209
American Telephone & Telegraph, 262
Ammoun, Fouad, 210, 211
Amsterdam Stock Exchange:
architecture, 80, 91
history and traditions of, 77–92
importance of, 80
Jewish members, 82–83
vs. New York Stock Exchange, 81–82, 83, 85–86, 87
regulation of, 83–86
statistics, 80–84
stocks listed on, 80–81
trading hours, 81, 87–88
woman member, 81
in World War II, 82–83
Andany Sanz, Ángel, 173, 174, 176
Andreu Domingo, Carlos, 163–64, 165, 166, 168
Armand-Ugon, Enrique C., 208
Arnaíz Moreno, Martín, 128–29
Azaña, Manuel, 121, 124, 126, 127, 128

Baer, Hans J., 237–38
Baer, Julius, & Cie., 237
Bagehot, Walter, 63, 64
Bahamas Exploration Company Ltd., 344–48, 353, 357, 358
See also Gulf Oil
Baird, David, 10
Baldwin, Robert, 32, 33–36, 46–47, 48, 49, 50–51
Balfour, John, 175–76
Baltimore & Ohio Railroad, 221
Banca March, 99, 119
Banco Commercial Mexicano, S.A., 247
Bangor Punta Corporation, 239
Bankers Trust Company, 261, 270
Banking Act of 1933, 43
Bank of England, 66, 70, 72, 75–76
Guard, 75–76
history and traditions, 75–76
Bank of France, 138–39
Bank of Italy, 140
Bank of Nova Scotia (Nassau), 334–45, 346
Banque Lambert, 242, 287
Banque Rothschild, 287
Bantam Books, 311
Barber, Anthony, 287, 296–97
Barcelona Traction, Light & Power Co., Ltd., 147–215 passim
Agreed Minute, 175–77, 178, 179, 205
auction of, 177–79
"bankruptcy" of, 95–96, 161–65, 170, 171, 172, 177, 179–80, 196, 209
bond issues, 152–55
"clean hands" issue, 205, 208
Commission of Experts, 173, 174–75
currency violations, 151
"duplicate" shares issued, 95–96, 177, 196, 214
financial history, 149–50
foreign government protests, 96

foreign shares voided, 95–96, 151
formation of, 106, 151
international character of, 95, 106,
    147, 148–52
International Court of Justice
    judgment on, 93–95, 207–10
    as precedent, 211–12
    judge replacement in trial, 113
    precedent cases, 206
    Reus (Spain) Court decree, 162–65,
        166–68, 169, 170, 171, 172, 177,
        178, 196, 209, 210
    seizure of, by March, 94, 95, 96, 97,
        148, 152–215 passim
    tax avoidance by, 151
    vulnerability of, as part of pyramid,
        151
    See also International Court of
        Justice
Barcelonesa Electric Company, 166
Barclays Bank, 223
Barnett, Frank E., 240
Barrientos, René, 353
Barron, W. G., 70
Baskin-Robbins, 311
Bear raids, 79, 265–66
Beecher, Henry Ward, 221
Beinecke, William S., 227
Belgian Kredietbank, 223
Belgium, 93
    in Barcelona Traction case, 94, 149,
        168, 171, 172, 173, 174, 177, 185,
        186–87, 190, 194–95, 197, 198,
        199, 201, 204–05, 206–09, 215
Benavides, Manuel Dominguez, Last
    Pirate of the Mediterranean, The,
    108–09
Bernanos, Georges, 138
Blair-Cunynghame, J. O., 240
Blosser, Raymond F., 18
Blough, Roger M., 223, 231–32, 242
Boeing Company, 220, 222, 229
    747 program, 228–29, 230–33, 235,
        240–41, 247
Bolín, Luis, 135
Bolivia, Gulf Oil illegal contributions,
    353
Bonaccorsi, Arconovaldo, 138
Bonds:
    in corporate finance, 36, 37–38
    history of, 90

Borbón, Juan de, 146, 147
Bos, M., 204
Boter Vaquer, Juan, 168, 170, 171
Bounds, Joseph E., 341–42, 343–44,
    345–46, 347–48, 358
Bourse. See Paris Bourse
Bowers, Claude G., 131, 132
Bradley, Albert, 37
Breedlove, Howell A., Jr., 311, 319,
    320, 321, 323
Brenan, Gerald, 119
Bretton Woods agreement, 288, 290,
    293, 298
Brisco, Milo M., 306
Britain, 294
    in Barcelona Traction case, 172,
        175–77, 178–79, 204, 215
British Economic Warfare Ministry,
    145
British Foreign Office, 155, 158–59,
    175–76
British Treasury, 95–96, 155, 158, 176
Brockett, E. D., 359
Bronx Community College, 327
Brown, Alex, & Sons, 239
Brown, James, 244
Brown, John A., & Co., 220
Brown, Moreau Delano, 222, 248
Brown & Williamson, 311
Brown Brothers Harriman & Co.:
    as private bank, 219, 220–21
    sesquicentennial program, 219–48
Bryan, Anthony J. A., 323
Burguera, Raimundo, 129
Burns, Arthur F., 287
Bush, Prescott, 222
Bustamente y Rivero, José Luis, 94,
    203, 211

Cady, Ware, 55–56
Calame, Byron E., 359
Call options, history of, 79
Cambó, Francisco, 113–15, 117
Canada, 294, 297
    in Barcelona Traction case, 165, 168,
        170, 171, 172, 173, 206–07, 211,
        215
Canals, José Antonio, 130, 131, 132
Carner, Jaime, 102–03, 107, 125, 128,
    133, 142, 200, 201
Carter, Arthur, 257

Carter, Berlind and Weill, 256, 257, 260
Carter, Don H., 10–11, 17
Carter, Jimmy, 362
Carter Auto Transport and Service Corporation, 256
Castro-Rial, J. M., 204
Celanese Corporation, 242
CHADE (holding company), 169
Chapman, E. G., 72–73
Charles, F. W., 173, 174, 176
Chartered Bank (People's Republic of China), 226
Chase National Bank, 8, 9, 10, 11, 13, 261, 270, 287
Chemical Bank New York Trust:
    and Leasco takeover attempt, 250, 261–81
    size of, 250, 263
Chesapeake & Ohio Railroad, 4, 6, 13, 17, 20
    New York Central stockholdings, 9, 10, 11, 12, 13
Christiana Bank Og Kreditkasse, 228
Chun Woo transaction, 352
Churchill, Winston, 178
Ciano, Galeazzo, 136
Citibank, 270
    See also First National Bank of the City of New York
City (London), 63–76
    banking jargon, 64
    geography, 64–66
    government of, 71
    history of, 71
    vs. Wall Street, 64–66, 71
City University Construction Fund, 327
Clayton Act, 277
Claytor, W. Graham, Jr., 227
Clegg, Cuthbert, 223, 227, 231, 242
Collins, Tim, 46, 47
Columbia Broadcasting System, 21, 223
Committee to Re-Elect the President (CREEP), 340, 356, 357
Commodity trading, as forerunner of stock trading, 79
Common Cause, 340
Common Market, 80
Connally, John B., 287, 291, 293, 295, 297–98, 299

Connor, John T., 223
Conservative Party (Britain), 71
Continental Illinois Bank & Trust Company, 268
Copland, Lammot du Pont, 262, 263, 280
Copperweld Corporation, Imetal takeover of, 310–23
Copps, Joseph, 8
Corporate bribery, 337–63
    See also indiv. companies
Corporate financing:
    bonds, 36, 37
    common stock, 36, 38–39
    convertible bonds, 37–38
    convertible preferred stock, 37
    debentures, 37
    mortgage bonds, 37
    preferred stock, 37
    preferred stock with sinking funds, 37
    See also indiv. companies
Cortina, Marquis of, 114
Cosell, Howard, 325
Cox, Archibald, 338, 340
Cravath, Swaine & Moore, 275, 280
Credit Commercial de France, 227
Curtice, Harlow H., 30–31, 37

Daily Mail, 131–32
Daily Telegraph, 129–30, 131–32
Data Processing Financial & General, 258
Dean, Arthur H., 96, 182–84, 211–12
De Capriles, Miguel, 328, 329
Deegan, Thomas J., Jr., 20
Deering, Fred, 360
De Gaulle, Charles, 232
De Graaf, J. J. N., 80, 82–83, 85, 86–88
Delaware and Hudson Railroad, 28
Delgado Curto, Antonio, 111–13
Depression, 43, 288
Deutsche Bundesbank, 243
Díaz Nosty, Bernardo, *Irresistible Rise of Juan March, The,* 108, 113, 134, 135, 137, 141, 146
Diebold, Inc., 16–18
Doar, Hand & Dawson, 13
Documentation, Inc., 256

Dollar:
  devaluations of, 287, 288, 291–92,
    295, 298, 299, 300
  as principal currency, 288–89, 295
  See also Gold
Donner, Frederic, 36–37, 38, 39, 47
Dorsey, Bob R., 341, 344, 350–51
  resignation of, 358–60
Drexel & Co., 43
Dualde, Joaquín, 163
Duncan, J. Donald, 163
Du Pont de Nemours, E. I. & Co., 262
  and 1955 General Motors offering,
    35, 42, 46–48, 52
Dutch East India Company, 77–79, 84,
    89
  early stock certificates, 89–90
  first stock split, 90
  stock price movements, 78–79
Dutch West India Company, 79
  Manhattan purchase by, 79
  stock price movements, 79

Ebbott, Percy J., 8, 10, 13
Ebro Irrigation and Power Company
    Ltd., 151, 156–57, 159–60, 161,
    166, 167, 172, 177, 214
Eckert, Seamans, Cherin & Mellott,
    357
Economist, 64
Eggers, H. H., 176
Ellis-Rees, Hugh, 158, 159, 176
Emminger, Otmar, 243
Ervin, Sam, 340
España Nueva, 112–13
European Economic Community, 291
Exxon Corporation:
  illegal contributions, 338, 341
  name change, 301–09
Ewing, William, 44

Fairchild Hiller Corporation, 353
Falange, 134
  See also Franco, Francisco
Farley, James A., 26
FECSA. *See* Fuerzas Eléctricas
Federal Reserve Bank, 226, 242
Federal Reserve Board, 58, 275, 278,
    280
Federal Trade Commission, 316

Federation of Women Shareholders in
    American Business, 20
Feeley, William P., 20–21
Fenchurch Nominees, Ltd., 155, 159
Ferris, Paul, 71
Ferronière, Jacques, 227–28
Finance Committee to Re-Elect the
    President, 340, 347, 357
Firestone Tire & Rubber Co., 338
First Boston Corporation, 42, 44, 268
First National Bank of New Jersey,
    258, 262, 263
First National Bank of the City of
    New York, 8, 13–14
  See also Citibank
Fitzmaurice, Gerald Gray, 210–11
Foote, Cone & Belding, 18
Forbes, 260
Ford, Gerald, 361
Ford, Henry, 100
Ford Foundation, 100
Ford Motor Company, 304
Foreign Corrupt Practices Act of 1977,
    362–63
Foremost-McKesson, Inc., 334–35
Fortune, "Sound and Fury of Robert
    R. Young, The," 19, 24
Fournier Cuadros, Adolfo, 164, 171
Fox Computer Services, 256
Fractional shares, history of, 79
France, 294
  currency devaluations, 292
Franco, Francisco, 134–36, 140–41,
    142, 145, 146, 150, 156, 157
  Barcelona Traction role, 94, 96, 97,
    99, 100, 147, 152, 181, 182, 183,
    184, 185
Freeport Sulphur, 228
Frère, Jean, 242
Frère, Maurice, 192–99, 201, 213
Frier, Harry W., 18
Fuerzas Eléctricas de Cataluña, S.A.
    (FECSA), 179, 184, 186, 196, 203,
    214
Funston, Keith, 262, 263, 280

Galarza, Ángel, 122, 123, 124
Gambús, Francisco, 164, 166, 171, 172
Garau, José, 111, 112, 113, 213
Garau, Rafael, 110–11, 213
Garau affair, 110–13, 124, 127

García del Cid, Francisco, 167
Garland, Charles S., 239, 240
Garriga, Ramón, *Juan March and His Time,* 108, 113, 134, 135, 137
Garrigues, Joaquín, 165
Geismar, Sydney J., 55, 56
General Agreement on Tariffs and Trade (G.A.T.T.), 286
General Electric, 81
General Motors Corporation, 30–31, 223, 242
  on Amsterdam Exchange, 81
  1955 stock rights offering, 31–32, 33, 36–43, 46–60
  rights price movements, 51–52, 53, 54
  stockholder statistics and anecdotes, 34, 35, 41, 55–57, 60
  stock price movements, 33, 39, 42, 47, 51, 52, 53, 54, 57, 58
Genora, S.A., 171
Georgeson & Co., 8, 16, 18, 23, 275
Gerry, Elbridge T., 222
Gestapo, 82
Gibbs, Michael A., 256, 257, 261
Gil Robles, José Maria, 134, 136, 145, 204
Giscard d'Estaing, Valéry, 287, 292–93
Glass-Steagall Act, 43
Gold, 289
  London fixing, 72
  March's deposits, 140
  price rises, 297, 298
  Spanish reserves, 138
  as standard, 288, 291, 295, 298
  U.S. redemptions, 286, 290, 293, 296, 299
Goodrich Tire and Rubber Company, 249
Gordon Riots, 76
Graham, Donald M., 268
Great Lakes Dredge & Dock Co., 21
Green, Hetty, 148, 252
Gros, André, 208
Group of Ten, 291, 293, 295, 296
Grummer, William T., 345
Gulf Good Government Fund, 355, 358
Gulf Oil Corporation:
  Fondo Nero (Black Fund), 353–54
  Gray Fund, 353–54
  illegal contributions, 339–61, 362

"Political Program," 343
Special Review Committee (McCloy committee), 341–42, 350, 351, 352, 354, 357–59

Hague Stock Exchange, 84
Hall, Herbert, 58
Hall, Perry, 33, 36–39, 40, 41–42, 44, 48, 52, 57, 58–59
Halsey Stuart & Co., 44
Hamilton, Thomas J., 142
Hand, Chauncey H., 13, 18
Harriman, E. H., 221, 222
Harriman, E. Roland, 221, 225, 229–30
Harriman, W. Averell, 222, 225–26, 248
Harriman Brothers & Co., 221
  See also Brown Brothers Harriman & Co.
Hartford Fire Insurance Co., 257
Harvard Business Review, 266
Hawker, Cyril, 223
Hayes, Alfred, 226–27, 242
Heineken's, 81
Heineman, Dannie N., 149, 153–54, 157, 159, 168, 191, 192, 213
Heinemann, H. Erich, 264, 266–67
Henry, William L., 356, 359–60
Hentsch, Conrad, 223, 227, 233–34, 246, 247–48
Hentsch & Compagnie, 233
Hernández, José Manuel, 193, 194, 197, 198
Hester, James M., 327, 329, 330
Hillgarth, Alan H., 156–57, 158
Hills, Roderick M., 338–39, 361
Hoare, Henry, 75
Hoare, Samuel, 157
Hoare & Company, 70, 73–75
  banking museum, 73–74
  history of, 74–75
Hoch, Frank, 238
Hodes, Robert, 274
Hoeken (trading posts), 81–82, 86–87
Hoekmen (stock specialists), 81–82, 86
Höglund, Rune, 231
Hongkong & Shanghai Banking Corporation, 234
Hornblower Weeks, 268
Hughes, Graham, 328–29
Humphrey, Hubert H., 355, 360

I.B.M., 81, 253–55, 262
Ideal Leasing Company. *See* Leasco
Iglesias, Emiliano, 106, 117, 122, 123, 124
Informaciones, 117, 131
Inouye, Daniel K., 342, 360
Insull, Samuel, 201
Internal Revenue Service, 338
International Court of Justice, 93, 188–90
    in Barcelona Traction case, 94, 95, 96, 156, 165, 185, 186–87, 190, 192–93, 195–96, 198, 199, 201–11, 214
    judges' opinions, 208–11
International Monetary Fund, 285–300
    Articles of Agreement, 286, 298
International Telephone and Telegraph, 257
Interstate Commerce Commission, 6, 13, 14, 22
Investment banking. *See* Underwriting; indiv. investment bankers and firms
Ireland, R. L., III, 222
Irving Trust Company, 261, 270
Isla de Tenerife, 144–45, 156
Istel, Jerome, 287
Italy, 297
    Gulf Oil illegal contributions, 353–54
    Spanish Civil War role, 136–38, 139, 140, 141

Jackson, Henry M., 340, 356, 360
Jamieson, J. K., 306
Japan, 294, 297
    currency revaluations, 287
    G.A.T.T. violations, 286
Javits, Jacob, 325
Jenkins, Walter, 346
Jessup, Philip C., 210
Jiskoot, Allard, 234, 246
Johnson, Lyndon B., 346, 360
Johnson, Malcolm, 19
Jones, A. N., 44
Jones, Thomas V., 362
Josephson, Matthew, 96

Kaplan, Louis, 59
Keynes, John Maynard, 288–89, 298

Khashoggi, Adnan M., 354–55
Kim, S. K., 350–51
King, Dudley, 275
Kirby, Allan, 4, 9, 10, 12, 21, 23
Kirby, James C., Jr., 329
Kissel Organization, 16
Klasen, Karl, 287
Kleinwor, Sons & Company Ltd., 135, 139, 155
Kleinwort, Cyril H., 135
K.L.M., 81
Korea (South), Gulf Oil illegal contributions, 341, 349–52, 353, 354, 360–61
Korean Democratic Republican Party, 341, 350
Kostyzak, William, 316–17, 321–22
Kouwenhoven, John A., *Partners in Banking*, 221
Kreuger, Ivar, 29, 201
Kuhn, Loeb & Company, 220, 268, 311, 316, 321
Kuwait, 350, 352
Kuwait Oil Company Ltd., 352

Labour Party (Britain), 70, 71
Lambert (Baron), 287
Lasell, Chester, 39, 40, 50, 53
Law, John, 90
Lazard Frères, 183
League of Nations, 187–88
Learson, T. Vincent, 262, 263, 280
Leasco Data Processing Equipment Corporation, 250–81
    acquisitions made by, 256–61
    Chemical Bank takeover attempt by, 250, 261–81
    Establishment pressure against, 262, 265–66, 268–69, 273, 275–81
    growth of, 255–56
    Reliance Insurance takeover by, 257–61, 273, 275
    stock price movement, 260–61, 265–66, 267, 275, 276, 277–78
Lehman Brothers, 273
Lemkau, Hudson, 32, 51
Lerroux, Alejandro, 106, 122, 126–27, 128, 132
Levinson, Jerome, 361–62
Levi Strauss & Co., 338
Libertad, La, 117–18, 130, 131

Liebhefer ("bull"), 87
Lipp, Robert I., 264
Lipton, Martin, 332, 333
Litton Industries, 223
Lloyd's of London, 70, 72–73
Lockheed Aircraft Corporation, 338, 341, 362
Loewenstein, Alfred, 150
London, Lord Mayor of, 71
    See also City (London)
London County Council, 71
London Stock Exchange, 66–70
    Committee on Damaged Bonds and Irregular American Certificates, 70
    memberships, 67, 69–70
    vs. New York Stock Exchange, 67, 68, 69–70
    public relations efforts, 67, 68, 70
    statistics, 69–70
    Stock Exchange Council, 69
    traditions, 67–68, 69
Long, Augustus C., 262, 263, 280
Lovett, Robert A., 220, 221, 222, 229, 230
Luca de Tena (Marquis), 135
Luz, 127

McAfee, Jerry, 360
McCall, Howard, 270, 272, 274
McCance, Thomas, 222
McCloy, John J., 13–14, 341, 360–61
    McCloy committee, 341, 344, 350, 351, 352, 354, 357–59
McCloy, John J., II, 224
McFadden, J. A., 263–64, 265, 274
McKay, Robert B., 329
McLean, Harold H., 13, 18, 25
Maffitt, Donald, 318
Maggin, Daniel, 17
Maluquer, Joaquín, 161
Manhattan, purchase of, 79
Mann, Francis, 179, 204, 209–10, 212–13
Manning, Herbert C., 349, 360
Manufacturers Hanover Trust, 261, 270
March, J., & Company Ltd., 142
March, Juan (son), 131
March, Juan, Foundation, 99–101, 194, 199

March Ordinas, Juan, 93–215
    adaptability to political regimes, 97, 102–03, 105, 115
    appearance, 98, 99, 100–01, 107–08, 124, 132, 146, 160
    biographies, 99, 104–05, 108–09
    bribery by, 97, 99, 111, 114–15, 123, 127, 132, 156
    British ties, 131, 135, 139, 142, 143, 145, 156–58, 176
    character, 97, 102–03, 107, 109–10, 111, 115–16, 123–24, 125, 131, 133–34, 160, 163, 169, 170, 185–86, 190–91, 194–95, 197, 199, 200–01
    death and obituaries, 96, 199–201
    as double dealer, 108–10, 143–47
    early life, 104–05
    election campaigns, 115–16, 127–28, 132, 133
    as forger, 113
    foundation, 99–101, 194, 199
    as Franco backer, 94, 97, 99, 100, 133, 134–37, 138, 139–42, 145, 152, 155
    in Garau affair, 110–13
    as Geneva resident, 160
    Jewish ancestry alleged, 144
    as Lisbon resident, 145–46
    national reputation, 99, 102–03
    newspaper control, 117–18, 127, 128
    as philanthropist, 97, 99–101, 118, 125
    as pirate and privateer, 103–04, 114
    in prison, 98, 125–26, 127–28, 130–31
    prison escape, 128–31
    as private expropriator, 147, 152–215 passim
    and Republicans, 102–03, 121–33, 213
    as robber baron, 96–99, 102–03, 106, 107–10, 142–43
    as smuggler, 94, 97, 103, 105–06, 110, 112, 113, 114–15
    tobacco monopoly, 107, 117, 118, 119, 123, 124–25
    wealth of, 113
    in World War I, 104, 107–10, 113
    in World War II, 143–47
    See also Barcelona Traction

March Severa, B., Library, 102
Martin, William McChesney, Jr., 58, 241, 245, 275
Martín Artajo, Alberto, 179, 183, 184
Martins Bank, 223
Matthews, Beverley, 341
Maura, Antonio, 116
Maura, Miguel, 121, 122
Mechem, Edwin L., 349
Medina, Harold R., 44
Mellon, T., & Sons, 342
Mellon family, 344, 359
Merck & Co., 338
Merlin, Jacques, 227, 231–32, 233
Metz, Robert, 264–65
Metzman, Gustav, 6
Midcaribbean Investments, Ltd., 357
    See also Bahamas Exploration; Gulf Oil
Miller, John L., 314, 318, 319
Mills, Wilbur, 340, 356, 360
Minnesota Mining & Manufacturing Co., 338, 362
Mississippi Bubble, 90–91
Mitchell, John, 356
Mizutai, Mikuo, 287
Mola, Emilio, 137
Monasterio, Juan O., 247
Montañés, Carlos, 148, 153
Morelli, Gaetano, 208
Morgan, Charles Francis, 49, 51
Morgan, Henry S., 44, 49
Morgan, J. P., & Co., 8, 43–44, 45, 52, 54–55, 56, 220, 221
    See also Morgan Stanley & Co.
Morgan Grenfell & Co., 46, 47, 223
Morgan Guaranty Trust, 261, 270
Morgan Stanley & Co., 30–60
    antitrust suit won, 44
    buying department, 39
    history, 43–45
    offices, 32–33
    selling department, 39
    statistics, 44, 59
    underwriting function, 34–35, 39
    See also General Motors stock offering
Motrico, Count of, 193, 194, 195, 196, 197, 198
Mueller, C. F., Company, 325–31

Foremost-McKesson purchase of, 334–35
"Multiple flogging." *See* Bear raids
Murchison, Clint W., 11–12, 13, 14, 16, 17, 22, 26, 28
Murray, Lawrence N., 8
Mussolini, Benito, 141
Myers, Frederick A., 348–49, 361

Nagle, Alexander C., 8
National Alliance of Democratic Organizations (Spain), 146, 147
National City Bank rights offering, 42
National Steel, 242
National Trust Company of Canada, 165, 167, 177
Nazis, 82, 83, 144, 145
Netter, Edward, 259
    "Financial Services Holding Company," 256–57
New Bridge (Amsterdam), 78, 79
New Court Securities Corporation, 316
New York Central and Hudson River Railroad, 5, 15
New York Central Railroad, 3–29
    directors' meetings, 7–8, 10
    proxy fight, 5–6, 8–28
    proxy vote, 27–28
    stock price movements, 10, 11–12, 28
New York State General Corporation Law, proxy provisions, 15
New York State Legislature, 276, 277, 278–79, 280
New York Stock Exchange, 10, 11, 43, 51, 52, 262
    vs. Amsterdam Stock Exchange, 81, 82
    vs. London Stock Exchange, 67, 68, 69–70
    regulation of, 81–82, 83, 85–86, 87
    trading posts, 82
New York Supreme Court, 22
New York Times, The, 128, 142, 264–65, 271, 313, 314
New York University:
    financial problems, 327–28, 330–31, 335
    and Mueller income attempt, 328–35
New York University School of Law, 324–36
    facilities, 325, 326–27, 331–33

Law Center Foundation, 326, 327, 330, 331, 334
Mueller income, 324, 327, 328, 329, 330–31
Mueller sale, 328, 334–36
Student Bar Association, 329
Nixon, Richard M., 290, 291, 299, 337, 340, 347, 355, 356, 360, 362, 363
Norman, H. G., 173, 174, 176
Northrop Corporation, 338, 354, 362
Northwest Industries, 249
Nye, Richard S., 18, 23

O'Brien, Leslie, 287
Ohio Department of Commerce, 314–15
Oliva, L. Jay, 335
O.P.E.C. oil embargo, 287, 299, 308
Opie, Redvers, 171
Organization for Economic Cooperation and Development (O.E.C.D.), 361
Overhoff, Carel, 83

Paley, William S., 223
Pan American World Airways, 223, 249
Paris Bourse, 80
Park Chung Hee, 350
Parsky, Gerald L., 318–19
Patman, Wright, 266
Pearson, Fred Stark, 148
Pearson, Nathan W., 341
Peat, Marwick Mitchell & Company, 173
Peire, Tomás, 146
Pemán, José Maria, 200, 201
Penn Central Railroad, 4
See also New York Central Railroad
Pepys, Samuel, 75
Perlman, Alfred, 28
Permanent Court of Arbitration, 187
Permanent Court of International Justice, 187–88
Philips Gloeilamp, 81
Phillips Petroleum Co., 338
Picasso, Pablo, 100
Pierson, Helding & Pierson, 234
Pittston Company, 21
Place, Willard F., 8, 18, 25
Political contributions, 337–63
See also indiv. companies and people
Pollack, Leslie, 332

Pompidou, Georges, 291
Popular Front (Spain), 133
Porto Pi Oil Company, 132
Powell, David G., 305, 307–08
Preston, Simon, 68, 69, 70
Price, Waterhouse & Company, 173
Prieto, Indalecio, 121, 123, 124, 127, 180–81
Primo de Rivera, José Antonio, 134, 136
Primo de Rivera, Miguel, 97, 116, 117, 118, 119–21, 123, 125, 213
Princeton University, 330
Prospectuses and registration statements, 40–41
Proxmire, William, 361
Proxy, history of, 15
Proxy fights. See indiv. companies
Prudential Insurance Company of America, 325, 327
Pueblo, El, 141
Pullen, W. G., 226
Put options, history of, 79

Radical Party (Spain), 106, 122–23, 124
Rambin, J. Howard, Jr., 238
Reader's Digest, 20
Redlich, Norman, 330–34, 336
Régulo Martínez (politician), 146
Reliance Group, Inc. See Leasco Data Processing
Reliance Insurance Co., 257, 262, 263, 273
Leasco takeover of, 257–61, 273, 275
stock price movement, 257
Renchard, William Shryock, 250, 251–53, 261
appearance, 252–53, 269
career, 252
and Leasco takeover attempt, 263–81
Resorts International, 249
Rialto (Venice), 78
Richardson, Elliot, 361
Richardson, Sid W., 12, 13, 14, 22, 26, 28
Rights offerings, 33–35, 42
See also indiv. companies
Riphagen, Willem, 208
Ritchie of Dundee (Lord), 69

Roberts, A. Addison, 258–59, 260, 273, 274
Robinson-Hannagan Associates, 8, 18, 19
Rockefeller, David, 183, 247, 277, 287
Rockefeller, Laurance, 277
Rockefeller, Nelson, 276, 277, 280
Rockefeller family, 315–16
Rodríguez Sastre, Antonio, 185, 203, 204
Rogers, William P., 209
Rolin, Henri, 204
Román, Carlos, 116
Romnes, H. I., 262, 263, 280
Roosa, Robert V., 222, 234, 243
Rothschild, Evelyn de, 71–72
Rothschild, Guy de, 312, 315, 317, 318, 319–20, 322
Rothschild, Meyer Amschild, 312
Rothschild, N. M. & Sons, 70, 71–72
  as bullion brokers, 72
  history and traditions, 72
Rothschild family, 313–14, 315–16, 322, 323
Rotterdam Stock Exchange, 84
Roudebush, Richard L., 349
Routh, Joseph, 21–22
Royal Bank of Scotland, 240
Royal Dutch Petroleum, 81, 87
Royal Exchange (London), 65–66, 78
  See also London Stock Exchange
Russell, George, 223, 242

St. Olof's Chapel (Amsterdam), 78, 79
Salazar, Antonio de Oliveira, 124
Salgo, Nicholas M., 238–39, 246
Sanjurjo, José, 126
Sarasin, Alfred E., 238
Sasaki, Tadashi, 287
Satoh, Kiichiro, 223
Saunders, J. A. H., 234, 235
Sawhill, John C., 330–32, 334, 335
Scandinavian Airlines System, 224
Schiller, Karl, 287
Schimmelpenninck van der Oije, C. J., 88–92
Schoeller, Fritz, 242
Scully, Jane, 359
Schweitzer, Pierre-Paul, 287, 291, 294, 299

S.D.R.s. *See* Special Drawing Rights
Securities Act of 1933, 40, 83
Securities and Exchange Commission, 39, 40, 51, 85, 314
  on illegal contributions, 338, 340, 342, 348, 349, 361, 362–63
  letters of comment ("deficiency letters"), 41, 50
Senate Banking and Currency Committee, 276, 278–79, 280
Senate Foreign Relations Subcommittee on Multinational Corporations, 341, 361–62
Senate Watergate Committee, 340
Serrano, Pablo, 100–01
Serrano Suñer, Ramón, 181–82
Servan-Schreiber, Jean-Jacques, *Défi Americain, Le,* 231–32
Short selling, 78–79, 84, 85–86
Shriver, Alfred, 59–60
Simmons, Richard, 275–76
Simó Bofarull, Jaime, 123
Simonson, Cortelyou, 57
Sloan, Alfred P., Jr., 30, 37
Smith, Phillip H., 311, 312–13, 314, 318, 319–20, 321, 322–23
Société Financière de Transports et d'Entreprises Industrielles (SO-FINA), 149–50, 168, 186, 191, 192, 193, 197
Société Générale, 228
Société Imetal:
  antitrust hearing, 314, 318–19, 322
  Copperweld takeover by, 310–23
  union opposition to, 315–18
Société Internationale d'Energie Hydro-Électrique (SIDRO), 150, 168, 169, 179, 181, 183, 186, 190, 191, 192, 196–97, 214
SOFINA-SIDRO, 154, 161, 166, 169–70, 173, 176, 182, 185, 190, 193, 201
Sol, El, 127
Sorg, H. Theodore, 325
Soss, Wilma, 20, 26–27
Southern Railway System, 227
Spain, 93
  in Barcelona Traction case, 148, 152–215 passim
  Cortes (Parliament), 102, 105, 106, 107, 110, 116, 122–25, 132, 133
  under Directory, 116–21, 122

industrial development of, 105–06, 119
under Republic, 122–33
as U.N. member, 147, 185
See also Barcelona Traction; Franco, Francisco; March, Juan; Spanish Civil War; indiv. people and institutions
Spanish Civil War, 94, 99, 133, 136–42, 150, 152
Italian role in, 136–38, 139, 140, 141
Sparkman, John J., 276, 278–79
Special Drawing Rights (S.D.R.s), 295–98
Spender, Percy, 203
Sperry & Hutchinson, 227
Stamper, Malcolm T., 228, 230, 231
Standard Oil trust breakup, 302
See also Exxon Corporation
Stanley, Harold, 44
Stans, Maurice, 355, 356
Stanton, Thomas J., Jr., 263
States General (Netherlands), 77–78
Steinberg, Julius (father), 253, 260
Steinberg, Meyer (uncle), 260
Steinberg, Robert (brother), 260
Steinberg, Saul Phillip, 250, 312
appearance, 253, 255, 269–70
in Chemical Bank takeover attempt, 261–81
as entrepreneur, 254–56, 257–58, 260, 263, 266, 267
Stevens, John, 223
Stinson, George A., 242
Stock Exchange Journal (London), 70
Stock trading, 77–81
Stoner, George, 232–33
Stouffer Company, 311
Suances, Juan Antonio, 147, 155–56, 159, 170, 175
Suez Canal, 72
Svenska Handelsbanken, 231
Switzerland, 287
Syndicates. *See* Underwriting

Takeover strategies, 312–13, 314
See also indiv. companies
Tanaka, Kakuei, 338
Tanaka, Kotaro, 208
Terlinck, Frans H., 213–14

Texaco (Texas Oil Company), 140, 238, 262
Thomas, Hugh, 121, 132
Thomson, John, 223
Thornton, Charles B. (Tex), 223
Tilden, Samuel J., 325
Time, Inc., 19
Times (London), 150, 157, 171, 175, 286
Tisch, Laurence A., 331
Tombstone advertisements, 36
Trading with the Enemy Act (U.S.), 144
Transmediterranean Company, 110, 132, 137, 144
Trippe, Juan T., 223, 228, 237
Tulipomania, 90
Tuohy, Walter J., 11, 12
Tyson, Robert C., 262, 263, 280

Underwriting, 34–35, 36, 40–41
See also indiv. companies
Unilever, 81
Union Carbide, 242
Union Pacific Railroad, 222, 225, 229, 236, 237–38
United Brands Co., 338
United States:
in Barcelona Traction case, 172–73
currency revaluation, 287, 288, 291–92, 295, 298, 299, 300
gold stocks, 290, 293, 296, 299–300
in I.M.F. negotiations, 285–300
trade deficits, 289–90
U.S. Code, corporate contributions, 339, 340
U.S. Congress, 43, 338, 348, 361, 362
See also Senate committees
U.S. Department of Justice, 145, 277, 362–63
U.S. Steel, 38, 223, 262, 322
U.S. Supreme Court, 302, 303
United Steelworkers of America, 315–16, 321–22

Vagts, Detlev F., 209
Vanderbilt, Arthur T., 325, 326–27
Vanderbilt, Cornelius, 3–4, 15, 28
Vanderbilt, Harold S., 3–4, 5, 6, 9, 16, 25
Vanderbilt, William H., 5, 26

Vanderbilt, William H. (great-grandson), 25–26
Vargas Rodríguez, Eugenio, 129, 131
Veblen, Thorstein, 152, 180
Vega, Joseph de la, 79
Vietnam war, 248, 289, 295
Viglia, William C., 345, 346–47, 356, 357, 358
Viig, Sven, 228
Villeméjane, Bernard de, 312, 320
Viñas, Angel, *Spanish Gold in the Civil War*, 138–39, 141
Voz, La, 127

Waldock, Humphrey, 151–52, 165, 204
Wallace, Lila Bell Acheson, 20
Wallenberg, Marcus, 223, 224, 239, 240, 243, 245
Wall Street Journal, 23, 276, 277, 359
Ward, Francis T., 58
War Office (Britain), 76
Watergate affair, 339, 363
Watergate Special Prosecution Force, 337, 357
Waterloo, Battle of, 72
Wauters, Luc, 223, 234
Weinfeld, Edward, 332
Wellington, Duke of, 72
West Germany, 80, 290
White, Harry Dexter, 288
White, Weld, 273

White, William, 3–4, 5, 6, 7, 26–27, 28, 29
    proxy-fight strategy, 8–9, 13–15, 18–19, 22–25
Whiteford, William K., 343–44, 345–46, 347–48, 358
Whitney, George, 8, 56–57
Wild, Claude C., Jr., 340, 342, 343, 346–47, 348, 349, 355–56, 357, 358–59, 360
Williams, Langbourne M., 228
Wilmers, Charles K., 161, 163, 168–70, 176, 182–84, 190, 191–92, 194, 213
Wilson, Walter W., 58
Winder, R. McD., 74–75
Windhandel (short selling), 78–79, 84, 85–86
Winiarski, Bohdan, 203
Wright, Thomas D., 342–47, 355

Xerox Corporation, 302, 304
Xonex Synthetic Lubricants, Inc., 309

York, E. H., 44
Young, John M., 38, 44, 47, 52–53
Young, Robert R., 4, 5–6, 7, 8
    suicide, 29
    takeover strategy, 9–19, 20–22, 23, 27–28

Zuloaga, Antonio, 197–98
Zuloaga, Ignacio, 98, 101, 197–98